THE IDEOLOGICAL ORIGINS
OF THE AMERICAN REVOLUTION

The

IDEOLOGICAL

ORIGINS

of the

AMERICAN

REVOLUTION

FIFTIETH ANNIVERSARY EDITION

BERNARD BAILYN

The Belknap Press of Harvard University Press

Cambridge, Massachusetts

London, England

2017

Fifth Printing

Figure pp. xvi–xvii: Giovanni Battista Piranesi, *The Basilica of Constantine, with a Street Seen through Arches on the Left*. Harvard Art Museums/Fogg Museum, Gift of Roderick K. MacLeod, M13622. Photograph: Imaging Department © President and Fellows of Harvard College.

Figure pp. xviii–xix: Giovanni Battista Piranesi, *The Temple of Portunas (?) (The Round Temple near S. Maria in Cosmedin)*. Harvard Art Museums/Fogg Museum, Permanent transfer from the Fine Arts Library, Harvard University, Gift of Thomas Palmer, Esq., of Boston, 1772, 2008.312.47. Photograph: Imaging Department © President and Fellows of Harvard College.

The Postscript, "Fulfillment: A Commentary on the Constitution," is adapted from *Faces of Revolution,* Copyright © 1990 by Bernard Bailyn, reprinted by permission of Alfred A. Knopf, Inc. "Mind" from *Things of This World,* Copyright © 1956 by Richard Wilbur, is reprinted by permission of Harcourt Brace Jovanovich, Inc.

Library of Congress Cataloging-in-Publication Data
available from the Library of Congress

ISBN 978-0-674-97565-1

PREFACE TO THE
FIFTIETH ANNIVERSARY EDITION

I am grateful to the Harvard University Press for giving this book a new lease on life and thereby, incidentally, leading me to review it—not to evaluate it but only to note my reactions to re-reading it now. For though the book remains exactly as it was first written and supplemented, the readers'—and my own—response to it may well have changed to reflect the circumstances of our time. But the book is not a tract. It is a work of history, the history, in part, of our national origins, which must forever concern us. I note in this new Preface what seem to be now some features of the book that I saw perhaps less clearly in earlier years.

The first is the sense of emergence, which is what much of the book is about. It traces one of those critical passages of history where elements of our own familiar present, still part of an unfamiliar past, begin to disentangle themselves, begin to emerge amid confusion and uncertainty. The crucial words in the pounding debate on constitutional principles and human rights in these initial years of the Revolution were not new, but their meanings were beginning to shift. These inner transformations were neither quick nor clear. They appeared contentiously, erratically from within the struggle for resistance to Britain's sovereignty. The leaders of resistance, as I wrote in the original Foreword to the book, were not philosophers or political theorists but merchants, lawyers, planters, and preachers. They did not write formal discourses, nor did they feel bound to adhere to traditional political maxims or to apparently logical reasoning that led to conclusions they feared. Edmund Burke, in his speech of 1774 on American taxation, caught their spirit exactly. If, he warned the British government, you keep making subtle arguments to justify a supreme sovereignty odious to those you govern, you will teach them to call your sovereignty into question.

> When you drive him hard, the boar will surely turn upon the hunters. If that sovereignty and their freedom cannot be reconciled, what will they take? They will cast your sovereignty in your face. Nobody will be argued into slavery.

So, defiantly and experimentally, the colonial leaders twisted and turned to find new meanings within familiar concepts that they could accept. Britain's "constitution" was famous for its protection of Britons' freedoms. But what was it? It was what was constituted—a loose bundle of statutes, common law, and sanctioned practices, without explicit boundaries. In the course of the American struggle with Britain a new meaning emerged; the term "constitution" remained but was transformed. It came to mean a written, foundational structure of powers and rights superior to and controlling any subsequent enactments. So it was with the age-old concept of the balance of powers in a free state. The formal concept remained dominant in their thinking, but by a complex process, protracted and difficult to trace, the units in balance shifted from social orders or estates to the functioning branches of government.

What strikes me now, looking back over *The Ideological Origins,* is how much of the book is devoted to tracing just such transforming processes. So it was with rights: indistinguishable in the past from the privileges and liberties granted by rulers and municipalities—gifts, as it were, entangled in ancient customs and inscribed in statutes and royal decrees. But as the struggle to find more secure grounds for resistance to Britain's powers developed, so did the transformation of the nature of rights, from sanctified privileges to the natural endowments of humanity based on the principles of reason and justice. None of the Revolutionary writers sought to repudiate the heritage of common and statutory law. Their aim was to establish the source of all rights in the laws of nature and the fundamental endowments of humanity, beyond the reach of legislative powers and executive mandates. It was left for the future to identify exactly what such rights were and to enact them into positive law, a struggle that we now know would have no end. But the Revolutionary generation created the basic transformation of the meaning of rights on what would prove to be the cusp of emerging modernity.

And so it was in other spheres of political thought: in the meaning of representation, in the nature of sovereignty, and in the amplitudes and boundaries of personal freedom. It was an emergent world, slowly becoming part of our familiar present.

I became keenly aware as well, as I went back through the book, of something quite different, something that had developed as the book was written. Some sections of the exposition proved to be a collage of quotations and paraphrases drawn from contributors to the Anglo-American debate—a contentious conversation, it would seem, among many speakers. Some of the writers I quoted or paraphrased were arguing with others directly but some were not; they simply joined the discussion to establish their views of the issues at hand. But however varied in their origins, their scattered comments, when brought together, became direct exchanges. Such constructed debates could produce useful results. A comment from one source could be brought together with its opposite, to show the outer boundaries of opinion, the limits of imagination. Or more commonly and more significantly, the complexity of opinion and the difficulty of establishing any kind of consensus could be shown by juxtaposing similar-seeming but in fact fundamentally different views, many of which became explicit conflicts as the controversy deepened.

But I knew that there were dangers in creating such quasi-conversational or confrontational collages. One could gather together similar sounding expressions to form an apparently consistent grouping, or tradition, or party line that in fact was an authorial construct, a tale of one's own devising. So was I then not assuming some kind of collective mind at work and simply illustrating its fortunes with the documentation I had? There was no such collective mind, but there were vital issues around which scattered opinions could be gathered. They could reasonably and without contextual distortion be grouped together to form virtual discussions that expressed the heart of the matter.

Looking back at the result now, I find this unplanned feature of the book in itself still interesting, and perhaps at this distant point especially useful in conveying a sense of the intellectual excitement of the pre-Revolutionary years of controversy, the raw conflicts and intractable difficulties of the problems the participants faced, and their constant experimentation in unknown territories of political and constitutional thought.

But of all my impressions on re-reading the book the most vivid is the Americans' obsession with Power. It was not one among many concerns; it was their central concern. Power and its ravages engrossed their minds; they wrote about it again and again, elaborately and imaginatively—in pamphlets, letters, newspapers, sermons—in any medium available. But seeing it now with a broader knowledge of early modern political thought and culture, I was struck not only by how fully it permeates the book but also by the curious ways in which the writers expressed their concerns about the uses and misuses of power.

They wrote about the specific agencies of power they feared—royal armies, crown prerogatives, Parliamentary mandates, arbitrary magistrates—and about all the "usurpations" of power that would be listed in the Declaration of Independence. But they wrote more often and more eloquently of power itself: power in its essence, in its nature, whatever its manifestation—as an autonomous entity, a dark, independent, primordial force, pervasive and malign. As such it could be described only in metaphors, similes, and analogies. Power, they wrote, however evoked, "is like the ocean, not easily admitting limits to be fixed in it." It is like "jaws . . . always open to devour." It is "like cancer, it eats faster and faster every hour." And it is everywhere in public life, and everywhere it is dominating, grasping, and absorbing. Liberty, its opposite, could not strongly stand before it. For liberty, as John Adams put it, always "skulking about in corners . . . hunted and persecuted in all countries by cruel power," was in its nature delicate and sensitive, weak in the presence of power. It was to overcome the dark, engrossing force of power that all efforts to liberate mankind had been directed.

I can now see more clearly than before how this essentualization and personification of power and the metaphoric descriptions of its character came to suffuse their thinking. In a situation of political conflict with established authority they drew on the legacy of the "Commonwealthmen," the "real Whigs," who had struggled in the generation after the Revolution of 1688 to carry forward against the Hanoverian court dominated by Robert Walpole the reform principles of the seventeenth century. The great spokesmen and publicists of that earlier age, the political pamphleteers John Trenchard and Thomas Gordon, had been eloquent and prolific on the need for reform and the dangers of powerful autocracies. Their two most famous weekly publications were the *Independent Whig* and *Cato's Letters,* which, republished in book form, together constituted 191 essays on "Liberty, Civil and Religious." These pamphleteers of the 1720s expressed in vivid, challenging, defiant prose the basic themes on the nature and uses of power that the later American Patriots would fervently embrace.

These earlier writings overflowed with examples of the havoc wrought by power—power unfettered, power released, power allowed to tear at the vitals of free institutions and at the liberties of ordinary folk. In a free state power is a trust acquired by consent and used only for the people's good. When it is acquired by force or deceit by those who use it to enhance their own glory and influence, power, they wrote, is arbitrary, and the people suffer deeply. Unconstrained monopolists of power become monsters, tyrants, savages, and they make the world "a slaughter-house," a "desart." They transform "blessings and plenty into curses and misery, great cities into gloomy solitudes, and their rich citizens into beggars and vagabonds." The "Daemons" of power become worse the longer they wield their illegal force, until their victims, refusing to "be slaves to their own servants," find it necessary for their survival to oppose them. And then, they wrote, the great upheavals ensue, as cities and nations are torn apart in the struggle for the uses of power.

These words of the earlier age on the dark progress of power lay deep in the American polemics of the 1760s and 1770s. Active resistance, the American Revolutionaries feared, was required against those who had gained, by brutality or guile or demagoguery, some measure of power's dark essence.

Some people, they knew, seemed never to have known freedom, having been ruled by powerful despots time out of mind: the Russians, the Turks, and the Ottomans, governed by vicious leaders backed by the power of personal janissary troops. But what interested the Americans more than such legendary despotisms were examples of once-free states whose descent into autocracies of power had happened within living memory and had been recorded in detail by participants or contemporary witnesses.

Poland was a case in point—a nation, they believed, sunk in human misery, its peasant people reduced to barbarism, its social condition "a scene of carnage." They could trace equally the loss of liberty in France under Louis XIV, the advent of autocracy in Sweden, and the revolts that shook Spain and severed its relation to Portugal. The most recent example of the loss of freedom was that of Denmark, a story that had been recorded in day-by-day, at times hour-by-hour detail by Viscount Molesworth, England's envoy to Copenhagen under William III. In four short days, they learned from Molesworth's *An Account of Denmark,* that country had "changed from an estate little different from aristocracy to as absolute a monarchy as any is at present." Molesworth, an eyewitness, knew exactly what had happened. At a critical moment, seeking safety from the impositions of the nobles, the two lower orders, the commons and the clergy, fearful and angry, gave the king, their supposed protector, the absolute power of the state, only to discover that "the little finger of an absolute prince can be heavier than the loins of many nobles."

But the greatest example they knew of the descent from freedom to autocracy was the most distant from them in time but so familiar to them as to be contemporaneous in their thinking. This was the fortunes of ancient Rome.

At the start of the book, I wrote at length of the Americans' deep immersion in the writings of antiquity. "Knowledge of classical authors," I wrote, "was universal among colonists with any degree of education," and I referred to the vast array of classical authors they knew and referred to—not merely the obvious Latin writers like Cicero, Tacitus, Sallust, Livy, Ovid, and Virgil, and not merely, among the Greeks, Homer, Sophocles, Herodotus, Plato, and Plutarch, but also lesser known writers like Strabo, Nepos, Petronius, Lucan, and Marcus Aurelius. There was much misunderstanding in their readings; but still, I wrote, they found in the classics their ideal selves, and to some extent their inner voices. And then I wrote:

> The classics of the ancient world are everywhere in the literature of the Revolution, but they are everywhere illustrative, not determinative, of thought. They contributed a vivid vocabulary but not the logic or grammar of thought, a universally respected personification but not the source of political and social beliefs.

The objections to these words by many writers on the classics in America have not subsided in the years since their appearance. It seems that everyone who writes about the subject seems obliged to register, upon reading these words, a sense of violation, of desecration, of lèse-majesté. But for those who knew Molesworth's *Account of Denmark,* the dismal fortunes of Poland, and the collapse of good order in Spain and Sweden, the destruction of the ancient Roman republic, the advent of Caesarian power and the resulting dictatorial principate, was one among many illustrations.

The fullest and most famous history of the destruction of Roman freedom and the rise of imperial power that left Rome in ruins was the detailed two-volume account by the Abbé René-Aubert Vertot, "one of the most popular writers of the first half of the eighteenth century" (Caroline Robbins). English translations of his *Revolutions That Happened in the Government of the Roman Republic* (1720) were in almost every library, private or institutional, in British North America. And so too were copies of Vertot's parallel accounts of the loss of freedom in Spain and Sweden. They were all illustrations of a universal phenomenon. What was unique about the Roman example was the vividness and drama of the personalities involved and the fame and familiarity of some of the major texts of the story. John Adams, age 23, recorded his joy in reading aloud, alone at night in his room, Cicero's four orations against Cataline. The "sweetness and grandeur of his sounds," Adams wrote, "give pleasure enough" to justify reading the great speeches even if one doesn't understand their meaning. His younger contemporary, Josiah Quincy, Jr., a neophyte lawyer with ambitions to play an important role as a learned public intellectual, far exceeded Adams as a classicist. His publications and private correspondence are laced with references to the classical authors. Scarcely a page goes by without one or more references to ancient writings. He seems intellectually to have inhabited the classical world. He and others as well educated knew not only the deeds of Cato but his stoicism as well, not only Brutus's role in history but his self-sacrificing nature, and not only what Tacitus recorded but the terse, sardonic style of his writing as well. And what they knew of these famous figures of the ancient past stirred their imaginations as nothing else could.

Drawing on all the sources they had available—Vertot's volumes and those of other historians of Rome as well as the mass of facts and comments that had appeared in the opposition press a generation earlier—the Americans rejoiced in the freedom of Rome's republic and celebrated its checks on the unlimited power of magistrates. They enjoyed reading about the magnificence of Rome at its height and lamented its decline and fall when freedom was destroyed by the power of imperial despots who lived in corrupt magnificence and left behind a broken and supine people wandering about in the wreckage around them. Their paraphrases of Vertot were dramatic. In the struggle of warring factions in the great contest for power at the end of the Republic

> Rome and all Italy was but one slaughter-house. Thousands, hundreds of thousands, fell sacrifices to the ambition

of a few. Rivers of blood ran in the publick streets, and pro-
scriptions and massacres were esteemed sport and pastime,
till at length two thirds of the people were destroyed and
the rest made slaves to the most wicked and contemptible
wretches of mankind.

Thus ended, Vertot had concluded, "the greatest, the noblest
state that ever adorned the worldly theatre." To which, in 1720
the English "Cato" had commented, "I wish I could say that the
Abbot Vertot's description of the Roman state in its last declension suited no other state in our own time. I hope that we ourselves have none of these corruptions and abuses to complain of."
But it was only a hope, of which the American leaders increasingly despaired. Many active in the struggle with Britain had
come to agree with the well-informed, well-educated member of
the Continental Congress who wrote in 1774: "From the fate of
Rome, Britain may trace the course of its present degeneracy and
its impending destruction. Similar causes will ever produce similar effects."

In Britain as in ancient Rome, the Americans believed, factions were tearing the nation apart. The ancient story of encroaching power and the growing corruption of the newly rich
that had been so clearly illustrated in the case of Rome were being reenacted in Britain, threatening the British empire as it had
the Roman.

There seems to have been no end to the torrent of writings the
Americans had at hand that dwelt on the beauties and the glory
of the ancient Roman republic and its ultimate destruction by the
advent of arbitrary power. So vast, so complex, and so rich in
meaning were the ancient world-historical events that no defini-
tive account of them, they believed, could ever be given. Properly
to describe the "noble" subject of liberty and power in ancient

Rome is a task, Trenchard and Gordon had written in 1722, "to which no human mind is equal,"

> for neither the sublimest wits of antiquity, nor the brightest geniuses of late or modern time, assisted with all the powers of rhetorick and all the stimulations of poetick fire . . . ever did, or ever could, or ever can, describe . . . sufficiently the beauty of the one [liberty] or the deformity of the other [power]. Language [they wrote] fails in it, and words are too weak.

But if language fails and words are not sufficient, how could one recover the Americans' vision of the power-driven corruption of the ancient world? I wondered about this and thought that where words fail, images might succeed.

What did eighteenth-century Rome look like? How did its appearance relate to the Americans' concerns? Few colonists of the Revolutionary years had visited continental Europe, fewer still knew the art world of contemporary Rome. But some did, and others were well informed. Thomas Hollis, Harvard's English benefactor, in constant touch with the American Patriots, was intimately involved with artists and their works in France and Italy, and especially in Rome. It was in the Roman art world that one finds the visual expressions of the Americans' concerns. They lie in the artistic achievements of their contemporary, the celebrated Roman engraver and print maker, Giovanni Battista Piranesi, whom Hollis knew well.

Piranesi's themes in his famous images of antiquity were theirs. Both he and the Americans dwelled on the glory of Rome as a free state and the squalor of its decline and fall. In his great series of prints of contemporary Rome, his *Vedute de Roma* and the *Antichità Romane,* copies of which Hollis sent to Harvard,

Giovanni Battista Piranesi, *The Basilica of Maxentius*

Veduta degli avanzi del Tablino
della Casa aurea di Nerone detti
volgarmente il Tempio della Pace
...

Giovanni Battista Piranesi, *The Temple of Portunas*

Piranesi depicted everything the colonists could have imagined about the greatness of the ancient city and its surroundings: the monumental structures of all kinds, the temples, the celebratory columns, the arches, the tombs, the fountains, the baths, the circuses, the colosseums, all enhanced in monumentality by mannerist exaggerations and by the manipulation of perspective. But the *Vedute* were not only scenes of magnificent architecture. Many of the structures were in ruins, and Piranesi portrayed them as they were: testimonies of the power-driven barbarism that had destroyed the classical world. Some of the crumbling buildings had been shabbily rebuilt to serve as churches, others had been patched together to form ragged habitations with farm equipment scattered about. A few people wander around like "human insects," in Marguerite Yourcenar's words, shuffling "through the rubble or the brush" aimlessly leaning on staves, occasionally gesturing to sights unseen as if guiding strangers through the crumbling ruins. In the shadows of once-great structures, washing is being hung out to dry, donkeys are balking, dogs are barking, goats are wandering among fallen segments of magnificent columns. Here and there people in small groups seem to be conversing, but mostly they are solitary, and everywhere they are "reduced to infinitesimal proportions by the enormity of the edifices."

These scenes of vast power and "minuscule humanity" appear in most concentrated form in Piranesi's earliest and most famous prints, the sixteen nightmarish, hallucinatory scenes of wildly imagined prisons, the *Carceri*—deep, gargantuan, cavernous, and darkly threatening spaces with sweeping ranges of staircases and platforms that lead nowhere, soaring ropes of heavy chains, spiked wheels, racks, and other instruments of torture. Everywhere in these vast inhuman halls is a sense of the brutality of power. The people scattered here and there on the platforms and stairs are simply watching, dwarfed by the monumental stone labyrinths that surround them.

There were, of course, no such prisons in Rome or anywhere else. They were products of Piranesi's imagination, his dark dreams, his *capricci,* his fantasies. But these imaginings were well within the range of the Americans' fears of uncontrolled power, which would appear also in the great popularity in the colonies as in Europe of Cesare Beccaria's tract, *On Crime and Punishment.* Written in 1764 to reform the entire judicial system of the *ancien régime,* it centered on the issues of arbitrary power.

Such are a few of the features of the book that stand out to me most clearly now. But they are part of the larger design of the book, which I hope in its entirety still conveys an understanding of the ideas, beliefs, fears, and aspirations that inspired the rebellion against Britain and ultimately the founding of the American nation.

B. B.

2017

PREFACE TO THE TWENTY-FIFTH
ANNIVERSARY EDITION

Thinking back to the inception of this book, almost three decades ago, I can recall the intense excitement and the sense of discovery I felt in studying freshly the ideological themes of Revolutionary America. I, and others who shared that excitement, had been surprised to see the dominant cluster of ideas, beliefs, and attitudes that came to light when the Enlightenment platitudes were put aside and one concentrated on what the leaders of the Revolutionary movement were actually saying, where their ideas had actually come from, how those ideas had cohered, and how, though derived from a different world, they had articulated circumstances unique to North America. Those discoveries emerged from a deeply contextualist approach to history—an immersion in the detailed circumstances of a distant era and an effort to understand that world not as it anticipated the future but as it was experienced by those who lived in it.

In that context it became clear that the ideology of the American Revolution was a blend of ideas and beliefs that were extremely radical for the time—and that are implicitly radical still. In fact, I called the book when it was first published *The Transforming Radicalism of the American Revolution,* and worked out some of the broader implications of that theme in Chapter VI: "The Contagion of Liberty." The ideology of the Revolution, derived from many sources, was dominated by a peculiar strand of British political thought. It was a cluster of convictions focused on the effort to free the individual from the oppressive misuse of power, from the tyranny of the state. But the spokesmen of the Revolution—the pamphleteers, essayists, and miscellaneous commentators—were not philosophers and they did not form a detached intelligentsia. They were active politicians, merchants, lawyers, plantation owners, and preachers, and they were not attempting to align their thought with that of major figures in the history of political philosophy whom modern scholars would declare to have been seminal. They did not think of themselves as "civic humanists," nor did I describe them as such in attempting to characterize their thought. They would have been surprised to hear that they had fallen into so neat a pattern in the history of political thought. They believed that any political system, certainly all republics, had to be based in some significant degree on virtue, but they had no illusions about the virtue of ordinary people, and all of them believed in the basic value of personal property, its preservation and the fostering of economic growth. They were both "civic humanists" and "liberals," though with different emphases at different times and in different circumstances. And indeed it is the flexibility of their ideas, the complex variations that could be harmoniously composed on the main themes, that has proven the most impressive product of the later studies of Revolutionary ideology. The force and cohesiveness of the original ideas and beliefs were clear from the start, but not their inclusiveness, their adaptability, and their resilience in the face of changing demands and circumstances. These qualities emerged as the story was carried forward beyond 1776, and one could examine in detail the encounters of these ideas with new and different problems.

In the first phase of their effort to think through and put to use the ideas they had inherited and valued most—the main subject of this book—they directed their attention to corruption abroad and the acute political dangers they faced at home, and concluded that perpetuation of the freedom they had known required, at whatever cost, the destruction of the political and constitutional system that had hitherto governed them. In the next phase—reforming, according to progressive principles, the public life of the separate states—they drew on ideas, implicit and explicit in what had gone before, related to the technical problems of liberalizing the small-scale governments with which they were deeply familiar and which made no claims to the powers of nation-states. The final phase—perverse, it seemed to many, in view of the main concerns of the pre-Revolutionary years—was the construction of a new national government of great potential power, a government that would rule over a diverse community and that previously had existed, feebly, only in the desperation of war. But to build such a nation-state to replace the power system from which they had only recently escaped seemed to reverse the direction of the ideological revolution they had created. To be certain that that did not happen, they had to return to their ideological origins, rethink the principles that had guided them into and through the Revolution, refine them, modernize them, and then reapply them in this new situation. In the end they found themselves fulfilling their original goals by creating power, on new principles, not by destroying it.

To probe this conclusive phase of the ideology of the Revolution in which the protean possibilities of the original ideas were deeply explored and daringly applied, I have expanded the original book by including a Postscript on the vast, sprawling, bitterly contentious debate on the ratification of the Constitution. Just as the original book was based on an examination of the corpus of writings, formal and informal, of those who undertook the Revolution, so this Postscript is a product of a close reading of the enormous documentation—the countless newspaper pieces, personal correspondences, state papers, and speeches pro and con in the ratifying conventions—produced in the tumultuous year when the fate of the Constitution hung in the balance.

PREFACE, 1992

This nationwide debate, in which every community and every politically conscious person participated, was a sequel to everything that had come before and it was a preface to what was to follow. But while a new national power system emerged from this struggle, it does not mark a sudden break in the ideological history of our national origins. The powerful set of ideas, ideals, and political sensibilities that shaped the origins and early development of the Revolution did not drop dead with the Constitution. That document, in my view, does not mark a Thermidorean reaction to the idealism of the early period engineered by either a capitalist junta or the proponents of rule by a leisured patriciate; nor did the tenth *Federalist* paper mark the death knell of earlier political beliefs or introduce at a crack a new political science. Modifications in the basic doctrines had to be made to accommodate the urgencies that had arisen; fundamental beliefs had to be tested, refined, modernized, and ingeniously reapplied—but they were not repudiated. The Constitution created, of course, a potentially powerful central government, with powers that served certain economic groups particularly well, and this new government could be seen—as many antifederalists saw it—as just the kind of arbitrary, absolute, and concentrated power that the Revolution had set out to destroy. But in fact, as almost all the antifederalists sooner or later realized, especially when the guarantees of the Bill of Rights were in place, it was not. The earlier principles remained, though in new, more complicated forms, embodied in new institutions devised to perpetuate the received tradition into the modern world. The essential spirit of eighteenth-century reform—its idealism, its determination to free the individual from the power of the state, even a reformed state—lived on, and lives on still.

B. B.
1992

FOREWORD TO THE ORIGINAL EDITION

This book has developed from a study that was first undertaken a number of years ago, when Howard Mumford Jones, then Editor-in-Chief of the John Harvard Library, invited me to prepare a collection of pamphlets of the American Revolution for publication in that series. Like all students of American history I knew well perhaps a half dozen of the most famous pamphlets of the Revolution, obviously worth republication, and I knew also of others, another half dozen or so, that would probably be worth considering. The project was attractive to me, it did not appear to be particularly burdensome, and since in addition it was related to a book I was then preparing on eighteenth century politics, I agreed to undertake it.

The starting point of the work was the compilation of a complete bibliography of the pamphlets. This alone proved to be a considerable task, and it was in assembling this list that I discovered the magnitude of the project I had embarked on. The full bibliography of pamphlets relating to the Anglo-American struggle published in the colonies through the year 1776 contains not a dozen or so items but over four hundred; in the end I concluded that no fewer than seventy-two of them ought to be republished. But sheer numbers were not the most important measure of the magnitude of the project. The pamphlets include all sorts of writings—treatises on political theory, essays on history, political arguments, sermons, correspondence, poems—and they display all sorts of literary devices. But for all their variety they have in common one distinctive characteristic: they are, to an unusual degree, *explanatory*. They reveal not merely positions taken but the reasons why positions were taken; they reveal motive and understanding: the assumptions, beliefs, and ideas—the articulated world view—that lay behind the manifest events of the time. As a result I found myself, as I read through these many documents, studying not simply a particular medium of publication but, through these documents, nothing less than the ideological origins of the American Revolution. And I found myself viewing these origins with surprise, for the "interior" view, from the vantage point of the pamphlets, was different from what I had expected. The task, consequently, took on an increasing excitement, for much of the history of the American Revolution has fallen into the condition that overtakes so many of the great events of the past; it is, as Professor Trevor-Roper has written in another connection, taken for granted: "By our explanations, interpretations, assumptions we gradually make it seem automatic, natural, inevitable; we remove from it the sense of wonder, the unpredictability, and therefore the freshness it ought to have." Study of the pamphlets appeared to lead back into the unpredictable reality of the Revolution, and posed a variety of new problems of interpretation. More, it seemed to me, was called for in preparing this edition than simply reproducing accurately and annotating a selected group of texts.

Study of the pamphlets confirmed my rather old-fashioned view that the American Revolution was above all else an ideological, constitutional, political struggle and not primarily a controversy between social groups undertaken to force changes in the organization of the society or the economy. It confirmed too my belief that intellectual developments in the decade before Independence led to a radical idealization and conceptualization of the previous century and a half of American experience, and that it was this intimate relationship between Revolutionary thought and the circumstances of life in eighteenth-century America that endowed the Revolution with its peculiar force and made it so

profoundly a transforming event.[1] But if the pamphlets confirmed this belief, they filled it with unexpected details and gave
it new meaning. They shed new light on the question of the
sources and character of Revolutionary thought. Most commonly
the thought of the Revolution has been seen simply as an expression of the natural rights philosophy: the ideas of the social contract, inalienable rights, natural law, and the contractual basis
of government. But some have denounced this interpretation as
"obtuse secularism," and, reading the sermons of the time with
acute sensitivity, argue that it was only a respect for world opinion that led the Founders to put their case "in the restricted language of the rational century," and that the success of the Revolutionary movement is comprehensible only in terms of the
continuing belief in original sin and the need for grace. Yet others have described the sermons of the time as a form of deliberate
propaganda by which revolutionary ideas were fobbed off on an
unsuspecting populace by a "black regiment" of clergy committed, for reasons unexplained, to the idea of rebellion. And still
others deny the influence of both Enlightenment theory and theology, and view the Revolution as no revolution at all, but
rather as a conservative movement wrought by practitioners of
the common law and devoted to preserving it, and the ancient
liberties embedded in it, intact.

The pamphlets do reveal the influence of Enlightenment
thought, and they do show the effective force of certain religious
ideas, of the common law, and also of classical literature; but
they reveal most significantly the close integration of these elements in a pattern of, to me at least, surprising design—surprising because of the prominence in it of still another tradition, interwoven with, yet still distinct from, these more familiar

---

[1] Bernard Bailyn, "Political Experience and Enlightenment Ideas in Eighteenth- Century America," *American Historical Review,* 67 (1961–62), 339–351.

strands of thought. This distinctive influence had been transmitted most directly to the colonists by a group of early eighteenth-century radical publicists and opposition politicians in England who carried forward into the eighteenth century and applied to the politics of the age of Walpole the peculiar strain of anti-authoritarianism bred in the upheaval of the English Civil War. This tradition, as it developed in the British Isles, has in part been the subject of extensive research by Caroline Robbins, forming the substance of her *Eighteenth-Century Commonwealthman;* in part too it has been the subject of recent research by students of other aspects of English history in this period: Archibald S. Foord, on the history of the opposition in eighteenth-century English politics; Alan D. McKillop, Bonamy Dobrée, and Louis I. Bredvold on the social and political background of early eighteenth-century literature; J. G. A. Pocock, J. W. Gough, Peter Laslett, and Corinne Weston on political thought in the seventeenth and eighteenth centuries; Ian Christie, George Rudé, Lucy Sutherland, and S. Maccoby on eighteenth-century radicalism. But little if any of this writing had hitherto been applied to the origins of the American Revolution. Convinced of the importance of this influence, I thought it would be useful to identify and analyze all the references found in the pamphlets, and on the basis of that analysis present in both the annotation to the texts and in essay form an interpretation of the sources and character of the American Revolutionary ideology. This essay on sources and patterns of ideas became the nucleus of the General Introduction to the edition of the pamphlets, and subsequently of this book, where it appears as Chapters II and III.

It was in the context of the sources and patterns of ideas presented in these two chapters that I began to see a new meaning in phrases that I, like most historians, had readily dismissed as mere rhetoric and propaganda: "slavery," "corruption," "conspiracy." These inflammatory words were used so forcefully by writers of

so great a variety of social statuses, political positions, and religious persuasions; they fitted so logically into the pattern of radical and opposition thought; and they reflected so clearly the realities of life in an age in which monarchical autocracy flourished,
in which the stability and freedom of England's "mixed" constitution was a recent and remarkable achievement, and in which
the fear of conspiracy against constituted authority was built into
the very structure of politics, that I began to suspect that they
meant something very real to both the writers and their readers:
that there were real fears, real anxieties, a sense of real danger
behind these phrases, and not merely the desire to influence by
rhetoric and propaganda the inert minds of an otherwise passive
populace. The more I read, the less useful, it seemed to me, was
the whole idea of propaganda in its modern meaning when applied to the writings of the American Revolution—a view that I
hope to develop at length on another occasion. In the end I was
convinced that the fear of a comprehensive conspiracy against
liberty throughout the English-speaking world—a conspiracy believed to have been nourished in corruption, and of which, it was
felt, oppression in America was only the most immediately visible part—lay at the heart of the Revolutionary movement. This
too seemed to me to be worth developing. It appeared as a chapter of the General Introduction to the edition of pamphlets, extended in a Note on Conspiracy; in expanded form it constitutes
Chapter IV, and the Note appended to that chapter, in the present volume.

Beyond all of this, however, I found in the pamphlets evidence
of a transformation that overtook the inheritance of political and
social thought as it had been received in the colonies by the early
1760's. Indeliberately, half-knowingly, as responses not to desire
but to the logic of the situation, the leaders of colonial thought
in the years before Independence forced forward alterations in,
or challenged, major concepts and assumptions of eighteenth-

century political theory. They reached—then, before 1776, in the debate on the problem of imperial relations—new territories of thought upon which would be built the commanding structures of the first state constitutions and of the Federal Constitution. This too deserved to be explored, it seemed to me; the results appear in Chapter V. Finally there was evidence that this transformation of thought, which led to conclusions so remarkably congruent with the realities of American life, was powerfully contagious. It affected areas not directly involved in the Anglo-American controversy, areas as gross as the institution of chattel slavery and as subtle as the assumptions of human relations. This "spill-over" effect I have also tried to analyze, with results that appear in Chapter VI.

At no point did I attempt to describe all shades of opinion on any of the problems discussed. I decided at the start to present what I took to be the dominant or leading ideas of those who made the Revolution. There were of course articulate and outspoken opponents of the Revolution, and at times I referred to their ideas; but the future lay not with them but with the leaders of the Revolutionary movement, and it is their thought at each stage of the developing rebellion that I attempted to present, using often the shorthand phrase "the colonists" to refer to them and their ideas.

In this way, topic by topic as the story unfolded in the study of the pamphlets, the chapters that first appeared as the General Introduction to the first volume of *Pamphlets of the American Revolution* (Harvard University Press, 1965) were conceived. Two considerations have led me to attempt to go beyond what I had written there and to develop the General Introduction into the present book. First, I found that there was some demand for a separate republication of the Introduction, the necessarily high price of the first volume of the *Pamphlets* having made its use particularly difficult for students. And second, my own subsequent work on early eighteenth-century politics and political thought led me to uncover a deeper and broader documentation of the story than that presented in the Introduction; and it led me, too, to see deeper implications in the story than those I had been able to see before. In this separate study of early eighteenth-century politics and political theory (published as *The Origins of American Politics*), I discovered that the configuration of ideas and attitudes I had described in the General Introduction as the Revolutionary ideology could be found intact as far back as the 1730's; in partial form it could be found even farther back, at the turn of the seventeenth century. The transmission from England to America of the literature of political opposition that furnished the substance of the ideology of the Revolution had been so swift in the early years of the eighteenth century as to seem almost instantaneous; and, for reasons that reach into the heart of early American politics, these ideas acquired in the colonies an importance, a relevance in politics, they did not then have—and never would have—in England itself. There was no sharp break between a placid pre-Revolutionary era and the turmoil of the 1760's and 1770's. The argument, the claims and counter-claims, the fears and apprehensions that fill the pamphlets, letters, newspapers, and state papers of the Revolutionary years had in fact been heard throughout the century. The problem no longer appeared to me to be simply why there was a Revolution but how such an explosive amalgam of politics and ideology first came to be compounded, why it remained so potent through years of surface tranquillity, and why, finally, it was detonated when it was.

These new materials and this new dimension I have tried to work into the revision and expansion of the original Introduction; and I have tried to do this without destroying the structure of the original chapters. One result has been a considerable enlargement of the annotation. For while the text proper

FOREWORD TO THE ORIGINAL EDITION

is expanded, especially in Chapters II–IV, and the phraseology elaborated in many places to convey the greater density of material and depth of argument, much of the new material will be found in the annotation. It is there, particularly, that I have sought to trace back into the early eighteenth century—and back into the European sources, wherever possible—the specific attitudes, conceptions, formulations, even in certain cases particular phrases, which together form the ideology of the American Revolution.

My debts to the people who assisted in one way or another in the preparation of the initial publication of this book I have gratefully acknowledged in the Foreword to volume I of the *Pamphlets*. Many of them have continued to help in the preparation of this enlarged version. I would like particularly to thank Jane N. Garrett, who assisted me in the research on the early eighteenth-century sources of the Revolutionary ideology, and Carol S. Thorne, who tracked elusive books through the most arcane windings of the Harvard library system, and typed the complicated manuscript accurately and with unfailing good cheer.

B. B.
1967

CONTENTS

ABBREVIATIONS

Adams, *Diary and Autobiography*	Lyman H. Butterfield, *et al.,* eds., *Diary and Autobiography of John Adams.* 4 vols. Cambridge, 1961.
Adams, *Works*	Charles Francis Adams, ed., *The Works of John Adams.* 10 vols. Boston, 1850–1856.
Bailyn, *Pamphlets*	Bernard Bailyn, ed., *Pamphlets of the American Revolution.* Cambridge, 1965, in progress.
CC	Commentaries on the Constitution: vols. XIII–XVI of *Doc. Hist.*
Doc. Hist.	Merrill Jensen, John P. Kaminski, and Gaspare J. Saladino, eds., *The Documentary History of the Ratification of the Constitution.* Madison, 1976, in progress.
Elliot, *Debates*	Jonathan Elliot, ed., *The Debates in the Several State Conventions, on the Adoption of the Federal Constitution . . .* 2d ed., 4 vols. Washington, D.C., 1836.
Evans	Charles Evans, comp., *American Bibliography: A Chronological Dictionary of All Books, Pamphlets and Periodical Publications Printed in the United States of America [1639–1800].* 14 vols. Chicago and Worcester, 1903–1959. (Volumes XIII and XIV were compiled by Clifford K. Shipton.)
Gipson, *British Empire*	Lawrence H. Gipson, *The British Empire before the American Revolution.* 15 vols. Caldwell, Idaho, and New York, 1936–1970.
JHL	The John Harvard Library
MHS *Colls.*	*Collections of the Massachusetts Historical Society*
MHS *Procs.*	*Proceedings of the Massachusetts Historical Society*
Pa. Mag.	*Pennsylvania Magazine of History and Biography*
W.M.Q.	*William and Mary Quarterly*

Chapter I
THE LITERATURE OF REVOLUTION

What do we mean by the Revolution? The war? That was no part of the Revolution; it was only an effect and consequence of it. The Revolution was in the minds of the people, and this was effected, from 1760 to 1775, in the course of fifteen years before a drop of blood was shed at Lexington. The records of thirteen legislatures, the pamphlets, newspapers in all the colonies, ought to be consulted during that period to ascertain the steps by which the public opinion was enlightened and informed concerning the authority of Parliament over the colonies.

— John Adams to Jefferson, 1815

WHATEVER deficiencies the leaders of the American Revolution may have had, reticence, fortunately, was not one of them. They wrote easily and amply, and turned out in the space of scarcely a decade and a half and from a small number of presses a rich literature of theory, argument, opinion, and polemic. Every medium of written expression was put to use. The newspapers, of which by 1775 there were thirty-eight in the mainland colonies, were crowded with columns of arguments and counter-arguments appearing as letters, official documents, extracts of speeches, and sermons. Broadsides — single sheets on which were often printed not only large-letter notices but, in three or four columns of minuscule type, essays of several thousand words — appeared everywhere; they could be found posted or passing from hand to hand in the towns of every colony. Almanacs, workaday publications universally available in the colonies, carried, in odd corners and occasional columns, a considerable freight of political comment.[1] Above all, there were pamphlets: booklets consisting of a few printer's sheets, folded in various ways so as to make various sizes and numbers of pages, and sold — the pages stitched together loosely, unbound and uncovered — usually for a shilling or two.[2]

It was in this form — as pamphlets — that much of the most important and characteristic writing of the American Revolution appeared. For the Revolutionary generation, as for its predecessors back to the early sixteenth century, the pamphlet had peculiar virtues as a medium of communication. Then, as now, it was seen that the pamphlet allowed one to do things that were not possible in any other form.

The pamphlet [George Orwell, a modern pamphleteer, has written] is a one-man show. One has complete freedom of expression, including, if one chooses, the freedom to be scurrilous, abusive, and seditious; or, on the other hand, to be more detailed, serious and "highbrow" than is ever possible in a newspaper or in most kinds of periodicals. At the same time, since the pamphlet is always short and unbound, it can be produced much more quickly than a book, and in principle, at any rate, can reach a bigger public. Above all, the pamphlet does not have to follow any prescribed pattern. It can be in prose or in verse, it can consist largely of maps or statistics or quotations, it can take the form of a story, a fable, a letter, an essay, a dialogue, or a piece of "reportage." All that is required of it is that it shall be topical, polemical, and short.[3]

[1] Arthur M. Schlesinger, *Prelude to Independence* (New York, 1958), pp. 215–216, part ii; Philip Davidson, *Propaganda and the American Revolution* (Chapel Hill, 1941), pp. 216–224.

[2] The precise bibliographical definition of a pamphlet is the following: a booklet formed by the folding and stitching loosely together of between two and five printer's sheets, which "gives to a pamphlet, in extreme, twenty pages when printed in folio; forty pages when printed in quarto; and eighty pages when printed in octavo." Charles Evans and Clifford K. Shipton, comps., *American Bibliography* . . . (Chicago and Worcester, Mass., 1903–1959), V, xv. Cf. Lester Condit, *A Pamphlet about Pamphlets* (Chicago, 1939), chap. i.

[3] George Orwell, "Introduction," in George Orwell and Reginald Reynolds, eds., *British Pamphleteers* (London, 1948–1951), I, 15. Orwell's spirited introductory essay was sparked by his belief that in twentieth-century society the

The pamphlet's greatest asset was perhaps its flexibility in size, for while it could contain only a very few pages and hence be used for publishing short squibs and sharp, quick rebuttals, it could also accommodate much longer, more serious and permanent writing as well. Some pamphlets of the Revolutionary period contain sixty or even eighty pages, on which are printed technical, magisterial treatises. Between the extremes of the squib and the book-length treatise, however, there lay the most commonly used, the ideally convenient, length: from 5,000 to 25,000 words, printed on anywhere from ten to fifty pages, quarto or octavo in size.

The pamphlet of this middle length was perfectly suited to the needs of the Revolutionary writers. It was spacious enough to allow for the full development of an argument — to investigate premises, explore logic, and consider conclusions; it could accommodate the elaborate involutions of eighteenth-century literary forms; it gave range for the publication of fully wrought, leisurely-paced sermons; it could conveniently carry state papers, collections of newspaper columns, and strings of correspondence. It was in this form, consequently, that "the best thought of the day expressed itself"; it was in this form that "the solid framework of constitutional thought" was developed; it was in this form that "the basic elements of American political thought of the Revolutionary period appeared first." [4] And yet pamphlets of

---

press does not adequately represent all shades of opinion. "At any given moment there is a sort of all-prevailing orthodoxy, a general tacit agreement not to discuss some large and uncomfortable fact." He looked back to the days of vigorous, highly individualistic pamphleteering with nostalgia, and hoped that people "would once again become aware of the possibilities of the pamphlet as a method of influencing opinion, and as a literary form." A. J. P. Taylor's introduction to volume II of the same collection is an acerb comment on Orwell's nostalgia.

[4] Davidson, *Propaganda*, pp. 209–210; Moses C. Tyler, *The Literary History of the American Revolution, 1763-1783* (New York, 1897), I, 17 ff.; Homer L. Calkin, "Pamphlets and Public Opinion during the American Revolution," *Pa. Mag.*, 64 (1940), 22–42.

this length were seldom ponderous; whatever the gravity of their themes or the spaciousness of their contents, they were always essentially polemical, and aimed at immediate and rapidly shifting targets: at suddenly developing problems, unanticipated arguments, and swiftly rising, controversial figures. The best of the writing that appeared in this form, consequently, had a rare combination of spontaneity and solidity, of dash and detail, of casualness and care.

Highly flexible, easy to manufacture, and cheap, pamphlets were printed in the American colonies wherever there were printing presses, intellectual ambitions, and political concerns. But in their origins most of them may be grouped within three categories. The largest number were direct responses to the great events of the time. The Stamp Act touched off a heavy flurry of pamphleteering in which basic American positions in constitutional theory were staked out; its repeal was celebrated by the publication of at least eleven thanksgiving sermons, all of them crowded with political theory; the Townshend Duties led to another intense burst of pamphleteering, as did the Boston Massacre and the precipitating events of the insurrection itself — the Tea Party, the Coercive Acts, and the meeting of the first Continental Congress.[5]

But if the writing of the pamphlets had been only a response to these overt public events, their numbers would have been far smaller than in fact they were. They resulted also, and to a considerable extent, from what might be called chain-reacting personal polemics: strings of individual exchanges — arguments, replies, rebuttals, and counter-rebuttals — in which may be found

---

[5] See, in general, Evans, *American Bibliography*, vols. III–V; and Thomas R. Adams, *American Independence, the Growth of an Idea: A Bibliographical Study of the American Political Pamphlets Published between 1764 and 1776* . . . (Providence, 1965). The published sermons delivered at the repeal of the Stamp Act are listed in William D. Love, Jr., *The Fast and Thanksgiving Days of New England* (Boston and New York, 1895), pp. 541–542.

heated personifications of the larger conflict. A bold statement on a sensitive issue was often sufficient to start such a series, which characteristically proceeded with increasing shrillness until it ended in bitter personal vituperation. Thus East Apthorp's tract of 1763 on the Church of England's Society for the Propagation of the Gospel, inflaming as it did New Englanders' fears of an American bishopric, was answered at once by Jonathan Mayhew in a 176-page blast, and then, in the course of the next two years, by no less than nine other pamphleteers writing in a melee of thrusts and counterthrusts. Similarly, a succession of seven or eight searing pamphlets followed Richard Bland's attack on the Reverend John Camm in the Two-Penny Act controversy in Virginia. Any number of people could join in such proliferating polemics, and rebuttals could come from all sides. Thomas Paine's *Common Sense* was answered not merely by two exhaustive refutations by Tories but also by at least four pamphlets written by patriots who shared his desire for independence but not his constitutional and religious views or his assumptions about human nature.[6]

A third type of pamphlet — besides those that surrounded the great public events and those that appeared in polemical series — was distinguished by the ritualistic character of its themes and language. In the course of the Revolutionary controversy, the regular, usually annual, publication in pamphlet form of commemorative orations came to constitute a significant addition to the body of Revolutionary literature. In an earlier period such publications had consisted mainly of sermons delivered on election day in New England, together with a few of those preached on official thanksgiving and fast days, and public letters addressed to "freeholders and qualified voters" that appeared regularly on

---

[6] Adams, *Bibliographical Study*, contains a separate listing of "Pamphlet Exchanges." On the Apthorp-Mayhew and Bland-Camm controversies, see Bailyn, *Pamphlets*, I, Introductions to Pamphlets 3, 4, 10, 11, and 13. See also below, pp. 96–97, 251–257.

the eve of the annual elections. But from the mid-1760's on, celebrations of more secular anniversaries were added: the anniversary of the repeal of the Stamp Act, of the Boston Massacre, of the landing of the Pilgrims, and of an increasing number of fast and thanksgiving days marking political rather than religious events.[7]

Such commemorative orations were stylized; but in the heat of controversy the old forms took on new vigor, new relevance and meaning: some of the resulting pamphlets of this type have remarkable force and originality. Massachusetts and Connecticut had been publishing sermons preached on election days for one hundred years before Independence; by 1760 these pamphlets had arrived not only at an apparent fulfillment in style but, in content, at a classically monitorial attitude to political authority as well. Yet Andrew Eliot's use of the familiar formulas in his election sermon of 1765 infused them with more direct power and gave them new point; for to proclaim from the pulpit in the year of the Stamp Act and before the assembled magistrates of Massachusetts that when tyranny is abroad "submission . . . is a crime" was an act of political defiance strengthened rather than weakened by the sanction of time and tradition the words had acquired. Similarly the title of John Carmichael's Artillery Company sermon, *A Self-Defensive War Lawful,* though it

[7] Love, *Fast and Thanksgiving Days, passim;* Robert W. G. Vail, "A Check List of New England Election Sermons," *Proceedings of the American Antiquarian Society,* new ser., 45 (1935), 233–266. *A Letter to the Freeholders, and Qualified Voters, Relating to the Ensuing Election* (Boston, 1749) is typical of its genre. The Massacre Orations were delivered annually from 1771 to 1784, when they were superseded by Fourth of July Orations. In 1785 Peter Edes published a collection of Massacre Orations under the title *Orations Delivered at the Request of Inhabitants . . .* (Boston, [1785]). Accounts of the orators and of the circumstances of their speaking appear in James S. Loring, *The Hundred Boston Orations Appointed by the Municipal Authorities . . .* (Boston, 1852). On the Pilgrim celebrations and the general significance of the pre-Revolutionary commemorations, see Wesley Frank Craven, *The Legend of the Founding Fathers* (New York, 1956), chap. ii.

merely repeated a traditional phrase, was, in 1775, in itself provocative; and the concluding passage of the pamphlet constitutes a significant transition in which clichés about the duties of Christian soldiers acquire the fervor of battlefield prayers. And if one of the later commemorative celebrations, that of the Boston Massacre, quickly became the occasion for the outpouring of some of the most lurid and naive rhetoric heard in eighteenth-century America, another of them, a thanksgiving day appointed by the Continental Congress, inspired an obscure Salem parson to write, in the most dignified and moving prose, a paean to the promise of American life, and to devise an original blend of theological and constitutional principles. Everywhere in New England, clerical orators celebrating these anniversary events invoked the power of the ancient "jeremiad" to argue that "any vindication of provincial privileges was inextricably dependent upon a moral renovation." [8]

Not all the pamphlets, of course, fall into these three categories. Some, like the *Votes and Proceedings of the Freeholders . . . of . . . Boston* (1772), written for circulation in pamphlet form, were in themselves political events to which other pamphleteers responded. Others, like Jefferson's *Summary View . . .* (1774), written as an instruction to the Virginia delegates to the first Continental Congress, were political "position" papers. And in addition there were literary pieces — poems like John Trumbull's *M'Fingal* and plays like Mercy Otis Warren's *The Blockheads* and *The Group* — which, though manifestly political, sprang from more deeply personal inspiration.

---

[8] Andrew Eliot, *A Sermon Preached before His Excellency Francis Bernard . . .* (Boston, 1765: JHL Pamphlet 15), pp. 47–48; John Carmichael, *A Self-Defensive War Lawful . . .* (Lancaster, Mass., [1775]), esp. p. 25; Samuel Williams, *A Discourse on the Love of Our Country . . .* (Salem, 1775: JHL Pamphlet 55); Perry Miller, "From the Covenant to the Revival," in *The Shaping of American Religion* (James W. Smith and A. Leland Jamison, eds., *Religion in American Life*, I, Princeton, 1961), p. 327. (Miller's important essay is being reprinted in the forthcoming collection of his writings, *Nature's Nation*.)

Expressing vigorous, polemical, and more often than not considered views of the great events of the time; proliferating in chains of personal vituperation; and embodying to the world the highly charged sentiments uttered on commemorative occasions, pamphlets appeared year after year and month after month in the crisis of the 1760's and 1770's. More than 400 of them bearing on the Anglo-American controversy were published between 1750 and 1776; over 1,500 appeared by 1783.[9] Explanatory as well as declarative, and expressive of the beliefs, attitudes, and motivations as well as of the professed goals of those who led and supported the Revolution, the pamphlets are the distinctive literature of the Revolution. They reveal, more clearly than any other single group of documents, the contemporary meaning of that transforming event.

Important above all else as expressions of the ideas, attitudes, and motivations that lay at the heart of the Revolution, the pamphlets published in the two decades before Independence are primarily political, not literary, documents. But form and substance are never wholly separate. The literary qualities of the pamphlets are also important, not only in themselves but for what they reveal of the people who wrote them, their goals and style of mind.

These pamphlets form part of the vast body of English polemical and journalistic literature of the seventeenth and eighteenth centuries to which the greatest men of letters contributed. Milton, Halifax, Locke, Swift, Defoe, Bolingbroke, Addison were all pamphleteers at least to the extent that Bland, Otis, Dickinson, the Adamses, Wilson, and Jefferson were. But there are striking differences in the quality of the British and American polemical writings considered simply as literature.

The differences do not lie in the presence or absence of literary

---

[9] On the figures for the later years, see Calkin, "Pamphlets and Public Opinion," p. 23.

techniques. One of the surprising aspects of the American writings is the extent to which they include the stylistic modes associated with the great age of English pamphleteering. Of satire, the protean artifice that dominated the most creative pamphleteering of the time, one scholar has identified no fewer than 530 examples published in America during the period 1763–1783; a large percentage of these appeared originally, or were reprinted, in pamphlets.[10] In addition to satire there is an abundance of other devices: elusive irony and flat parody; extended allegory and direct vituperation; sarcasm, calculated and naive. All the standard tropes and a variety of unusual figurations may be found in the pamphlet literature.

The results are at times remarkable. Who has ever heard of Ebenezer Chaplin? He was parson of the second parish of the town of Sutton, Massachusetts, in the years before the Revolution; in conventional form he preached regularly and published occasionally on the problems of the church. But in a sermon published as a pamphlet in 1773 he suddenly revealed a remarkably self-conscious literary bent. The sermon is entitled *The Civil State Compared to Rivers,* and in it Chaplin managed for the better part of twenty-four pages to sustain the single simile announced in the title; the figure winds steadily through the argument, dramatizing it, coloring it, raising the aesthetic level of the piece far above what could have been attained by direct exposition. It is a noteworthy literary invention, and it gleams amid the hundreds of artistically drab sermons of the period.[11]

Similarly unexpected in its literary effects, though of a quite different genre, is Philip Livingston's *Other Side of the Question,* which appeared in the heavy bombardment of polemics of 1774. Where most of the writers in those exchanges used invective,

[10] Bruce I. Granger, *Political Satire in the American Revolution, 1763–1783* (Ithaca, 1960), p. viii.
[11] Ebenezer Chaplin, *The Civil State Compared to Rivers, All under God's Control and What People Have To Do When Administration Is Grievous . . .* (Boston, 1773).

Livingston used ironic ridicule, and he did so with such agility and lightness of touch that a device reminiscent of *Tristram Shandy* fits in naturally; two scatological passages seem normal exaggerations of a smart and worldly style.[12]

Effective in another way is the extended sham of a Christian catechism that was published anonymously in 1771 as an attack on sycophantic officemongering. No work of genius, it nevertheless gave a twist of originality to a familiar theme, exaggerating the abjectness of bought loyalty by its burlesque of sacred obligations. In a somewhat similar vein is what has been described as "the most ambitious and nearly successful of half a dozen Biblical imitations which appeared in the Revolutionary period," *The First Book of the American Chronicles of the Times,* a parody in six parts of an entire book of the Bible. It is so complete in its plot and characterization as to make identification of people and places an engaging puzzle. By its extensiveness and detail, by the sheer number of its imaginative touches, it attains a considerable effect.[13]

[12] [Philip Livingston], *The Other Side of the Question* . . . (New York, 1774: JHL Pamphlet 51), p. 11: "Pray read the eighth and ninth pages ———— ———— ———— ———— ———— ———— ———— Have you read them? ———— Why now, your honor, I will undertake to confute everything contained there." See also pp. 20, 25.

[13] *A Ministerial Catechise, Suitable To Be Learned by All Modern Provincial Governors, Pensioners, Placemen, &c. Dedicated to T[homas] H[utchinson], Esq.* (Boston, 1771: JHL Pamphlet 34); *The First Book of the American Chronicles of the Times* (1774–1775: JHL Pamphlet 57); Granger, *Political Satire,* p. 70. *The First Book,* which was enormously popular, was published in six chapter segments in Philadelphia, Boston, New Bern, N.C., and Norwich, Connecticut. On the complicated printing history of this pamphlet, or series of pamphlets, see J. R. Bowman, "A Bibliography of *The First Book* . . . ," *American Literature,* I (1929–30), 69–74. Political satire in the form of Biblical parodies was popular throughout the Revolutionary period, as it had been in earlier years. Cf. Davidson, *Propaganda,* p. 212; Granger, *Political Satire,* pp. 34–35, 68–70, 236–237. For an example characteristic of the earlier years, see Stephen Hopkins', or his party's, *The Fall of Samuel the Squomicutite, and the Overthrow of the Sons of Gideon,* referring to Samuel Ward and Gideon Wanton, described in Edward Field, ed., *State of Rhode Island and Providence Plantations* . . . (Boston, 1902), I, 209–210.

In other ways, by other devices, literary effects were sought and achieved. The most commonly attempted was the satire associated with pseudonymous authorship. Governor Stephen Hopkins of Rhode Island, for example, fell upon the opportunity offered to him when his antagonist, Judge Martin Howard, Jr., characterized him as a "ragged country fellow"; he replied with an earthy, vicious attack which he justified by the argument that rags go together with a crude directness of speech. And Richard Bland, in what was probably the most intricate literary conceit written in the entire period, succeeded to such an extent in ridiculing his antagonist by reversing roles with him and condemning him from his own mouth that his victim was forced to reply weakly by explaining to his readers who was really who. Even the more common and transparent forms of pseudonymity provided an opportunity for literary invention. The pastoral pose was more useful to the Reverend Samuel Seabury, arguing the case for the agrarian interests in New York against nonimportation, than it had been to the most famous "farmer" of them all, John Dickinson; it provided not only a consistent point of view but figures of speech and the opportunity for fanciful self-characterization.[14]

All sorts of literary twists and turns were used. Thomas Bradbury Chandler's *The American Querist,* one of the most popular of the Tory pamphlets, consisted of an even one hundred rhetorical questions aimed at the pretensions of the first Continental Congress; the queries were printed for emphasis as one hundred separate paragraphs spread across twenty-one octavo pages. Elephantine footnoting attached to nine stanzas of lampooning verse

[14] [Stephen Hopkins], *A Letter to the Author of the Halifax Letter* . . . ([Newport], 1765); [Richard Bland], *The Colonel Dismounted: Or the Rector Vindicated* . . . (Williamsburg, 1764: JHL Pamphlet 4); [John Camm], *Critical Remarks on a Letter Ascribed to Common Sense . . . with a Dissertation on Drowsiness* . . . (Williamsburg, 1765), pp. vi–ix; [Samuel Seabury], *Free Thoughts on the Proceedings of the Continental Congress Held at Philadelphia September 5, 1774* . . . ([New York], 1774), reprinted in Clarence H. Vance, ed., *Letters of a Westchester Farmer (1774–1775)* (*Publications of the Westchester County Historical Society,* VIII, White Plains, 1930), pp. 43–68.

was the form one response took to Mayhew's extended attacks on the Society for the Propagation of the Gospel. Dramatic dialogues —*"Between the Ghost of General Montgomery, Just Arrived from the Elysian Fields, and An American Delegate"*; *"Between a Southern Delegate and His Spouse"* — were convenient frames for lurid caricatures, and since they made fewer demands on the skills of the dramatist, they were on the whole more successful than the half-dozen more fully evolved plays that were written for pamphlet publication.[15]

And all the detailed linguistic tactics of the classic era of English pamphleteering were present. The pamphlets abound in aphorisms: a section of one sermon is in effect nothing but a mosaic of aphorisms.[16] There are apostrophes, hyperboles, and vivid personifications. There are subtle transitions that seek to ease the flow of thought, and others contrived to interrupt it, to surprise and fix attention. Even the most crudely bombastic harangues contain artful literary constructions.

And yet, for all of this — for all of the high self-consciousness of literary expression, the obvious familiarity with cosmopolitan models and the armory of sophisticated belles-lettres — the pamphlets of the American Revolution that seek artistic effects are not great documents. Next to the more artful pamphlets of eighteenth-century England they are pallid, imitative, and crude. And the higher, the more technically demanding the mode of expression, the more glaring the contrast. There is nothing in

[15] [Thomas Bradbury Chandler], *The American Querist: or, Some Questions Proposed* . . . ([New York], 1774: JHL Pamphlet 47); [John Aplin], *Verses on Doctor Mayhew's Book of Observations* (Providence, 1763: JHL Pamphlet 3). The dialogues, in the order cited, were published in Philadelphia, 1776 (cf. Richard Gimbel, *Thomas Paine: A Bibliographical Check List of Common Sense* . . . , New Haven, 1956, CS 9, p. 74) and [New York], 1774. They are reprinted in *Magazine of History*, 13 [Extra Number 51] (1916); and 18 [Extra Number 72] (1920–21).

[16] Samuel Cooke, *A Sermon Preached at Cambridge, in the Audience of His Honor Thomas Hutchinson Esq.* . . . (Boston, 1770), pp. 11 ff.

the American literature that approaches in sheer literary skill such imaginatively conceived and expertly written pamphlets as Swift's *Modest Proposal* and Defoe's *Shortest Way with the Dissenters*; there is no allegory as masterful as Arbuthnot's *History of John Bull,* and no satire as deft as his *Art of Political Lying.* Indeed, there are not many of the American pamphlets that are as successful in technique as any number of the less imaginative, straight expository essays published in seventeenth- and eighteenth-century England, essays of which Shebbeare's *Letter to the People of England,* lamenting corruption and excoriating the mismanagement of Braddock's expedition, may be taken as average in quality and Swift's *Conduct of the Allies* as a notable refinement. Why this should be so — why the more imaginative and self-consciously literary of the pamphlets of the Revolution should be manifestly inferior in quality to the English models — is an important even if not a wholly answerable question. For it helps locate and explain the qualities of these documents that are of the greatest distinction.

First and foremost, the American pamphleteers, though participants in a great tradition, were amateurs next to such polemicists as Swift and Defoe. Nowhere in the relatively undifferentiated society of colonial America had there developed before 1776 a group of penmen professional in the sense that Defoe or Franklin's friend James Ralph were professional: capable, that is, of earning their living by their pens, capable of producing copy on order as well as on inspiration, and taught by the experience of dozens of polemical encounters the limits and possibilities of their craft. The closest to having attained such professionalism in the colonies were a few of the more prominent printers; but with the exception of Franklin they did not transcend the ordinary limitations of their trade: they were rarely principals in the controversies of the time. The American pamphleteers were almost to a man lawyers, ministers, merchants, or planters heavily engaged in their regular occupations. For them political writing was an uncommon diversion, peripheral to their main concerns. They wrote easily and readily, but until the crisis of Anglo-American affairs was reached, they had had no occasion to turn out public letters, tracts, and pamphlets in numbers at all comparable to those of the English pamphleteers. The most experienced polemical writer in the colonies was probably William Livingston of New York, who, together with two or three of his friends, had sustained *The Independent Reflector* through enough issues in 1752 and 1753 to fill one good-sized volume.[17] But Swift's formal prose work alone fills fourteen volumes, and Defoe is known to have written at least 400 tracts, pamphlets, and books: his contributions to a single periodical during a ten year period total 5,000 printed pages, and they represent less than half of what he wrote in those years. It appears to have been no great matter for a professional like James Ralph, who attained success as a paid political writer after years of effort in poetry, drama, and criticism and who late in life published an eloquent *Case of Authors by Profession or Trade,* to turn out, amid a stream of pamphlets and periodical pieces, a massive *History of England* whose bibliographical and critical introduction alone covers 1,078 folio pages.[18]

No American writer in the half century between the death of Cotton Mather and the Declaration of Independence had anything like such experience in writing; and it is this amateurism,

[17] William Livingston, *et al., The Independent Reflector* . . . (Milton M. Klein, ed., Cambridge, 1963).

[18] On the professionalism of the English political writers in general, see Laurence Hanson, *Government and the Press, 1695–1763* (Oxford, 1936) (on Defoe's productivity, p. 94); William T. Laprade, *Public Opinion and Politics in Eighteenth Century England* (New York, 1936); Robert R. Rea, *The English Press in Politics, 1760–1774* (Lincoln, Nebraska, 1963). On Ralph, whose *History* was used by the colonists (see *Letter to the People of Pennsylvania,* JHL Pamphlet 2, text note 1) and whose career stands in such striking contrast to those of the American pamphleteers, see Robert W. Kenny, "James Ralph . . . ," *Pa. Mag.,* 64 (1940), 218–242.

this lack of practiced technique, that explains much of the crudeness of the Revolutionary pamphlets considered simply as literature. For while the colonial writers were obviously acquainted with and capable of imitating the forms of sophisticated polemics, they had not truly mastered them; they were rarely capable of keeping their literary contrivances in control. All of the examples cited above for their literary qualities (and as self-conscious artistic efforts they are among the most noteworthy documents of the group) suffer from technical weaknesses. By virtue of its extended simile Chaplin's *Civil State* shines among the sermons of the time, but in the end the effect is almost overcome by insistence; the figure is maintained too long; it becomes obtrusive, and the reader ends more aware of it than of the thought it is supposed to be illuminating. The *Ministerial Catechism* lacks the verbal cleverness necessary to keep it from falling into a jog-trotting substitution-play of words. And while *The First Book of . . . American Chronicles* is a more intricate and extended burlesque, its diction, one critic has noted, "has a synthetic ring and at one point a brief passage of French dialect is jarring." [19] Most of the pseudonymous poses, including Hopkins' cited above, were transparent to begin with, and they were unevenly, even sloppily, maintained; often they were simply cast aside after the opening passages, to be snatched up again hurriedly at the end in a gesture of literary decorousness. Even Bland, as artful a litterateur as America produced in the period, was incapable of fully controlling his own invention. If his elaborate conceit threw his intended victim into confusion, it must have had a similar effect on many of its other readers, for at times the point is almost lost in a maze of true and facetious meanings. Chandler's *Querist* is notably original, but strings of syntactically identical questions can become monotonous unless their contents are unusually clever; fifty of them are almost certain to become wearying;

[19] Granger, *Political Satire*, p. 70.

Chandler's one hundred will exhaust the patience of any reader.

And these are among the strongest of the efforts made to attain literary effects. The weakest are, on technical grounds, quite remarkably bad. The poetry — or, more accurately, the versification — is almost uniformly painful to read. There is scarcely a single group of stanzas that can be read with any satisfaction as poetry. Most of the verses are a kind of limping jingle-jangle in which sense and sound are alternatively sacrificed to each other, and both, occasionally, to the demands of termination. The dramatic dialogues, whatever their political importance might be, as literary expressions are wooden and lifeless. And the plays, especially the verse plays, are almost totally devoid of characterization or any other form of verisimilitude.

But there is more than amateurism behind the relative crudeness of the artistic efforts in the American pamphlets. For if writers like Adams and Jefferson were amateur pamphleteers, their writings in other ways display formidable literary talents. Jefferson had an extraordinary gift for supple and elegant if abstract expression; it was well known and appreciated at the time. And Adams, seemingly so stolid and unimaginative an embodiment of prosaic virtues, had a basically sensuous apprehension of experience which he expressed in brilliantly idiomatic and figurative prose — but in diary notations and in letters. Neither, as pamphleteers, sought literary effects: Jefferson's sole effort is a straightforward if gracefully written political policy statement, and Adams' major piece is a treatise on government.[20]

It is not simply a question of the presence or absence of literary

[20] Jefferson's style has been frequently discussed, most fully by Carl Becker, *The Declaration of Independence* (New York, 1922), chap. v. Cf. Bernard Bailyn, "Boyd's Jefferson: Notes for a Sketch," *New England Quarterly,* 33 (1960), 392–393. On Adams' prose, see Bernard Bailyn, "Butterfield's Adams: Notes for a Sketch," *W.M.Q.,* 3d ser., 19 (1962), 246–247. The writings referred to are Jefferson's *A Summary View of the Rights of British America* . . . (Williamsburg, [1774]: JHL Pamphlet 43) and Adams' *Thoughts on Government* . . . (Philadelphia, 1776: JHL Pamphlet 65).

imagination or technical skill but of their employment. The more deliberately artful writings were in a significant way — for reasons that reach into the heart of the Revolutionary movement — peripheral to the main lines of intellectual force developing through the period. They were peculiarly incongruous to the deeper impulses of the time, and they never attracted the major talents nor fully excited those that were drawn to them. Beneath the technical deficiencies of the belletristic pieces lies an absence of motivating power, of that "peculiar emotional intensity" that so distinguishes the political writing of Jonathan Swift.[21] The American pamphlets are essentially decorous and reasonable. Not that they are all mild in tone, prissy, anemic, or lacking in emphasis. Vigor of one sort or another was common enough; at times, as in the frantic Tory outpouring of 1774-1775, there was something akin to verbal violence. And mud-slinging invective was everywhere; for in an age when gross public accusations were commonplace, it took a degree of restraint no one sought to employ to keep from depicting George Washington as the corrupter of a washerwoman's daughter, John Hancock as both impotent and the stud of an illegitimate brood, William Drayton as a disappointed office seeker whose fortune had been ruined by "the nicks of *seven* and *eleven,*" and Judge Martin Howard, Jr., as a well-known cardsharper.[22]

But mere vigor and lurid splash are not in themselves expressions of imaginative intensity. Among all those who wrote pamphlets, in fact, there appear to have been only three — James Otis,

[21] F. R. Leavis, "The Irony of Swift," *Determinations: Critical Essays* (London, 1934), p. 81.

[22] *The Battle of Brooklyn, A Farce in Two Acts* . . . (New York, 1776: JHL Pamphlet 72), p. 11 (cf. Allen French, "The First George Washington Scandal," MHS *Procs.,* 65 [1932–1936], 469 ff.); [John Mein], *Sagittarius's Letters and Political Speculations* . . . (Boston, 1775), pp. 103–104; Thomas Bolton, *An Oration Delivered March Fifteenth, 1775* . . . ([Boston], 1775), p. 5; *Some Fugitive Thoughts on a Letter Signed Freeman* . . . ([Charleston], 1774), p. 10; Hopkins, *Letter to the Author of the Halifax Letter,* p. 7.

Thomas Paine, and that strange itinerant Baptist John Allen — who had anything like the concentrated fury that propelled Swift's thought and imagination through the intensifying indirections of literary forms. And in all three cases there were singular circumstances. Otis' passion, the wildness that so astonished his contemporaries, already by 1765 was beginning to lack control: it would soon slip into incoherence. The "daring impudence," the "uncommon frenzy" which gave *Common Sense* its unique power, Paine brought with him from England in 1774; it had been nourished in another culture, and was recognized at the time to be an alien quality in American writing. And Allen too — in any case no equal, as a pamphleteer, of Paine — had acquired his habits of literary expression abroad.[23]

The American writers were profoundly reasonable people. Their pamphlets convey scorn, anger, and indignation; but rarely blind hate, rarely panic fear. They sought to convince their opponents, not, like the English pamphleteers of the eighteenth

[23] On Otis, see Bailyn, *Pamphlets*, I, Introductions to Pamphlets 7 and 11. The quoted phrases on Paine are from John Adams, *Diary and Autobiography*, III, 330–335, and Charles Inglis, *The True Interest of America . . . Strictures on a Pamphlet Intitled Common Sense . . .* (Philadelphia, 1776), p. vi. Inglis notes later in the pamphlet that Paine's "main attack is upon the passions of his readers, especially their pity and resentment . . . he seems to be everywhere transported with rage — a rage that knows no limits, and hurries him along like an impetuous torrent . . . such fire and fury . . . indicate that some mortifying disappointment is rankling at heart, or that some tempting object of ambition is in view, or probably both" (p. 34). Allen, author of *The American Alarm . . . for the Rights, and Liberties, of the People* and the immensely popular *Oration upon the Beauties of Liberty,* both published in 1773 (JHL Pamphlets 39 and 38), left London in 1769, where he had been a Baptist preacher, after various vicissitudes, including a trial for forgery and some time in debtor's prison. Before arriving in the colonies he had published *The Spiritual Magazine . . .* (3 vols.) and a half-dozen pamphlets, and during his tumultuous stay in New York, 1770–1772, added *The Spirit of Liberty, or Junius's Loyal Address* (1770). His wanderings after he left Boston in 1773 are obscure, but apparently he continued to publish religious tracts; a poem, *Christ the Christian's Hope . . .* (Exeter, N. H., 1789), may also be his. See references cited in Bailyn, *Pamphlets*, I, 17n, and, generally, John M. Bumsted and Charles E. Clark, "New England's Tom Paine: John Allen and the Spirit of Liberty," *W.M.Q.,* 3d ser., 21 (1964), 561–570.

century, to annihilate them. In this rationality, this everyday, businesslike sanity so distant from the imaginative mists where artistic creations struggle into birth, they were products of their situation and of the demands it made in politics. For the primary goal of the American Revolution, which transformed American life and introduced a new era in human history, was not the overthrow or even the alteration of the existing social order but the preservation of political liberty threatened by the apparent corruption of the constitution, and the establishment in principle of the existing conditions of liberty. The communication of understanding, therefore, lay at the heart of the Revolutionary movement, and its great expressions, embodied in the best of the pamphlets, are consequently expository and explanatory: didactic, systematic, and direct, rather than imaginative and metaphoric. They take the form most naturally of treatises and sermons, not poems; of descriptions, not allegories; of explanations, not burlesques. The reader is led through arguments, not images. The pamphlets aim to persuade.

What was essentially involved in the American Revolution was not the disruption of society, with all the fear, despair, and hatred that that entails, but the realization, the comprehension and fulfillment, of the inheritance of liberty and of what was taken to be America's destiny in the context of world history. The great social shocks that in the French and Russian Revolutions sent the foundations of thousands of individual lives crashing into ruins had taken place in America in the course of the previous century, slowly, silently, almost imperceptibly, not as a sudden avalanche but as myriads of individual changes and adjustments which had gradually transformed the order of society. By 1763 the great landmarks of European life — the church and the idea of orthodoxy, the state and the idea of authority: much of the array of institutions and ideas that buttressed the society of the *ancien régime* — had faded in their exposure to the open, wilderness environment of America. But until the disturbances of the 1760's these changes had not been seized upon as grounds for a reconsideration of society and politics. Often they had been condemned as deviations, as retrogressions back toward a more primitive condition of life. Then, after 1760 — and especially in the decade after 1765 — they were brought into open discussion as the colonists sought to apply advanced principles of society and politics to their own immediate problems.[24]

The original issue of the Anglo-American conflict was, of course, the question of the extent of Parliament's jurisdiction in the colonies. But that could not be discussed in isolation. The debate involved eventually a wide range of social and political problems, and it ended by 1776 in what may be called the conceptualization of American life. By then Americans had come to think of themselves as in a special category, uniquely placed by history to capitalize on, to complete and fulfill, the promise of man's existence. The changes that had overtaken their provincial societies, they saw, had been good: elements not of deviance and retrogression but of betterment and progress; not a lapse into primitivism, but an elevation to a higher plane of political and social life than had ever been reached before. Their rustic blemishes had become the marks of a chosen people. "The liberties of mankind and the glory of human nature is in their keeping," John Adams wrote in the year of the Stamp Act. "America was designed by Providence for the theatre on which man was to make his true figure, on which science, virtue, liberty, happiness, and glory were to exist in peace."[25]

The effort to comprehend, to communicate, and to fulfill this destiny was continuous through the entire Revolutionary generation — it did not cease, in fact, until in the nineteenth century its

---

[24] Bernard Bailyn, "Political Experience and Enlightenment Ideas in Eighteenth-Century America," *American Historical Review,* 67 (1961–62), 339–351.

[25] *Diary and Autobiography,* I, 282.

creative achievements became dogma. But there were three phases of particular concentration: the period up to and including 1776, centering on the discussion of Anglo-American differences; the devising of the first state governments, mainly in the years from 1776 to 1780; and the reconsideration of the state constitutions and the reconstruction of the national government in the last half of the eighties and in the early nineties. In each of these phases important contributions were made not only to the skeletal structure of constitutional theory but to the surrounding areas of social thought as well. But in none was the creativity as great, the results as radical and as fundamental, as in the period before Independence. It was then that the premises were defined and the assumptions set. It was then that explorations were made in new territories of thought, the first comprehensive maps sketched, and routes marked out. Thereafter the psychological as well as intellectual barriers were down. It was the most creative period in the history of American political thought. Everything that followed assumed and built upon its results.

In the pamphlets published before Independence may be found the fullest expressions of this creative effort. There were other media of communication; but everything essential to the discussion of those years appeared, if not originally then as reprints, in pamphlet form. The treatises, the sermons, the speeches, the exchanges of letters published as pamphlets — even some of the most personal polemics — all contain elements of this great, transforming debate.

Chapter II
SOURCES AND TRADITIONS

I give to my son, when he shall arrive to the age of fifteen years, Algernon Sidney's works, — John Locke's works, — Lord Bacon's works, — Gordon's *Tacitus,* — and *Cato's Letters.* May the spirit of liberty rest upon him!
— Last Will and Testament of Josiah Quincy, Jr., 1774

THE INTELLECTUAL history of the years of crisis from 1763 to 1776 is the story of the clarification and consolidation under the pressure of events of a view of the world and of America's place in it only partially seen before. Elements of this picture had long been present in the colonies — some dated from as far back as the settlements themselves — but they had existed in balance, as it were, with other, conflicting views. Expressed mainly on occasions of controversy, they had appeared most often as partisan arguments, without unique appeal, status, or claim to legitimacy. Then, in the intense political heat of the decade after 1763, these long popular, though hitherto inconclusive ideas about the world and America's place in it were fused into a comprehensive view, unique in its moral and intellectual appeal. It is the development of this view to the point of overwhelming persuasiveness to the majority of American leaders and the meaning this view gave to the events of the time, and not simply an accumulation of grievances, that explains the origins of the American Revolution. For this peculiar configuration of ideas constituted in effect an intellectual switchboard wired so that certain combinations of events would activate a distinct set of signals — danger signals, indicating hidden impulses and the likely trajectory of events impelled by them. Well before 1776 the signals registered on this switchboard led to a single, unmistakable conclusion — a conclusion that had long been feared and to which there could be only one rational response.

What were the sources of this world view? From whom, from what, were the ideas and attitudes derived?

Study of the sources of the colonists' thought as expressed in the informal as well as the formal documents, in the private as well as the public utterances, and above all in the discursive, explanatory pamphlets, reveals, at first glance, a massive, seemingly random eclecticism. To judge simply from an enumeration of the colonists' citations, they had at their finger tips, and made use of, a large portion of the inheritance of Western culture, from Aristotle to Molière, from Cicero to "Philoleutherus Lipsiensis" [Richard Bentley], from Vergil to Shakespeare, Ramus, Pufendorf, Swift, and Rousseau. They liked to display authorities for their arguments, citing and quoting from them freely; at times their writings become almost submerged in annotation: in certain of the writings of John Dickinson the text disappears altogether in a sea of footnotes and footnotes to footnotes.[1] But ultimately this profusion of authorities is reducible to a few, distinct groups of sources and intellectual traditions dominated and harmonized into a single whole by the influence of one peculiar strain of thought, one distinctive tradition.

Most conspicuous in the writings of the Revolutionary period was the heritage of classical antiquity. Knowledge of classical authors was universal among colonists with any degree of education,

---

[1] Most notably in his *Essay on the Constitutional Power of Great-Britain over the Colonies in America* . . . (Philadelphia, 1774), reprinted in *Pennsylvania Archives*, 2d ser., III, 565 ff. See also Josiah Quincy, Jr.'s *Observations on the . . . Boston Port-Bill; with Thoughts on . . . Standing Armies* (Boston, 1774), reprinted in Josiah Quincy, *Memoir of the Life of Josiah Quincy Jun. . . .* (Boston, 1825), pp. 355 ff.

and references to them and their works abound in the literature. From the grammar schools, from the colleges, from private tutors and independent reading came a general familiarity with and the habit of reference to the ancient authors and the heroic personalities and events of the ancient world. "Homer, Sophocles, Plato, Euripides, Herodotus, Thucydides, Xenophon, Aristotle, Strabo, Lucian, Dio, Polybius, Plutarch, and Epictetus, among the Greeks; and Cicero, Horace, Vergil, Tacitus, Lucan, Seneca, Livy, Nepos, Sallust, Ovid, Lucretius, Cato, Pliny, Juvenal, Curtius, Marcus Aurelius, Petronius, Suetonius, Caesar, the lawyers Ulpian and Gaius, and Justinian, among the Romans" — all are cited in the Revolutionary literature; many are directly quoted. "It was an obscure pamphleteer indeed who could not muster at least one classical analogy or one ancient precept." [2]

But this elaborate display of classical authors is deceptive. Often the learning behind it was superficial; often the citations appear to have been dragged in as "window dressing with which to ornament a page or a speech and to increase the weight of an argument," for classical quotation, as Dr. Johnson said, was "the *parole* of literary men all over the world." So Jonathan Mayhew casually lumped Plato with Demosthenes and Cicero as the ancients who in his youth had initiated him "in the doctrines of civil liberty"; Oxenbridge Thacher too thought Plato had been a liberty-loving revolutionary, while Jefferson, who actually read the *Dialogues,* discovered in them only the "sophisms, futilities, and incomprehensibilities" of a "foggy mind" — an idea concurred in with relief by John Adams, who in 1774 had cited Plato as an advocate of equality and self-government but who

---

[2] Charles F. Mullett, "Classical Influences on the American Revolution," *Classical Journal,* 35 (1939–40), 93, 94. On the classics in general in colonial and Revolutionary America, see Richard M. Gummere, *The American Colonial Mind and the Classical Tradition* (Cambridge, 1963); on the teaching of the classics in the secondary schools, see Robert Middlekauff, *Ancients and Axioms* (New Haven, 1963).

was so shocked when he finally studied the philosopher that he concluded that the *Republic* must have been meant as a satire.[3]

Yet Jefferson was a careful reader of the classics, and others too — James Otis, for example, who wrote treatises on Latin and Greek prosody — were thorough scholars of the ancient texts. What is basically important in the Americans' reading of the ancients is the high selectivity of their real interests and the limitation of the range of their effective knowledge. For though the colonists drew their citations from all portions of the literature of the ancient world, their detailed knowledge and engaged interest covered only one era and one small group of writers. What gripped their minds, what they knew in detail, and what formed their view of the whole of the ancient world was the political history of Rome from the conquests in the east and the civil wars in the early first century B.C. to the establishment of the empire on the ruins of the republic at the end of the second century A.D. For their knowledge of this period they had at hand, and needed only, Plutarch, Livy, and above all Cicero, Sallust, and Tacitus — writers who had lived either when the republic was being fundamentally challenged or when its greatest days were already past and its moral and political virtues decayed. They had hated and feared the trends of their own time, and in their writing had contrasted the present with a better past, which they endowed with qualities absent from their own, corrupt era. The earlier age had been full of virtue: simplicity, patriotism, integrity, a love of justice and of liberty; the present was venal, cynical, and oppressive.[4]

For the colonists, arguing the American cause in the con-

---

[3] Mullett, "Classical Influences," pp. 93, 99; Peter Gay, *The Party of Humanity* (New York, 1963), p. 10; Lester J. Cappon, ed., *The Adams-Jefferson Letters* (Chapel Hill, 1959), II, 433, 437. Cf. Gummere, *Classical Tradition*, pp. 178-179.

[4] Mullett, "Classical Influences," pp. 96 ff. Cf. Harold T. Parker, *The Cult of Antiquity and the French Revolutionaries* (Chicago, 1937), pp. 22, 23.

troversies of the 1760's and 1770's, the analogies to their own times were compelling. They saw their own provincial virtues — rustic and old-fashioned, sturdy and effective — challenged by the corruption at the center of power, by the threat of tyranny, and by a constitution gone wrong. They found their ideal selves, and to some extent their voices, in Brutus, in Cassius, and in Cicero, whose Catilinarian orations the enraptured John Adams, aged 23, declaimed aloud, alone at night in his room. They were simple, stoical Catos, desperate, self-sacrificing Brutuses, silver-tongued Ciceros, and terse, sardonic Tacituses eulogizing Teutonic freedom and denouncing the decadence of Rome. England, the young John Dickinson wrote from London in 1754, is like Sallust's Rome: "'Easy to be bought, if there was but a purchaser.'" Britain, it would soon become clear, was to America "what Caesar was to Rome." [5]

The classics of the ancient world are everywhere in the literature of the Revolution, but they are everywhere illustrative, not determinative, of thought. They contributed a vivid vocabulary but not the logic or grammar of thought, a universally respected personification but not the source of political and social beliefs. They heightened the colonists' sensitivity to ideas and attitudes otherwise derived.

More directly influential in shaping the thought of the Revolutionary generation were the ideas and attitudes associated with the writings of Enlightenment rationalism — writings that expressed not simply the rationalism of liberal reform but that of enlightened conservatism as well.

Despite the efforts that have been made to discount the influ-

---

[5] Adams, *Diary and Autobiography*, I, 63; Mullett, "Classical Influences," p. 102; H. Trevor Colbourn, ed., "A Pennsylvania Farmer at the Court of King George: John Dickinson's London Letters, 1754-1756," *Pa. Mag.*, 86 (1962), 268. Quincy, *Observations*, in Quincy, *Memoir*, p. 435. American views of corruption in English life are described below, pp. 86–93, 130–138.

ence of the "glittering generalities" of the European Enlightenment on eighteenth-century Americans, their influence remains, and is profusely illustrated in the political literature. It is not simply that the great *virtuosi* of the American Enlightenment — Franklin, Adams, Jefferson — cited the classic Enlightenment texts and fought for the legal recognition of natural rights and for the elimination of institutions and practices associated with the *ancien régime*. They did so; but they were not alone. The ideas and writings of the leading secular thinkers of the European Enlightenment — reformers and social critics like Voltaire, Rousseau, and Beccaria as well as conservative analysts like Montesquieu — were quoted everywhere in the colonies, by everyone who claimed a broad awareness. In pamphlet after pamphlet the American writers cited Locke on natural rights and on the social and governmental contract, Montesquieu and later Delolme on the character of British liberty and on the institutional requirements for its attainment, Voltaire on the evils of clerical oppression, Beccaria on the reform of criminal law, Grotius, Pufendorf, Burlamaqui, and Vattel on the laws of nature and of nations, and on the principles of civil government.

The pervasiveness of such citations is at times astonishing. In his two most prominent pamphlets James Otis cited as authorities, and quoted at length, Locke, Rousseau, Grotius, and Pufendorf, and denounced spokesmen, such as Filmer, for more traditional ideas of political authority. Josiah Quincy, Jr., referred with approval to a whole library of enlightened authors, among them Beccaria, Rousseau, Montesquieu, and the historian Robertson; and the young Alexander Hamilton, seeking to score points against his venerable antagonist, Samuel Seabury, recommended with arch condescension that his adversary get himself at the first opportunity to some of the writings of Pufendorf, Locke, Montesquieu, and Burlamaqui to discover the true principles of politics.

Examples could be multiplied almost without end. Citations, respectful borrowings from, or at least references to, the eighteenth-century European illuminati are everywhere in the pamphlets of Revolutionary America.[6]

The citations are plentiful, but the knowledge they reflect, like that of the ancient classics, is at times superficial. Locke is cited often with precision on points of political theory, but at other times he is referred to in the most offhand way, as if he could be relied on to support anything the writers happened to be arguing.[7] Bolingbroke and Hume are at times lumped together with radical reformers, and secondary figures like Burlamaqui are treated on a level with Locke.[8] Nor were the critical, reforming writings of the Enlightenment, even some of the most radical, used exclusively by the left wing of the Revolutionary movement. Everyone, whatever his position on Independence or his judgment of Parliament's actions, cited them as authoritative; almost no one, Whig or Tory, disputed them or introduced them with apology. Writers the colonists took to be opponents of Enlightenment rationalism — primarily Hobbes, Filmer, Sibthorpe, Mandeville, and Mainwaring — were denounced as frequently by loyalists as by

[6] James Otis, *Rights of the British Colonies Asserted and Proved* (Boston, 1764: JHL Pamphlet 7), pp. 9, 15, 22–23, 25, 26, 27, 30, 37; [James Otis], *A Vindication of the British Colonies . . .* (Boston, 1765: JHL Pamphlet 11), pp. 10–12; Quincy, *Observations,* in Quincy, *Memoir,* pp. 394, 402, 404, 406, 415, 452; [Hamilton], *The Farmer Refuted . . .* (New York, 1775), reprinted in *The Papers of Alexander Hamilton* (Harold C. Syrett, *et al.,* eds., New York and London, 1961–), I, 86.

[7] Thus Simeon Howard validates his offhand description of the state of nature with the footnote "See Locke on government." *A Sermon Preached to the Ancient and Honorable Artillery-Company . . .* (Boston, 1773), p. 8.

[8] Hume was greatly respected in America, but his *History of Great Britain,* though often referred to, was commonly believed to be, in Daniel Dulany's words, "a studied apology for the Stuarts, and particularly Charles I." Elihu S. Riley, ed., *Correspondence of "First Citizen" — Charles Carroll of Carrollton, and "Antilon" — Daniel Dulany, Jr. . . .* (Baltimore, 1902), p. 191; see also note 25 below. On Bolingbroke, see below, and note 22; on Burlamaqui, see Ray F. Harvey, *Jean Jacques Burlamaqui, A Liberal Tradition in American Constitutionalism* (Chapel Hill, 1937).

patriots; but almost never, before 1776, were Locke, Montesquieu, Vattel, Beccaria, Burlamaqui, Voltaire, or even Rousseau.[9] Mercy Otis Warren listed the contents of a hypothetical Tory library in her play *The Group;* but with the exception of Filmer none of the authors she mentions there were in fact referred to favorably by the Tories. James Chalmers, the Maryland loyalist, attacked Paine not with Hobbes, Sibthorpe, Wedderburn's speeches, and the statutes of Henry VIII, which, according to Mrs. Warren, he should have done, but with Montesquieu, Hutcheson, even Voltaire and Rousseau. The New York loyalist Peter Van Schaack reached his decision to oppose Independence on the basis of a close and sympathetic reading of Locke, Vattel, Montesquieu, Grotius, Beccaria, and Pufendorf, and in 1777 justified his defiance of the state of New York with reference to "the sentiments of Mr. Locke and those other advocates for the rights of mankind whose principles have been avowed and in some instances carried into practice by the congress." The Pennsylvania loyalist Joseph Galloway also cited Locke and Pufendorf as readily as his antagonists did; and when Charles Inglis looked for the source of Paine's anti-monarchism in order to attack it, he found it not in Enlightenment theory, whose exponents he praised, but in an obscure treatise by one John Hall, "pensioner under Oliver Cromwell." [10]

[9] On those universally despised apologists of Stuart authoritarianism, Robert Sibthorpe and Roger Mainwaring (Manwaring), minor figures of the time of Charles I made famous by the condemnations of Locke, Sidney, and the early eighteenth-century libertarians, see besides Bailyn, *Pamphlets,* I, 696, and below, note 39, Francis D. Wormuth, *The Royal Prerogative, 1603–1649* (Ithaca, 1939), pp. 16, 43, 93–98. The only sustained attack on Locke and systematic effort to justify Filmer in the Revolutionary literature appears to be Jonathan Boucher's remarkable sermon of 1775, "On Civil Liberty, Passive Obedience, and Non-resistance," published in his *View of the Causes and Consequences of the American Revolution* . . . (London, 1797), discussed at length below, chap. VI, sec. 4.

[10] [Mercy Otis Warren], *The Group, A Farce* . . . (Boston, 1775), reprinted in Montrose J. Moses, ed., *Representative Plays by American Dramatists* . . . *1765–1819* (New York, 1918), p. 227; [James Chalmers], *Plain Truth* . . . *Containing Remarks on . . . Common Sense* . . . (Philadelphia, 1776: JHL

Referred to on all sides, by writers of all political viewpoints in the colonies, the major figures of the European Enlightenment and many of the lesser, contributed substantially to the thought of the Americans; but except for Locke's, their influence, though more decisive than that of the authors of classical antiquity, was neither clearly dominant nor wholly determinative.

Also prominent and in certain ways powerfully influential was yet another group of writers and ideas. Just as the colonists cited with enthusiasm the theorists of universal reason, so too did they associate themselves, with offhand familiarity, with the tradition of the English common law. The great figures of England's legal history, especially the seventeenth-century common lawyers, were referred to repeatedly — by the colonial lawyers above all, but by others as well. Sir Edward Coke is everywhere in the literature: "Coke upon Littleton," "my Lord Coke's Reports," "Lord Coke's 2nd Institute" — the citations are almost as frequent as, and occasionally even less precise than, those to Locke, Montesquieu, and Voltaire. The earlier commentators Bracton and Fortescue are also referred to, casually, as authorities, as are Coke's contemporary Francis Bacon, and his successors as Lord Chief Justice, Sir Matthew Hale, Sir John Vaughan, and Sir John Holt.[11] In

---

Pamphlet 64), pp. 1–3, 67, 72; Henry C. Van Schaack, *The Life of Peter Van Schaack* (New York, 1842), pp. 58, 74, 72–73, 122; [Joseph Galloway], *A Candid Examination of the Mutual Claims of Great Britain and the Colonies* . . . (New York, 1775), pp. 21–22 (see also 4–5, 8, 15, 17–18); [Charles Inglis], *The True Interest of America . . . Strictures on a Pamphlet Intitled Common Sense* . . . (Philadelphia, 1776), p. 22. For a particularly striking example of a favorable reference to Locke by a Tory who believed that "in the *body politic* all inferior jurisdictions should flow from *one superior fountain*," see Isaac Hunt, *The Political Family; or . . . the Reciprocal Advantages Which Flow from an Uninterrupted Union Between Great-Britain and Her American Colonies* (Philadelphia, 1775), pp. 6, 7.

[11] On Coke, see Charles F. Mullett, "Coke and the American Revolution," *Economica*, 12 (1932), 457–471. Of the other jurists mentioned (on whom see Index listings in Bailyn, *Pamphlets*, I), Hale was a particularly well-known and attractive figure; the *Newport Mercury*, for example, ran a biography of him, January 23 and 30, 1764.

the later years of the Revolutionary period, Blackstone's *Commentaries* and the opinions of Chief Justice Camden became standard authorities. Throughout the literature, trial reports — Raymond's, Salkeld's, Williams', Goldsboro's — are referred to, and use is made of standard treatises on English law: Sullivan's *Lectures on the Laws of England*; Gilbert's *Law of Evidence*; Foster's *Crown Law*; Barrington's *Observations on the More Ancient Statutes.*

The common law was manifestly influential in shaping the awareness of the Revolutionary generation. But, again, it did not in itself determine the kinds of conclusions men would draw in the crisis of the time. Otis and Hutchinson both worshiped Coke, but for reasons that have nothing to do with the great chief justice, they read significantly different meanings into his opinion in *Bonham's Case*.[12] The law was no science of what to do next. To the colonists it was a repository of experience in human dealings embodying the principles of justice, equity, and rights; above all, it was a form of history — ancient, indeed immemorial, history; constitutional and national history; and, as history, it helped explain the movement of events and the meaning of the present. Particularly revealing, therefore, though vague in their intent, are the references in the pamphlets to the seventeenth-century scholars of the law, especially of the history of the law, whose importance in the development of English historical thought we have only recently become aware: Henry Spelman, Thomas Madox, Robert Brady, and William Petyt. English law — as authority, as legitimizing precedent, as embodied principle, and as the framework of historical understanding — stood side by side with Enlightenment rationalism in the minds of the Revolutionary generation.[13]

---

[12] See Introduction to Otis' *Rights of the British Colonies* (JHL 7), in Bailyn, *Pamphlets*, I.

[13] J. G. A. Pocock, *The Ancient Constitution and the Feudal Law* (Cambridge, 1957), p. 31, chap. viii; David C. Douglas, *English Scholars, 1660–1730* (rev. ed., London, 1951), chaps. vi, xi. For instances of the use of the seventeenth-

Still another tradition, another group of writers and texts, that emerges from the political literature as a major source of ideas and attitudes of the Revolutionary generation stemmed ultimately from the political and social theories of New England Puritanism, and particularly from the ideas associated with covenant theology. For the elaborate system of thought erected by the first leaders of settlement in New England had been consolidated and amplified by a succession of writers in the course of the seventeenth century, channeled into the main stream of eighteenth-century political and social thinking by a generation of enlightened preachers, and softened in its denominational rigor by many hands until it could be received, with minor variations, by almost the entire spectrum of American Protestantism.[14]

In one sense this was the most limited and parochial tradition that contributed in an important way to the writings of the Revolution, for it drew mainly from local sources and, whatever the extent of its newly acquired latitudinarianism, was yet restricted in its appeal to those who continued to understand the world, as the original Puritans had, in theological terms. But in another sense it contained the broadest ideas of all, since it offered a context for everyday events nothing less than cosmic in its dimensions. It carried on into the eighteenth century and into the minds of the Revolutionaries the idea, originally worked out in the sermons and tracts of the settlement period, that the colonization of British America had been an event designed by the hand of God to satisfy his ultimate aims. Reinvigorated in its historical

century scholars by the American pamphleteers, see, besides references indexed in Bailyn, *Pamphlets*, I, Maurice Moore, *The Justice and Policy of Taxing the American Colonies* . . . (Wilmington, N. C., 1765: JHL Pamphlet 16), p. 3; Richard Bland, *An Inquiry into the Rights of the British Colonies* . . . (Williamsburg, 1766: JHL Pamphlet 17), pp. 7, 22; and Riley, *Correspondence of "First Citizen"* . . . *and "Antilon,"* pp. 84–85, 193, 231–232.

[14] Perry Miller, "From the Covenant to the Revival," in *The Shaping of American Religion* (James W. Smith and A. Leland Jamison, eds., *Religion in American Life*, I, Princeton, 1961), pp. 322–334.

meaning by newer works like Daniel Neal's *History of the Puritans* (1732–1738), his *History of New England* (1720), and Thomas Prince's uncompleted *Chronological History of New England in the Form of Annals* (1736), this influential strain of thought, found everywhere in the eighteenth-century colonies, stimulated confidence in the idea that America had a special place, as yet not fully revealed, in the architecture of God's intent. "Imparting a sense of crisis by revivifying Old Testament condemnations of a degenerate people," it prepared the colonists for a convulsive realization by locating their parochial concerns at a critical juncture on the map of mankind's destiny. Their own history, it was clear, would provide the climax for those remarkable *"Connections"* from which they liked to quote, Samuel Shuckford's *Sacred and Profane History of the World Connected* (which contains a map fixing the exact geographical location of the garden of Eden) and Humphrey Prideaux's *The Old and New Testament Connected.*[15]

But important as all of these clusters of ideas were, they did not in themselves form a coherent intellectual pattern, and they do not exhaust the elements that went into the making of the Revolutionary frame of mind. There were among them, in fact, striking incongruities and contradictions. The common lawyers the colonists cited, for example, sought to establish right by appeal to precedent and to an unbroken tradition evolving from time immemorial, and they assumed, if they did not argue, that the accumulation of the ages, the burden of inherited custom, contained within it a greater wisdom than any man or group of men could devise by the power of reason. Nothing could have been more alien to the Enlightenment rationalists whom the colonists also quoted — and with equal enthusiasm. These theorists

---

[15] E.g., Benjamin Trumbull, *A Discourse Delivered at . . . the Town of New-Haven . . .* (New Haven, 1773), pp. 7–8; Dan Foster, *A Short Essay on Civil Government, the Substance of Six Sermons . . .* (Hartford, 1775), pp. 23, 61. Miller, "From the Covenant to the Revival," p. 340.

felt that it was precisely the heavy crust of custom that was weighing down the spirit of man; they sought to throw it off and to create by the unfettered power of reason a framework of institutions superior to the accidental inheritance of the past. And the covenant theologians differed from both in continuing to assume the ultimate inability of man to improve his condition by his own powers and in deriving the principles of politics from divine intent and from the network of obligations that bound redeemed man to his maker.

What brought these disparate strands of thought together, what dominated the colonists' miscellaneous learning and shaped it into a coherent whole, was the influence of still another group of writers, a group whose thought overlapped with that of those already mentioned but which was yet distinct in its essential characteristics and unique in its determinative power. The ultimate origins of this distinctive ideological strain lay in the radical social and political thought of the English Civil War and of the Commonwealth period; but its permanent form had been acquired at the turn of the seventeenth century and in the early eighteenth century, in the writings of a group of prolific opposition theorists, "country" politicians and publicists.

Among the seventeenth-century progenitors of this line of eighteenth-century radical writers and opposition politicians united in criticism of "court" and ministerial power, Milton was an important figure — not Milton the poet so much as Milton the radical tractarian, author of *Eikonoklastes* and *The Tenure of Kings and Magistrates* (both published in 1649). The American Revolutionary writers referred with similar respect if with less understanding to the more systematic writing of Harrington and to that of the like-minded Henry Neville; above all, they referred to the doctrines of Algernon Sidney, that "martyr to civil liberty" whose *Discourses Concerning Government* (1698) became, in Caroline Robbins' phrase, a "textbook of revolution" in America.[16]

The colonists identified themselves with these seventeenth-century heroes of liberty: but they felt closer to the early eighteenth-century writers who modified and enlarged this earlier body of ideas, fused it into a whole with other, contemporary strains of thought, and, above all, applied it to the problems of eighteenth-century English politics. These early eighteenth-century writers — coffeehouse radicals and opposition politicians, spokesmen for the anti-Court independents within Parliament and the disaffected without, draftsmen of a "country" vision of English politics that would persist throughout the eighteenth century and into the nineteenth — faded subsequently into obscurity and are little known today. But more than any other single group of writers they shaped the mind of the American Revolutionary generation.

To the colonists the most important of these publicists and intellectual middlemen were those spokesmen for extreme libertarianism, John Trenchard (1662–1723) and Thomas Gordon (d. 1750). The former, a west-country squire of ample means and radical ideas, was a 57-year-old veteran of the pamphlet wars that surrounded the Glorious Revolution when in 1719 he met Gordon, "a clever young Scot . . . fresh from Aberdeen University,

[16] George Sensabaugh, *Milton in Early America* (Princeton, 1964), chaps. ii, iii; on Milton cf., e.g., Howard, *Sermon*, p. 28; Quincy, *Observations*, in Quincy, *Memoir*, p. 411; and the Hollis-Mayhew and Hollis-Eliot exchanges, in MHS *Procs.*, 69 (1956), 116, 117, 125, and MHS *Colls.*, 4th ser., IV, 403, 412–413. On Harrington, see especially J. G. A. Pocock, "Machiavelli, Harrington, and English Political Ideologies in the Eighteenth Century," *W.M.Q.*, 3d ser., 22 (1965), 549–583; also, H. F. Russell Smith, *Harrington and His Oceana: . . . and Its Influence in America* (Cambridge, England, 1914), chaps. vii, viii; cf., e.g., Otis, *Rights of the British Colonies* (JHL 7), p. 15 and text note 6; John Adams ("Novanglus"), in *Works*, IV, 103–105. On Sidney, see Caroline Robbins, "Algernon Sidney's *Discourses* . . . ," *W.M.Q.*, 3d ser., 4 (1947), 267–296; and cf., e.g., [Stephen Hopkins], *The Rights of Colonies Examined* (Providence, 1765: JHL Pamphlet 9), p. 4; William Stearns, *A View of the Controversy . . .* (Watertown, 1775), p. 18; Adams ("Novanglus"), in *Works*, IV, 80 ff.

[who had come] to London to make his fortune, equipped with little but a sharp tongue and a ready wit." They joined forces to produce, first, the weekly *Independent Whig* to attack High Church pretensions and, more generally, the establishment of religion, fifty-three papers of which were published in book form in 1721; and *Cato's Letters,* a searing indictment of eighteenth-century English politics and society written in response to the South Sea Bubble crisis, which appeared first serially in *The London Journal* and then, beginning in 1720, in book form.[17] Incorporating in their colorful, slashing, superbly readable pages the major themes of the "left" opposition under Walpole, these libertarian tracts, emerging first in the form of denunciations of standing armies in the reign of William III,[18] left an indelible imprint on the "country" mind everywhere in the English-speaking world. In America, where they were republished entire or in part again and again, "quoted in every colonial newspaper from Boston to Savannah," and referred to repeatedly in the pamphlet literature, the writings of Trenchard and Gordon ranked with the treatises of Locke as the most authoritative statement of the nature of political liberty and above Locke as an exposition of the social sources of the threats it faced.[19]

[17] Charles B. Realey, *The London Journal and Its Authors, 1720–1723* (*Bulletin of the University of Kansas*, XXXVI, no. 23, Dec. 1, 1935), pp. 1–34; J. M. Bulloch, *Thomas Gordon, the "Independent Whig"* (Aberdeen, 1918); William T. Laprade, *Public Opinion and Politics in Eighteenth Century England* (New York, 1936), pp. 237–269; Caroline Robbins, *The Eighteenth-Century Commonwealthman* (Cambridge, 1959), pp. 115–125, 392–393.

[18] On Trenchard and Walter Moyle's influential *Argument, Shewing, that a Standing Army Is Inconsistent with a Free Government* . . . (London, 1697), see, generally, Lois G. Schwoerer, "The Literature of the Standing Army Controversy, 1697–1699," *Huntington Library Quarterly*, 28 (1965), 189 ff.; on its ideological force, see Pocock, "English Political Ideologies," esp. p. 566; and below, pp. 61–63, 116.

[19] Elizabeth C. Cook, *Literary Influences in Colonial Newspapers, 1704–1750* (New York, 1912), pp. 81–83, 89, 125–126, 129, 137, 139, 159, 257, 265. On the Quaker merchants' interest in these writers, see Frederick B. Tolles, *Meeting House and Counting House* (Chapel Hill, 1948), pp. 178–179. On their influence on William Livingston and others in New York, see William Livingston, *et al.*,

SOURCES AND TRADITIONS

Standing with Trenchard and Gordon as early eighteenth-century "preceptors of civil liberty" was the liberal Anglican bishop, Benjamin Hoadly. This "best hated clergyman of the century amongst his own order," as Leslie Stephen described him — honored and promoted by an administration that despised him but could not do without him — achieved fame, or notoriety, in England for his role in the elaborate clerical polemics of the "Bangorian Controversy" (1717–1720), in which he had been assisted by Gordon. In the course of this bitter and voluminous debate he had become an object of scorn and vituperation as well as of admiration in England; but in the colonies he was widely held to be one of the notable figures in the history of political thought. Anglicans in America, it was true, like their co-denominationalists at home, could scarcely endorse his extraordinary denial of sacerdotal powers for the Church hierarchy or his almost unbelievable repudiation of the whole idea of the church visible, nor could they, in theory at least, accept his extreme toleration of dissent. But their attention focused not on his views of the Church but on the crucial battles he had fought early in the century against the nonjurors and their doctrines of divine right and passive obedience, and on the extreme statements of Whig political theory in his treatise *The Original and Institution of Civil Government Discussed* (1710) and in certain of his many tracts, especially *The Measures of Submission to the Civil Magistrates Considered*

The Independent Reflector . . . (Milton M. Klein, ed., Cambridge, 1963), pp. 21–28, 365, 450–452. For examples of the use of *Cato's Letters* by the American pamphleteers, besides those that appear below and that are indexed in Bailyn, *Pamphlets*, I, see [Joseph Galloway], *A True and Impartial State of the Province of Pennsylvania* . . . (Philadelphia, 1759), title page; H. Trevor Colbourn, "The Historical Perspective of John Dickinson," *Early Dickinsoniana* (The Boyd Lee Spahr Lectures in Americana, Dickinson College, 1951–1961, Carlisle, Pa., 1961), pp. 13, 14, 18; Jonathan Mayhew to Thomas Hollis, August 19, 1765, MHS *Procs.*, 69 (1956), 176; [John Dickinson], *Letters from a Farmer in Pennsylvania* . . . (Philadelphia, 1768: JHL Pamphlet 23), p. 28n; Chalmers, *Plain Truth* (JHL 64), p. 72. On the importance of *Cato's Letters* in the political controversies of the early and mid-eighteenth century, see Bernard Bailyn, *The Origins of American Politics* (New York, 1968), pp. 54, 117, 137, 141, 143–144.

(1705). Ultimately, Hoadly came to embody physically the continuity of the conglomerate tradition of English radical and opposition thought, for though he had been active at the end of the seventeenth century, he lived on until 1761, associating in his very old age with the English radicals of Jefferson's generation and establishing contact with such spokesmen of advanced American thought as Jonathan Mayhew.[20]

[20] Leslie Stephen, *History of English Thought in the Eighteenth Century* (London, 1876), II, 152. Hoadly has yet to be excavated from the scorn and abuse Stephen heaped on him, but some indication of his importance emerges from Norman Sykes's essay in F. J. C. Hearnshaw, ed., *Social and Political Ideas of Some English Thinkers . . . 1650–1750* (London, 1928), chap. vi. Hoadly's significantly ambiguous relationship to the government under George II, especially his value as the administration's go-between with the dissenting interests, is revealed in detail in the memoirs of his friend John, Lord Hervey, edited by Romney Sedgwick as *Some Materials Towards Memoirs of the Reign of King George II . . .* (London, 1931), I, 123 ff., 190–92; II, 394–99, 498–500; III, 794–95. For illustrations of the way Hoadly's ideas entered into the mainstream of American Revolutionary thought, see Jonathan Mayhew's *Discourse Concerning Unlimited Submission* (Boston, 1750: JHL Pamphlet 1), Introduction and notes 11 and 12, in Bailyn, *Pamphlets,* I; [William Livingston?], *The Occasional Reverberator,* September 14, 1753; [John Allen], *The American Alarm . . . for the Rights, and Liberties, of the People . . .* (Boston, 1773: JHL Pamphlet 39), 4th sec., p. 10; Gad Hitchcock, *A Sermon Preached before . . . Gage . . .* (Boston, 1774), pp. 23, 27; Howard, *Sermon,* p. 23; [John Dickinson], "Letters to the Inhabitants of the British Colonies," in Paul L. Ford, ed., *The Writings of John Dickinson* (*Memoir of the Historical Society of Pennsylvania,* XIV, Philadelphia, 1895), pp. 494–496n; and R. C. Nicholas' reply to "Hoadleianus" in *Virginia Gazette* (R), June 10, 1773. There is perhaps no better testimony to Hoadly's role in the growth of a Revolutionary frame of mind than the recollection of the arch-Tory Jonathan Boucher, who, hearing that a rival preacher proposed to deliver a sermon against absolute monarchy, concluded that he must have "found such a sermon in Hoadly, and having transcribed it, showed it to the Committee, by whom it was approved, as any and every thing was and would have been, however loose and weak, that but seemed to be against power and for liberty." Jonathan Bouchier, ed., *Reminiscences of an American Loyalist . . .* (Boston and New York, 1925), p. 120. Similarly, an anonymous English writer at the end of the century attributed the origins of the French Revolution to the fact that "every class of Frenchman . . . became familiarly acquainted with Sidney, Locke, and Hoadly." *An Historical View of the French Revolution . . .* (Newcastle upon Tyne, 1796), p. 18. (I owe this reference to Mr. John Dunn.) From the earliest years of the century the public prints had depicted Hoadly as "the embodiment of faction, rebellion, and profane Latitudinarianism": M. Dorothy George, *English Political Caricature to 1792* (Oxford, 1959), I, 68.

With Hoadly, among his contemporaries, though below him in importance to the Americans, was the outstanding opponent in Parliament of Walpole's administration, the leader of a coterie of early eighteenth-century freethinking Whigs, Robert Viscount Molesworth. Friend of Trenchard and Gordon, encomiast of *Cato's Letters* (they were frequently attributed to him), he was known particularly in the colonies for his *Account of Denmark* (1694), which detailed the process by which free states succumb to absolutism.[21] An opposition leader of another sort who contributed in a more complicated way to the colonists' inheritance of early eighteenth-century thought was the spectacular Jacobite politician, writer, and philosopher, Henry St. John, Viscount Bolingbroke. His *Craftsman,* appearing weekly or semiweekly for a full ten years, from 1726 to 1736, roasted Walpole's administration in crackling fires of ridicule and denunciation. Its savage, bitter, relentless attacks were indistinguishable from *Cato's* polemics on major points of political criticism. *The Craftsman,* in fact, quoted the writings of Trenchard and Gordon freely, and otherwise, in almost identical language, decried the corruption of the age and warned of the dangers of incipient autocracy.[22]

[21] On Molesworth, see Robbins, *Commonwealthman,* chap. iv, pp. 393–394; and Realey, *London Journal,* pp. 4–5. Cf. *Newport Mercury,* July 30, 1764; John Dickinson, *A Speech Delivered in the House of Assembly . . . 1764* (Philadelphia, 1764), in Ford, *Writings,* p. 24; Gilbert Chinard, ed., *The Commonplace Book of Thomas Jefferson* (Baltimore, 1926), pp. 212–213, 225–226; Arthur Lee, *An Appeal to the Justice and Interests of the People of Great Britain . . .* (New York, 1775), p. 32.

[22] On Bolingbroke, whose *Freeholder's Political Catechism* (1733), which originally appeared in the pages of *The Craftsman,* was reprinted in Boston in 1757 and in New London in 1769 and whose *Works* John Adams professed to have read through five times, see, e.g., Colbourn, "Historical Perspective," p. 11; "Dickinson's London Letters," pp. 246–247; H. Trevor Colbourn, *The Lamp of Experience* (Chapel Hill, 1965), pp. 84, 85, 87, 90, 123, 124, 128, 159; *Newport Mercury,* July 30, 1764; Quincy, *Observations,* in Quincy, *Memoir,* p. 386. For a particularly dramatic illustration of the direct use of *The Craftsman* in mid-century America, see Paul S. Boyer, "Borrowed Rhetoric: The Massachusetts Excise Controversy of 1754," *W.M.Q.,* 3d ser., 21 (1964), 328–351. Bolingbroke's importance in the shaping of eighteenth-century opposition ideology has only

The Scottish philosopher, Francis Hutcheson, and the nonconformist schoolmaster, Philip Doddridge, were also figures of this
generation the colonists knew and cited in the same general context, as was Isaac Watts, the hymnologist and writer on questions
of church and education.[23]

The tradition continued into the Revolutionaries' own generation, promoted by Richard Baron, republican and dissenter,
associate and literary heir of Thomas Gordon, who republished
in the 1750's political works of Milton and Sidney and issued also
an anthology of the writings of the later radicals, including Jonathan Mayhew; and promoted even more effectively by that extraordinary one-man propaganda machine in the cause of liberty,
the indefatigable Thomas Hollis, whose correspondence in the
1760's first with Mayhew and then with Andrew Eliot illustrates
vividly the directness of the influence of this radical and opposition tradition on the ideological origins of the Revolution. In the

---

recently been appreciated, notably by Pocock in "English Political Ideologies," pp.
552, 572, 578, and by Isaac Kramnick in *Bolingbroke and His Circle: The Politics
of Nostalgia in the Age of Walpole* (Cambridge, 1968). The overlap of Bolingbroke's arguments and attitudes with those of the extreme libertarians continued
through the century: just as Bolingbroke had quoted Trenchard on the necessary independence of the House of Commons and *"Cato's immortal Letters"*
on a wide range of topics (*Craftsman,* nos. 198, 179, 268, 269, 271, 272, 275
["*Cato's Letters* and the Writings of the *Craftsman* Compared"], 278, 288, 292,
303, 356, 372, 403, 407), so James Burgh quoted him in his *Political Disquisitions* (1774: reprinted in Philadelphia, 1775) as he had in his *Britain's Remembrancer: or, The Danger Not Over* (1746: reprinted in Philadelphia, 1747 and
1748; in Boston, 1759), and thus conveyed his thought in a radical context to an
eager colonial audience. Americans had long been habituated to think of Bolingbroke in a libertarian context. Passages from his *Dissertation on Parties,* for example ("the most masterly performance that ever was wrote upon the *British*
constitution"), were used in Maryland in 1748 to gloss Locke's theory of the
contract basis of government. *The Maryland Gazette Extraordinary; An Appendix
to No. 162,* June 4, 1748, p. 3. Cf. Colbourn, *Lamp of Experience,* pp. 23, 50;
and Bailyn, *Origins of American Politics,* pp. 140–141.

[23] All of these figures are discussed in Robbins' *Commonwealthman,* but on the
link to America the same author's essay on Hutcheson in *W.M.Q.,* 3d ser., 11
(1954), 214–251, is especially important.

Revolutionary years proper a group of still younger writers renewed the earlier ideas, extended them still further, and, together with the leading spokesmen for the colonies, applied them to the Anglo-American controversy. Foremost among these later English advocates of reform in politics and religion were Richard Price, Joseph Priestley, and John Cartwright; but the key book of this generation was the three-volume *Political Disquisitions* published in 1774 by the schoolmaster, political theorist, and moralist, James Burgh.[24] The republican historian Catharine Macaulay, whose *History of England* has aptly been called "an imaginative work in praise of republican principles under the title of a History of England," was also an important intellectual figure of this generation to the colonists, but among the many Whig historians the Americans knew and referred to — including Bulstrode Whitelock, Gilbert Burnet, William Guthrie, and James Ralph — their preference was for the exiled Huguenot, Paul de Rapin-Thoyras. His "inestimable treasure," the vast, radically Whiggish *Histoire d'Angleterre,* published in English between 1725 and 1731, together with his earlier sketch of the whole, *A Dissertation on the . . . Whigs and Tories* (1717: reprinted in Boston in 1773), provided indisputable proof of the theories of all of the radical and anti-establishment writers by demonstrating their validity through a thousand years of English history.[25] But all history, not only

[24] On Baron and Hollis, see Mayhew, *Discourse* (JHL 1), Introduction and references in notes 16 and 17. The Mayhew-Hollis correspondence is published in MHS *Procs.,* 69 (1956), 102–193; the Eliot-Hollis correspondence is in MHS *Colls.,* 4th ser., IV, 399–461. The later radicals are discussed in Robbins' *Commonwealthman*; but see particularly Oscar and Mary F. Handlin, "James Burgh and American Revolutionary Theory," MHS *Procs.,* 73 (1961), 38–57; Nicholas Hans, "Franklin, Jefferson, and the English Radicals at the End of the Eighteenth Century," *Proceedings of the American Philosophical Society,* 98 (1954), 406–426; and Ian R. Christie, *Wilkes, Wyvill and Reform* (London, 1962), chaps. i–iii.

[25] "Rapin . . . in my opinion . . . carries the palm among the writers of our story, and wants nothing but a reduction of his enormous bulk to about half the present size, and to have his language a little enlivened . . . to render him an inestimable treasure of knowledge": William Livingston to Noah Welles, August

English history, was vital to the thought of the Revolutionary generation, and it is a matter of particular consequence that among the best, or at least the most up-to-date, translations of Sallust and Tacitus available to the colonists were those by the ubiquitous Thomas Gordon, "under whose hands [Tacitus] virtually became an apologist for English Whiggery"; he prefaced his translations with introductory "Discourses" of prodigious length in which he explained beyond all chance of misunderstanding the political and moral meaning of those ancient historians.[26]

18, 1759, quoted by Klein in Livingston, *Independent Reflector*, p. 284. For indications of Rapin's great popularity in the colonies, see, besides the passages indexed in Colbourn's *Lamp of Experience*, H. Trevor Colbourn, "John Dickinson, Historical Revolutionary," *Pa. Mag.*, 83 (1959), 277, 281, 282, 289; "Dickinson's London Letters," pp. 448–449; Dickinson, *Farmer's Letters* (JHL 23), pp. 60, 62. [James Wilson], *Considerations on the . . . Authority of the British Parliament* (Philadelphia, 1774: JHL Pamphlet 44), p. 5; John Lathrop, *A Sermon Preached to the Ancient and Honorable Artillery-Company . . .* (Boston, 1774), p. 20; [John Joachim Zubly], *Calm and Respectful Thoughts on the Negative of the Crown . . .* [Savannah, 1772], p. 14. For Jefferson's admiration of Rapin, whom a contemporary of Bolingbroke called *"The Craftsman's* own political *evangelist"* (John, Lord Hervey, *Ancient and Modern Liberty . . .* , London, 1734, p. 51) and his widely shared dislike of Hume's *History*, see E. M. Sowerby, ed., *Catalogue of the Library of Thomas Jefferson* (Washington, D.C., 1952–1959), I, 156–157, and Colbourn, *Lamp of Experience*, pp. 177, 179, 181, 86, 104; cf. Dulany's opinion of Hume, note 8 above. For a revealing and characteristic use of Rapin by John Adams, see *Works*, III, 543. Rapin's *Dissertation* is an effort to explain the party structure under George I as the logical outcome of England's entire ideological and constitutional history; its stress on the "formed design" of the Tories to restore Stuart absolutism to the throne made it, for reasons explained in Chapter IV below, of particular relevance to American Revolutionary thought. The characterization of Mrs. Macaulay's *History* is from Christie, *Wilkes, Wyvill and Reform*, p. 17; for examples of the colonists' enthusiasm for the book, see Mayhew's and Washington's rhapsodies, the former in a letter to Hollis, August 8, 1765, in MHS *Procs.*, 69 (1956), 173, the latter in direct correspondence with Mrs. Macaulay, quoted in Colbourn, *Lamp of Experience*, pp. 153–154.

[26] Tolles, *Meeting House and Counting House*, p. 189. For examples of the use of these translations, see [Stephen Hopkins'] compliment to the "fine English" of Gordon's *Tacitus*, in his letter to Goddard, *Providence Gazette*, April 8, 1765; Charles Carroll, in Riley, *Correspondence of "First Citizen" . . . and "Antilon,"* p. 48; Colbourn, "Dickinson, Historical Revolutionary," p. 280; H. Trevor Col-

To say simply that this tradition of opposition thought was quickly transmitted to America and widely appreciated there is to understate the fact. Opposition thought, in the form it acquired at the turn of the seventeenth century and in the early eighteenth century, was devoured by the colonists. From the earliest years of the century it nourished their political thought and sensibilities. There seems never to have been a time after the Hanoverian succession when these writings were not central to American political expression or absent from polemical politics. James Franklin's *New England Courant* began excerpting *Cato's Letters* eleven months after the first of them appeared in London; before the end of 1722 his brother Benjamin had incorporated them into his Silence Dogood papers.[27] Isaac Norris I in 1721 ordered his London bookseller to send him the separate issues of *The Independent Whig* as they appeared, and that whole collection was reprinted in Philadelphia in 1724 and 1740. John Peter Zenger's famous *New York Weekly Journal* (1733 ff.) was in its early years a veritable anthology of the writings of Trenchard and Gordon.[28] By 1728, in fact, *Cato's Letters* had already been fused with Locke, Coke, Pufendorf, and Grotius to produce a prototypical American treatise in defense of English liberties overseas, a tract indistinguishable from any number of publications that would appear in the Revolutionary crisis fifty years later.[29]

---

bourn, "Thomas Jefferson's Use of the Past," *W.M.Q.* 3d ser., 15 (1958), 61–62; Quincy, *Observations*, in Quincy, *Memoir*, pp. 443, 444. See also, David L. Jacobson, "Thomas Gordon's Works of Tacitus in Pre-Revolutionary America," *Bulletin of the New York Public Library*, 69 (1965), 58–64.

[27] *New England Courant*, October 2–9, 9–16, 16–23, 23–30, 1721. The ten paragraphs quoted in Silence Dogood no. 8 (July 9, 1722) as well as the two quoted in no. 9 (July 23) were copied by Franklin from *Cato's Letters*, nos. 15 and 31. (I owe this information to Mr. Max Hall.) See Leonard W. Labaree, *et al.*, eds., *The Papers of Benjamin Franklin* (New Haven, 1959–), I, 27–32.

[28] Frederick B. Tolles, *Meeting House and Counting House* (New York, 1963 ed.), p. 179. On the *New York Weekly Journal*'s use of Trenchard and Gordon, see, e.g., the issues of February 4 and December 10, 1733.

[29] [Daniel Dulany, Sr.], *The Right of the Inhabitants of Maryland to the Benefit of the English Laws* (Annapolis, 1728: reprinted in St. George L. Sioussat, *The*

So popular and influential had *Cato's Letters* become in the colonies within a decade and a half of their first appearance, so packed with ideological meaning, that, reinforced by Addison's universally popular play *Cato*[30] and the colonists' selectively Whiggish reading of the Roman historians, it gave rise to what might be called a "Catonic" image, central to the political theory of the time, in which the career of the half-mythological Roman and the words of the two London journalists merged indistinguishably. Everyone who read the *Boston Gazette* of April 26, 1756, understood the double reference, bibliographical and historical, that was intended by an anonymous writer who concluded an address to the people of Massachusetts — as he put it without further explanation — "in the words of Cato to the freeholders of Great Britain."

Testimonies to the unique influence of this opposition literature — evidences of this great "hinterland of belief"[31] from which would issue the specific arguments of the American Revolution

---

English Statutes in Maryland, Baltimore, 1903), pp. [i], 7, 10, 19. For further identification of Dulany's sources, which include Henry Care's perennially popular *English Liberties* . . . (London, [1680?]), a combination casebook in law, guide to legal procedures, and Anglophile propaganda piece, the fifth edition of which was reprinted in Boston by James Franklin in 1721, and the sixth in Providence in 1774, see Bailyn, *Pamphlets,* I, 742–743.

[30] On the complex political history of the play in England, see John Loftis, *The Politics of Drama in Augustan England* (Oxford, 1963), esp. pp. 57–62; on its enthusiastic reception as a libertarian document in America, where it was reprinted four times after 1766, see Colbourn, *Lamp of Experience,* pp. 24, 153. For characteristic uses of the play in political polemics, see *New York Weekly Journal,* January 28, 1733, and the untitled three-page squib, prefaced and concluded by quotations from the play, on the dangers threatening the New York legislature from the governor's "prudent application of posts and pensions" (Evans 3595 [New York, 1732]).

[31] W. H. Greenleaf, *Order, Empiricism and Politics . . . 1500–1700* (London, 1964), p. 12: "The great books of an age, it may be suggested, are never fully intelligible without an acquaintance with their intellectual background, with . . . 'the great hinterland' of belief. To understand these notions, which men often saw little need to explain because they were so obvious, means a familiarity with more ordinary opinions whatever their coherence or logical status in modern eyes."

— are everywhere in the writings of eighteenth-century Americans. Sometimes they are explicit, as when Jonathan Mayhew wrote that, having been "initiated, in youth, in the doctrines of civil liberty, as they were taught by such men . . . as Sidney and Milton, Locke, and Hoadly, among the moderns, I liked them; they seemed rational"; or when John Adams insisted, against what he took to be the massed opinion of informed Englishmen, that the root principles of good government could be found only in "Sidney, Harrington, Locke, Milton, Nedham, Neville, Burnet, and Hoadly"; or again, when he listed the great political thinkers of 1688 as "Sidney, Locke, Hoadly, Trenchard, Gordon, Plato Redivivus [Neville]"; or when Josiah Quincy, Jr., bequeathed to his son in 1774 "Algernon Sidney's works, — John Locke's works, — Lord Bacon's works, — Gordon's *Tacitus,* — and *Cato's Letters.* May the spirit of liberty rest upon him!" [32] More often, the evidence is implicit, in the degree to which the pamphleteers quoted from, plagiarized, and modeled their writings on *Cato's Letters* and *The Independent Whig.* Above all, their influence may be seen in the way the peculiar bent of mind of the writers in this tradition was reflected in the ideas and attitudes of the Americans.

The fact is easily mistaken because on the main points of theory the eighteenth-century contributors to this tradition were not original. Borrowing heavily from more original thinkers, they were often, in their own time and after, dismissed as mere popularizers. Their key concepts — natural rights, the contractual basis of society and government, the uniqueness of England's liberty-preserving "mixed" constitution — were commonplaces of the liberal thought of the time. But if the elements of their thought were ordinary, the emphasis placed upon them and the use made of them were not. Pride in the liberty-preserving con-

[32] Jonathan Mayhew, *The Snare Broken* . . . (Boston, 1766: JHL Pamphlet 20), p. 35; John Adams, *Thoughts on Government* . . . (Philadelphia, 1776: JHL Pamphlet 65), p. 7; Adams, *Works,* VI, 4; Quincy, *Memoir,* p. 350.

stitution of Britain was universal in the political literature of the age, and everyone agreed on the moral qualities necessary to preserve a free government. But where the mainstream purveyors of political thought spoke mainly with pride of the constitutional and political achievements of Georgian England, the opposition writers, no less proud of the heritage, viewed their circumstances with alarm, "stressed the danger to England's ancient heritage and the loss of pristine virtue," studied the processes of decay, and dwelt endlessly on the evidences of corruption they saw about them and the dark future these malignant signs portended. They were the Cassandras of the age, and while their maledictions "were used for party purposes . . . what [they] said about antique virtue, native liberty, public spirit, and the dangers of luxury and corruption was of general application" and was drawn from the common repository of political lore. They used the commonplaces of the age negatively, critically. They were the enemies of complacence in one of the most complacent eras in England's history. Few of these writers would have agreed with the sentiment expressed by the Lord Chancellor of England in 1766 and concurred in by the overwhelming majority of eighteenth-century Englishmen: "I seek for the liberty and constitution of this kingdom no farther back than the [Glorious] Revolution: there I make my stand." [33] Few of them accepted the Glorious

[33] So too the New York Tory William Smith, Jr., declared, "I am a Whig of the old stamp. No Roundhead — one of King William's Whigs, for Liberty and the Constitution." William H. W. Sabine, ed., *Historical Memoirs . . . 1776 to . . . 1778 . . . of William Smith . . .* (New York, 1958), p. 278. The earlier quotations in the paragraph are from Alan D. McKillop's revealing study "The Background of Thomson's *Liberty*," *The Rice Institute Pamphlet*, XXXVIII, no. 2 (July 1951), 87, 92, where it is argued that "It can hardly be said that one party in this age is for Gothic liberty, the other against it, any more than it can be said that one coherent group opposed or defended luxury. But it came to be the Opposition, the shifting coalition of Tories and dissident Whigs, that stressed the danger to England's ancient heritage and the loss of pristine virtue; and it was the apologists for Walpole who at this point were likely to belittle primordial liberty in comparison with England's gains since 1688." For further discussion of

Revolution and the lax political pragmatism that had followed as the final solution to the political problems of the time. They refused to believe that the transfer of sovereignty from the crown to Parliament provided a perfect guarantee that the individual would be protected from the power of the state. Ignoring the complacence and general high level of satisfaction of the time, they called for vigilance against the government of Walpole equal to what their predecessors had shown against the Stuarts. They insisted, at a time when government was felt to be less oppressive than it had been for two hundred years, that it was necessarily — by its very nature — hostile to human liberty and happiness; that, properly, it existed only on the tolerance of the people whose needs it served; and that it could be, and reasonably should be, dismissed — overthrown — if it attempted to exceed its proper jurisdiction.

It was the better to maintain this vigil against government that they advocated reforms — political reforms, not social or economic reforms, for these were eighteenth- not nineteenth- or twentieth-century English radicals[34] — beyond anything admissible in Walpole's age, or indeed in any age that followed in England until well into the nineteenth century. At one time or another, one or another of them argued for adult manhood suffrage; elimination of the rotten borough system and the substitution of regular units of representation systematically related to the distribution of population; the binding of representatives to their constituencies by residential requirements and by instructions; alterations in the definition of seditious libel so as to permit full freedom of the press to criticize government; and the total withdrawal of government control over the practice of religion.

---

this monograph — the most sensitive effort yet made, as far as the present writer is aware, to distinguish opposition themes from the mainstream tradition of eighteenth-century political thought — see note 37 below.

[34] See below, pp. 283–284.

Such ideas, based on extreme solicitude for the individual and an equal hostility to government, were expressed in a spirit of foreboding and fear for the future. For while they acknowledged the existing stability and prosperity of England, they nevertheless grounded their thought in pessimism concerning human nature and in the discouraging record of human weakness. Their resulting concern was continuously deepened by the scenes they saw around them. Politics under Walpole may have been stable, but the stability rested, they believed, on the systematic corruption of Parliament by the executive, which, they warned, if left unchecked, would eat away the foundations of liberty. The dangers seemed great, for they saw, as J. G. A. Pocock has written in outlining "the 'Country' vision of English politics as it appears in a multitude of writings in the half century that follows 1675," that

the executive possesses means of distracting Parliament from its proper function; it seduces members by the offer of places and pensions, by retaining them to follow ministers and ministers' rivals, by persuading them to support measures — standing armies, national debts, excise schemes — whereby the activities of administration grow beyond Parliament's control. These means of subversion are known collectively as corruption, and if ever Parliament or those who elect them — for corruption may occur at this point too — should be wholly corrupt, then there will be an end of independence and liberty.[35]

This was their major theme, their obsessive concern, and they hammered away at it week after week, year after year, in ringing denunciations of Walpole's manipulation of Parliament and of the dissoluteness of the age that permitted it. The outcries were as loud, the fear as deep, on the "left" of the opposition spectrum as on the "right." So "Cato" warned, again and again, that

public corruptions and abuses have grown upon us; fees in most, if not all, offices, are immensely increased; places and employments,

[35] Pocock, "English Political Ideologies," p. 565.

48

which ought not to be sold at all, are sold for treble value; the necessities of the public have made greater impositions unavoidable, and yet the public has run very much in debt; and as those debts have been increasing, and the people growing poor, salaries have been augmented, and pensions multiplied.[36]

Bolingbroke was even more insistent that England was faced with the age-old and associated dangers of ministerial usurpation and political corruption. And the prose of his jeremiads — echoed in the more artistic productions of the great Tory satirists of the age, in the writings of Swift, Pope, Gay, Mandeville, even in the less partisan, critical-patriotic rhapsodies of James Thomson, *Liberty* and *Britannia*[37] — was even more vivid, more memorable than that of "Cato." He devised a new terminology to describe the urgent danger. "*Robinocracy*," he wrote, was what was developing under the "prime"-ministry (a term of derogation) of

[36] *Cato's Letters*, no. 20, March 11, 1720 (in the London, 1748 ed., I, 140). See also, e.g., no. 17, February 18, 1720 ("What Measures Are Actually Taken by Wicked and Desperate Ministers to Ruin and Enslave Their Country"), and no. 98, October 13, 1722.

[37] For the broad literary context of Bolingbroke's pessimism, see particularly Louis I. Bredvold, "The Gloom of the Tory Satirists," in James L. Clifford and Louis A. Landa, eds., *Pope and His Contemporaries* (Oxford, 1949); see also Bonamy Dobrée, *The Theme of Patriotism in the Poetry of the Early Eighteenth Century* (London, 1949). Thomson's *Liberty* (1735–36), a vast, unreadable autobiography of the goddess of that name, detailing the long history of her ancient greatness, her decline in "Gothic darkness," and her ultimate revival in Hanoverian England, proves, in the excellent analysis by Alan McKillop (cited in note 33 above), to be of the greatest importance in the ideological history of the eighteenth century. For not only does this "sweeping synthesis or elaborate piece of syncretism" expose the great array of sources that fed the early eighteenth-century ideas of liberty, but it demonstrates the degree of deviation from the normal pattern that opposition thought involved as it traces the shifts that took place in Thomson's views in the course of writing the poem — from confidence in English politics to concern, from support of the administration to opposition — and that are reflected in it. For the text of *Britannia* (1729), in which Thomson "had already made the transition from 'pointing with pride' to 'viewing with alarm,'" and for a commentary on it, see McKillop's edition of Thomson's *Castle of Indolence and Other Poems* (Lawrence, Kansas, 1961); see also John E. Wells, "Thomson's *Britannia* . . . ," *Modern Philology*, 40 (1942–43), 43–56. For references to *Liberty* in the Revolutionary pamphlets, see Index listings in Bailyn, *Pamphlets*, I.

Robert Walpole. Robinocracy, he explained, was a form of government in which the chief minister maintained the façade of
constitutional procedures while he in fact monopolized the whole
of governmental power:

> The *Robinarch*, or chief ruler, is nominally a *minister* only and crea-
> ture of the prince; but in reality he is a sovereign, as despotic, ar-
> bitrary a sovereign as this part of the world affords . . . The *Robin-
> arch* . . . hath unjustly engrossed the whole power of a nation into
> his own hands . . . [and] admits no person to any considerable post
> of trust and power under him who is not either a *relation*, a *creature*,
> or a *thorough-paced tool* whom he can lead at pleasure into any dirty
> work without being able to discover his designs or the consequences
> of them.

The modes of Robinarcal control of a once-free legislature were
clear enough. The corrupt minister and his accomplices systematically encourage "*luxury* and *extravagance*, the certain forerunners
of *indigence, dependance*, and *servility*." Some deputies

> are tied down with *honors, titles*, and *preferments*, of which the
> *Robinarch* engrosses the disposal to himself, and others with *bribes*,
> which are called *pensions* in these countries. Some are persuaded to
> prostitute themselves for the lean reward of *hopes* and *promises;*
> and others, more senseless than all of them, have sacrificed their prin-
> ciples and consciences to a set of *party names*, without any meaning,
> or the vanity of appearing in favor at *court*.

Once in power the Robinarcal ministry feeds on its own corruption. It loads the people with taxes and with debts, and ends by
creating a mercenary army ostensibly for the purpose of protecting the people but in fact to perfect its dominance in just those
ways, Bolingbroke wrote, that Trenchard had explained years
before in his tracts on standing armies.[38]

Solutions of different forms were advocated by "left" and
"right": the former urged those institutional, political, and legal

[38] *The Craftsman*, nos. 172, October 18, 1729; and 198, April 18, 1730 (in the
London, 1731 ed., V, 152–153, 155, 156; VI, 138 ff.).

reforms which would finally be realized a full century later in the Reform Acts of the nineteenth century; the latter argued the need for that romantic ideal, the Patriot Prince, who should govern as well as reign, yet govern above parties and factions, in harmony with a loyal and independent commons. But if their solutions were different their basic observations and the fears they expressed were identical. Everywhere, they agreed, there was corruption — corruption technically, in the adroit manipulation of Parliament by a power-hungry ministry, and corruption generally, in the self-indulgence, effeminizing luxury, and gluttonous pursuit of gain of a generation sunk in new and unaccustomed wealth. If nothing were done to stop the growth of these evils, England would follow so many other nations into a tyranny from which there would be no recovery.

But if these dark thoughts, in the England of Walpole and Gibbon, attained popularity in certain opposition, radical, and nonconformist circles, they had relatively little political influence in the country at large. In the mainland colonies of North America, however, they were immensely popular and influential. There, an altered condition of life made what in England were considered to be extreme, dislocating ideas sound like simple statements of fact. There, the spread of independent landholding had insensibly created a broad electorate. There, the necessity of devising systems of representation at a stroke and the presence of persistent conflict between the legislatures and the executives had tended to make representation regular and responsible and had limited the manipulative influence of any group in power. There, the multiplicity of religious groupings, the need for continuous encouragement of immigration, and the distance from European centers of ecclesiastical authority had weakened the force of religious establishments below anything known in Europe. There the moral basis of a healthy, liberty-preserving polity seemed already to exist in the unsophisticated lives of the independent, uncorrupted, landowning yeoman farmers who comprised so large a part of the colonial population. Yet there the threat of ministerial aggrandizement seemed particularly pressing and realistic, for there, in all but the charter colonies, the executive branches of government — venal surrogates, it so often seemed, of ill-informed if not ill-disposed masters — held, and used, powers that in England had been stripped from the crown in the settlement that had followed the Glorious Revolution as inappropriate to the government of a free people.[39]

In such a situation the writings of the English radical and opposition leaders seemed particularly reasonable, particularly relevant, and they quickly became influential. Everywhere groups seeking justification for concerted opposition to constituted governments turned to these writers. When in 1735 John Peter Zenger's lawyer sought theoretical grounds for attacking the traditional concept of seditious libel, he turned for authority to Trenchard and Gordon's *Cato's Letters.* When, four years later, an opposition writer in Massachusetts drew up an indictment of the governor so vehement the Boston printers would not publish it, he did so, he wrote, with "some helps from *Cato's Letters,* which were wrote upon the glorious cause of liberty." When in 1750 Jonathan Mayhew sought to work out, in his celebrated *Discourse Concerning Unlimited Submission,* a full rationale for resistance to constituted government, he drew on — indeed, cribbed wholesale — not Locke, whose ideas would scarcely have supported what he was saying, but a sermon of Benjamin Hoadly, from whom he borrowed not only ideas and phrases but, in abusing the nonjuror Charles Leslie, the Bishop's enemies as

---

[39] The argument that English opposition theory had a special utility and unique attractiveness in early- and mid-eighteenth-century America as a result of the existence of an archaic preponderance of executive power coupled with an almost total elimination of the kind of political "influence" that Walpole was able to exert over opposition forces in Parliament, I have developed in *The Origins of American Politics.*

well.[40] When in 1752-1753 William Livingston and his friends undertook to publish in a series of periodical essays a sweeping critique of public life in New York, and in particular to assault the concept of a privileged state, they modeled their publication, *The Independent Reflector,* on Trenchard and Gordon's *Independent Whig,* and borrowed from it specific formulations for their central ideas. And when in Massachusetts in 1754 opponents of a stringent excise act sought models for a campaign of opposition, they turned not only generally to the literature of opposition that had been touched off by Walpole's excise proposal of 1733 but specifically to Bolingbroke's *Craftsman* of that year, from which they freely copied arguments and slogans, even figures of speech.[41] Everywhere in America the tradition that had originated in seventeenth-century radicalism and that had been passed on, with elaborations and applications, by early eighteenth-century English opposition publicists and politicians brought forth congenial responses and provided grounds for opposition politics.

But it did more. It provided also a harmonizing force for the other, discordant elements in the political and social thought of

[40] Trenchard and Gordon helped similarly to transmit to the Revolutionary generation the reputations of the more notorious clerical absolutists and the belief that "priestcraft and tyranny are ever inseparable, and go hand-in-hand." For their condemnation of Leslie, and of Robert Sibthorpe and Roger Mainwaring, chaplains to Charles I who advocated passive obedience to royal authority and threatened damnation to opponents of crown taxation, see *Cato's Letters,* nos. 128, May 11, 1723; and 130, May 25, 1723 (in the London, 1775 ed., IV, 192, 213).

[41] Leonard W. Levy, *Legacy of Suppression* (Cambridge, 1960), pp. 115-121, 129-137; Stanley N. Katz, ed., *A Brief Narrative of the Case and Trial of John Peter Zenger* (Cambridge, 1963), pp. 15, 9, 10. [Americanus, pseud.], *A Letter to the Freeholders and Other Inhabitants of the Massachusetts-Bay* . . . ([Newport], 1739), p. 1. Mayhew's use of Hoadly's *Measures of Submission to the Civil Magistrates* is detailed in the Introduction to his *Discourse Concerning Unlimited Submission* (JHL 1) in Bailyn, *Pamphlets,* I. On Livingston's reliance on Trenchard and Gordon, see Klein's comments in Livingston, *Independent Reflector,* pp. 21-28, 450-452; and Livingston's quotation, p. 365. On *The Craftsman* and the Massachusetts excise controversy, see Boyer, "Borrowed Rhetoric," cited in note 22 above.

the Revolutionary generation. Within the framework of these ideas, Enlightenment abstractions and common law precedents, covenant theology and classical analogy — Locke and Abraham, Brutus and Coke — could all be brought together into a comprehensive theory of politics. It was in terms of this pattern of ideas and attitudes — originating in the English Civil War and carried forward with additions and modifications not on the surface of English political life but in its undercurrents stirred by doctrinaire libertarians, disaffected politicians, and religious dissenters — that the colonists responded to the new regulations imposed by England on her American colonies after 1763.

Chapter III

POWER AND LIBERTY:
A THEORY OF POLITICS

In Europe, charters of liberty have been granted by power. America has set the example and France has followed it, of charters of power granted by liberty. This revolution in the practice of the world may, with an honest praise, be pronounced the most triumphant epoch of its history and the most consoling presage of its happiness.

— James Madison, 1792

THE THEORY of politics that emerges from the political literature of the pre-Revolutionary years rests on the belief that what lay behind every political scene, the ultimate explanation of every political controversy, was the disposition of power. The acuteness of the colonists' sense of this problem is, for the twentieth-century reader, one of the most striking things to be found in this eighteenth-century literature: it serves to link the Revolutionary generation to our own in the most intimate way.

The colonists had no doubt about what power was and about its central, dynamic role in any political system. Power was not to be confused, James Otis pointed out, with unspecified physical capacity — with the "mere physical quality" described in physics. The essence of what they meant by power was perhaps best revealed inadvertently by John Adams as he groped for words in drafting his *Dissertation on the Canon and Feudal Law*. Twice choosing and then rejecting the word "power," he finally selected as the specification of the thought he had in mind "dominion,"

55

and in this association of words the whole generation concurred. "Power" to them meant the dominion of some men over others, the human control of human life: ultimately force, compulsion.[1] And it was, consequently, for them as it is for us "a richly connotative word": some of its fascination may well have lain for them, as it has been said to lie for us, in its "sado-masochistic flavor,"[2] for they dwelt on it endlessly, almost compulsively; it is referred to, discussed, dilated on at length and in similar terms by writers of all backgrounds and of all positions in the Anglo-American controversy.

Most commonly the discussion of power centered on its essential characteristic of aggressiveness: its endlessly propulsive tendency to expand itself beyond legitimate boundaries. In expressing this central thought, which explained more of politics, past and present, to them than any other single consideration, the writers of the time outdid themselves in verbal ingenuity. All sorts of metaphors, similes, and analogies were used to express this view of power. The image most commonly used was that of the act of trespassing. Power, it was said over and over again, has "an encroaching nature"; ". . . if at first it meets with no control [it] creeps by degrees and quick subdues the whole." Sometimes the image is of the human hand, "the hand of power," reaching out to clutch and to seize: power is "grasping" and "tenacious" in its nature; "what it seizes it will retain." Sometimes power "is like the ocean, not easily admitting limits to be fixed in it." Sometimes it is "like a cancer, it eats faster and faster every hour." Sometimes it is motion, desire, and appetite all at once, being "restless, aspiring, and insatiable." Sometimes it is like "jaws . . . always opened to devour." It is everywhere in public life, and

---

[1] [James Otis], *Brief Remarks on the Defence of the Halifax Libel . . .* (Boston, 1765), p. 24; Adams, *Diary and Autobiography*, I, 255. Cf. Charles Carroll: "power (understood as force)," *Maryland Historical Magazine*, 12 (1917), 187.

[2] K. R. Minogue, "Power in Politics," *Political Studies*, 7 (1959), 271.

everywhere it is threatening, pushing, and grasping; and too often in the end it destroys its benign — necessarily benign — victim.[3]

What gave transcendent importance to the aggressiveness of power was the fact that its natural prey, its necessary victim, was liberty, or law, or right. The public world these writers saw was divided into distinct, contrasting, and innately antagonistic

[3] The examples quoted here, selected from innumerable discussions of power in the literature before 1776, are from: *America, A Poem. By Alexander Martin . . . to Which Is Added, Liberty. A Poem. By Rusticus . . .* ([Philadelphia, 1769?]: JHL Pamphlet 31), p. [17]; [William Hicks], *Considerations upon the Rights of the Colonists to the Privileges of British Subjects . . .* (New York, 1766: JHL Pamphlet 18), p. 15; Richard J. Hooker, ed., "John Dickinson on Church and State," *American Literature*, 16 (1944–45), 90; John Adams, *Dissertation on the Canon and Feudal Law*, in *Works*, III, 457; [Moses Mather], *America's Appeal to the Impartial World . . .* (Hartford, 1775: JHL Pamphlet 59), p. 22; and John Adams ("Novanglus"), in *Works*, IV, 43. So also Jonathan Mayhew: "Power is of a grasping, encroaching nature . . . [it] aims at extending itself and operating according to mere *will* wherever it meets with no balance, check, control, or opposition of any kind." *The Snare Broken . . .* (Boston, 1766: JHL Pamphlet 20), p. 34; and "Power is like avarice, its desire increases by gratification," *Newport Mercury*, July 30, 1764.

The discussion of power, in precisely these terms, may be traced back through the political literature of mid eighteenth-century America to seventeenth- and early eighteenth-century sources. See, for example, *Boston Gazette and Country Journal*, May 10, 1756, which contains a discourse on power and liberty; *New York Mercury*, October 15, 1753, where an essay on balance in government as "the firmest barrier against unlimited power . . . our whole constitution, so nicely poised between too much power and too much liberty," is fashioned from extracts from William Oldisworth's *A Dialogue Between Timothy and Philatheus . . .* (London, 1709), one of the many answers to Matthew Tindall's proscribed *Rights of the Christian Church Asserted* (1706); *New York Evening Post*, December 7, 1747, on disputes between power and liberty; John Wright's speech of 1741, quoting "a noted professor of law" who said that power "may justly be compared to a great river, which, while kept within due bounds, is both beautiful and useful, but when it overflows its banks . . . brings destruction and desolation where it comes" (Robert Proud, *History of Pennsylvania . . .* [Philadelphia, 1798], II, 224n); *Cato's Letters*, nos. 25, 33, 73, 115 ("Unlimited power is so wild and monstrous a thing that however natural it be to desire it, it is as natural to oppose it; nor ought it to be trusted with any mortal man, be his intentions ever so upright . . . It is the nature of power to be ever encroaching . . . It is dominion, it is power which [the Jacobite clergy] court" [6th ed., London, 1755, IV, 81–82, 214]); *The Craftsman*, nos. 180, 213; Benjamin Hoadly, *Works* (John Hoadly, ed., London, 1773), II, 25; Locke, *Second Treatise of Government*, i, 3; iii, 17.

spheres: the sphere of power and the sphere of liberty or right. The one was brutal, ceaselessly active, and heedless; the other was delicate, passive, and sensitive. The one must be resisted, the other defended, and the two must never be confused. "Right and power," Richard Bland stated, "have very different meanings, and convey very different ideas"; "power abstracted from right cannot give a just title to dominion," nor is it possible legitimately, or even logically, to "build right upon power." When the two are intermingled, when "brutal power" becomes "an irresistible argument of boundless right" as it did, John Dickinson explained, under the Cromwellian dictatorship, innocence and justice can only sigh and quietly submit.[4]

Not that power was in itself — in some metaphysical sense — evil. It was natural in its origins, and necessary. It had legitimate foundations "in compact and mutual consent" — in those covenants among men by which, as a result of restrictions voluntarily accepted by all for the good of all, society emerges from a state of nature and creates government to serve as trustee and custodian

[4] [Richard Bland], *An Inquiry into the Rights of the British Colonies* . . . (Williamsburg, 1766: JHL Pamphlet 17), pp. 5, 25; [John Joachim Zubly], *An Humble Enquiry* . . . ([Charleston], 1769: JHL Pamphlet 28), p. 26; [John Dickinson], *An Essay on the Constitutional Power of Great-Britain over the Colonies in America* . . . (Philadelphia, 1774), p. 108 (reprinted in *Pennsylvania Archives*, 2d ser., III, 610). See also, [William Hicks], *The Nature and Extent of Parliamentary Power Considered* . . . (Philadelphia, 1768: JHL Pamphlet 24), pp. 21, 27. Cf. *Cato's Letters*, no. 33: "Now, because liberty chastises and shortens power, therefore power would extinguish liberty; and consequently liberty has too much cause to be exceeding jealous, and always upon her defense. Power has many advantages over her . . . and whereas power can, and for the most part does, subsist where liberty is not, liberty cannot subsist without power, so that she has, as it were, the enemy always at her gates." So also, no. 73: "Alas! Power encroaches daily upon liberty, with a success too evident, and the balance between them is almost lost." The implicitly sexual character of the imagery is made quite explicit in passages of the libertarian literature, e.g., in Marchamont Nedham's *Excellencie of a Free State* (1656): "the interest of freedom is a virgin, that everyone seeks to deflower"; if it is not properly protected "(so great is the lust of mankind after dominion) there follows a rape upon the first opportunity" (in Richard Baron's 1767 ed., pp. 18-19).

of the mass of surrendered individual powers. Power created legitimately by those voluntary compacts which the colonists knew from Lockean theory to be logical and from their own experience to be practical, power in its legitimate form inhered naturally in government and was the possession and interest of those who controlled government, just as liberty, always weak, always defensive, always, as John Adams put it, "skulking about in corners . . . hunted and persecuted in all countries by cruel power," inhered naturally in the people and was their peculiar possession and interest. Liberty was not, therefore, for the colonists, as it is for us, professedly the interest and concern of all, governors and governed alike, but only of the governed. The wielders of power did not speak for it, nor did they naturally serve it. Their interest was to use and develop power, no less natural and necessary than liberty but more dangerous. For "as great a blessing as government is," the Rev. Peter Whitney explained, "like other blessings, it may become a scourge, a curse, and severe punishment to a people." What made it so, what turned power into a malignant force, was not its own nature so much as the nature of man — his susceptibility to corruption and his lust for self-aggrandizement.[5]

[5] Andrew Eliot, *A Sermon Preached before His Excellency Francis Bernard* . . . (Boston, 1765: JHL Pamphlet 15), p. 17; Adams, *Diary and Autobiography.* I, 282; II, 58; Peter Whitney, *The Transgressions of a Land* . . . (Boston. 1774), pp. 21–22. Whitney's thought — indeed his very phraseology — echoes through the opposition literature of early eighteenth-century England and in the many discussions of power and government published in the colonies. Thus, for example, Prideaux's doubt *"whether the benefit which the world receives from government be sufficient to make amends for the calamities which it suffers from the follies, mistakes, and maladministration of those that manage it"* was quoted in *Cato's Letters,* no. 31, May 27, 1721 ("Considerations on the Weakness and Inconsistencies of Human Nature," as republished, fifth ed., London, 1758. I, 241); the same quotation, properly attributed and identical in every detail. appears at the head of an essay on the "propensity of *men in power* to oppress the *people*" that was copied from an unnamed "northern paper" into the *South Carolina Gazette,* July 29–August 1, 1748. This borrowed essay, which is a classic example of the application to colonial politics of the language of English opposition ideology, appears between two issues of the *South Carolina Gazette*

On this there was absolute agreement. Everyone, of course, knew that if "weak or ignorant men are entrusted with power" there will be "universal confusion," for "such exaltation will . . . make them giddy and vain and deprive them of the little understanding they had before." But it was not simply a question of what the weak and ignorant will do. The problem was more systematic than that; it concerned "mankind in general." And the point they hammered home time and again, and agreed on — freethinking Anglican literati no less than neo-Calvinist theologians — was the incapacity of the species, of mankind in general, to withstand the temptations of power. Such is "the depravity of mankind," Samuel Adams, speaking for the Boston Town Meeting, declared, "that ambition and lust of power above the law are . . . predominant passions in the breasts of most men." These are instincts that have "in all nations combined the worst passions of the human heart and the worst projects of the human mind in league against the liberties of mankind." Power always and everywhere had had a pernicious, corrupting effect upon men. It "converts a good man in private life to a tyrant in office." It acts upon men like drink: it "is known to be intoxicating in its nature" — "too intoxicating and liable to abuse." And nothing within man is sufficiently strong to guard against these effects of power — certainly not "the united considerations of reason and religion," for they have never "been sufficiently powerful to restrain these lusts of men." [6]

---

made up almost entirely of selections from *Cato's Letters*, the issue of July 25–29 republishing in its entirety *Cato's Letters*, no. 37 ("Character of a Good and of an Evil Magistrate, Quoted from Algernon Sidney, Esq."), the issue of August 1–8 republishing no. 38 ("The Right and Capacity of the People to Judge of Government"). The "northern paper" was in all probability *The Independent Advertiser* of Boston, which ran the same two numbers of *Cato's Letters*, also without attribution, on May 16 and February 29 of the same year.

[6] Eliot, *Sermon* (JHL 15), pp. 10–11; [Daniel Dulany], *Considerations on the Propriety of Imposing Taxes* (Annapolis, 1765: JHL Pamphlet 13), p. 41: "for mankind are generally so fond of power that they are oftener tempted to

POWER AND LIBERTY

From these central premises on the nature of power and man's weakness in face of its temptations, there followed a series of important conclusions. Since power "in proportion to its extent is ever prone to wantonness," Josiah Quincy wrote, and since in the last analysis "the supreme power is ever possessed by those who have arms in their hands and are disciplined to the use of them," the absolute danger to liberty lay in the absolute supremacy of "a veteran army" — in making "the civil subordinate to the military," as Jefferson put it in 1774, "instead of subjecting the military to the civil powers." Their fear was not simply of armies but of *standing armies*, a phrase that had distinctive con-

---

exercise it beyond the limits of justice than induced to set bounds to it from the pure consideration of the rectitude of forbearance"; *The Votes and Proceedings of the Freeholders . . . of . . . Boston* . . . (Boston, [1772]: JHL Pamphlet 36), p. 20; [Jonathan Boucher], *A Letter from a Virginian* . . . ([New York], 1774: JHL Pamphlet 46), p. 7; Oliver Noble, *Some Strictures upon the . . . Book of Esther* . . . (Newburyport, 1775: JHL Pamphlet 58), p. 5; *The Genuine Principles of the Ancient Saxon, or English Constitution* . . . (Philadelphia, 1776: JHL Pamphlet 70), p. 5 (quoting [Obadiah Hulme's] *An Historical Essay on the English Constitution* [1771]); Josiah Quincy, Jr., *Observations on the . . . Boston Port-Bill; with Thoughts on . . . Standing Armies* (Boston, 1774), in Josiah Quincy, *Memoir of the Life of Josiah Quincy Jun.* . . . (Boston, 1825), pp. 372–373; Whitney, *Transgressions*, pp. 21–22; Zabdiel Adams, *The Grounds of Confidence and Success in War* . . . (Boston, 1775), p. 5; Adams, *Diary and Autobiography*, II, 59.

This basic concept of human nature, which would attain its greatest fame in the *Federalist*, appears full blown in the colonies well before the Revolutionary years, and may be traced back, intact, to the early eighteenth-century transmitters of English opposition thought. Thus, in words that may be found duplicated almost endlessly in the public prints of the mid-century, a writer in the *New York Mercury*, March 24, 1755, wrote: "A lust of domination is more or less natural to all parties; and hence the stupidity of entrusting any set of people with more power than necessity requires. Ambition and a thirst for sway are so deeply implanted in the human mind that one degree of elevation serves only as a step by which to ascend the next; nor can they ever mount the ladder so high as not to find the top still equally remote." The passage is indistinguishable from any number of discussions of the same topic in *Cato's Letters* (e.g., nos. 31, 39, 40, 43, 44, 134), and in the writings of the later English radicals (e.g., Catharine Macaulay, *Observations on a Pamphlet, Entitled, Thoughts on the Cause of the Present Discontents*, 3d ed., London, 1770, p. 9: "All systematical writers on the side of freedom plan their forms and rules of government on the just grounds of the known corruption and wickedness of the human character").

notations, derived, like so much of their political thought, from the seventeenth century and articulated for them by earlier English writers — in this case most memorably by Trenchard in his famous *An Argument, Shewing, that a Standing Army Is Inconsistent with a Free Government . . .* (1697). With him the colonists universally agreed that "unhappy nations have lost that precious jewel *liberty* . . . [because] their necessities or indiscretion have permitted a standing army to be kept amongst them." There was, they knew, no "worse state of thraldom than a military power in any government, unchecked and uncontrolled by the civil power"; and they had a vivid sense of what such armies were: gangs of restless mercenaries, responsible only to the whims of the rulers who paid them, capable of destroying all right, law, and liberty that stood in their way.[7]

[7] Quincy, *Observations,* in Quincy, *Memoir,* pp. 373, 428; [Thomas Jefferson], *A Summary View of the Rights of British America* . . . (Williamsburg, [1774]: JHL Pamphlet 43), p. 22; [John Trenchard and Walter Moyle], *An Argument,* p. 4 (reprinted in *The Pamphleteer* . . . , X [1817], 114); [Samuel Seabury], *An Alarm to the Legislature of the Province of New-York* . . . (New York, 1775), in Clarence H. Vance, ed., *Letters of a Westchester Farmer (Publications of the Westchester County Historical Society,* VIII, White Plains, 1930), p. 159. For other examples of the almost obsessive concern in the colonies with standing armies, see *No Standing Army in the British Colonies* . . . (New York, 1775); Noble, *Some Strictures* (JHL 58), pp. 28–29; *Genuine Principles* (JHL 70), p. 23; Simeon Howard, *A Sermon Preached to the Ancient and Honorable Artillery-Company* . . . (Boston, 1773), pp. 26–28 (quoting Trenchard); James Lovell, *An Oration* . . . (Boston, 1771), pp. 8–9 (also quoting Trenchard); and above all, Quincy, *Observations,* in Quincy, *Memoir,* pp. 400–445. Lois Schwoerer discusses the original context and literature of standing armies in England (see above, Chap. II, n. 18), and Caroline Robbins, *The Eighteenth-Century Commonwealthman* (Cambridge, 1959), deals with the subsequent English background at many points (see Index under "militia"). But the fullest discussion of the ideological meaning of standing armies is J. G. A. Pocock, "Machiavelli, Harrington, and English Political Ideologies in the Eighteenth Century," *W.M.Q.,* 3d ser., 22 (1965), 560 ff. Pocock, who dates the origins of "that concept or bogey" in 1675, argues that by the end of the seventeenth century it had come to mean not praetorians or janissaries but "a permanent professional force maintained by the administration and supplied out of the public ᵻxchequer"; as such, standing armies were feared as instruments in the systematic corruption of Parliament by the administration and hence of

This fear of standing armies followed directly from the colonists' understanding of power and of human nature: on purely logical grounds it was a reasonable fear. But it went beyond mere logic. Only too evidently was it justified, as the colonists saw it, by history and by the facts of the contemporary world. Conclusive examples of what happened when standing armies were permitted to dominate communities were constantly before their minds' eyes. There was, first and foremost, the example of the Turks, whose rulers — cruel, sensuous "bashaws in their little divans" — were legendary, ideal types of despots who reigned unchecked by right or law or in any sense the consent of the people; their power rested on the swords of their vicious janissaries, the worst of standing armies. So too had the French kings snuffed out the liberties of their subjects "by force" and reduced to nothing the "puny privilege of the French parliaments." The ranks of "despotic kingdoms" included also Poland, Spain, and Russia; India and Egypt were occasionally mentioned too.[8]

---

the overthrow of the balanced constitution. The colonists echoed this concern: see John Dickinson's association of standing armies and excise collection in his *Letters from a Farmer in Pennsylvania* . . . (Philadelphia, 1768: JHL Pamphlet 23), pp. 60–61; and Simeon Howard's definition of a standing army as "a number of men paid by the public to devote themselves wholly to the military profession," who, though "really servants of the people and paid by them," come to think of themselves as the King's men exclusively and become "the means, in the hands of a wicked and oppressive sovereign, of overturning the constitution of a country and establishing the most intolerable despotism" (*Sermon*, pp. 26, 27). But the phrase was also commonly used loosely to mean simply the personal troops of the prince in states already lacking balanced constitutions; e.g., John Hancock, *An Oration* . . . (Boston, 1774: JHL Pamphlet 41), pp. 13–14.

[8] Turkey as the ultimate refinement of despotism fascinated eighteenth-century Americans and Englishmen alike, their fascination doubtless heightened by the salacious details furnished in such perennial best sellers as Sir Paul Rycaut (or Ricaut), *History of the Present State of the Ottoman Empire* (first published 1668; 6th ed. 1686; reprinted continuously for a century afterward and lifted bodily into such comprehensive works as *A Compleat History of the Turks*, 4 vols., London, 1719), which jumbles together under the heading "Maxims of the Turkish Polity" chapters on the absolutism of the Turkish government, "The Affection and Friendship the Pages of the Seraglio Bear to Each Other" and

More interesting than these venerable despotisms, bywords for the rule of force unrestrained by countervailing influences, were a number of despotic states that had within living memory been free and whose enslavement, being recent, had been directly observed. Venice was one: it had once, not so long ago, been a republic, but now it was governed "by one of the worst of despotisms." Sweden was another; the colonists themselves could remember when the Swedish people had enjoyed liberty to the full; but now, in the 1760's, they were known to "rejoice at being subject to the caprice and arbitrary power of a tyrant, and

---

"The Apartments of the Women." From at least the mid-seventeenth century, writings on the absolutism of the Turks had served in England as disguised tracts for the times, commentaries "upon the English polity from a safe vantage point" (Felix Raab, *The English Face of Machiavelli*, London, 1964, p. 164). The early eighteenth-century polemicists continued to probe the inner characteristics of absolutism, and by contrast the nature of liberty, by examining the society and government of the Turks. There are innumerable discussions and references to Turkish despotism in *Cato's Letters*; Letter 50, dilating on "that horrible and destroying government [of the Turks], a government fierce and inhuman, founded in blood, supported by barbarity," includes eight pages of quotations from Rycaut. As a result, long before the Revolution the colonists were habituated to conceive of "the difference between free and enslaved countries" as "the difference between *England and Turkey*" (*Boston Gazette or Country Journal*, May 19, 1755); to see the ultimate in political oppression as "worse than Turkish cruelties" (M. G. Hall, *et al.*, eds., *The Glorious Revolution in America*, Chapel Hill, 1964, p. 45); and to think of total power "as absolute as that of the Great Turk" (*Boston Evening Post*, July 4, 1737). This terminology and this mode of thought were carried over directly into the Revolutionary literature. See, for example, [William H. Drayton], *A Letter from Freeman of South-Carolina* . . . Charleston, 1774: JHL Pamphlet 45), p. 8; and [Richard Bland], *The Colonel Dismounted: Or the Rector Vindicated* . . . (Williamsburg, 1764: JHL Pamphlet 4), p. 26.

For an elaborate discussion of the "awful lesson" of Poland entirely in the spirit of the Revolutionary pamphleteers, see Mercy Otis Warren, *History of the . . . American Revolution* . . . (Boston, 1805), II, 182–184. On France and the other familiar tyrannies, see the characteristic background in *New York Evening Post*, December 7, 1747, and the examples in Quincy, *Observations*, in Quincy, *Memoir*, pp. 443, 450–451; Dickinson, *Farmer's Letters* (JHL 23), pp. 12, 46; [Stephen Johnson], *Some Important Observations* . . . (Newport, 1766: JHL Pamphlet 19), p. 11; [Alexander Hamilton], *The Farmer Refuted* . . . (New York, 1775), in *The Papers of Alexander Hamilton* (Harold C. Syrett, *et al.*, eds., New York and London, 1961–), I, 122.

kiss their chains." But the most vivid of these sad cases, because the most closely studied, was that of Denmark. The destruction of parliamentary liberties in Denmark had in fact taken place a century before, but that event, carefully examined in a treatise famous in opposition circles and in America, was experienced as contemporary by the colonists.

Molesworth's *An Account of Denmark* (1694) established the general point, implicit in all similar histories but explicit in this one, that the preservation of liberty rested on the ability of the people to maintain effective checks on the wielders of power, and hence in the last analysis rested on the vigilance and moral stamina of the people. Certain forms of government made particularly heavy demands on the virtue of the people. Everyone knew that democracy — direct rule by all the people — required such spartan, self-denying virtue on the part of all the people that it was likely to survive only where poverty made upright behavior necessary for the perpetuation of the race. Other forms, aristocracies, for example, made less extreme demands; but even in them virtue and sleepless vigilance on the part of at least the ruling class were necessary if privilege was to be kept responsible and the inroads of tyranny perpetually blocked off. It had been the lack of this vigilance that had brought liberty in Denmark to its knees, for there a corrupt nobility, more interested in using its privileges for self-indulgence than for service to the state, had dropped its guard and allowed in a standing army which quickly destroyed the constitution and the liberties protected by it.

The converse of all of this was equally true and more directly relevant. The few peoples that had managed to retain their liberties in the face of all efforts of would-be tyrants propelled by the lust for power had been doughty folk whose vigilance had never relaxed and whose virtue had remained uncontaminated. The Swiss, a rustic people locked in mountain sanctuaries, were ancient members of this heroic group; they had won their liberty long ago and had maintained it stubbornly ever after. The Dutch were more recent members, having overthrown the despotic rule of Spain only a century earlier; they too were industrious people of stubborn, Calvinist virtue, and they were led by an alert aristocracy. More recent in their emergence from darkness were the Corsicans, whose revolt against Genoese overlords backed by French power had begun only in 1729; they were still, at the time of the Stamp Act, struggling under the leadership of Pasquale Paoli to maintain their independence and liberty.[9]

Above all, however, there were the English themselves. The colonists' attitude to the whole world of politics and government was fundamentally shaped by the root assumption that they, as Britishers, shared in a unique inheritance of liberty. The English people, they believed, though often threatened by despots who had risen in their midst, had managed to maintain, to a greater degree and for a longer period of time than any other people, a tradition of the successful control of power and of those evil tendencies of human nature that would prevent its proper uses.

In view of the natural obstacles that stood in the way of such a success and in view of the dismal history of other nations, this,

[9] On the more recent despotisms, especially Denmark and Sweden, see *Votes and Proceedings of Boston* (JHL 36), p. 35; Dulany, *Considerations* (JHL 13), p. 46n; Samuel Williams, *A Discourse on the Love of Our Country* . . . (Salem, 1775: JHL Pamphlet 55), p. 21; H. Trevor Colbourn, *The Lamp of Experience* (Chapel Hill, 1965), pp. 74, 137. On the surviving free states, see, for example, John Joachim Zubly, *The Law of Liberty* . . . (Philadelphia, 1775), Appendix, pp. 33–41; [Carter Braxton], *An Address to . . . Virginia; on the Subject of Government* . . . (Philadelphia, 1776: JHL Pamphlet 66), p. 18; [James Chalmers], *Plain Truth . . . Containing Remarks on . . . Common Sense* . . . (Philadelphia, 1776: JHL Pamphlet 64), pp. 9 ff.; [Charles Inglis], *The True Interest of America . . . Strictures on a Pamphlet Intitled Common Sense* . . . (Philadelphia, 1776), pp. 46, 61. For a detailed discussion of Moleworth's influential *Account of Denmark*, see Robbins, *Commonwealthman*, pp. 98–109, 393–394. On the Corsicans, see e.g., Arthur Lee's equation of their effort against the French and Genoese to those of the Athenians against Xerxes, the starving Romans against their various besiegers, the Flemish against "a very potent monarch," and the Georgians against the Turks. "Monitor V," *Virginia Gazette* (R), March 24, 1768.

as the colonists saw it, had been an extraordinary achievement. But it was not a miraculous one. It could be explained historically. The ordinary people of England, they believed, were descended from simple, sturdy Saxons who had known liberty in the very childhood of the race and who, through the centuries, had retained the desire to preserve it. But it had taken more than desire. Reinforcing, structuring, expressing the liberty-loving temper of the people, there was England's peculiar "constitution," described by John Adams, in words almost every American agreed with before 1763, as "the most perfect combination of human powers in society which finite wisdom has yet contrived and reduced to practice for the preservation of liberty and the production of happiness." [10]

The word "constitution" and the concept behind it was of central importance to the colonists' political thought; their entire understanding of the crisis in Anglo-American relations rested upon it. So strategically located was this idea in the minds of both English and Americans, and so great was the pressure placed upon it in the course of a decade of pounding debate that in the end it was forced apart, along the seam of a basic ambiguity, to form the two contrasting concepts of constitutionalism that have remained characteristic of England and America ever since.[11]

At the start of the controversy, however, the most distinguishing feature of the colonists' view of the constitution was its apparent traditionalism. Like their contemporaries in England and like their predecessors for centuries before, the colonists at the beginning of the Revolutionary controversy understood by the word "constitution" not, as we would have it, a written

---

[10] Adams, *Works*, III, 477. For characteristic encomiums on the constitution and descriptions of its operating balance, see James Otis, *Rights of the British Colonies Asserted and Proved* (Boston, 1764: JHL Pamphlet 7), p. 47; Dulany, *Considerations* (JHL 13), p. 15; Johnson, *Some Important Observations* (JHL 19), pp. 27 ff.; Whitney, *Transgressions*, p. 10; Mather, *America's Appeal* (JHL 59), pp. 7–8, 34 ff.

[11] See below, Chap. V, sec. 2.

document or even an unwritten but deliberately contrived design of government and a specification of rights beyond the power of ordinary legislation to alter; they thought of it, rather, as the constituted — that is, existing — arrangement of governmental institutions, laws, and customs together with the principles and goals that animated them. So John Adams wrote that a political constitution is like "the constitution of the human body"; "certain contextures of the nerves, fibres, and muscles, or certain qualities of the blood and juices" some of which "may properly be called *stamina vitae,* or essentials and fundamentals of the constitution; parts without which life itself cannot be preserved a moment." A constitution of government, analogously, Adams wrote, is "a frame, a scheme, a system, a combination of powers for a certain end, namely, — the good of the whole community." [12]

The elements of this definition were traditional, but it was nevertheless distinctive in its emphasis on the animating prin-

---

[12] Adams, *Works,* III, 478–479. The conception of "constitution" as the arrangement of existing laws and practices of government may be traced back through the literature of the early eighteenth and the seventeenth centuries. So, traditionally, David Lloyd referred in 1706 to "the best constitution we could find, to wit: the common and statute laws of England" (Roy N. Lokken, *David Lloyd,* Seattle, 1959, p. 168). Similarly, in 1748 *The Maryland Gazette* printed a series of essays elaborating the idea that parliaments "are the very constitution itself," that "our constitution is at present but a series of alterations made by Parliament," and ridiculing the notion that *"the Parliament cannot alter the constitution"* (issues of April 27 and May 4 and Supplement to issue of May 11). Bolingbroke's views are particularly interesting since, while he insisted that the constitution was immutable, that even kings must subject themselves to it, and that obedience was justified by the degree to which magistrates conformed to the constitution, he nevertheless defined a constitution as "that assemblage of laws, institutions, and customs, derived from certain fixed principles of reason, directed to certain fixed objects of public good, that compose the general system according to which the community hath agreed to be governed": "Dissertation on Parties," Letter X, in *Works* . . . (London, 1754), II, 130. Cf. J. H. Burns, "Bolingbroke and the Concept of Constitutional Government," *Political Studies,* 10 (1962), 264–276. For particularly close anticipations of Adams' imagery and understanding of constitutions, see the discussion of the "natural or political body . . . composed of springs, wheels, and ligaments," and of the "stamina, first principles, or original constitution" of government, in *Cato's Letters,* nos. 69 and 84.

ciples, the *stamina vitae,* those "fundamental laws and rules of the constitution, which ought never to be infringed." Belief that a proper system of laws and institutions should be suffused with, should express, essences and fundamentals — moral rights, reason, justice — had never been absent from English notions of the constitution. But not since the Levellers had protested against Parliament's supremacy in the mid-seventeenth century had these considerations seemed so important as they did to the Americans of the mid-eighteenth century. Nor could they ever have appeared more distinct in their content. For if the ostensible purpose of all government was the good of the people, the particular goal of the English constitution — "its end, its use, its designation, drift, and scope" — was known to all, and declared by all, to be the attainment of liberty. This was its peculiar "grandeur" and excellence; it was for this that it should be prized "next to our Bibles, above the privileges of this world." It was for this that it should be blessed, supported and maintained, and transmitted "in full, to posterity." [13]

[13] *A Letter to the People of Pennsylvania* (Philadelphia, 1760: JHL Pamphlet 2), p. 3; Adams, *Works,* III, 479; Otis, *Rights of the British Colonies* (JHL 7), p. 47; Johnson, *Some Important Observations* (JHL 19), p. 28. For a characteristic pre-Revolutionary statement of the relation between fundamental law and the constitution, see *Boston Gazette and Country Journal,* May 10, 1756, where an anonymous essayist explained that Magna Carta "is only *declaratory* of the *principal* grounds, of the *fundamental* laws and liberties of England . . . so that it seems rather to be a collection of ancient privileges from the common law ratified by the suffrage of the people and claimed by them as their *reserved rights.* It is in short the constitution of *English* government — the basis of English law — the compact — the standing perpetual rule over which no man nor any body of men distinct from the whole may claim any just superiority." There was an obvious answer, the writer made clear, to the question "whether the three branches [of Parliament] is the constitution, or whether they are not circumscribed by some rules established previous to their existence, which they may not depart from." If Parliament were to pass a law that altered the constitution, the writer argued in phrases that anticipate both James Otis' famous self-contradictions and the ultimate grounds of American defiance of Parliament, "would the people, if they did not like the alteration, think themselves obliged to abide by such a law? Notwithstanding the veneration which is justly due to an act of Parliament, *the known wisdom of British Parliament* will hardly admit of the supposition." (Italics added.)

But how had this been achieved? What was the secret of this success of the British constitution? It lay in its peculiar capacity to balance and check the basic forces within society. It was common knowledge, expressed in such familiar clichés, a Virginian complained, "that the merest sciolist, the veriest smatterer in politics must long since have had them all by rote," [14] that English society consisted of three social orders, or estates, each with its own rights and privileges, and each embodying within it the principles of a certain form of government: royalty, whose natural form of government was monarchy; the nobility, whose natural form was aristocracy; and the commons, whose form was democracy. In the best of worlds, it had been known since Aristotle, each of these forms independently was capable of creating the conditions for human happiness; in actuality all of them, if unchecked, tended to degenerate into oppressive types of government — tyranny, oligarchy, or mob rule — by enlarging their own rights at the expense of the others' and hence generating not liberty and happiness for all but misery for most. In England, however, these elements of society, each independently dangerous, entered into government in such a way as to eliminate the dangers inherent in each. They entered simultaneously, so to speak, in a balanced sharing of power. The functions, the powers, of government were so distributed among these components of society that no one of them dominated the others. So long as each component remained within its proper sphere and vigilantly checked all efforts of the others to transcend their proper boundaries there would be a stable equilibrium of poised forces each of which, in protecting its own rights against the encroachments of the others, contributed to the preservation of the rights of all.

Such was the theoretical explanation, universally accepted in the eighteenth century, of the famous "mixed" constitution of

---

[14] [Robert Carter Nicholas], *Considerations on the Present State of Virginia Examined* ([Williamsburg], 1774), in the Earl G. Swem edition (New York, 1919), p. 40.

England.[15] It was an arrangement of power that appeared to the colonists as it did to most of Europe as "a system of consummate wisdom and policy." But if the theory was evident and unanimously agreed on, the mechanics of its operation were not. It was not clear how the three social orders were related to the functioning branches of government. The clarity of the modern assumption of a tripartite division of the functions of government into legislative, executive, and judicial powers did not exist for the colonists (the term "legislative," for example, was used to mean the whole of government as well as the lawmaking branch), and in any case the balance of the constitution was not expected to be the result of the symmetrical matching of social orders with powers of government: it was not assumed that each estate would singly dominate one of the branches or functions of government.[16] What was generally agreed on was what Molesworth

[15] On the origins and development of this theory of the English constitution, see Corinne C. Weston, *English Constitutional Theory and the House of Lords, 1556–1832* (London, 1965), where it is argued that, though the idea of mixed government was an ancient one, it acquired its classic English form in Charles I's *His Majesties Answer to the XIX. Propositions of Both Houses of Parliament* (London, 1642). Before the appearance of that pamphlet "the term three estates had been used officially and popularly to designate the lords spiritual, the lords temporal, and the commons" (p. 31). For a model statement of the concept as it was transmitted to the colonists in the early eighteenth century, see *The Spectator*, no. 287 (January 29, 1711/12), where the roots of the idea in classical antiquity are traced and where the main emphasis is placed on the liberty-preserving force of dividing government among persons "of different ranks and interests, for where they are of the same rank, it differs but little from a despotical government in a single person." Safety would be found in a government in which power was divided among "persons so happily distinguished that by providing for the particular interests of their several ranks they are providing for the whole body of the people." For a view of the theory of the mixed constitution as an expression of the fundamental change in intellectual orientation from medieval scholasticism to modern empiricism, see W. H. Greenleaf, *Order, Empiricism and Politics . . . 1500–1700* (London, 1964), chap. ix. See also Stanley Pargellis, "The Theory of Balanced Government," in Conyers Read, ed., *The Constitution Reconsidered* (New York, 1938), pp. 37–49, and below, Chap. VI, sec. 3.

[16] Robert Shackleton argues ("Montesquieu, Bolingbroke, and the Separation of Powers," *French Studies*, III [1949], 25–38, and *Montesquieu* [Oxford, 1961], pp. 298–301) that Montesquieu interpreted the balance of the English constitution

wrote in defining a "real Whig" in his Introduction to Hotman's *Franco-Gallia* (1711): "one who is exactly for keeping up to the strictness of the true old *Gothic constitution,* under the *three estates* of *King* (or *Queen*), *Lords,* and *Commons,* the *legislature* being seated in all three together, the executive entrusted with the first but accountable to the whole body of the people, in case

in terms of the modern idea of the separation of functioning powers, and that he derived this idea from Bolingbroke's *Craftsman.* The argument seems unconvincing on both points from the evidence presented. The most that can be said, it would seem, is that in discussing the English constitution Montesquieu did attempt to show the matching of social powers with the functioning powers of government (which he did, indeed, clearly define as legislative, executive, and judicial) but that he did not succeed in doing so with any clarity. See *Spirit of the Laws* (Franz Neumann, ed., New York, 1949), bk. xi, sec. 6 (esp. p. 156; cf. p. lviii). His partial and confused mingling of the idea of the mixed state with the modern idea of the separation of powers (which the colonists did, on occasion, unambiguously extract from his writing: e.g., *Boston Gazette and Country Journal,* January 2, 1758) is described in Weston, *English Constitutional Theory,* pp. 124–125; in Betty Kemp, *King and Commons, 1660–1832* (London, 1959), pp. 82–85; and above all in W. B. Gwyn, *The Meaning of the Separation of Powers (Tulane Studies in Political Science,* IX, New Orleans, 1965), pp. 104, 109—a work of particular importance that came to hand too late to be used in the writing of this book. Bolingbroke in his debate with Walpole's publicists over whether balance in government is properly attained by the independence or by the mutual dependence of powers, assumed, as did his opponents, that the object of discussion was England's mixed government, or constitution, of King, Lords, and Commons. See Isaac Kramnick, *Bolingbroke and His Circle: The Politics of Nostalgia in the Age of Walpole* (Cambridge, 1968), esp. chap. vi, and Gwyn, *Separation of Powers,* pp. 91–99. Bolingbroke's arguments, jumbling the concepts of balances and checks, the mixed constitution and the separation of powers, are echoed by Thomas Hutchinson in his notable message of July 14, 1772, to the Massachusetts House in which he sought to justify the proposed independent salary of the Massachusetts governor by analogy to the independence of King, Lords, and Commons in England. Thomas Hutchinson, *The History of . . . Massachusetts-Bay* (Lawrence S. Mayo, ed., Cambridge, 1936), III, Appendix W (esp. pp. 408–409). It is suggested below, Chap. VI, sec. 3, that in America the origins of the modern doctrine of the separation of functioning powers lay in the Revolutionary effort to recreate balance in governments within a society systematically lacking in divisions of rank or estate. For an account of the intense and revealing discussion of Montesquieu and the doctrine of the separation of power in Massachusetts on the eve of the Revolutionary controversy, see Ellen E. Brennan, *Plural Office-Holding in Massachusetts, 1760–1780* (Chapel Hill, 1945), chap. ii; on the English origins of the doctrine, see Gwyn, *Separation of Powers,* chaps. iii–v.

of maladministration." What was agreed on, in other words, primarily and most significantly was that all three social orders did and should enter into and share, by representation or otherwise, the legislative branch. In the legislative functioning of government, Moses Mather explained in terms that commanded universal assent, power was

so judiciously placed as to connect the force and to preserve the rights of all; each estate, armed with a power of self-defense against the encroachments of the other two, by being enabled to put a negative upon any or all of their resolves, neither the King, Lords, or Commons could be deprived of their rights or properties but by their own consent in Parliament and no laws could be made or taxes imposed but such as were necessary and in the judgment of the three estates in Parliament, for the common good and the interest of the realm.[17]

It was also agreed that the executive function was largely if not completely the proper responsibility of the first order of society, the crown. The rights exercised there were understood to be the rights of power: prerogative rights, privileges properly enjoyed by the monarch and his servants. But there the agreement stopped. There were several explanations of how the balance of social forces worked to check the undue exercise of prerogative power. Some writers found a sufficient balance and check in the fact that executive action was confined to bounds laid down by

[17] Francis Hotman, *Franco-Gallia* . . . (Molesworth trans., 2nd ed., London, 1721), p. vii (Molesworth's Introduction was republished separately in 1775 as *The Principles of a Real Whig*); Mather, *America's Appeal* (JHL 59), p. 8. Cf. Trenchard's formulation in his *History of Standing Armies*, copied with approval by Bolingbroke in his *Craftsman*, no. 198 (in collected edition, London, 1731, VI, 142): "All wise governments endeavor, as much as possible, to keep the *legislative* and *executive parts* asunder, that they may be a check upon one another. Our government trusts the King with no part of the *legislative* but a *negative voice*, which is absolutely necessary to preserve the *executive*. One part of the duty of the *House of Commons* is to punish offenders and redress the grievances occasioned by the *executive* part of the government; and how can that be done if they should happen to be the *same persons*, unless they would be public-spirited enough to *hang* or *drown themselves*?"

laws in the making of which all three powers had shared. But others were able to perceive a subtler kind of check upon prerogative power. For John Adams an essential point was that the commons, or the democracy, of society shared too in the execution of laws through the institution of trial by jury. This ancient device was critical, as Adams saw it, in establishing the equipoise of the English constitution in that it introduced into the "executive branch of the constitution . . . a mixture of popular power" and as a consequence "the subject is guarded in the execution of the laws." [18] Most writers, however, turned for explanation not so much to the popular recruitment of juries and hence to a social balance within the executive branch as to the pressure exerted against the executive from outside, by an independent judiciary. It was taken as a maxim by all, whether or not they used the point to explain how the executive branch entered into the separation of powers, that it was the function of the judges "to settle the contests between prerogative and liberty . . . to ascertain the bounds of sovereign power, and to determine the rights of the subject," and that in order for them to perform this duty properly they must be "perfectly free from the influence of either." The threat to this independence — liberty being passive and power active — came most commonly from prerogative because of the effect of "its natural weight and authority" working upon the almost universal "love of promotion and private advantage." Unless the judiciary could stand upon its own firm and independent foundations — unless, that is, judges held their positions by a permanent tenure in no way dependent upon the will and pleasure of the executive — it would be ridiculous "to look for strict impartiality and a pure administration of justice, to

[18] Adams, *Works*, III, 481; cf. *Four Letters on Interesting Subjects* (Philadelphia, 1776: JHL Pamphlet 69), p. 21. On the background of the problem in European thought, see Gwyn, *Separation of Powers*, pp. 5–8, 101, 103, 106, 110–111.

expect that power should be confined within its legal limits, and right and justice done to the subject." [19]

The difficulty of explaining how, precisely, the natural divisions of society expressed themselves in the English government so as to pit power against power for the mutual benefit of all was compounded when the unit involved was seen to be not the single community of Britain but an empire of communities each with its own separate social groupings and governmental institutions yet each part of a greater society and government as well. But until the Revolutionary crisis was well under way no one sought to settle this complicated constitutional problem.[20] The

[19] *Letter to the People of Pennsylvania* (JHL 2), pp. 4, 5, 7.

[20] Thus Dickinson: ". . . the government here is not only *mixed* but *dependent*, which circumstance occasions *a peculiarity in its form* of a very delicate nature" (*Farmer's Letters* [JHL 23], p. 58). This peculiarity, and the constitutional difficulties it involved, had long been noticed. In 1711 the astute Governor Hunter of New York warned Bolingbroke, then Secretary of State, that if the New York Council successfully claimed the "rights and privileges of a House of Peers," since the Assembly already claimed the privileges of a House of Commons, the colony would become "a body politic coordinate with (claiming equal powers) and consequently independent of the Great Council of the realm," adding for authority Harrington's idiosyncratic formula, which he quoted exactly, but without attribution: "as national or independent empire is to be exercised by them that have the proper balance of dominion in the nation, so provincial or dependent empire is not to be exercised by them that have the balance of dominion in the province, because that would bring the government from provincial and dependent to national and independent." E. B. O'Callaghan and Berthold Fernow, eds., *Documents Relative to the Colonial History of the State of New-York* . . . (Albany, 1856–1887), V, 255–256; cf. *Oceana* (S. B. Liljegren, ed., Heidelberg, 1924), p. 18. While by the mid-eighteenth century there was general agreement that the colonial governments were miniatures of the English government whose discrepancies from the model "doubtless in time will be rectified" (William Douglass, *A Summary, Historical and Political* . . . , Boston, 1749–1751, I, 215), it was equally apparent that the colonial legislatures did not have "a corresponding power with that of the Parliament in *Great Britain* . . . If the three branches [of the colonial Assemblies] united have equal power [with that of Parliament], then each of them have separately the same: and so a house of representatives has power equal to the House of Commons, the council to the House of Lords, and a governor to the King, which is absurd . . . The truth is, we are all of us *British* subjects, from the

colonists were content to celebrate the wonderful balance of forces they understood to exist in England, and to assume that in some effective way the same principles operated both in epitome within each colony and in the over-all world of the empire as well.

The result of this balanced counterpoise of social and governmental forces in the British constitution was the confinement of social and political powers to specified, limited spheres. So long as the crown, the nobility, and the democracy remained in their designated places in government and performed their designated political tasks, liberty would continue to be safe in England and its dominions. But if any of them reached beyond the set boundaries of their rightful jurisdictions; if, particularly, the agencies of power — the prerogative, administration — managed, by corrupt practices, to insinuate their will into the assembly of the commons and to manipulate it at pleasure, liberty would be endangered.

The very idea of liberty was bound up with the preservation

---

greatest to the least, subject to British laws and entitled to *British* privileges . . . that a government in America is not equal there to the Parliament of *Great Britain* is evident from this one consideration, that the former have not power to make laws repugnant or contrary to the laws of the latter." *Boston Gazette and Country Journal,* May 10, 1756. Yet it could also be assumed — and the assumption would ultimately flower into the most advanced Revolutionary views of the imperial constitution — that the colonists upon leaving England had "totally disclaim[ed] all *subordination* to a dependence upon the two inferior estates of their mother country" (Hicks, *Nature and Extent of Parliamentary Power* [JHL 24], p. 6), and that therefore from the start their Assemblies had been equivalent bodies to the Houses of Parliament, forming complete mixed polities in their separate affiliation with the King. As a consequence the question of how the colonies shared in "the democracy" of the English constitution became a matter of critical importance at the height of the crisis. See, e.g., Joseph Warren, *An Oration* . . . (Boston, 1772: JHL Pamphlet 35), pp. 9–10; Adams ("Novanglus"), *Works,* IV, pp. 100 ff., and Hutchinson's message of 1772 cited in note 16 above. Behind the lack of definition of the imperial constitution before 1763 and of the colonies' involvement in it lay the more basic question of the meaning of the British "empire" itself. The concept when applied to the American colonies had only a special and restricted meaning. See Richard Koebner, *Empire* (Cambridge, England, 1961), chap. iii, esp. pp. 77.

of this balance of forces. For political liberty, as opposed to the theoretical liberty that existed in a state of nature, was traditionally known to be "a natural power of doing or not doing whatever we have a mind" so long as that doing was "consistent with the rules of virtue and the established laws of the society to which we belong"; it was "a power of acting agreeable to the laws which are made and enacted by the consent of the PEOPLE, and in no ways inconsistent with the natural rights of a single person, or the good of the society." Liberty, that is, was the capacity to exercise "natural rights" within limits set not by the mere will or desire of men in power but by non-arbitrary law — law enacted by legislatures containing within them the proper balance of forces.[21]

But what were these all-important "natural rights"? They were defined in a significantly ambiguous way. They were understood to be at one and the same time the inalienable, indefeasible rights inherent in people as such, and the concrete specifications of English law. Rights, John Dickinson wrote,

are created in us by the decrees of Providence, which establish the laws of our nature. They are born with us; exist with us; and cannot be taken from us by any human power without taking our lives. In short, they are founded on the immutable maxims of reason and justice.

Such God-given, natural, inalienable rights, distilled from reason and justice through the social and governmental compacts, were expressed in the common law of England, in the statutory enact-

---

[21] *New York Evening Post*, November 16, 1747; Levi Hart, *Liberty Described and Recommended* . . . (Hartford, 1775), p. 13 (cf. p. 9); [John Allen], *The Watchman's Alarm to Lord N - - - h* . . . (Salem, 1774), p. [5]. As Allen points out, his definition of liberty — "the true etymology of the word" — was taken from Daniel Fenning's *Royal English Dictionary* (London, 1761). He might equally well have attributed his discussion of liberty in *Cato's Letters*, nos. 62 and 63; to the casual reference in *The Spectator*, no. 287; or to various passages in Montesquieu, Rapin, or Bolingbroke. Cf. Neumann's Introduction to *The Spirit of the Laws*, pp. xlix–liii.

ments of Parliament, and in the charters of privileges promulgated by the crown. The great corpus of common law decisions and the pronouncements of King and Commons were but expressions of "God and nature . . . The natural absolute personal rights of individuals are . . . the very basis of all municipal laws of any great value." Indeed, "Magna Carta itself is in substance but a constrained declaration, or proclamation and promulgation in the name of King, Lords, and Commons of the sense the latter had of their original, inherent, indefeasible, natural rights." [22]

But this relationship between human rights and English law — so simple sounding when expressed in casual phrases like Daniel Dulany's "unalienable rights of the subject" — was in fact complicated even before the events of the 1760's and seventies placed the whole issue under severe pressure. Even then the identification between the two was known to be necessarily incomplete, for the provision of English law did not and properly could not wholly exhaust the great treasury of human rights. No documentary specification ever could. Laws, grants, and charters merely stated the essentials (which everyone summarized, with minor variations in phrasing, as "personal security, personal liberty, and private property") insofar, and only insofar, as they had come under attack in the course of English history. They marked out the minimum not the maximum boundaries of right. To claim more, to assert that all rights might be written into a comprehensive bill or code was surely, James Otis declared, "the insolence of a haughty and imperious minister . . . the flutter of a coxcomb, the pedantry of a quack, and the nonsense of a pettifogger." The "strange gallimaufry" of "codes, pandects, nov-

---

[22] [John Dickinson], *An Address to the Committee of Correspondence in Barbados* . . . (Philadelphia, 1766), in Paul L. Ford, ed., *The Writings of John Dickinson* (*Memoirs of the Historical Society of Pennsylvania*, XIV, Philadelphia, 1895), p. 262; [James Otis], *A Vindication of the British Colonies* . . . (Boston, 1765: JHL Pamphlet 11), p. 8; *Votes and Proceedings of Boston* (JHL 36), pp. 7-8.

els, decretals of popes, and the inventions of the d——l" may be suitable for "the cold bleak regions [of] Brandenburg and Prussia or the scorching heats of Jamaica or Gambia" but not for Britain's more temperate climate.[23]

Conceiving of liberty, then, as the exercise, within the boundaries of the law, of natural rights whose essences were minimally stated in English law and custom, the colonists saw in the balance of powers of the British constitution "a system of consummate wisdom" that provided an effective "check upon the power to oppress."[24] Yet they were far from optimistic about the future of liberty. They looked ahead with anxiety rather than with confidence, for they knew, from the whole of their received tradition, of the desperate plight of liberty everywhere: "new tyrannies have sprung up, like so many new plagues, within the memory of man, and . . . [have] engrossed almost the whole earth," rendering "the world a slaughterhouse." Rulers of the East were "almost universally absolute tyrants . . . The states of Africa are scenes of tyranny, barbarity, confusion, and every form of violence. And even in Europe, where human nature and society are arrived at the highest improvements, where can we find a well constituted government or a well governed people?" France "has an arbitrary authority"; Prussia, "an absolute government"; Sweden and Denmark "have sold or betrayed their liberties"; Rome "groans under a medley of civil and ecclesiastical bondage"; Germany "is a hundred-headed hydra"; and Poland a ruin of "extravagant licentiousness and anarchy . . . the nobility and gentry arbitrary despotic tyrants, and the populace a race of slaves." Only in Britain — and her colonies — had liberty emerged from its trials intact; only in Britain had the battle repeatedly been won. Yet even in Britain the margin of victory

---

[23] Dulany, *Considerations* (JHL 13), p. 30; *Votes and Proceedings of Boston* (JHL 36), p. 8; Otis, *Vindication* (JHL 11), p. 32.
[24] Mather, *America's Appeal* (JHL 59), p. 8; Lovell, *Oration*, p. 11.

had been narrow, especially in the last, bitter struggle with would-be despots of the house of Stuart. And the dangers were known to persist.[25]

The historical phasing of the defense of liberty in England was a matter of great importance to the colonists not merely because it illustrated the characteristic dangers liberty faced but also because it made clear their own special role in history. "Liberty," James Otis wrote in a sentence that reveals much of the structure of the colonists' historical thought, "was better understood and more fully enjoyed by our ancestors before the coming in of the first Norman tyrants than ever after, till it was found necessary for the salvation of the kingdom to combat the arbitrary and wicked proceedings of the Stuarts." The period before the Norman conquest was the greatest age of English history.

> . . . it is a fact as certain as history can make it that the present civil constitution of England derives its original from those Saxons who . . . established a form of government in [England] similar to that they had been accustomed to live under in their native country . . . This government, like that from whence they came, was founded upon principles of the most perfect liberty. The conquered lands were divided among the individuals in proportion to the rank they held in the nation, and every freeman, that is, every freeholder, was a member of their Witan Moot or Parliament . . . or, which was the same thing in the eye of the constitution, every freeholder had a right to vote at the election of members of Parliament, and therefore

---

[25] *Cato's Letters*, no. 73; *New York Gazette: or, The Weekly Post Boy*, November 1, 1756, quoting at length "a survey of the kingdoms of the earth" that appeared in the eleventh essay by "Virginia-Centinel," originally published in the *Virginia Gazette* in September or October 1756. (Essay 10, the only one of the original group that is extant, was published in the September 3, 1756, issue of the *Virginia Gazette*.) For an almost identical account of "the deplorable state of your fellow-creatures in other countries," see the *New York Mercury*, May 22, 1758, reprinting an essay from the *Pennsylvania Journal* which in turn quoted long extracts from "a late writer in an address to the farmers of England."

might be said, with great propriety, to be present in that assembly either in his own person or by representation.

Political liberty, based upon a landholding system "the wisest and most perfect ever yet devised by the wit of man, as it stood before the eighth century," had flourished in this ancient, pre-feudal elysium. But then had come the conquest, and with it the imposition of feudal tyranny upon gothic liberty. "The spirit of the English nation, depressed and broken by the Norman conquest, for many years quietly gave way to the rage of despotism, and peaceably submitted to the most abject vassallage." Not only had the King himself been rapacious and cruel, eagerly snatching at the liberties of the ancient, Saxon constitution, but the barons, "domineering and turbulent . . . capricious and inconstant . . . sometimes abetted the King in his projects of tyranny, and at other times excited the people to insurrections and tumults. For these reasons the constitution was ever fluctuating from one extreme to another. Now despotism, now anarchy prevailed." Gradually, safeguards against such evils were built up — that great array of documents starting with Magna Carta that outlined the inner boundaries of English liberties — which remained effective until, in the seventeenth century, that "execrable race of the Stuarts" precipitated a "formidable, violent, and bloody" struggle between the people and the confederacy "of temporal and spiritual tyranny." In the end liberty, as all the world knew, had been re-established in England, for the Glorious Revolution had created "that happy establishment which Great Britain has since enjoyed." But it had been a close victory which would require the utmost vigilance to maintain.[26]

[26] Otis, *Rights of the British Colonies* (JHL 7), p. 31; Bland, *Inquiry* (JHL 17), pp. 7–8; Jefferson to Edmund Pendleton, August 13, 1776, *Papers of Thomas Jefferson* (Julian P. Boyd, ed., Princeton, 1950–), I, 492; Hicks, *Considerations* (JHL 18) p. 2; [James Wilson], *Considerations on the . . . Authority of the British Parliament* (Philadelphia, 1774: JHL Pamphlet 44), p. 12; Adams, *Dissertation*, in *Works*, III, 451; Otis, *Rights of the British Colonies* (JHL 7),

ORIGINS OF THE AMERICAN REVOLUTION

It had been at this critical juncture in the history of England and of liberty, when Englishmen had been forced to struggle with tyranny as they had not since the conquest, that America had been settled. The conjunction had not been accidental. "It

---

p. 70. The pamphlets contain a good deal of discussion of English history, for much of the intellectual coherence of the colonists' political arguments rested on their views of the past. The ancient, presumably Saxon, origins of the English constitution was of particular importance to them, though, as John Adams pointed out, the Saxon constitution was "involved in much obscurity . . . the monarchical and democratic factions in England, by their opposite endeavors to make the Saxon constitutions swear for their respective systems, have much increased the difficulty of determining . . . what that constitution, in many important particulars, was" (*Works*, III, 543). Most agreed with Charles Carroll that "the liberties which the English enjoyed under their Saxon kings were wrested from them by the Norman conqueror," but differed with him on the idea (which seems to have been Rapin's view also) that only at the close of the reign of Henry III could there be found "the first faint traces of the House of Commons" (Elihu S. Riley, ed., *Correspondence of "First Citizen" — Charles Carroll of Carrollton, . . . and "Antilon" — Daniel Dulany, Jr. . . .* , Baltimore, 1902, p. 212). Maurice Moore admitted that "whether the Commons of England made up a part of the Saxon Witan Moot hath been a subject of great dispute," but cited Spelman and Madox to the effect that the Commons in the ancient constitution, while not apparently meeting regularly, was summoned when taxation was to be discussed, a practice abolished at the conquest and only slowly thereafter recovered (*The Justice and Policy of Taxing the American Colonies* . . . [Wilmington, N. C., 1765: JHL Pamphlet 16], pp. 3–4). Richard Bland cited Petyt, Brady, Rapin, and particularly Tacitus to establish the ancient, Saxon antecedents of the actual representation of all freeholders in Parliament, but, concentrating on the lack of such a franchise in eighteenth-century England ("the putrid part of the constitution"), ignored the conquest altogether (*Inquiry* [JHL 17], pp. 7–10). William Hicks too passed silently over the "Saxon" era and wrote vaguely of the establishment of constitutional liberty in post-conquest struggles (*Considerations* [JHL 18], pp. 2–4; *Nature and Extent of Parliamentary Power* [JHL 24], p. 3). But the view most characteristic of the Revolutionary pamphleteers is that summarized in the text paragraph above, which postulated an ideal constitution based on an elected assembly in Saxon England, destroyed by the conquest, regained with modifications in the course of centuries of struggle that culminated in the Glorious Revolution, and that was once again challenged by the corruption of eighteenth-century politics. In accepting this view the colonists sought not to undermine Parliamentary authority as such but to establish its true character in its ancient origins in such a way as to emphasize the corruptions of the Parliament of George III. Cf. Colbourn, *Lamp of Experience*, esp. chap. ii, and the same author's articles on Dickinson and Jefferson, in *Pa. Mag.*, 83 (1959), 280–292, and *W.M.Q.*, 3d ser., 15 (1958), 56–70. For

was this great struggle that peopled America . . . a love of universal liberty, and a hatred, a dread, a horror, of the infernal confederacy [of temporal and spiritual tyranny] projected, conducted, and accomplished the settlement of America." Just as their Saxon ancestors had left "their native wilds and woods in the north of Europe," the settlers of America had emigrated to create in a new land civil and ecclesiastical governments purer, freer than those they had left behind. The transplantation had been made from an undefiled branch of the nation, strong, healthy, brimming with the juices of liberty, and it had been placed in a soil perfect for its growth. In the colonies, "sought and settled as an asylum for liberty, civil and religious," virtue continued to be fortified by the simplicity of life and the lack of enervating luxury.[27]

This was not merely a parochial view. Though the idea that America was a purer and freer England came largely from local, nonconformist readings of history, it was reinforced by powerful elements within Enlightenment thought. European illuminati continued to identify America, as John Locke had done, with

Rapin's account of the ancient origins of the English constitution, linking pre-conquest institutions to eighteenth-century politics, see his *Dissertation on the . . . Whigs and Tories* [1717] (Boston, 1773), pp. 6–16; for his elaborate and inconclusive discussion of the pre-conquest origins of Parliament, see his *Dissertation on the Government, Laws . . . of the Anglo-Saxons, Particularly, the Origin, Nature, and Privileges of Their Wittena-Gemot, or Parliament . . .*, published in volume II (London, 1728) of his *History of England*, pp. [135]–210. On the historiographical background of these views, see J. G. A. Pocock, *The Ancient Constitution and the Feudal Law* (Cambridge, England, 1951), esp. chap. ii; Christopher Hill, "The Norman Yoke," *Puritanism and Revolution* (London, 1958), chap. iii; David C. Douglas, *English Scholars, 1660–1730* (London, 1951), esp. chap. vi; and Samuel Kliger, *The Goths in England* (Cambridge, 1952), chap. ii, esp. pp. 146 ff.

[27] Adams, *Dissertation*, in *Works*, III, 451; Jefferson, *Summary View* (JHL 43), p. 6; Amos Adams, *A Concise Historical View of the . . . Planting . . .* (Boston, 1769), p. 51. See also Judah Champion, *A Brief View of the Distresses . . . Our Ancestors Encountered in Settling New-England . . .* (Hartford, 1770), pp. 10 ff.; and, for an even more local application of the same point of view, James Dana, *A Century Discourse . . .* (New Haven, [1770]), pp. 18 ff.

something approximating a benign state of nature and to think of the colonies as special preserves of virtue and liberty. They could not help but note the refreshing simplicity of life and the wholesome consequences of the spread of freehold tenure. Nor could they deny the argument of Trenchard that the colonies demonstrated the military effectiveness of militia armies whose members were themselves the beneficiaries of the constitution and hence not likely to wish to destroy it.[28] No less a figure than Voltaire stated that America was the refinement of all that was good in England, writing in his *Lettres philosophiques* that Penn and the Quakers had actually brought into existence "that golden age of which men talk so much and which probably has never existed anywhere except in Pennsylvania." At lower levels of sophistication too — in the propaganda turned out by promoters of emigration — the idea was broadcast that inhabitants of the colonies enjoyed a unique simplicity and rectitude in their social life and a special freedom in their politics.

Not all, of course, agreed. A contrary picture of the colonists as provincial rustics steadily degenerating in a barbarous environment distant from civilizing influences persisted.[29] But on the eve of the Revolutionary controversy Americans, if not all Europeans and if not the crown officials who legally ruled them, could see themselves as peculiarly descended, and chosen for a special destiny. English successes in the Seven Years' War made this seem particularly realistic, for it seemed reasonable, after the conquest of Canada, to envision, as Jonathan Mayhew did in 1759, "a mighty empire" in America "(I do not mean an independent one) in numbers little inferior perhaps to the greatest in Europe, and in felicity to none." There would be "a great and flourishing kingdom in these parts of America," with cities "rising

[28] *An Argument*, pp. 21–22 (in *The Pamphleteer*, X, 132–133).
[29] Durand Echeverria, *Mirage in the West* (Princeton, 1957), chap. i; Koebner, *Empire*, pp. 93–96.

84

on every hill . . . happy fields and villages . . . [and] religion professed and practiced throughout this spacious kingdom in far greater purity and perfection than since the times of the apostles." [30]

It was at least possible. What would in fact happen in England and America would be the result, the colonists knew, of the degree of vigilance and the strength of purpose the people could exert. For they believed with Trenchard, with Bolingbroke, Hume, and Machiavelli — with the basic presupposition of eighteenth-century history and political theory — that "what happened yesterday will come to pass again, and the same causes will produce like effects in all ages," the laws of nature, as James Otis explained, being "uniform and invariable." [31] The preservation of liberty would continue to be what it had been in the past, a bitter struggle with adversity; and if at the moment the prospects for success in that struggle seemed excellent in the colonies, they appeared to be considerably less than that in the home country. By 1763, before any of the major problems of Anglo-

[30] *Two Discourses Delivered October 25, 1759 . . .* (Boston, 1759), pp. 60, 61.

[31] *An Argument*, p. 5 (in *The Pamphleteer*, X, 115); Otis, *Vindication* (JHL 11), p. [3]. This fundamental presumption was repeatedly expressed in the political writings of eighteenth-century America. See, e.g., Zenger's *New York Weekly Journal*, December 24, 1733 (". . . as causes and effects are things correlative, and the same causes ever had and ever will have the same effects"); *O Liberty, Thou Goddess Heavenly Bright . . .* ([New York, 1732] Evans 3595), p. [1] ("men in the same circumstances will do the same things, call them by what names of distinction you please"); the Carrolls' remarks to the same effect quoted pp. 91–92 below; William Hooper to James Iredell, April 26, 1774, in W. L. Saunders, ed., *Colonial Records of North Carolina* (Raleigh, N. C., 1886–1890), V, 985 ("From the fate of Rome, Britain may trace the cause of its present degeneracy and its impending destruction. Similar causes will ever produce similar effects."); and [James Chalmers], *Additions to Plain Truth . . .* (Philadelphia, 1776), p. 128. For an explanation of this belief, see Daniel J. Boorstin, *The Mysterious Science of the Law* (Cambridge, 1941), chap. ii, esp. pp. 32–33; on the relation of this notion to the idea of progress, see Wallace K. Ferguson, *The Renaissance in Historical Thought* (Cambridge, 1948), chap. iv, esp. pp. 79–86, and Stow Persons, "The Cyclical Theory of History in Eighteenth-Century America," *American Quarterly*, 6 (1954), 147–163.

American relations had appeared, the belief was widespread in America that while liberty had been better preserved in England than elsewhere in the Old World, the immediate circumstances in the home country were far from conducive to the continued maintenance of liberty — that it was not unreasonable to believe, in fact, that a new crisis of liberty might be approaching. Writings popular in the colonies insisted that the environment of eighteenth-century England was, to a dangerous degree, hostile to liberty: that Jacobite remnants flourished, that effeminizing luxury and slothful negligence continued to soften the moral fiber of the nation, and that politics festered in corruption. Specifically, the colonists were told again and again that the prime requisite of constitutional liberty, an independent Parliament free from the influence of the crown's prerogative, was being undermined by the successful efforts of the administration to manipulate Parliamentary elections to its advantage and to impose its will on members in Parliament.

How widespread the fear was in America that corruption was ripening in the home country, sapping the foundations of that most famous citadel of liberty, may be seen not only in the general popularity of periodicals like *The Craftsman* and *Cato's Letters,* which repeatedly excoriated the degeneracy of the age and the viciousness of ministerial corruption, but in the deliberateness with which some of the most vituperative of the English jeremiads were selected for republication in the colonies. There is no more sustained and intense attack on the corruption of Augustan England than James Burgh's *Britain's Remembrancer: or, The Danger Not Over* . . . (London, 1746), which had been touched off by the shock of the 'Forty-five. Its perfervid denunciation of "our degenerate times and corrupt nation" — a people wallowing in "luxury and irreligion . . . venality, perjury, faction, opposition to legal authority, idleness, gluttony, drunken-

ness, lewdness, excessive gaming, robberies, clandestine mar-
riages, breach of matrimonial vows, self-murders . . . a legion
of furies sufficient to rend any state or empire that ever was in
the world to pieces" — this blasting denunciation could scarcely
have been improved upon by the most sulphurous of Puritan
patriarchs. The pamphlet was reprinted by Franklin the year
after its initial appearance; reprinted again the following year
by another printer in Philadelphia; and reprinted still again in
Boston in 1759. So too the lengthy lament, *An Estimate of the
Manners and Principles of the Times,* written by the fashionable
belletrist and Church of England preacher, Dr. John Brown,
despairing of the prospects of liberty in England ("We are roll-
ing to the brink of a precipice that must destroy us"), decrying
the *"vain, luxurious,* and *selfish* EFFEMINACY" of the British
people, and attributing the "weaken[ing of] the *foundations* of
our *constitution*" to the deliberate corruption of the Commons
by Robert Walpole, was reprinted in Boston in 1758, a year after
its first publication.[32]

Such charges were not allowed to dissipate. They were repeatedly reinforced by the testimony of direct experience. Letters
from England expressed in personal terms what print imperson-
ally conveyed — letters not only from such doctrinaire libertarians
as Thomas Hollis but also from such undogmatic conservatives
as the printer William Strahan, who wondered, he wrote David
Hall in Philadelphia in 1763, whether England had "virtue

[32] Burgh, *Britain's Remembrancer,* p. 6; *An Estimate* (Boston ed.), pp. 11, 19,
60. The phrases quoted from *An Estimate* are among the many that are under-
scored in Thomas Hollis' copy of the book, now in the Houghton Library,
Harvard University (see pp. 15, 29, 115). At the word "weaken" in the
passage concerning Walpole, Hollis inked in the words "read: ruined." Brown's
Estimate was being quoted in Boston even before it was reprinted there: a writer
in the *Boston Gazette and Country Journal,* January 2, 1758, identified the
author of *The Spirit of the Laws* to his readers as a writer "whom Dr. Brown,
in his late celebrated *Estimates,*" approved of!

enough to be saved from that deluge of corruption with which we have been so long overwhelmed." [33] The same question had long since occurred to Americans visiting England for business, pleasure, or education. Lewis Morris, in London in 1735-36 to recover the political losses he had sustained in New York at the hands of Governor Cosby, returned home with so intense a disgust at the scenes he had beheld that he took to poetry to relieve his feelings. His 700-line poem, "The Dream and Riddle" echoed the many despairing pamphlets, poems, and squibs published in London in the 1720's and early 1730's in ridiculing the justice of the English government ("Complaints if just are very shocking things; / And not encouraged in the courts of Kings"); the venality of the court (". . . our noble Prince's ear / Is open to complaints, and he will hear; / The difficulty's how to get them there"); the mores of shopkeepers ("The gaudy shops of this tumultuous hive / By several arts of cheating only thrive"); and the corruption of Parliament ("Both senates and their chosers vote for pay / And both alike their liberty betray"). He ended with what would become a characteristic American response: "If bound unto that land of liberty / I just described, then know it is not nigh [i.e., in England], / But lies far distant from this place somewhere / Not in this, but some other hemisphere." [34]

But Morris had been a casual visitor, and, as he discovered to his dismay, he was ignorant of the intricacies of backroom politics in England. Benjamin Franklin knew England and its

---

[33] William Strahan to David Hall, London, February 21, 1763, *Pa. Mag.*, 10 (1886), 89. So also the bookseller, pamphleteer, and printer John Almon, who was to be responsible for so much of the most effective pro-American publicity in England in the 1760's and 1770's and who was continuously in touch with American writers, observed in 1765 that "in no age except that which produced the destruction of the Roman liberty were venality and corruption so prevalent as at this time in Britain." Quoted in Ian Christie, *Wilkes, Wyvil and Reform* (London, 1962), p. 38.

[34] "The Dream and Riddle. A Poem." MS in papers relating to Lewis Morris, Robert Morris Papers, Rutgers University Library.

politics better, and loved that country and its people. Yet he wrote to Peter Collinson in 1753: "I pray God long to preserve to Great Britain the English laws, manners, liberties, and religion notwithstanding the complaints so frequent in your public papers of the prevailing corruption and degeneracy of your people. I know you have a great deal of virtue still subsisting among you, and I hope the constitution is not so near a dissolution as some seem to apprehend. I do not think you are generally become such slaves to your vices as to draw down that *justice* Milton speaks of" in *Paradise Lost*. The tide, he comfortingly added, "is never so low but it may rise again." Yet it might not; and should the worst happen,

should this dreaded fatal change happen in my time, how should I, even in the midst of the affliction, rejoice if we [in America] have been able to preserve those invaluable treasures, and can invite the good among you to come and partake of them! O let not Britain seek to oppress us, but like an affectionate parent endeavor to secure freedom to her children; they may be able one day to assist her in defending her own.[35]

So too John Dickinson, in England in the election year 1754 as a student of law, was enthralled by the sophistication and variety of life in London, and "filled with awe and reverence" by his contact with scenes of ancient greatness and by the opportunity to hear "some of the greatest men in England, perhaps in the world." But he was shocked, too, beyond all expectation, by

[35] Franklin to Collinson, Philadelphia, May 9, 1753, *The Papers of Benjamin Franklin* (Leonard W. Labaree, *et al.*, eds., New Haven, 1959–), IV, 485–486. Among the many English writers Franklin read who confirmed his troubled views of England's prospects was his old friend James Ralph, whose *Of the Use and Abuse of Parliaments* . . . (2 vols., London, 1744) argued "that the constitution is everywhere undermined; at the first sound of the trumpet . . . it will sink at once into a heap of ruins . . . So great is the influence of the crown become, so servile the spirit of our grandees, and so depraved the hearts of the people, that hope itself begins to sicken." Colbourn, *Lamp of Experience*, p. 128.

Hogarthian election scenes and by the callous disregard of freedom exhibited in Parliament. Over £1,000,000, he wrote his father, had been expended in efforts to manipulate the general election. The starting price for the purchase of votes in one northern borough, he reported, was 200 guineas.

It is astonishing to think what impudence and villainy are practiced on this occasion. If a man cannot be brought to vote as he is desired, he is made dead drunk and kept in that state, never heard of by his family or friends till all is over and he can do no harm. The oath of their not being bribed is as strict and solemn as language can form it, but is so little regarded that few people can refrain from laughing while they take it. I think the character of Rome will equally suit this nation: "Easy to be bought, if there was but a purchaser."

The fact that over seventy elections were disputed, he continued a few months later, is "one of the greatest proofs perhaps of the corruption of the age that can be mentioned."

Bribery is so common that it is thought there is not a borough in England where it is not practiced, and it is certain that many very flourishing ones are ruined, their manufactories decayed, and their trade gone by their dependence on what they get by their votes. We hear every day in Westminster Hall leave moved to file informations for bribery, but it is ridiculous and absurd to pretend to curb the effects of luxury and corruption in one instance or in one spot without a general reformation of manners, which everyone sees is absolutely necessary for the welfare of this kingdom. Yet Heaven knows how it can be effected. It is grown a vice here to be virtuous . . . People are grown too polite to have an old-fashioned religion, and are too weak to find out a new, from whence follows the most unbounded licentiousness and utter disregard of virtue, which is the unfailing cause of the destruction of all empires.

And in the House of Lords he heard speeches that could only be interpreted as acquiescence in the creation of a standing army. "But such is the complacency these great men have for the smiles of their prince that they will gratify every desire of ambition and power at the expense of truth, reason, and their country." [36]

So too Charles Carroll of Carrollton wrote from London in 1760 after twelve years of study and travel abroad that "a change in our constitution is I think near at hand. Our dear-bought liberty stands upon the brink of destruction." His father, who had also been educated abroad, agreed: "Things seem to be tending hastily to anarchy in England;" he wrote his son in 1763, "corruption and freedom cannot long subsist together . . . for my part I think an absolute government preferable to one that is only apparently free; and this must be the case of your present constitution, if it be true that whoever presides in the treasury can command in Parliament." At home in Maryland two years later it seemed more evident than ever to the younger Carroll that the English constitution was "hastening to its final period of dissolution, and the symptoms of a general decay are but too visible." Sell your estate in England, he advised an English friend, and

purchase lands in this province where liberty will maintain her empire till a dissoluteness of morals, luxury, and venality shall have prepared the degenerate sons of some future age to prefer their own mean lucre, the bribes, and the smiles of corruption and arbitrary ministers to patriotism, to glory, and to the public weal. No doubt the same causes will produce the same effects, and a period is already set to the reign of American freedom; but that fatal time seems to be at a great distance. The present generation at least, and I hope many succeeding ones, in spite of a corrupt Parliament, will enjoy the blessings and the sweets of liberty.

Later, Carroll's father, further informed of the realities of European life not only by his well-traveled son but by "daily papers,

[36] H. Trevor Colbourn, ed., "A Pennsylvania Farmer at the Court of King George: John Dickinson's London Letters, 1754–1756," *Pa. Mag.*, 86 (1962), 257, 268, 421, 445.

periodical and occasional pamphlets" as well, enlarged upon the theme in letters to his English friends:

> What must be the end of this shameless, long-continued want of honor, public spirit, and patriotism? Will not your profligacy, corruption, and versatility sink you into anarchy and destruction? All states laboring under the same vices have met with the fate which will be your lot. That fate is impending; it cannot be far off. The same causes will ever produce similar effects . . . are you not a people devoted to and on the brink of destruction? I began to be acquainted with the world in the year 1720, memorable by the ruin of not only the unthinking adventurers in the South Sea stock but of numberless widows, helpless minors, and innocent infants . . . Soon after Sir Robert Walpole was made premier he reduced corruption into a regular system which since his time to the present period has been improved and founded on so broad and solid a basis as to threaten the constitution with immediate ruin and already to have left to the people little more than the appearance of liberty.[37]

In the context of such beliefs the question inevitably arose "whether we are obliged to yield," as Jonathan Mayhew put it in his famous *Discourse* of 1750, "an absolute submission to our prince, or whether disobedience and resistance may not be justifiable in some cases." The answer was clear. Submission is not required "to all who bear the *title* of rulers in common, but only to those who *actually* perform the duty of rulers, by exercising a reasonable and just authority for the good of human society." When government fails to serve its proper ends then "a regard to the public welfare ought to make us withhold from our rulers that obedience and subjection which it would, otherwise, be our

---

[37] Charles Carroll of Carrollton to Charles Carroll, Sr., London, January 29, 1760, *Maryland Historical Magazine,* 10 (1915), 251; Charles Carroll, Sr., to Charles Carroll of Carrollton, September 3, 1763, Thomas M. Field, ed., *Unpublished Letters of Charles Carroll of Carrollton* . . . (New York, 1902), p. 78; Charles Carroll of Carrollton to Mr. Bradshaw, November 21, 1765, *ibid.,* p. 97; Charles Carroll, Sr., to William Graves, December 23, 1768, *Maryland Historical Magazine,* 12 (1917), 185. See also, William L. Sachse, *The Colonial American in Britain* (Madison, 1956), pp. 204–207.

duty to render to them." In such situations one is "bound to throw off [his] allegiance"; not to do so would be tacitly to conspire "in promoting slavery and misery."

For a nation thus abused to arise unanimously and to resist their prince, even to the dethroning him, is not criminal, but a reasonable way of vindicating their liberties and just rights; it is making use of the means, and the only means, which God has put into their power, for mutual and self-defense. And it would be highly criminal in them not to make use of this means. It would be stupid tameness and unaccountable folly for whole nations to suffer *one* unreasonable, ambitious, and cruel man to wanton and riot in their misery. And in such a case it would, of the two, be more rational to suppose that they that did NOT resist [rather] than that they who did, would *receive to themselves damnation.*

When tyranny is abroad, "submission," Andrew Eliot wrote quite simply in 1765, "is a crime." [38]

[38] *A Discourse Concerning Unlimited Submission* (Boston, 1750: JHL Pamphlet 1), pp. 13, 20, 29, 30, 40; Eliot, *Sermon* (JHL 13), pp. 47–48.

Chapter IV

THE LOGIC OF REBELLION

Lord Chancellor *Camden* . . . declared . . . that for some time he had beheld with silent indignation the arbitrary measures which were pursuing by the ministry; . . . that, however, he would do so no longer, but would openly and boldly speak his sentiments . . . In a word, he accused the ministry . . . of having formed a conspiracy against the liberties of their country.

— Report of Speech in the House of Lords, 1770

A series of occurrences, many recent events, . . . afford great reason to believe that a deep-laid and desperate plan of imperial despotism has been laid, and partly executed, for the extinction of all civil liberty . . . The august and once revered fortress of English freedom — the admirable work of ages — the BRITISH CONSTITUTION seems fast tottering into fatal and inevitable ruin. The dreadful catastrophe threatens universal havoc, and presents an awful warning to hazard all if, peradventure, we in these distant confines of the earth may prevent being totally overwhelmed and buried under the ruins of our most established rights.

— Boston Town Meeting to its Assembly Representatives, 1770

IT IS the meaning imparted to the events after 1763 by this integrated group of attitudes and ideas that lies behind the colonists' rebellion. In the context of these ideas, the controversial issues centering on the question of Parliament's jurisdiction in America acquired as a group new and overwhelming significance. The colonists believed they saw emerging from the welter of events during the decade after the Stamp Act a pattern whose meaning was unmistakable. They saw in the·measures taken by the British government and in the

94

actions of officials in the colonies something for which their peculiar inheritance of thought had prepared them only too well, something they had long conceived to be a possibility in view of the known tendencies of history and of the present state of affairs in England. They saw about them, with increasing clarity, not merely mistaken, or even evil, policies violating the principles upon which freedom rested, but what appeared to be evidence of nothing less than a deliberate assault launched surreptitiously by plotters against liberty both in England and in America. The danger to America, it was believed, was in fact only the small, immediately visible part of the greater whole whose ultimate manifestation would be the destruction of the English constitution, with all the rights and privileges embedded in it.

This belief transformed the meaning of the colonists' struggle, and it added an inner accelerator to the movement of opposition. For, once assumed, it could not be easily dispelled: denial only confirmed it, since what conspirators profess is not what they believe; the ostensible is not the real; and the real is deliberately malign.

It was this — the overwhelming evidence, as they saw it, that they were faced with conspirators against liberty determined at all costs to gain ends which their words dissembled — that was signaled to the colonists after 1763, and it was this above all else that in the end propelled them into Revolution.

Suspicion that the ever-present, latent danger of an active conspiracy of power against liberty was becoming manifest within the British Empire, assuming specific form and developing in coordinated phases, rose in the consciousness of a large segment of the American population before any of the famous political events of the struggle with England took place. No adherent of a nonconformist church or sect in the eighteenth century was free from suspicion that the Church of England, an arm of the English state, was working to bring all subjects of the crown into the community of the Church; and since toleration was official and nonconformist influence in English politics formidable, it was doing so by stealth, disguising its efforts, turning to improper uses devices that had been created for benign purposes. In particular, the Society for the Propagation of the Gospel in Foreign Parts, an arm of the Church created in 1701 to aid in bringing the Gospel to the pagan Indians, was said by 1763 to have "long had a formal design to root out Presbyterianism, etc., and to establishing both episcopacy and bishops." [1]

This suspicion, which had smoldered in the breasts of New Englanders and nonconformists throughout the colonies for half a century or more, had burst into flame repeatedly, but never so violently as in 1763, in the Mayhew-Apthorp controversy which climaxed years of growing anxiety that plans were being made secretly to establish an American episcopate. To Mayhew, as to Presbyterian and Congregational leaders throughout the colonies, there could be little doubt that the threat was real. Many of the facts were known, facts concerning maneuvers in London and in America. Anglican leaders in New York and New Jersey had met almost publicly to petition England for an American episcopate, and there could be little doubt also of the role of the Society for the Propagation of the Gospel in this undercover operation. For if the ostensible goal of the Society was the gospelizing of the pagan Indians and Negroes, its true goal was manifestly revealed when it established missions in places like Cambridge, Massachusetts, which had not had a resident Indian since the seventeenth century and was well equipped with "orthodox" preachers. Such missions, Mayhew wrote, have "all the appearance of entering wedges . . . carrying on the crusade, or spiritual

[1] Jonathan Mayhew, *Observations on the Charter and Conduct of the Society for the Propagation of the Gospel in Foreign Parts* . . . (Boston, 1763), pp. 103–108.

siege of our churches, with the hope that they will one day submit to an episcopal sovereign." Bishops, he wrote unblinkingly in reply to the Archbishop of Canterbury, have commonly been instruments in arbitrary reigns of "establishing a tyranny over the bodies and souls of men," and their establishment in America would mark the end of liberty in Massachusetts and elsewhere. By 1765, when the final exchanges in this pamphlet war were published, it was commonly understood in New England and elsewhere that "the stamping and episcopizing [of] our colonies were . . . *only different branches of the same plan of power.*"[2]

Fear of an ecclesiastical conspiracy against American liberties, latent among nonconformists through all of colonial history, thus erupted into public controversy at the very same time that the first impact of new British policies in civil affairs was being felt. And though it was, in an obvious sense, a limited fear (for large parts of the population identified themselves with the Anglican Church and were not easily convinced that liberty was being threatened by a plot of Churchmen) it nevertheless had a profound indirect effect everywhere, for it drew into public discussion — evoked in specific form — the general conviction of eighteenth-century Englishmen that the conjoining of "temporal and spiritual tyranny" was, in John Adams' words, an event totally "calamitous to human liberty" yet an event that in the mere nature of things perpetually threatened. For, as David Hume had explained, "in all ages of the world priests have been enemies to liberty . . . Liberty of thinking and of expressing our thoughts is always fatal to priestly power . . . and, by an infallible connection which prevails among all kinds of liberty, this

[2] Mayhew, *Observations,* p. 57; Jonathan Mayhew, *Remarks on an Anonymous Tract . . . Being a Second Defence . . .* (Boston, 1764), p. 12; Alden Bradford, *Memoir of the Life and Writings of Rev. Jonathan Mayhew . . .* (Boston, 1838), p. 372. For a full account of "the Anglican Plot," see Carl Bridenbaugh, *Mitre and Sceptre* (New York, 1962), chaps. vii–ix. See also Introduction to [John Aplin], *Verses on Doctor Mayhew's Book of Observations* (Providence, 1763: JHL Pamphlet 3), in Bailyn, *Pamphlets,* I, and pp. 254–257 below.

privilege can never be enjoyed . . . but in a free government. Hence . . . all princes that have aimed at despotic power have known of what importance it was to gain the established clergy; as the clergy, on their part, have shown a great facility in entering into the views of such princes." Fear of the imposition of an Anglican episcopate thus brought into focus a cluster of ideas, attitudes, and responses alive with century-old Popish-Stuart-Jacobite associations that would enter directly into the Revolutionary controversy in such writings as John Adams' *Dissertation on the Canon and Feudal Law* (1765) and Samuel Adams' "A Puritan" pieces published in the *Boston Gazette* in 1768. And more than that, it stimulated among highly articulate leaders of public opinion, who would soon be called upon to interpret the tendency of civil affairs, a general sense that they lived in a conspiratorial world in which what the highest officials professed was not what they in fact intended, and that their words masked a malevolent design.[3]

---

[3] Adams, *Dissertation*, in *Works*, III, 450, 451; Hume, "Of the Parties of Great Britain," in Charles W. Hendel, ed., *David Hume's Political Essays* (New York, 1953), pp. 86, 87; Henry A. Cushing, ed., *The Writings of Samuel Adams* (New York, 1904–1908), I, 201–212. Fear of the conjunction of civil and ecclesiastical tyrannies was central to John Adams' understanding of American history as well as of the Revolutionary crisis. It had been, he wrote, "a hatred, a dread, a horror, of the infernal confederacy before described that projected, conducted, and accomplished the settlement of America," and it was this same confederacy that confronted Americans in 1765: "There seems to be a direct and formal design on foot to enslave all America. This, however, must be done by degrees. The first step that is intended seems to be an entire subversion of the whole system of our fathers by the introduction of the canon and feudal law into America (*Works*, III, 464). "Popery," the conjunction of the Church of Rome with aggressive civil authority, was felt to be the greatest threat, the classic threat; but "popery" was only a special case, though the superlative one, of the more general phenomenon: "it has been a general mistake," Molesworth had pointed out, to think "that the popish religion is the only one of all the Christian sects proper to introduce and establish slavery in a nation insomuch that popery and slavery have been thought inseparable . . . Other religions, and particularly the *Lutheran,* has [sic] succeeded as effectually in this design as ever popery did . . . It is not popery as such but the doctrine of a blind obedience, in what religion soever it be found, that is the destruction of the

THE LOGIC OF REBELLION

Reinforcement for this belief came quickly. Even for those who had in no way been concerned with the threat of an episcopal establishment, the passage of the Stamp Act was not merely an impolitic and unjust law that threatened the priceless right of the individual to retain possession of his property until he or his chosen representative voluntarily gave it up to another; it was to many, also, a danger signal indicating that a more general threat existed. For though it could be argued, and in a sense proved by the swift repeal of the act, that nothing more was involved than ignorance or confusion on the part of people in power who really knew better and who, once warned by the reaction of the colonists, would not repeat the mistake — though this could be, and by many was, concluded, there nevertheless appeared to be good reason to suspect that more was involved. For from whom had the false information and evil advice come that had so misled the English government? From officials in the colonies, said John Adams, said Oxenbridge Thacher, James Otis, and Stephen Hopkins — from officials bent on overthrowing the constituted forms of government in order to satisfy their own lust for power, and not likely to relent in their passion. Some of these local plotters were easily identified. To John Adams, Josiah Quincy, and others the key figure in Massachusetts from the beginning to the end was Thomas Hutchinson who by "serpentine wiles" was befuddling and victimizing the weak, the avaricious, and the in-

liberty and consequently of all the happiness of any nation." *An Account of Denmark* . . . (London, 1694), pp. 258–259. Fear of the association of priesthood and magistracy in arbitrary rule runs through Eliot's and Mayhew's correspondences with Thomas Hollis; Mayhew contributed to the fear not only indirectly in his attacks on the Society for the Propagation of the Gospel but directly in his Dudleian lecture, *Popish Idolatry* . . . (Boston, 1765). On the persistence of the fear of episcopacy and its spillover into secular problems, see, for example, Eliot to Hollis, January 26, 1771, MHS *Colls.*, 4th ser., IV, 255: "The design will never be abandoned — we fear a *coup de main*"; and, in general, Bridenbaugh, *Mitre and Sceptre*, chap. ix: "Bishops and Stamps, 1764–1766." For John Adams' final summary of the Mayhew-Apthorp affair, see below, pp. 256–257.

cautious in order to increase his notorious engrossment of public office. In Rhode Island it was, to James Otis, that "little, dirty, drinking, drabbing, contaminated knot of thieves, beggars, and transports . . . made up of Turks, Jews, and other infidels, with a few renegado Christians and Catholics" — the Newport junto, led by Martin Howard, Jr., which had already been accused by Stephen Hopkins and others in Providence of "conspiring against the liberties of the colony." [4]

But even if local leaders associated with power elements in England had not been so suspect, there were grounds for seeing more behind the Stamp Act than its ostensible purpose. The official aim of the act was, of course, to bring in revenue to the English treasury. But the sums involved were in fact quite small, and "some persons . . . may be inclined to acquiesce under it." But that would be to fall directly into the trap, for the smaller the taxes, John Dickinson wrote in the most influential pamphlet

[4] For a succinct explanation of the manifest threat of the Stamp Act, see Stephen Hopkins, *The Rights of Colonies Examined* (Providence, 1765: JHL Pamphlet 9), pp. 16–17. Adams' almost paranoiac suspicions of Hutchinson's hidden motives run through his *Diary and Autobiography; e.g.,* I, 306; II, 39; III, 430. See also his "Novanglus" papers, in *Works,* IV, esp. pp. 62–63, 67–71, 87; and references in his correspondence: *Works,* X, 285–286, 298. It is the generality of such suspicions that accounts for the furor caused by the publication in 1773 of Hutchinson's innocuous letters of 1768 — letters in which, the publishers wrote in the pamphlet's title, *"the Judicious Reader Will Discover the Fatal Source of the Confusion and Bloodshed"* (JHL Pamphlet 40). Josiah Quincy thought he saw the final proof of Hutchinson's conspiratorial efforts in his maneuverings with the North administration in London in 1774 and 1775: "Journal of Josiah Quincy Jun. . . . in England . . . ," MHS *Procs.,* 50 (1916–17), 444, 446, 447, 450, 452. Thacher's suspicions of Hutchinson (whom he called "Summa Potestatis," or "Summa" for short) are traced in the Introduction to his *Sentiments of a British American* (Boston, 1764: JHL Pamphlet 8), in Bailyn, *Pamphlets,* I. Otis' phrase is quoted from his abusive pamphlet, *Brief Remarks on the Defence of the Halifax Libel . . .* (Boston, 1765), p. 5. The charge against Howard appeared in the *Providence Gazette,* September 15, 1764, and is part of the intense antipathy that built up in Providence against the royalist group in Newport. See, in general, Edmund S. Morgan and Helen M. Morgan, *The Stamp Act Crisis* (Chapel Hill, 1953), chap. iv; and Introduction to Howard's *Letter from a Gentleman at Halifax* (Newport, 1765: JHL Pamphlet 10).

published in America before 1776, the more dangerous they were, since they would the more easily be found acceptable by the incautious, with the result that a precedent would be established for making still greater inroads on liberty and property.

Nothing is wanted at home but a PRECEDENT, the force of which shall be established by the tacit submission of the colonies . . . If the Parliament succeeds in this attempt, other statutes will impose other duties . . . and thus the Parliament will levy upon us such sums of money as they choose to take, *without any other* LIMITATION *than their* PLEASURE.

Others saw more drastic hidden meanings and implications in the passage of the Stamp Act. "If the real and only motive of the minister was to raise money from the colonies," Joseph Warren wrote in 1766, "that method should undoubtedly have been adopted which was least grievous to the people." Choice of so blatantly obnoxious a measure as the Stamp Act, consequently, "has induced some to imagine that the minister designed by this act to force the colonies into a rebellion, and from thence to take occasion to treat them with severity, and, by military power, to reduce them to servitude." Such a supposition was perhaps excessive: "charity forbids us to conclude [the ministry] guilty of so black a villainy. But . . . it is known that tyrannical ministers have, at some time, embraced even this hellish measure to accomplish their cursed designs," and speculation based on "admitting this to have been his aim" seemed well worth pursuing. To John Adams it seemed "very manifest" that the ultimate design behind the Stamp Act was an effort to forge the fatal link between ecclesiastical and civil despotism, the first by stripping the colonists "in a great measure of the means of knowledge, by loading the press, the colleges, and even an almanac and a newspaper with restraints and duties," the second, by recreating the inequalities and dependencies of feudalism "by taking from the poorer sort of people all their little subsistence, and conferring it on a set of stamp officers, distributors, and their deputies." This last point was the most obvious: "as the influence of money and places generally procures to the minister a majority in Parliament," Arthur Lee wrote, so an income from unchecked taxation would lead to a total corruption of free government in America, with the result that the colonies would "experience the fate of the *Roman* people in the deplorable times of their slavery." [5]

But by then, in 1768, more explicit evidence of a wide-ranging plot was accumulating rapidly. Not only had the Townshend Duties, another revenue act, been passed by Parliament despite all the violence of the colonists' reaction to the Stamp Act, but it was a measure that enhanced the influence of the customs administration, which for other reasons had already come under suspicion. There had been, it was realized by the late 1760's, a sudden expansion in the number of "posts in the [colonial] 'government' . . . worth the attention of persons of influence in Great Britain" — posts, Franklin explained, like the governorships, filled by persons who were

generally strangers to the provinces they are sent to govern, have no estate, natural connection, or relation there to give them an affection for the country . . . they come only to make money as fast as they can; are sometimes men of vicious characters and broken fortunes, sent by a minister merely to get them out of the way.[6]

By the late 1760's, in the perspective of recent events, one could see that the invasion of customs officers "born with long claws

[5] *Letters from a Farmer in Pennsylvania* . . . (Philadelphia, 1768: JHL Pamphlet 23), p. 55; Warren to Edmund Dana, Boston, March 19, 1766, in Richard Frothingham, *Life and Times of Joseph Warren* (Boston, 1865), pp. 21–22; Adams, *Dissertation*, in *Works*, III, 464; [Arthur Lee], "Monitor VI," in *Virginia Gazette* (R), March 31, 1768. For an elaboration of Dickinson's argument on the special dangers of "imperceptible" taxes, see Mercy Otis Warren, *History of the . . . American Revolution* . . . (Boston, 1805), I, 45.

[6] Dickinson, *Farmer's Letters* (JHL 23), p. 54; Albert H. Smyth, ed., *Writings of Benjamin Franklin* (New York, 1905–1907), V, 83. Cf. Verner W. Crane, *Benjamin Franklin's Letters to the Press, 1758–1775* (Chapel Hill, 1950), pp. 106–107, 277.

like eagles," had begun as far back as the last years of the Seven
Years' War and was now being reinforced by the new tax measures. The wartime Orders in Council demanding stricter enforcement of the Navigation Laws; the Sugar Act of 1764, which had
multiplied the customs personnel; and the American Board of
Customs Commissioners created in 1767 with "power," Americans
said, "to constitute as many under officers as they please" — all
of these developments could be seen to have provided for an "almost incredible number of inferior officers," most of whom the
colonists believed to be "wretches . . . of such infamous characters that the merchants cannot possibly think their interest safe
under their care." More important by far, however, was their influence on government.

For there was an obvious political and constitutional danger in
having such "a set of *idle drones,*" such "lazy, proud, worthless
pensioners and *placemen,*" in one's midst. It was nothing less
than "a general maxim," James Wilson wrote,

that the crown will take advantage of every opportunity of extending
its prerogative in opposition to the privileges of the people, [and]
that it is the interest of those who have *pensions* or *offices at will*
from the crown to concur in all its measures.

These "baneful harpies" were instruments of power, of prerogative. They would upset the balance of the constitution by extending "*ministerial influence* as much beyond its former bounds as
the late war did the British dominions." Parasitic officeholders,
thoroughly corrupted by their obligations to those who had appointed them, would strive to "*distinguish themselves* by their
sordid zeal in defending and promoting measures which *they
know beyond all question* to be *destructive* to the *just rights* and
true interests of their country." Seeking to "*serve the ambitious
purposes of great men* at home," these "*base-spirited wretches*"
would urge — were already urging — as they logically had to, the
specious attractions of "SUBMISSIVE behavior." They were arguing

with a plausible affectation of *wisdom* and *concern* how *prudent* it is to please the *powerful* — how *dangerous* to provoke them — and then comes in the perpetual incantation that freezes up every generous purpose of the soul in cold, inactive expectation — "that if there is any request to be made, compliance will obtain a favorable attention."

In the end, this extension of executive patronage, based on a limitless support of government through colonial taxation, would make the whole of government "merely a ministerial engine"; by throwing off the balance of its parts, it would destroy the protective machinery of the constitution.[7]

[7] [Silas Downer], *A Discourse Delivered in Providence . . . at the Dedication of the Tree of Liberty* . . . (Providence, 1768: JHL Pamphlet 25), p. 10; Ebenezer Baldwin, . . . *An Appendix Stating the Heavy Grievances* . . . , published in Samuel Sherwood, *A Sermon Containing Scriptural Instructions to Civil Rulers* . . . (New Haven, [1774]: JHL Pamphlet 52), pp. 52–53; *Observations on Several Acts of Parliament . . . and Also on the Conduct of the Officers of the Customs* . . . ([Boston], 1769: JHL Pamphlet 27), p. 15; William Gordon, *Discourse Preached December 15th 1774* . . . (Boston, 1775), p. 11; [James Wilson], *Considerations on the . . . Authority of the British Parliament* (Philadelphia, 1774: JHL Pamphlet 44), pp. 6–7; Dickinson, *Farmer's Letters* (JHL 23), pp. 51n (citing at length the portentous example of the Irish establishment, honeycombed with "pensions . . . purloined out of the national treasure of Ireland under the MASK OF SALARIES ANNEXED TO PUBLIC OFFICES USELESS TO THE NATION, newly invented FOR THE PURPOSES OF CORRUPTION"), 55, 66; *The Votes and Proceedings of the Freeholders . . . of . . . Boston* . . . (Boston, [1772]: JHL Pamphlet 36), p. 21. See also, among the myriad expressions of resentment and fear of the extension of patronage offices in the colonies, [Henry Laurens], *Extracts from the Proceedings of the High Court of Vice-Admiralty in Charlestown . . . with . . . Observations on American Custom-House Officers* . . . (Charleston, 1769: JHL Pamphlet 26); Andrew Eliot's excoriation of the "pitiful sycophants, court parasites, and hungry dependents" whom the colonists' tax money would have to maintain "in luxury and extravagance" in letters to Hollis, MHS *Colls.*, 4th ser., IV, 420, 438; *A Ministerial Catechise, Suitable To Be Learned by All Modern Provincial Governors, Pensioners, Placemen, &c. Dedicated to T[homas] H[utchinson], Esq.* (Boston, 1771: JHL Pamphlet 34); *A [Sixteenth] Report of the Record Commissioners of the City of Boston* . . . (Boston, 1886), p. 258; and the citations in H. Trevor Colbourn, *The Lamp of Experience* (Chapel Hill, 1965), pp. 76, 141; and in Gipson, *British Empire*, XI, 199, 201, 221, 523, 551, 552, 558. For a pre-Revolutionary expression of these same fears, illustrating the process of transmission of early eighteenth-century ideas into the Revolutionary ideology, see "A Letter to the Freeholders . . . ," *Boston Gazette and Country Journal*, April 26, 1756.

THE LOGIC OF REBELLION

But even this did not exhaust the evidence that a design against liberty was unfolding. During the same years the independence of the judiciary, so crucial a part of the constitution, was suddenly seen to be under heavy attack, and by the mid-1760's to have succumbed in many places.[8]

This too was not a new problem. The status of the colonial judiciary had been a controversial question throughout the century. The Parliamentary statute of 1701 which guaranteed judges in England life tenure in their posts had been denied to the colonies, in part because properly trained lawyers were scarce in the colonies, especially in the early years, and appointments for life would prevent the replacement of ill-qualified judges by their betters, when they appeared; and in part because, judicial salaries being provided for by temporary legislative appropriations, the removal of all executive control from the judiciary, it was feared, would result in the hopeless subordination of the courts to popular influences. The status of the judiciary in the eighteenth century was therefore left open to political maneuvering in which, more often than not, the home government managed to carry its point and to make the tenure of judges as temporary as their salaries. Then suddenly, in the early 1760's, the whole issue exploded. In 1759 the Pennsylvania Assembly declared that the judges of that province would thereafter hold their offices by the same permanence of tenure that had been guaranteed English judges after the Glorious Revolution. But the law was disallowed forthwith by the crown. Opposition newspapers boiled with resentment; angry speeches were made in the Assembly; and a

[8] For further details on the problem of the judiciary — which had been discussed in terms indistinguishable from those of the Revolutionary era probably as early as 1701 (Louis B. Wright, ed., *An Essay upon the Government of the English Plantations* . . . , San Marino, 1945, p. 40), certainly as early as 1707 (Roy N. Lokken, *David Lloyd,* Seattle, 1959, pp. 173–175) — and for documentation of the paragraphs that follow, see the Introduction and notes to *A Letter to the People of Pennsylvania* (Philadelphia, 1760: JHL Pamphlet 2), in Bailyn, *Pamphlets,* I.

pamphlet appeared explaining in the fullest detail the bearing of judicial independence on constitutional freedom.

In New York the issue was even more inflamed and had wider repercussions. There, the judges of the Supreme Court, by a political maneuver of 1750, had managed to secure their appointments for life. But this tenure was interrupted by the death of George II in 1760 which required the reissuance of all crown commissions. An unpopular and politically weak lieutenant governor, determined to prevent his enemies from controlling the courts, refused to recommission the judges on life tenure. The result was a ferocious battle in which the opposition asserted New York's *undoubted right* of having the judges of our courts on a constitutional basis," and demanded the "liberties and privileges" of Englishmen in this connection as in all others. But they were defeated, though not by the governor. In December 1761 orders were sent out from the King in Council to all the colonies, permanently forbidding the issuance of judges' commissions anywhere on any tenure but that of "the pleasure of the crown." [9]

All the colonies were affected. In some, like New Jersey, where the governor's incautious violation of the new royal order led to his removal from office, or like North Carolina, where opposition forces refused to concede and managed to keep up the fight for permanent judicial tenure throughout the entire period from 1760 to 1776, the issue was directly joined. In others, as in Massachusetts, where specific Supreme Court appointments were vehemently opposed by anti-administration interests, the force of the policy was indirect. But everywhere there was bitterness at the decree and fear of its implications, for everywhere it was known that judicial tenure "at the will of the crown" was "dangerous to the liberty and property of the subject," and that if the bench

[9] Milton M. Klein, "Prelude to Revolution in New York: Jury Trials and Judicial Tenure," *W.M.Q.*, 3d ser., 17 (1960), 452.

were occupied by "men who depended upon the smiles of the crown for their daily bread," the possibility of having an independent judiciary as an effective check upon executive power would be wholly lost.[10]

This fear was magnified by the rumor, which was circulating vigorously as early as 1768, that it was part of the administration's policy to have the salaries of the colonial judges "appointed for them by the crown, independent of the people." If this ever happened, the Boston Town Meeting asserted when the rumor was becoming actuality, it would "complete our slavery." The reasoning was simple and straightforward:

if taxes are to be raised from us by the Parliament of Great Britain without our consent, and the men on whose opinions and decisions our properties, liberties, and lives in a great measure depend receive their support from the revenues arising from these taxes, we cannot, when we think of the depravity of mankind, avoid looking with horror on the danger to which we are exposed!

"More and more," as the people contemplated the significance of crown salaries for a judiciary that served "at pleasure," was it clear that "the designs of administration [were] totally to subvert the constitution." Any judge, the House in Massachusetts ultimately stated, who accepted such salaries would thereby declare "that he has not a due sense of the importance of an impartial administration of justice, that he is an enemy to the constitution,

---

[10] [William H. Drayton], *A Letter from Freeman of South-Carolina* . . . (Charleston, 1774: JHL Pamphlet 45), pp. 10, 20. For other characteristic expressions of the fear of a corrupt judiciary, see [John Allen], *An Oration upon the Beauties of Liberty* . . . (Boston, 1773; JHL Pamphlet 38), pp. 21 ff.; *The Conduct of Cadwallader Colden* . . . ([New York], 1767), reprinted in *Collections of the New-York Historical Society*, X (New York, 1877), 433–467; [John Allen], *The American Alarm* . . . *for the Rights, and Liberties, of the People* . . . (Boston, 1773: JHL Pamphlet 39), 1st sec., pp. 17, 20, 27, 28; *Votes and Proceedings of Boston* (JHL 36), pp. 37–38; Adams, *Diary and Autobiography*, II, 36, 65–67; III, 297 ff.

and has it in his heart to promote the establishment of an arbitrary government in the province." [11]

Long before this, however, another aspect of the judicial system was believed also to have come under deliberate attack. The jury system, it was said, in New York particularly but elsewhere as well, was being systematically undermined. In New York the same executive who had fought the permanent tenure of judges insisted on the legality of allowing jury decisions, on matters of fact as well as of law, to be appealed to the governor and Council. This effort, though defeated within a year by action of the Board of Trade in England, had a lasting impact on the political consciousness of New Yorkers. It was publicly assailed, in the year of the Stamp Act, as "arbitrary" and "scandalous" in its deliberate subversion of the British constitution. [12]

Associated with this but more important because more widespread in its effect was the extension and enforcement of the jurisdiction of the vice-admiralty courts — "prerogative" courts composed not of juries but of single judges whose posts were "political offices in the hands of the royal governors, to be bestowed upon deserving friends and supporters." Since these courts had jurisdiction over the enforcement of all laws of trade and navigation as well as over ordinary marine matters, they had always been potentially threatening to the interests of the colonists. But in the past, by one means or another, they had been curtailed in their effect, and much of their business had been shunted off to common law courts dominated by juries. Suddenly in the 1760's they acquired a great new importance, for it was into their hands that the burden of judicial enforcement of the new Parliamentary legislation fell. It was upon them, consequently, and

[11] *Votes and Proceedings of Boston* (JHL 36), p. 20; Thomas Hutchinson, *The History of . . . Massachusetts-Bay* (Lawrence S. Mayo, ed., Cambridge, 1936), III, 278, 279. See also, Gipson, *British Empire*, XII, 47, 139 ff., and Hutchinson, *History*, III, Appendices V, W.

[12] Klein, "Prelude to Revolution in New York," pp. 453–459.

upon the whole principle of "prerogative" courts that abuse was hurled as the effect of their enhanced power was felt. "What has America done," victims of the decisions of these courts asked, "to be thus particularized, to be disfranchised and stripped of so invaluable a privilege as the trial by jury?" The operations of the vice-admiralty courts, it was felt, especially after their administrative reorganization in 1767, denied Americans a crucial measure of the protection of the British constitution. "However respectable the judge may be, it is however an hardship and severity which distinguishes [defendants before this court] from the rest of Englishmen." The evils of such prerogative invasion of the judiciary could hardly be exaggerated: their "enormous created powers . . . threatens future generations in America with a curse tenfold worse than the Stamp Act." [13]

The more one looked the more one found evidences of deliberate malevolence. In Massachusetts, Thomas Hutchinson's elaborate patronage machine, long in existence but fully organized only after the arrival of Governor Francis Bernard in 1760, appeared to suspicious tribunes like Oxenbridge Thacher and John Adams to constitute a serious threat to liberty. The Hutchinsons and the Olivers and their ambitious allies, it was said (and the view was widely circulated through the colonies), had managed, by accumulating a massive plurality of offices, to engross the power of all branches of the Massachusetts government thereby building a "foundation sufficient on which to erect a tyranny."

[13] Carl Ubbelohde, *The Vice-Admiralty Courts and the American Revolution* (Chapel Hill, 1960), pp. 125–126, 112. For further expressions of antipathy to the admiralty courts, see especially the Laurens pamphlet cited in note 7 above, and also, besides the references indexed in Bailyn, *Pamphlets*, I, Adams, *Works*, III, 466–467; *Votes and Proceedings of Boston* (JHL 36), p. 24; and Oliver M. Dickerson, comp., *Boston under Military Rule, 1768–1769* . . . (Boston, 1936), pp. 46, 54, 56, 68, 72, which documents the popular comparison of vice-admiralty courts and the Court of Star Chamber.

Bernard had all the executive, and a negative of the legislative; Hutchinson and Oliver, by their popular arts and secret intrigues, had elevated to the [Council] such a collection of crown officers and their own relations as to have too much influence there; and they had three of a family on the superior bench . . . This junto, therefore, had the legislative and executive in their control, and more natural influence over the judicial than is ever to be trusted to any set of men in the world.

With encouragement, no doubt, from England, they were stretching their power beyond all proper bounds, becoming "conspirators against the public liberty." [14]

The same evil of plural officeholding, tending to destroy the protective mechanism of the separation of powers, was observed to be at work in South Carolina. In both cases the filiation between the engrossing of offices in England and in America could be said to be direct. The self-seeking monopolists of office in the colonies, advancing themselves and their faithful adherents "to the exclusion of much better men," Adams wrote somewhat plaintively, were as cravenly obedient to their masters in power in England as their own despicable "creatures" were to them.[15] How deep this issue ran, how powerful its threat, could be seen best when one noted the degree to which it paralleled cognate developments in England.

John Wilkes's career was crucial to the colonists' understanding of what was happening to them; his fate, the colonists came to believe, was intimately involved with their own.[16] Not only was

[14] John Adams ("Novanglus"), *Works*, IV, 53 ff., 63, and citations in note 29 below; Ellen E. Brennan, *Plural Office-Holding in Massachusetts, 1760–1780* (Chapel Hill, 1945), chaps. i, ii. See also references to Hutchinson, above, note 4.

[15] Drayton, *Letter from Freeman* (JHL 45), pp. 9, 18–19, 32–33; Edward McCrady, *The History of South Carolina under the Royal Government, 1719–1776* (New York, 1899), pp. 533–535, 710–713; Adams, *Diary and Autobiography*, I, 306; II, 39.

[16] For a detailed discussion of the Wilkes affair in the context of the present discussion, see Pauline Maier, "John Wilkes and American Disillusionment with Britain," *W.M.Q.*, 3d ser., 20 (1963), 373–395.

he associated in their minds with general opposition to the government that passed the Stamp Act and the Townshend Duties, that was flooding the colonies with parasitic placemen, and that appeared to be making inroads into the constitution by weakening the judiciary and bestowing monopolies of public offices on pliant puppets — not only was he believed to be a national leader of opposition to such a government, but he had entered the public arena first as a victim and then as the successful antagonist of general warrants, which, in the form of writs of assistance, the colonists too had fought in heroic episodes known throughout the land. He had, moreover, defended the sanctity of private property against confiscation by the government. His cause was their cause. His *Number 45 North Briton* was as celebrated in the colonies at it was in England, and more generally approved of; its symbolism became part of the iconography of liberty in the colonies. His return from exile in 1768 and subsequent election to Parliament were major events to Americans. Toasts were offered to him throughout the colonies, and substantial contributions to his cause as well as adulatory letters were sent by Sons of Liberty in Virginia, Maryland, and South Carolina. A stalwart, independent opponent of encroaching government power and a believer in the true principles of the constitution, he was expected to do much in Parliament for the good of all: so the Bostonians wrote him in June 1768 "your perseverance in the *good old cause* may still prevent the great system from dashing to pieces. 'Tis from your endeavors we hope for a royal 'Pascite, ut ante, boves,' and from our attachment to 'peace and good order' we wait for a constitutional redress: being determined that the King of Great Britain shall have subjects but not slaves in these remote parts of his dominions." [17]

[17] Boston Sons of Liberty to Wilkes, June 6, 1768, MHS *Procs.*, 47 (1913–14), 191. The quotation is from Vergil, *Eclogues*, i, 45: "pasture your cattle as of old."

By February 1769 it was well known that *"the fate of Wilkes and America must stand or fall together."* [18] The news, therefore, that by the maneuvers of the court party Wilkes had been denied the seat in Parliament to which he had been duly elected came as a profound shock to Americans. It shattered the hopes of many that the evils they saw around them had been the result not of design but of inadvertence, and it portended darker days ahead. When again, and then for a second, a third, and a fourth time Wilkes was re-elected to Parliament and still denied his seat, Americans could only watch with horror and agree with him that the rights of the Commons, like those of the colonial Houses, were being denied by a power-hungry government that assumed to itself the privilege of deciding who should speak for the people in their own branch of the legislature. Power had reached directly and brutally into the main agency of liberty. Surely Wilkes was right: the constitution was being deliberately, not inadvertently, torn up by its roots.

Meanwhile an event even more sinister in its implications had taken place in the colonies themselves. On October 1, 1768, two regiments of regular infantry, with artillery, disembarked in Boston. For many months the harassed Governor Bernard had sought some legal means or excuse for summoning military help in his vain efforts to maintain if not an effective administration then at least order in the face of Stamp Act riots, circular letters, tumultuous town meetings, and assaults on customs officials. But the arrival of troops in Boston increased rather than decreased his troubles. For to a populace steeped in the literature of eighteenth-century English politics the presence of troops in a peaceful town had such portentous meaning that resistance instantly stiffened. It was not so much the physical threat of the troops that affected the attitudes of the Bostonians; it was the bearing their

[18] William Palfrey to Wilkes, February 21, 1769, MHS *Procs.*, 47 (1913–14), 197.

arrival had on the likely tendency of events. Viewed in the perspective of Trenchard's famous tracts on standing armies and of the vast derivative literature on the subject that flowed from the English debates of the 1690's, these were not simply soldiers assembled for police duties; they were precisely what history had proved over and over again to be prime movers of the process by which unwary nations lose "that precious jewel *liberty*." The mere rumor of possible troop arrivals had evoked the age-old apprehensions. "The raising or keeping a standing army within the kingdom in time of peace, unless it be with the consent of Parliament, is against the law," the alarmed Boston Town Meeting had resolved. It is, they said,

the indefeasible right of [British] subjects to be *consulted* and to give their *free consent in person* or by representatives of their own free election to the raising and keeping a standing army among them; and the inhabitants of this town, being free subjects, have the same right derived from nature and confirmed by the British constitution as well as the said royal charter; and therefore the raising or keeping a standing army without their consent in person or by representatives of their own free election would be an infringement of their natural, constitutional, and charter rights; and the employing such army for the enforcing of laws made without the consent of the people, in person or by their representatives, would be a grievance.[19]

But the troops arrived, four regiments in all: in bold, stark actuality a standing army — just such a standing army as had snuffed out freedom in Denmark, classically, and elsewhere throughout the world. True, British regulars had been introduced into the colonies on a permanent basis at the end of the Seven Years' War; that in itself had been disquieting. But it had then been argued that troops were needed to police the newly acquired territories, and that they were not in any case to be regularly garrisoned in

---

[19] *Sixteenth Report of the Boston Record Commissioners*, p. 263.

peaceful, populous towns.[20] No such defense could be made of the troops sent to Boston in 1768. No simple, ingenuous explanation would suffice. The true motive was only too apparent for those with eyes to see. One of the classic stages in the process of destroying free constitutions of government had been reached.

To those most sensitive to the ideological currents of the day, the danger could scarcely have been greater. "To have a standing army!" Andrew Eliot wrote from Boston to Thomas Hollis in September, 1768, "Good God! What can be worse to a people who have tasted the sweets of liberty! Things are come to an unhappy crisis; there will never be that harmony between Great Britain and her colonies that there hath been; all confidence is at an end; and the moment there is any blood shed all affection will cease." He was convinced, he wrote, that if the English government "had not had their hands full at home they would have crushed the colonies." As it was, England's most recent actions tended only "to hasten that independency which at present the warmest among us deprecate." "I fear for the nation," he concluded, and his fears were shared not only by all liberty-minded Bostonians but also, through the stimulation of the "Journal of the Times," a day-by-day account of Boston "under military rule" that was, in effect, syndicated throughout the colonies, it was shared by politically and ideologically sensitive Americans everywhere. Time did not ease these anxieties; it merely complicated them. Fear and hatred became edged with contempt. "Our people begin to despise a military force," Eliot observed a year after the troops had first appeared; they coolly woo away the soldiers and drag offending officers before the courts — which, he grimly added, continue to function "notwithstanding all their efforts." But "things cannot long remain in the state they are now in;

---

[20] Gipson, *British Empire*, X, 200–201, 328–329, 408; cf. Bernhard Knollenberg, *Origin of the American Revolution, 1759–1766* (New York, 1960), pp. 87–96.

they are hastening to a crisis. What will be the event, God knows."[21]

And again significant corroboration for America's fears could be found in developments in England, and support furnished for the belief that events in America were only part of a larger whole. On May 10, 1768, a mob, assembled in St. George's Fields, London, in support of the imprisoned Wilkes, was fired upon by the regiment of Foot Guards that had been summoned by the nervous magistrates. Several deaths resulted, the most dramatic being that of a boy, wrongly identified as a leader of the mob, who was tracked down and shot to death on orders of the commander. The political capital made of this episode by the Wilkesites and other anti-government groups in London, who declared it to have been a deliberately planned "massacre," was echoed loudly in the colonies, the more so when it appeared that convictions of the guilty soldiers by normal processes of law were being quashed by the government. Could it be believed to be a coincidence that in February 1770 an eleven-year-old boy was also shot to death in a Boston riot by a suspected customs informer? This was more than a parallel to what had happened in London: the two events were two effects of the same cause.[22]

[21] Eliot to Hollis, Boston, September 27, 1768; July 10, September 7, 1769, in MHS *Colls.*, 4th ser., IV, 428, 442, 444. The "Journal of the Times" was a series of newspaper articles published from October 13, 1768, to November 30, 1769. The pieces, dilating on day-by-day offenses of the military in Boston, were apparently written in Boston but were sent to New York for weekly publication in the *New York Journal* and to Pennsylvania for reprinting in the *Pennsylvania Chronicle.* After these two initial appearances the articles were again reprinted in the *Boston Evening Post,* and thereafter generally copied in American and English publications. The series has been collected by Oliver M. Dickerson as *Boston under Military Rule, 1768–1769.*

[22] George Rudé, *Wilkes and Liberty* (Oxford, 1962), pp. 49 ff.; Maier, "Wilkes and American Disillusionment," pp. 386–387; Gipson, *British Empire,* XI, 275, 281. For an example of the currency in personal correspondence of the St. George's Fields "massacre," see William Strahan to David Hall, London, December 30, 1768, *Pa. Mag.* 10 (1886), 468–469. On the role of the shooting of the

And then, a few weeks later, came the Boston Massacre. Doubts that the troops in Boston constituted a standing army and that it was the purpose of standing armies to terrify a populace into compliance with tyrannical wills were silenced by that event, which, Eliot assured Hollis, had obviously been coming. It "serves to show the impossibility of our living in peace with a standing army. A free people will sometimes carry things too far, but this remedy will always be found worse than the disease. Trenchard's *History of Standing Armies,* with which you formerly obliged me, is excellent . . . Unless there is some great alteration in the state of things the era of the independence of the colonies is much nearer than I once thought it, or now wish it." [23] The same response was generally broadcast in the narrative of the Massacre, written by James Bowdoin and others for the Boston Town Meeting, which was distributed everywhere in the English-speaking world. This famous pamphlet stressed the deliberateness of the shooting and the clarity of the design that lay behind the lurid event; nor was the parallel to the St. George's Fields murders neglected. The acquittal of the indicted soldiers did not alter the conviction that the Massacre was the logical work of a standing army, for it accentuated the parallel with the English case which also had concluded with acquittal; and in Boston too there was suspicion of judicial irregularities. How the murderers managed to escape was known to some, it was said, but was "too dark to explain." [24]

Snider boy in the Revolutionary movement in Boston, see John Cary, *Joseph Warren* (Urbana, 1961), pp. 91–92.

[23] Eliot to Hollis, June 28, 1770, MHS *Colls.,* 4th ser., IV, 452.

[24] Allen, *Oration upon the Beauties of Liberty* (JHL 38), p. xiii; [Bowdoin, *et al.*], *A Short Narrative of the Horrid Massacre in Boston* . . . (Boston, 1770: JHL Pamphlet 32), reprinted within the year three times in Boston, three times in London and once (retitled) in Dublin; for the association of the Massacre with the problem of standing armies, see *Short Narrative,* p. 8. The annual Massacre Day orators played up this association in lurid detail: see, for example, Joseph Warren, *An Oration* . . . (Boston, 1772: JHL Pamphlet 35), pp. 11–12; John Hancock, *An Oration* . . . (Boston, 1774: JHL Pamphlet 41), pp. 13–15.

THE LOGIC OF REBELLION

Unconstitutional taxing, the invasion of placemen, the weakening of the judiciary, plural officeholding, Wilkes, standing armies — these were major evidences of a deliberate assault of power upon liberty. Lesser testimonies were also accumulating at the same time: small episodes in themselves, they took on a large significance in the context in which they were received. Writs of assistance in support of customs officials were working their expected evil: "our houses, and even our bedchambers, are exposed to be ransacked, our boxes, trunks, and chests broke open, ravaged and plundered by wretches whom no prudent man would venture to employ even as menial servants." Legally convened legislatures had been "adjourned . . . to a place highly inconvenient to the members and greatly disadvantageous to the interest of the province"; they had been prorogued and dissolved at executive whim. Even the boundaries of colonies had been tampered with, whereby *"rights of soil"* had been eliminated at a stroke. When in 1772 the Boston Town Meeting met to draw up a full catalogue of the "infringements and violations" of the "rights of the colonists, and of this province in particular, as men, as Christians, and as subjects," it approved a list of twelve items, which took seventeen pamphlet pages to describe.[25]

But then, for a two-year period, there was a détente of sorts created by the repeal of the Townshend Duties, the withdrawal

---

The view of the Massacre held by John Adams and Josiah Quincy, Jr., the lawyers who successfully defended the soldiers in court, is especially important. Both thought the Massacre was "the strongest of proofs of the danger of standing armies" despite their efforts on the soldiers' behalf; Adams saw nothing incompatible between the verdict of the jury and his being invited to deliver one of the orations commemorating the Massacre, and Quincy publicly urged continued discussion of the "fatal effects of the policy of standing armies and . . . quartering troops in populous cities in time of peace." Josiah Quincy, *Memoir of the Life of Josiah Quincy Jun.* . . . (Boston, 1825), p. 67; Adams, *Diary and Autobiography*, II, 74, 79; Gipson, *British Empire*, XI, 281. For the complete documentation and an excellent analysis of the trial, see L. Kinvin Wroth and Hiller B. Zobel, eds., *Legal Papers of John Adams* (Cambridge, 1965), III.

[25] *Votes and Proceedings of Boston* (JHL 36), pp. 13–30.

of troops from Boston, and the failure of other provocative measures to be taken. It ended abruptly, however, in the fall and winter of 1773, when, with a rush, the tendencies earlier noted were brought to fulfillment. In the space of a few weeks, all the dark, twisted roots of malevolence were finally revealed, plainly, for all to see.

The turning point was the passage of the Tea Act[26] and the resulting Tea Party in Boston in December 1773. Faced with this defiant resistance to intimidation, the powers at work in England, it was believed, gave up all pretense of legality — "threw off the mask," John Adams said in a phrase that for a century had been used to describe just such climactic disclosures[27] — and moved swiftly to complete their design. In a period of two months in the spring of 1774 Parliament took its revenge in a series of coercive actions no liberty-loving people could tolerate: the Boston Port Act, intended, it was believed, to snuff out the economic life of the Massachusetts metropolis; the Administration of Justice

[26] For an analysis of the motivation behind the opposition to the Tea Act on the part of the merchant community, explicitly contradicting the interpretation of A. M. Schlesinger's *Colonial Merchants and the American Revolution* (1918), see Arthur L. Jensen, *The Maritime Commerce of Colonial Philadelphia* (Madison, Wis., 1963), pp. 193 ff. Jensen concludes that "it is difficult to see how the constitutional question can be lightly dismissed as mere window dressing for the more fundamental economic questions when there is an impressive amount of contemporary testimony, private as well as public, to the contrary."

[27] Thus the commonwealthman and regicide Edmund Ludlow described in his *Memoirs* (written 1663–1673) how Charles I, fatally attracted to French and Spanish despotism, "immediately after his ascent to the throne pulled off the mask, and openly discovered his intentions to make the crown absolute and independent" (C. H. Firth, ed., Oxford, 1894, I, 10). Similarly — or perhaps conversely — Governor Hunter of New York, who had for months been seething with indignation at the arrogance of the New York Assembly, finally wrote the Secretary of State in 1712 that "now the mask is thrown off; they have called in question the Council's share in the legislation . . . and have but one short step to make towards what I am unwilling to name [i.e., independence]." E. B. O'Callaghan and Berthold Fernow, eds., *Documents Relative to the Colonial History of the State of New-York* . . . (Albany, 1856–1887), V, 296; cf. pp. 255–256. The Secretary of State involved was Bolingbroke, who himself used the phrase in similar circumstances: e.g., *Works* (Philadelphia, 1841), I, 116.

THE LOGIC OF REBELLION

Act, aimed at crippling judicial processes once and for all by permitting trials to be held in England for offenses committed in Massachusetts; the Massachusetts Government Act, which stripped from the people of Massachusetts the protection of the British constitution by giving over all the "democratic" elements of the province's government — even popularly elected juries and town meetings — into the hands of the executive power; the Quebec Act, which, while not devised as a part of the coercive program, fitted it nicely, in the eyes of the colonists, by extending the boundaries of a "papist" province, and one governed wholly by prerogative, south into territory claimed by Virginia, Connecticut, and Massachusetts; finally, the Quartering Act, which permitted the seizure of unoccupied buildings for the use of troops on orders of the governors alone even in situations, such as Boston's, where barracks were available in the vicinity.

Once these coercive acts were passed there could be little doubt that "the system of slavery fabricated against America . . . is the offspring of mature deliberation." To the leaders of the Revolutionary movement there was, beyond question, "a settled, fixed plan for *enslaving* the colonies, or bringing them under arbitrary government, and indeed the nation too." By 1774 the idea "that the British government — the *King, Lords,* and *Commons* — have laid a regular plan to enslave America, and that they are now deliberately putting it in execution" had been asserted, Samuel Seabury wrote wearily but accurately, "over, and over, and over again." The less inhibited of the colonial orators were quick to point out that "the MONSTER of a standing ARMY" had sprung directly from "a PLAN . . . *systematically* laid, and pursued by the British *ministry,* near twelve years, for enslaving America"; the Boston Massacre, it was claimed, had been "planned by Hillsborough and a knot of treacherous knaves in Boston." Careful analysts like Jefferson agreed on the major point; in one of the most closely reasoned of the pamphlets of 1774 the Virginian stated unambiguously that though "single

119

acts of tyranny may be ascribed to the accidental opinion of a day . . . a series of oppressions, begun at a distinguished period and pursued unalterably through every change of ministers, too plainly prove a deliberate and systematical plan of reducing us to slavery." So too the fastidious and scholarly John Dickinson, though in 1774 he still clung to the hope that inadvertence, at least on the part of the King, was involved, believed that "a plan had been deliberately framed and pertinaciously adhered to, unchanged even by frequent changes of ministers, unchecked by any intervening gleam of humanity, to sacrifice to a passion for arbitrary dominion the universal property, liberty, safety, honor, happiness, and prosperity of us unoffending yet devoted Americans." So too Washington, collaborating with George Mason in writing the Fairfax Resolves of 1774, agreed that the trouble had arisen from a "regular, systematic plan" of oppression, the English government "endeavoring by every piece of art and despotism to fix the shackles of slavery upon us"; he was convinced "beyond the smallest doubt," he wrote privately, "that these measures are the result of deliberation . . . I am as fully convinced as I am of my own existence that there has been a regular, systematic plan formed to enforce them." The more sensitive observers were to ideological issues — the more practiced in theoretical discourse — the more likely they were to find irrefutable evidence of what Richard Henry Lee called "designs for destroying our constitutional liberties." In 1766 Andrew Eliot had been unsure; the Stamp Act, he wrote, had been "calculated (I do not say designed) to enslave the colonies." By 1768 things had worsened, and the distinction between "calculation" and "design" disappeared from his correspondence. "We have everything to fear and scarce any room to hope," he then wrote to Hollis; "I am sure this will put you in mind of 1641." He was convinced that the English government "had a design to new-model our constitution, at least in this province," and they would already have succeeded had they not been so occupied with other business at home. His friends in Boston concurred, and, beginning in 1770 wrote out in a series of town resolutions, instructions to representatives, and House declarations their conviction that

a deep-laid and desperate plan of imperial despotism has been laid, and partly executed, for the extinction of all civil liberty . . . The august and once revered fortress of English freedom — the admirable work of ages — the BRITISH CONSTITUTION seems fast tottering into fatal and inevitable ruin.[28]

Specifics were sought, especially as to the date of the origins of the plot. Josiah Quincy — "Wilkes Quincy," Hutchinson called him — found it in the Restoration of Charles II; others traced it to the administration of Robert Walpole; and though John Adams, with one eye on Hutchinson, wrote in 1774 that "the conspiracy was first regularly formed and begun to be executed in 1763 or 4," later he traced it back to the 1750's and 1740's and the administration of Governor Shirley of Massachusetts. Nor were the specific stages of its development neglected. They could be traced, if in no other place, in the notorious Hutchinson letters of 1768–69, those "profoundly secret, dark, and deep" letters which, published in 1773, totally exposed Hutchinson's "machia-

[28] [Alexander Hamilton], *A Full Vindication of the Measures of the Congress* . . . (New York, 1774), in Harold C. Syrett, *et al.*, eds., *Papers of Alexander Hamilton* (New York and London, 1961–), I, 50; Baldwin, *Appendix* (JHL 52), p. 67; [Samuel Seabury], *A View of the Controversy* . . . (New York, 1774), in Clarence H. Vance, ed., *Letters of a Westchester Farmer (1774-1775)* (*Publications of the Westchester County Historical Society*, VIII, White Plains, 1930), p. 123; Oliver Noble, *Some Strictures upon the . . . Book of Esther* . . . (Newburyport, 1775: JHL Pamphlet 58), pp. 28, 26; Hancock, *Oration* (JHL 41), p. 9; [Jefferson], *A Summary View of the Rights of British America* . . . (Williamsburg, [1774]: JHL Pamphlet 43), p. 11; on the development of Dickinson's understanding of the cause of the crisis, see the Introduction to his *Late Regulations* (Philadelphia, 1765: JHL Pamphlet 14), in Bailyn, *Pamphlets*, I; Colbourn, *Lamp of Experience*, p. 155; Washington to Bryan Fairfax, August 27, 1774, in John C. Fitzpatrick, ed., *Writings of George Washington* . . . (Washington, D. C., 1931–1944), III, 241, 242; Gipson, *British Empire*, XII, 36n; MHS *Colls.*, 4th ser., IV, 400, 429, 444; [*Eighteenth*] *Report of the Record Commissioners of the City of Boston* . . . (Boston, 1887), p. 26 (cf. pp. 83–86).

vellian dissimulation," John Adams wrote, and convicted him of "junto conspiracy"; they gave proof, the Boston Committee of Correspondence wrote, that God had "wonderfully interposed to bring to light the plot that has been laid for us by our malicious and invidious enemies." [29]

But who, specifically, were these enemies, and what were their goals? Josiah Quincy, at the center of affairs in London in the winter of 1774–75, was convinced "that all the measures against America were planned and pushed on by Bernard and Hutchinson." But most observers believed that local plotters like Hutchinson were only "creatures" of greater figures in England coordinating and impelling forward the whole effort. There were a number of specific identifications of these master influences. One of the most common was the claim that at the root of the evil stood the venerable John Stuart, Lord Bute, whose apparent absence from politics since 1763 could be seen as one of his more successful dissimulations: "he has been aiming for years . . . to destroy the ancient right of the subjects," and now was finally taking steps to "overthrow both . . . King and state; to bring on a revolution, and to place another whom he [is] more nearly allied to upon the throne." Believing the people to "have too much liberty," he intended to reduce them to the "spiritless SLAVES" they had been "in the reign of the *Stuarts.*" So it had seemed to Arthur Lee, who had written from London at the beginning of the period that "Lord Bute, though seemingly re-

[29] Quincy, *Observations on the . . . Boston Port-Bill; with Thoughts on . . . Standing Armies* (Boston, 1774), in Quincy, *Memoir*, p. 446 (cf. pp. 464–465); Adams, *Works*, X, 242–243 (for Adams' full elaboration of the ministry's "dark intrigues and wicked machinations" so clearly dovetailed with the Hutchinson clique's maneuverings, see *Works*, IV, 18 ff., 62–64, 70, 91–92; *Diary and Autobiography*, II, 80, 90, 119); John C. Miller, *Origins of the American Revolution* (Boston, 1943), p. 332. For other expressions of the fear of "a constant, unremitted, uniform aim to enslave us," see *Votes and Proceedings of Boston* (JHL 36), pp. 30, 37; Allen, *American Alarm* (JHL 39), 1st sec., pp. 8–9, 17, 18, 33; Edmund S. Morgan, *The Gentle Puritan* (New Haven, 1962), pp. 263–265.

tired from the affairs of court, too plainly influences all the operations of government"; the hard facts, he said, lead one to condemn "the unprincipled ambition and partiality of the Scots lord as having produced all the mischiefs of the present period." Eliot too feared "this mysterious THANE," declaring in 1769 that "he has too much influence in the public measures." Five years later John Dickinson still lumped together "the Butes, Mansfields, Norths, Bernards, and Hutchinsons" as the people "whose falsehoods and misrepresentations have enflamed the people," and as late as 1775 an informed American could write confidently from London that "this plan you may be assured was devised by Lords North, Bute, and Jenkinson only." [30] A more general version of this view was that a Stuart-Tory party, the "corrupt, Frenchified party in the nation," as it was described in 1766 — "evil-minded individuals," Jonathan Mayhew believed, "not improbably in the interests of the houses of Bourbon and the Pretender" — was at work seeking to reverse the consequences of the Glorious Revolution. It was a similar notion that in all probability accounts for the republication of Rapin's *Dissertation on . . . the Whigs and Tories* in Boston in 1773; and it was this notion that furnished Jefferson with his ultimate understanding of the "system" that sought to destroy liberty in America. Still another explanation, drawing no less directly on fears that had lain at the root of opposition ideology in England since the turn of the century, emphasized the greed of a "monied interest" created by the crown's financial necessities and the power of a newly risen, arrogant, and irresponsible capitalist group, that battened on wars and stock manipulation. The creation of this group was accompanied "by levying of taxes, by a host of tax gatherers, and a long

---

[30] Allen, *American Alarm* (JHL 39), 1st sec., pp. 18–19 (cf. the same author's reference to *"Scotch-barbarian troops"* at the St. George's Fields riot, in *Oration upon the Beauties of Liberty* [JHL 38], p. xiii); Arthur Lee Papers (MSS in Houghton Library, Harvard University), I, 2; II, 26, 33; Eliot to Hollis, December 25, 1769, MHS *Colls.*, 4th ser., IV, 445.

train of dependents of the crown. The practice grew into system, till at length the crown found means to break down those barriers which the constitution had assigned to each branch of the legislature, and effectually destroyed the independence of both Lords and Commons." [31]

The most common explanation, however — an explanation that rose from the deepest sources of British political culture, that was a part of the very structure of British political thought — located "the spring and cause of all the distresses and complaints of the people in England or in America" in "a kind of fourth power that the constitution knows nothing of, or has not provided against." This "overruling arbitrary power, which absolutely controls the King, Lords, and Commons," was composed, it was said, of the "ministers and favorites" of the King, who, in defiance of God and man alike, "extend their usurped authority

[31] [Stephen Johnson], *Some Important Observations* . . . (Newport, 1766: JHL Pamphlet 19), p. 15; Jonathan Mayhew, *The Snare Broken* . . . (Boston, 1766: JHL Pamphlet 20), p. 9; [Carter Braxton], *An Address to* . . . *Virginia; on the Subject of Government* . . . (Philadelphia, 1776: JHL Pamphlet 66), p. 10. Jefferson's explanation appeared first as notes he jotted down on reading François Soulé's *Histoire des troubles de l'Amérique anglaise* (London, 1785) at the point where George III's education is mentioned: "The education of the present King was Tory. He gave decisive victories to the Tories. To these were added sundry rich persons sprung up in the E. I. America would have been too formidable a weight in the scale of the Whigs. It was necessary therefore to reduce them by force to concur with the Tories." Later he wrote more formally to Soulé: "The seeds of the war are here traced to their true source. The Tory education of the King was the first preparation for that change in the British government which that party never ceases to wish. This naturally ensured Tory administrations during his life. At the moment he came to the throne and cleared his hands of his enemies by the peace of Paris, the assumptions of unwarrantable right over America commenced; they were so signal, and followed one another so close as to prove they were part of a system either to reduce it under absolute subjection and thereby make it an instrument for attempts on Britain itself, or to sever it from Britain so that it might not be a weight in the Whig scale. This latter alternative however was not considered as the one which would take place. They knew so little of America that they thought it unable to encounter the little finger of Great Britain." *The Papers of Thomas Jefferson* (Julian P. Boyd, ed., Princeton, 1950–), X, 373n2, 369.

infinitely too far," and, throwing off the balance of the constitution, make their "despotic will" the authority of the nation.

For their power and interest is so great that they can and do procure whatever laws they please, having (by power, interest, and the application of the people's money to *placemen* and *pensioners*) the whole legislative authority at their command. So that it is plain (not to say a word of a particular reigning arbitrary *Stuarchal* power among them) that the rights of the people are ruined and destroyed by ministerial *tyrannical* authority, and thereby . . . become a kind of slaves to the ministers of state.

This "junto of courtiers and state-jobbers," these "court-locusts," whispering in the royal ear, "instill in the King's mind a divine right of authority to command his subjects" at the same time as they advance their "detestable scheme" by misinforming and misleading the people.[32]

The notion that, as Eliot put it, "If the King can do no wrong, his ministers may; and when they do wrong, they ought to be h g d," had served for generations in England to justify opposition to constituted government. It had been the standard argument of almost every opposition group from the earliest years of the eighteenth century, and it had been transmitted intact to the colonies, where now it received its final, apocalyptic application. Its expression in the writings of the seventies is legion. It was heard in inland towns, like Farmington, Connecticut, where in 1774 an assembly of 1,000 inhabitants resolved:

That the present ministry, being instigated by the devil and led by their wicked and corrupt hearts, have a design to take away our liberties and properties, and to enslave us forever . . . That those pimps and parasites who dared to advise their masters to such detestable measures be held in utter abhorrence by . . . every American, and their names loaded with the curses of all succeeding generations.

[32] Allen, *American Alarm* (JHL 39), 1st sec., pp. 8–9; Noble, *Some Strictures* (JHL 58), p. 6; Allen, *Oration upon the Beauties of Liberty* (JHL 38), p. 29.

It was heard in the cities — in Philadelphia, where handbills addressed to tradesmen and mechanics warned that "a corrupt and prostituted ministry are pointing their destructive machines against the sacred liberties of the Americans, [attempting] . . . by every artifice to enslave the American colonies and plunder them of their property and, what is more, their birthright, *liberty*." It was heard continuously in Boston, whose Committee of Correspondence condemned the Coercive Acts as "glaring evidence of a fixed plan of the British administration to bring the whole continent into the most humiliating bondage," and whose Suffolk Resolves, addressed to the first Continental Congress, condemned "the arbitrary will of a licentious minister" and "the attempts of a wicked administration to enslave America." And it was heard in the Congress itself. The formal address of the first Continental Congress to the people of Great Britain dilated on "the ministerial plan for enslaving us." The second Congress justified its actions by reference to "the rapid progress of a tyrannical ministry," and explained in detail, in its plea for support from Canada, "the designs of an arbitrary ministry to extirpate the rights and liberties of all America," arguing that armed resistance alone would induce the King at long last to "forbid a licentious ministry any longer to riot in the ruins of the rights of mankind." It was this same protest against the "delusive pretenses, fruitless terrors, and unavailing severities" of what Arthur Lee called "the most unprincipled administration that ever disgraced humanity" that shaped the Congress' Declaration of the Causes and Necessity for Taking up Arms and its more conciliatory Olive Branch Petition.[33]

No fear, no accusation, had been more common in the history of opposition politics in eighteenth-century England; none was

---

[33] Eliot to Hollis, December 25, 1769, MHS *Colls.*, 4th ser., IV, 446; Gipson, *British Empire*, XII, 173, 91, 150n, 245, 255, 326, 328; Boyd, *Jefferson Papers*, I, 220, 214; Lee Papers, II, 62.

more familiar to Americans whose political awareness had been formed by the literature of English politics. It had, moreover, a special resonance in New England and elsewhere in the colonies where people generally were acquainted with the Biblical Book of Esther and hence had a special model for a ministerial conspiracy in the story of that "tyrannic *bloodthirsty* MINISTER OF STATE," Haman, at the court of Ahasuerus. There he was, wrote the Newbury, Massachusetts, minister Oliver Noble in 1775, "*Haman* the *Premier,* and his junto of court *favorites, flatterers,* and *dependents* in the royal city, together with *governors* of provinces, *councilors, boards of trade, commissioners* and their *creatures, officers* and *collectors* of REVENUE, *solicitors,* assistants, *searchers,* and *inspectors,* down to *tide-waiters* and their *scribes,* and the good Lord knows whom and how many of them, together with the coachmen and servants of the whole . . ." — [*footnote:*] "Not that I am certain the *Persian* state had all these *officers* . . . or that the underofficers of state rode in *coaches* or chariots . . . But as the *Persian* monarchy was despotic . . . it is highly probable . . ." The story was so well known: ". . . now behold the DECREE obtained! The *bloody* PLAN ripened!" The "*cruel perpetrators of the horrid PLOT* and a *banditti* of ministerial tools through the provinces" had everything in readiness. "But behold! . . . A merciful GOD heard the cries of this oppressed people . . ." The parallels were closely drawn; Haman: Lord North; Esther and the Jews: the colonists; and Mordecai: Franklin.[34]

But why were not these manipulators of prerogative satisfied

[34] Archibald S. Foord, *His Majesty's Opposition, 1714–1830* (Oxford, 1964), pp. 37–38, 51, 53–54, 147–148, 170, 291, 318–319; Noble, *Some Strictures* (JHL 58), pp. 10, 17–18, 12. See also Richard Salter, *A Sermon* . . . (New London, 1768); Johnson, *Some Important Observations* (JHL 19), pp. 39, 55–56; Elisha Fish, *Joy and Gladness* . . . (Providence, 1767). For an earlier use of this Biblical imagery, see Philip Livingston's angry description in 1747 of Cadwallader Colden as New York's "Haman," quoted by Milton Klein in *W.M.Q.*, 3d ser., 17 (1960), 445.

with amassing power at home? Why the attention to faraway provinces in America? Several answers were offered, besides the general one that power naturally seeks to drive itself everywhere, into every pocket of freedom. One explanation was that the court, having reached a limit in the possibilities of patronage and spoils in the British Isles, sought a quarrel with the colonies as an excuse for confiscating their wealth. "The long and scandalous list of placemen and pensioners and the general profligacy and prodigality of the present reign exceed the annual supplies. England is drained by taxes, and Ireland impoverished to almost the last farthing . . . America was the only remaining spot to which their oppression and extortion had not fully reached, and they considered her as a fallow field from which a large income might be drawn." When the colonists' reaction to the Stamp Act proved that "raising a revenue in America quietly" was out of the question, it was decided to destroy their power to resist: the colonies were to be "politically broken up." And so the Tea Act was passed, not to gain a revenue but, as in the case of the Massacre, to provoke a quarrel. The ministry wished "to see America in arms . . . because it furnished them with a pretense for declaring us rebels; and persons conquered under that character forfeit their all, be it where it will or what it will, to the crown." England did not desire an accommodation of any sort, Lord North's conciliatory plan notwithstanding. "From motives of political avarice," she sought an excuse for conquest: "it is on this ground only that the continued obstinacy of her conduct can be accounted for." Not that the crown was necessarily implicated. Most commentators, until 1776, considered the crown equally the victim of ministerial machinations, one writer reporting to London from Philadelphia late in 1774 that "it is suspected here that a design is regularly prosecuted by the ministry to make His Majesty dethrone himself by the calamities and convulsions his reign is likely to bring on his whole people. Please to inform me what is thought on this point in England." [35]

Perhaps the most explicit and detailed explanation of the assault upon America by a conspiratorial ministry, encapsulating a century of opposition thought, came from the pen of a country parson in Connecticut writing "to enlighten the people of a country town not under the best advantages for information from the newspapers and other pieces wrote upon the controversy." Seeking to rouse the villagers "to a sense of the danger to which their liberties are now involved," the Rev. Ebenezer Baldwin of Danbury explained that during the last war "the state of the colonies was much more attended to than it had been in times past," and "a very exalted idea of the riches of this country" had been conveyed back to England by the returning officers and soldiers. This exciting information fitted the plans of the ministry neatly, for

notwithstanding the excellency of the British constitution, if the ministry can secure a majority in Parliament who will come into all their measures [and] will vote as they bid them, they may rule as absolutely as they do in *France* or *Spain,* yea as in *Turkey* or *India.* And this seems to be the present plan: to secure a majority of Parliament, and thus enslave the nation with their own consent. The more places or pensions the ministry have in their gift the more easily they can *bribe* a majority of Parliament by bestowing those places on them or their friends. This makes them erect so many new and unnecessary offices in America, even so as to swallow up the whole of the revenue . . . by bestowing these places — places of considerable profit and no labor — upon the children or friends or dependents of the members of Parliament, the ministry can secure them in their interest. This doubtless is the great thing the ministry are driving at, to establish

[35] *Four Letters on Interesting Subjects* (Philadelphia, 1776: JHL Pamphlet 69), p. 5; [John Dickinson?] to Arthur Lee, October 27, 1774, Lee Papers, II, 26. For the argument that the Massacre was a deliberate effort of the enemies of Massachusetts "to drive it into that state [of rebellion], whereby in the end they might hope to gratify both their malice and avarice," see Bowdoin, *et al., Short Narrative,* p. 44 (cf. p. A:86).

arbitrary government with the consent of Parliament. And to keep the people of England still, the first exertions of this power are upon the colonies.[36]

Thus the balance of the constitution had been thrown off by a gluttonous ministry usurping the prerogatives of the crown and systematically corrupting the independence of the Commons. Corruption was at the heart of it — the political corruption built on the general dissoluteness of the populace, so familiar in the history of tyranny and so shocking to observers of mid-eighteenth-century England. The evil, public and private, that had appalled Dickinson in 1754 had ripened, it seemed clear, in the subsequent decade. As early as 1765 there had been nervous speculation in the colonies about what would happen

if the British empire should have filled up the measure of its iniquity and become ripe for ruin; if a proud, arbitrary, selfish, and venal spirit of corruption should ever reign in the British court and diffuse itself through all ranks in the nation; if lucrative posts be multiplied without necessity, and pensioners multiplied without bounds; if the policy of governing be by bribery and corruption, and the trade and manufactures of the nation be disregarded and trampled under foot; if all offices be bought and sold at a high and extravagant price . . . ; and if, to support these shocking enormities and corruptions, the subjects in all quarters must be hard squeezed with the iron arms of oppression.

But the writer was still confident, as Franklin had been a decade earlier, that enough virtue remained in England to overcome the deepening corruption. Three years later, however, it was stated that

The present involved state of the British nation, the rapacity and profuseness of many of her great men, the prodigious number of their dependents who want to be gratified with some office which may enable them to live lazily upon the labor of others, must convince us that we shall be taxed so long as we have a penny to pay,

[36] Baldwin, *Appendix* (JHL 52), pp. 51, 67–68.

and that new offices will be constituted and new officers palmed upon us until the number is so great that we cannot by our constant labor and toil maintain any more.

By 1769 a Boston correspondent of Wilkes commented on "that torrent of corruption which 'like a general flood, has deluged all' to the eternal disgrace of the British nation," and suggested that the reason the "arbitrary and despotic" English government had "extended their ravages to America" was because they had found the British Isles too restricted an area for the full gratification of their "incessant cravings of luxury, extravagance and dissipation." In 1770 Eliot wrote Hollis: "The Lord have mercy on Great Britain! for among the great, I fear, there is scarce a virtuous character to be found. I should be glad to hope it was better among the other ranks, but the people could not be sold if they did not first sell themselves." Charles Carroll was even more emphatic: "I despair of seeing the constitution recover its former vigor. The vast influence of the crown, the luxury of the great, and the depravity of the common people are unsurmountable obstacles to Parliamentary independence . . . The English seem to be arrived to that degree of liberty and of servitude which Galba ascribes to the Roman people in his speech to Piso: *imperaturus es hominibus, qui nec totam servitutem pati possunt, nec totam libertatem.* Those same Romans, a few years after that period, deified the horse of Caligula." Three years later, in 1774, he saw the same, ultimate degradation in England: "The insatiable avarice or worse ambition of corrupt ministers intent on spreading that corruption through America by which they govern absolutely in Great Britain, brought the British empire to the brink of ruin, armed (the expression is not too strong) subject against subject, the parent against the child, ready to add unnatural murders to the horrors of civil war."[37]

[37] Johnson, *Some Important Observations* (JHL 19), p. 20; Thomas Bradbury, *The Ass, or, the Serpent* . . . (1712: reprinted in Boston, 1768), p. 12n; William

That by 1774 the final crisis of the constitution, brought on by political and social corruption, had been reached was, to most informed colonists, evident; but if they had not realized it themselves they would soon have discovered it from the flood of newspapers, pamphlets, and letters that poured in on them from opposition sources in England. Again and again reports from the home country proclaimed that the English nation had departed, once and for all and completely, from the true principles of liberty: the principles not of "certain modern Whigs," as one English pamphlet of 1774, reprinted in the colonies no less than seven times within a year of its first appearance, explained, but of "Whigs before the [Glorious] Revolution and at the time of it; I mean the principles which such men as Mr. Locke, Lord Molesworth, and Mr. Trenchard maintained with their pens, Mr. Hampden and Lord [William] Russell with their blood, and Mr. Algernon Sidney with both." To those Englishmen who in the 1770's most directly inherited and most forcefully propagated these principles — Richard Price, Joseph Priestley, James Burgh — the situation at home if not abroad justified, even exaggerated, the worst fears for the future of liberty that their predecessors had expressed. For these latter-day radicals had witnessed personally the threatening rise of prerogative influence in the English government and its dramatic manifestation in the Wilkes affair; and they had seen revealed the rapacity and bankruptcy of the swollen East India Company, a revelation which illuminated to them the corruption of their era as dramatically as the collapse of the South Sea Company had revealed the rottenness

Palfrey to Wilkes, February 21 and April 12, 1769, MHS *Procs.*, 47 (1913–14), 197, 199; Eliot to Hollis, June 28, 1770, MHS *Colls.*, 4th ser., IV, 453; Carroll to Edmund Jennings and to William Graves, August 9, 1771, August 15, 1774, in *Maryland Historical Magazine*, 32 (1937), 197, 225. The Latin quotation is from Tacitus, *Histories*, I, xvi; it was translated in *Cato's Letters*, no. 41 (which reprints the whole of Galba's speech, after a discursive introduction), as: "You are about to govern the Romans, a people of too little virtue to support complete liberty, of too much spirit to bear absolute bondage."

of the era of George I to Trenchard and Gordon. Everywhere there was cynicism and gluttonous self-seeking. What more was needed to convince one that affairs in Britain were plummeting toward complete and irrecoverable collapse? The long-awaited signs of the total degeneration of the moral qualities necessary to preserve liberty were unmistakable, and these English radicals said so, vigorously, convincingly, in a series of increasingly shrill pamphlets and letters that were read avidly, circulated, published and republished, in America.[38]

But it was not only the radicals. A wide range of public figures and pamphleteers, known and read in America, carried forward the cries of corruption that had been heard in earlier years and directed them to the specific political issues of the day. William Bollan, the former agent and advocate-general of Massachusetts, still well known in America and experienced in analyzing colonial affairs, produced in London in 1768 two pamphlets of blasting condemnation, one "wherein the great mischief and danger of corruption are set forth and proved from its operations in *Greece* and *Rome*," the other covering, as the title indicated, the whole range of *Continued Corruption, Standing Armies, and Popular Discontents*. In the same vein the prominent London printer and publicist (and political conservative) William Strahan wondered, in letters to the Philadelphian David Hall, publisher

[38] [Matthew Robinson-Morris, Lord Rokeby], *Considerations on the Measures Carrying on with Respect to the British Colonies in North America* (2d ed., London, 1774), p. 10. This pamphlet was reprinted three times in Boston, twice in Philadelphia, and once in New York and Hartford in 1774 and 1775. For Abigail Adams' awareness of the identity between Rokeby's views and those of her husband writing as "Novanglus," see her letter of May 22, 1775, in L. H. Butterfield, *et al.*, eds., *Adams Family Correspondence* (Cambridge, 1963), I, 202, 203n11. See also [Joseph Priestley], *An Address to Protestant Dissenters* (Boston, 1774), p. 6; this pamphlet, first published in London in 1773, appeared in three American editions in 1774. And see, in general, Oscar and Mary F. Handlin, "James Burgh and American Revolutionary Theory," MHS *Procs.*, 73 (1961), 38–57; H. Trevor Colbourn, "John Dickinson, Historical Revolutionary," *Pa. Mag.*, 83 (1959), 284; Caroline Robbins, *The Eighteenth-Century Commonwealthman* (Cambridge, 1959), chap. ix.

of the *Pennsylvania Gazette,* whether England had "virtue enough to be saved from that deluge of corruption with which we have been so long overwhelmed" — a concern that gnawed at him as he contemplated the "immense sums [that] are daily given to secure seats in Parliament" and that resulted in the selection of "men who in the east, by rapine and plunder, in most cases attended with the most shocking instances of barbarity, have suddenly acquired immense wealth. Such you will perhaps think not the most proper guardians of our constitution and liberties." He could only hope, he wrote, that "before matters come to extremity the nation . . . the happiest nation this world ever contained . . . will come to their senses, and not suffer a fabric, the work of ages and the envy of the rest of the world, to be materially injured."

But far greater voices than these were heard, some in the highest reaches of the English government. In the year of Burke's *Thoughts on the Present Discontents,* the most famous of all the attacks on the plots of "a certain set of intriguing men . . . *to secure to the court the unlimited and uncontrolled use of its own vast influence under the sole direction of its own private favor* . . . [pursuing] a scheme for undermining all the foundations of our freedom," Burke's patron, the Marquis of Rockingham, explained in a speech in the House of Lords the "total change in the old system of English government" which could be traced to the accession of George III and which alone could explain the secret motivations behind the Stamp Act. But it was left for the colonists' Olympian champion, William Pitt, now Earl of Chatham, to probe the ultimate sources of English corruption. The reason "the constitution at this moment stands violated," this grandson of "Diamond Pitt," East India merchant and governor of Madras, declared, is perfectly clear:

For some years past there has been an influx of wealth into this country which has been attended with many fatal consequences, because it has not been the regular, natural produce of labor and industry. The riches of Asia have been poured in upon us, and have brought with them not only Asiatic luxury but, I fear, Asiatic principles of government. Without connections, without any natural interest in the soil, the importers of foreign gold have forced their way into Parliament by such a torrent of private corruption as no private hereditary fortune could resist. My Lords, I say nothing but what is within the knowledge of us all; the corruption of the people is the great original cause of the discontents of the people themselves, of the enterprise of the crown, and the notorious decay of the internal vigor of the constitution.

Something, he said, must be done, immediately, "to stop the rapid progress of corruption"; he advocated strengthening the health of Parliament as a representative body by increasing the number of representatives from the still independent, unbought constituencies, the counties and the great and growing cities, at the expense of the rotten, purchasable, boroughs.[39]

All of this was borne to America, and there carried conviction to a far larger part of the population, and bore more dramatic implications than it did in England. "Liberty," John Adams wrote, "can no more exist without virtue and independence than the body can live and move without a soul," and what liberty can be expected to flow from England where "luxury, effeminacy, and venality are arrived at such a shocking pitch" and where "both electors and elected are become one mass of corruption"? It was not hard to see where England stood: it was, Adams declared, precisely at the point "where the Roman republic was

[39] The first of Bollan's pamphlets of 1768 is *An Epistle from Timolean* . . . ; for an indication of the curious complication of Bollan's reputation in Massachusetts, see Bailyn, *Pamphlets*, I, 721–722. Strahan to Hall, February 23, 1763; February 13 and March 12, 1768, in *Pa. Mag.*, 10 (1886), 89, 329, 333. (For the publisher Edmund Dilly's similar fear of "bribery and corruption . . . swarms of placemen and pensioners . . . [which] like leeches suck the very vitals . . . of the constitution," see *ibid.*, 83 [1959], 284.) The Rockingham and Chatham speeches are in T. C. Hansard, *The Parliamentary History of England* . . . (London, 1806–1820), XVI, 742, 747, 752.

when Jugurtha left it, and pronounced it 'a venal city, ripe for destruction, if it can only find a purchaser.' " The analogy to the decline and fall of Rome and its empire was intriguing and informative; others carried it further and became more specific. Like Rome in its decline, England, "from being the nursery of heroes, became the residence of musicians, pimps, panders, and catamites." The swift decline of her empire, which, it was observed, had reached its peak only between 1758 and the Stamp Act, resulted from the same poison that had proved so fatal to free states in classical antiquity: the corruption, effeminacy, and languor that came from "the riches and luxuries of the East" and led to a calamitous "decay of virtue" and the collapse of the constitution. Even Franklin, his old caution and careful optimism gone, agreed, writing in 1775 to his one-time political ally Joseph Galloway, that he would himself, reluctantly, have to oppose Galloway's plan for reconciliation.

. . . when I consider the extreme corruption prevalent among all orders of men in this old rotten state, and the glorious public virtue so predominant in our rising country, I cannot but apprehend more mischief than benefit from a closer union. I fear they will drag us after them in all the plundering wars which their desperate circumstances, injustice, and rapacity may prompt them to undertake; and their wide-wasting prodigality and profusion is a gulf that will swallow up every aid we may distress ourselves to afford them. Here numberless and needless places, enormous salaries, pensions, perquisites, bribes, groundless quarrels, foolish expeditions, false accounts or no accounts, contracts and jobs, devour all revenue and produce continual necessity in the midst of natural plenty. I apprehend, therefore, that to unite us intimately will only be to corrupt and poison us also.

Patrick Henry used a variation of the same argument in discussing Galloway's proposal in Congress: "We shall liberate our constituents from a corrupt House of Commons but throw them into the arms of an American legislature that may be bribed by that nation which avows, in the face of the world, that bribery is a part of her system of government." Even Galloway himself had to agree that "Parliament and ministry is wicked and corrupt." So often, so stridently, and so convincingly was it said in the colonies that in England "luxury has arrived to a great pitch; and it is a universal maxim that luxury indicates the declension of a state" — so often was it argued that vigor was gone, exhaustion and poverty approaching, that those who would defend British policy were obliged to debate the point: to assert the health and strength of English society, arguing, as Samuel Seabury did, that England was a "vigorous matron, just approaching a green old age; and with spirit and strength sufficient to chastise her undutiful and rebellious children" and not at all, as his adversary Alexander Hamilton had pictured her, "an old, wrinkled, withered, worn-out hag." [40]

[40] Adams ("Novanglus"), *Works*, IV, 31, 28, 54–55; William Hooper to James Iredell, April 26, 1774, in W. L. Saunders, ed., *Colonial Records of North Carolina* (Raleigh, N.C., 1886–1890), IX, 985–986; William H. Drayton, *A Charge on the Rise of the American Empire* . . . (Charleston, 1776), pp. 2–3; Seabury, *A View*, in Vance, *Letters of a Westchester Farmer*, p. 140; Albert H. Smyth, ed., *Writings of Benjamin Franklin*, VI, 311–312; Edmund C. Burnett, ed., *Letters of Members of the Continental Congress* (Washington, D. C., 1921–1938), I, 53, 54. Analogies to the decline and fall of Rome sprang to the lips of almost every commentator as the crisis in Anglo-American affairs deepened; Arthur Lee's "Monitor" letters, for example — to pick almost at random — are replete with such references (see especially no. II, *Virginia Gazette* [R], March 3, 1768), as are the letters of Charles Carroll. Adams' quotation of Jugurtha's description of Roman venality is from Sallust, *War with Jugurtha*, xxxv, 12–13. Sallust was an invaluable treasury of apothegms and warnings on the consequences of public corruption; it was this theme in Sallust that Thomas Gordon had exploited most fully in the introductory Discourses to his popular translation (1744); note especially Discourse VI. The sentence Adams quotes as of Jugurtha was perhaps Sallust's most memorable phrase for the eighteenth century. It had appeared in *Cato's Letters* (no. 18), and it had been used by Americans to describe England at least as early as 1754 (see Dickinson's letter quoted above, p. 90); it continued to be used throughout the pre-Revolutionary years. Hooper's letter contains a particularly elaborate discussion of Britain, corruption, and the fall of Rome; in it Rome as observed by Jugurtha and England since Walpole are explicitly compared.

The fact that the ministerial conspiracy against liberty had risen from corruption was of the utmost importance to the colonists. It gave a radical new meaning to their claims: it transformed them from constitutional arguments to expressions of a world regenerative creed. For they had long known — it had been known everywhere in the English-speaking world in the eighteenth century — that England was one of the last refuges of the ancient gothic constitution that had once flourished everywhere in the civilized world. And now, in the outpourings of colonial protest, it was again repeated, but with new point and urgency, that by far "the greatest part of the human race" already lies in "total subjection to their rulers." Throughout the whole continent of Asia people are reduced "to such a degree of abusement and degradation"

that the very idea of liberty is unknown among them. In *Africa*, scarce any human beings are to be found but barbarians, tyrants, and slaves: all equally remote from the true dignity of human nature and from a well-regulated state of society. Nor is *Europe* free from the curse. Most of her nations are forced to drink deep of the bitter cup. And in those in which freedom seem to have been established, the vital flame is going out. Two kingdoms, those of *Sweden* and *Poland*, have been betrayed and enslaved in the course of one year. The free towns of *Germany* can remain free no longer than their potent neighbors shall please to let them. *Holland* has got the forms if she has lost the spirit of a free country. *Switzerland* alone is in the full and safe possession of her freedom.

And if now, in this deepening gloom, the light of liberty went out in Britain too — in Britain, where next to "self-preservation, political liberty is the main aim and end of her constitution" — if, as events clearly portended and as "senators and historians are repeatedly predicting . . . continued corruption and standing armies will prove mortal distempers in her constitution" — what then? What refuge will liberty find?

"To our own country," it was answered, "must we look for

the biggest part of that liberty and freedom that yet remains, or is to be expected, among mankind . . . For while the greatest part of the nations of the earth are held together under the yoke of universal slavery, the North American provinces yet remain *the country of free men:* the *asylum,* and the last, to which such may yet flee from the common deluge." More than that: "our native country . . . bids the fairest of any to promote *the perfection and happiness of mankind."* No one, of course, can predict "the state of mankind in future ages." But insofar as one can judge the ultimate "designs of providence by the number and power of the causes that are already at work, we shall be led to think that the perfection and happiness of mankind is to be carried further in America than it has ever yet been in any place." Consider the growth the colonies had enjoyed in so short a time — growth in all ways, but especially in population: a great natural increase it had been, supplemented by multitudes from Europe, "tired out with the miseries they are doomed to at home," migrating to America "as the only country in which they can find food, raiment, and rest." Consider also the physical vigor of the people. But above all consider the moral health of the people and of the body politic.

The fatal arts of luxury and corruption are but comparatively beginning among us . . . Nor is corruption yet established as the common principle in public affairs. Our representatives are not chosen by bribing, corrupting, or buying the votes of the electors. Nor does it take one half of the revenue of a province to manage her house of commons . . . We have been free also from the burden and danger of standing armies . . . Our defense has been our *militia* . . . the general operation of things among ourselves indicate strong tendencies towards a state of greater perfection and happiness than mankind has yet seen.

No one, therefore, can conceive of the cause of America as "the cause of a mob, of a party, or a faction." The cause of America "is the cause of *self-defense,* of *public faith,* and of the *liberties of mankind* . . . 'In our destruction, liberty itself expires, and human nature will despair of evermore regaining its first and original dignity.' "[41]

This theme, elaborately orchestrated by the colonial writers, marked the fulfillment of the ancient idea, deeply embedded in the colonists' awareness, that America had from the start been destined to play a special role in history. The controversy with England, from its beginning in the early 1760's, had lent support to that belief, so long nourished by so many different sources: the covenant theories of the Puritans, certain strands of Enlightenment thought, the arguments of the English radicals, the condition of life in the colonies, even the conquest of Canada. It had been the Stamp Act that had led John Adams to see in the original settlement of the colonies "the opening of a grand scene and design in providence for the illumination of the ignorant and the emancipation of the slavish part of mankind all over the earth." And Jonathan Mayhew, celebrating the conclusion of the same episode, had envisioned future streams of refugees escaping from a Europe sunk in "luxury, debauchery, venality, intestine quarrels, or other vices." It was even possible, Mayhew had added, "who knows?" that "our liberties being thus established, . . . on some future occasion . . . we or our posterity may even have the great felicity and honor to . . . keep Britain herself from ruin."[42]

[41] Samuel Williams, *A Discourse on the Love of Our Country* . . . (Salem, 1775: JHL Pamphlet 55), pp. 21, 22, 23, 25, 26. Cf., e.g., Thomas Coombe, *A Sermon Preached* . . . (Philadelphia, 1775), pp. 19–20; [Richard Wells], *A Few Political Reflections* . . . (Philadelphia, 1774), pp. 38–40, 50.

[42] Adams, *Dissertation*, in *Works*, III, 452n; Mayhew, *Snare Broken* (JHL 20), pp. 36, 38. The concept of America as a refuge for liberty was by no means an exclusively American notion. As early as 1735 James Thomson had celebrated the idea in his book-length poem *Liberty* (the relevant passage is quoted, and the secondary literature cited, in Bailyn, *Pamphlets*, I, 730). The idea that liberty was drifting steadily westward was commonly accepted; Thomas Pownall invoked the notion explicitly in the opening section of his *Administration of the Colonies*: he had long assumed, he wrote, "from the spirit and genius of the

THE LOGIC OF REBELLION

Now, in 1774, that "future occasion" was believed to be at hand. After the passage of the Coercive Acts it could be said that "all the spirit of patriotism or of liberty now left in England" was no more than "the last snuff of an expiring lamp," while "the same sacred flame . . . which once showed forth such wonders in Greece and in Rome . . . burns brightly and strongly in America." Who ought then to suppress as "whimsical and enthusiastical" the belief that the colonies were to become "the foundation of a great and mighty empire, the largest the world ever saw to be founded on such principles of liberty and freedom, both civil and religious . . . [and] which shall be the principal seat of that glorious kingdom which Christ shall erect upon earth in the latter days"? America "ere long will build an empire upon the ruins of Great Britain; will adopt its constitution purged of its impurities, and from an experience of its defects will guard against those evils which have wasted its vigor and brought it to an untimely end." The hand of God was "in America now giving a new epocha to the history of the world."[43]

In the invigorating atmosphere of such thoughts, the final conclusion of the colonists' logic could be drawn not with regret but with joy. For while everyone knew that when tyranny is abroad "submission is a crime"; while they readily acknowledged

people" that the colonies would "become in some future and perhaps not very distant age an asylum to that liberty of mankind which, as it hath been driven by corruption and the consequent tyranny of government, *hath been constantly retiring westward*" (4th ed., 1768, pp. 44–45). Beyond these specific references to America was the more abstract and general notion that overseas territories were the natural sanctuaries for liberty and virtue bedeviled by domestic corruption and authoritarianism. See, e.g., Andrew Eliot's confession of his thrill in reading of the regicide "honest General [Edmund] Ludlow's account of the generous protection afforded him by the magistrates of Berne, and felt a secret pleasure in the thought that there was such a land of liberty to be an asylum to patriots and virtue in distress." To Hollis, January 29, 1769, MHS *Colls.*, 4th ser., IV, 436.
[43] Rokeby, *Considerations*, p. 148; Ebenezer Baldwin, *The Duty of Rejoicing under Calamities and Afflictions* . . . (New York, 1776), p. 38; Hooper to Iredell, cited in note 40 above, pp. 985, 986.

that "no obedience is due to arbitrary, unconstitutional edicts calculated to enslave a free people"; and while they knew that the invasion of the liberties of the people "constitutes a state of war with the people" who may properly use "all the power which God has given them" to protect themselves — nevertheless they hesitated to come to a final separation even after Lexington and Bunker Hill. They hesitated, moving slowly and reluctantly, protesting "before God and the world that the utmost of [our] wish is that things may return to their old channel." They hesitated because their *"sentiments of duty and affection"* were sincere; they hesitated because their respect for constituted authority was great; and they hesitated too because their future as an independent people was a matter of doubt, full of the fear of the unknown.[44]

What would an independent American nation be? A republic, necessarily — and properly, considering the character and circumstances of the people. But history clearly taught that republics were delicate polities, quickly degenerating into anarchy and tyranny; it was impossible, some said, to "recollect a single instance of a nation who supported this form of government for any length of time or with any degree of greatness." Others felt that independence might "split and divide the empire into a number of petty, insignificant states" that would easily fall subject to the will of "some foreign tyrant, or the more intolerable despotism of a few American demagogues"; the colonies might end by being "parceled out, Poland-like."

But if what the faint-hearted called "the ill-shapen, diminutive brat, INDEPENDENCY" contained within it all that remained of freedom; if it gave promise of growing great and strong and becoming the protector and propagator of liberty everywhere;

[44] Johnson, *Some Important Observations* (JHL 19), pp. 21, 23; [Robert Carter Nicholas], *Considerations on the Present State of Virginia Examined* ([Williamsburg], 1774), in the Earl G. Swem edition (New York, 1919), pp. 68, 42.

if it were indeed true that "the cause of America is in a great measure the cause of all mankind"; if " 'Tis not the concern of a day, a year, or an age; posterity are virtually involved in the contest, and will be more or less affected even to the end of time by our proceedings now" — if all of this were true, ways would be found by men inspired by such prospects to solve the problems of a new society and government. And so let every lover of mankind, every hater of tyranny,

stand forth! Every spot of the old world is overrun with oppression. Freedom hath been hunted round the globe. Asia and Africa have long expelled her. Europe regards her like a stranger, and England hath given her warning to depart. O! receive the fugitive, and prepare in time an asylum for mankind.[45]

[45] Braxton, *Address* (JHL 66), p. 19; Seabury, *A View,* in Vance, *Letters of a Westchester Farmer,* pp. 12, 117; [Daniel Leonard] ("Massachusettensis"), *The Origin of the American Contest with Great-Britain* . . . (New York, 1775: JHL Pamphlet 56), p. 84; [Joseph Galloway], *A Candid Examination of the Mutual Claims of Great-Britain and the Colonies* . . . (New York, 1775), p. 31; [Thomas Paine], *Common Sense* . . . (Philadelphia, 1776: JHL Pamphlet 63), pp. [ii], 30, 60.

A NOTE ON CONSPIRACY

As I have indicated at length in Chapters III and IV, the conviction on the part of the Revolutionary leaders that they were faced with a deliberate conspiracy to destroy the balance of the constitution and eliminate their freedom had deep and widespread roots — roots elaborately embedded in Anglo-American political culture. How far back in time one may trace these roots it is difficult to say, but I have attempted at least to illustrate in the pages above, and to show in considerable detail elsewhere,[1] that the configuration of attitudes and ideas that would constitute the Revolutionary ideology was present a half-century before there was an actual Revolution, and that among the dominant elements in this pattern were the fear of corruption — of its anticonstitutional destructiveness — and of the menace of a ministerial conspiracy. At the very first signs of conflict between the colonies and the administration in the early 1760's the question of motivation was openly broached and the imputation of secret purposes discussed. Early in the controversy anti-administration leaders like Oxenbridge Thacher could only "suppose" for the sake of discussion "that no design is formed to enslave them," while pro-administration partisans, like Martin Howard, Jr., were forced to refute the charge of design.[2] To be

---

[1] *The Origins of American Politics* (New York, 1968).

[2] [Oxenbridge Thacher], *The Sentiments of a British American* (Boston, 1764: JHL Pamphlet 8), p. 4; [Martin Howard, Jr.], *A Letter from a Gentleman at Halifax* . . . (Newport, 1765: JHL Pamphlet 10), p. 6. Similarly, Daniel Dulany felt obliged to argue the point, writing in 1773, when he was neutral in his sympathies, that "I should hardly expect to find [substantial merchants] in a plot against liberty, since commerce is ever engrafted on the stock of liberty, and must feel every wound that is given to it." Elihu S. Riley, ed., *Correspondence of "First Citizen" — Charles Carroll of Carrollton, and "Antilon" — Daniel Dulany, Jr.* . . . (Baltimore, 1902), p. 35.

sure, the conviction that the colonies, and England itself, were faced with a deliberate, anti-libertarian design grew most quickly where the polarization of politics was most extreme and where radical leaders were least inhibited in expressing and reinforcing general apprehensions. But in some degree it was present every-where; it was almost universally shared by sympathizers of the American cause. The views of John Dickinson are particularly interesting, not merely because, though the most cautious and reluctant of Revolutionary leaders, he so forcefully conveyed the idea of conspiracy, but because he understood so well the psycho-logical and political effects of thinking in precisely these con-spiratorial terms. Reviewing the crisis of Charles I's reign, he pointed out that

acts that might *by themselves* have been upon many considerations excused or extenuated derived a contagious malignancy and odium from other acts with which they were connected. They were not re-garded according to the simple force of each but as parts of a system of oppression. Every one, therefore, however small in itself, became alarming as an additional evidence of tyrannical designs. It was in vain for prudent and moderate men to insist that there was no neces-sity to abolish royalty. Nothing less than the utter destruction of the monarchy could satisfy those who *had* suffered and thought they had reason to believe they always *should* suffer under it. The consequences of these mutual distrusts are well known.[3]

The explosion of long-smoldering fears of ministerial con-spiracy was by no means an exclusively American phenomenon. It was experienced in England too, in a variety of ways, by a wide range of the English political public. Under George III, George Rudé has pointed out, it was

widely believed . . . that the influence of the Crown was being used to staff the administration with new Favourites and "King's Friends," who formed a secret Closet party, beyond the control of Parliament and guided behind the scenes by the sinister combination of the Earl

[3] Dickinson, *Farmer's Letters* (JHL 23), pp. 58–59 (cf. pp. 62–64).

of Bute (who had resigned office in 1763) and the Princess Dowager of Wales. Opponents of the new system talked darkly of a repetition of "the end of Charles II's reign" — and such talk was not confined to the circles of the Duke of Newcastle and others, who might be inclined to identify the eclipse of their own public authority with that of the national interest.

Such expressions, Rudé concludes, "were common currency and abound throughout this period both in the press, in Burke's *Thoughts on the Present Discontents* (1770), in personal correspondence, pamphlet literature and speeches in Parliament." [4] Burke's *Thoughts* is particularly relevant to the American situation, for the apprehension that dominates that piece is in essence interchangeable with that of innumerable Revolutionary writers. Its argument that Parliament was on the brink of falling "under the control of an unscrupulous gang of would-be despots" who would destroy the constitution "was sufficiently widely believed," Ian Christie has written, "to give momentum in due course to a radical movement in the metropolis." [5] The specific identification in *Thoughts* of the conspiratorial cabal at work was distinctively Burke's, but those who most vehemently disagreed with him about the source and nature of the conspiracy were

[4] Rudé, *Wilkes and Liberty*, p. 186.

[5] Ian R. Christie, *Wilkes, Wyvill and Reform* (London, 1962), p. 32. Burke expressed his more general fears privately to his friend Charles O'Hara in the year the *Thoughts* was published: "Without some extraordinary change . . . the court [working with the mob] may assume as uncontrolled a power in this country as the King of Sweden has done in his, without running any risks or meeting any more opposition than is just convenient to give their measures the sort of countenance that things receive from the supposition of their having been fairly debated. I know that this has been said ever since the Crown has got its great influence in Parliament. But it was not truly said while the people preferred one man to another; it was not said truly while a new ministry supposed a new Parliament; it was not said truly whilst it required art, address, and influence to secure a majority. Whether or no things were prepared for this in the last reign I cannot justly say; but this sort of power was then either not fully discovered, or nobody chose to venture upon it." Burke to O'Hara, September 30, 1770, *The Correspondence of Edmund Burke* (Thomas W. Copeland, *et al.*, eds., Cambridge and Chicago, 1958–), II, 336–337.

no less convinced that a conspiratorial cabal of some sort was in fact at work. Catharine Macaulay, speaking for the extreme radicals, found it in the "maneuvers of aristocratic faction and party" of which Burke and the Rockinghams were themselves the inheritors and which was based on "a system of corruption [that] began at the very period of the [Glorious] Revolution and . . . was the policy of every succeeding administration." Horace Walpole too felt that Burke had not gone back far enough: "The canker had begun in the administration of the Pelhams," in the effort of the clique around the Princess Dowager "to inspire arbitrary principles into her son [the future George III] and to instruct him how to . . . establish a despotism that may end in tyranny in his descendants." [6]

For Horace Walpole, therefore, the immediate villain was Bute, who had arrived on the scene, Walpole wrote, with the triple disability of being "unknown, ungracious, and a Scot"; his influence, it was believed, continued through the sixties un-abated, and by the early 1770's "Lord North had flung himself into the hands of Lord Bute's junto." In believing this, Walpole was scarcely alone. The conviction that Bute's secret influence lay behind the troubles of the time was widespread in opposition circles in England as it was in America. Seven years after Bute left office, Chatham delivered a speech in the Lords against "the secret influence of an invisible power — of a favorite, whose pernicious counsels had occasioned all the present unhappiness and disturbances in the nation, and who, notwithstanding he was abroad, was at this moment as potent as ever." Rockingham, who was convinced that Bute's secret influence had destroyed his administration in 1765–66, wrote in 1767 that his party's "fundamental principle" was to resist and restrain "the power

[6] Catharine Macaulay, *Observations on a Pamphlet, Entitled, Thoughts on the Cause of the Present Discontents* (3d ed., London, 1770), pp. 7, 13; Romney Sedgwick, ed., *Letters from George III to Lord Bute, 1756–1766* (London, 1939), p. xli.

and influence of Lord Bute." More ordinary opinion was reflected by the printer and publicist William Strahan, who in fact thought well of Bute but who agreed that his secret influence remained paramount long after his resignation from office. Strahan's colleague in the press, John Almon, not only blamed the evils of the time on Bute but believed that the Rockinghams were secretly cooperating with him. Indeed, the image of Bute as a malevolent and well-nigh indestructible machinator was almost universal among the opposition. Propagated endlessly in pamphlets and newssheets of all sorts, caricatured in a torrent of lurid cartoons depicting " 'the thane' as the lover of the Princess Dowager of Wales . . . and thus the bestower of posts and pensions to hordes of hungry barbarous Scots to the exclusion of the English," the idea of Bute as the central plotter became one of the keystones in the structure of opposition ideology, and it contributed forcefully to the belief, in England as well as in America, that an active conspiracy against the constitution was underway.[7]

Not everyone, of course, even within opposition circles, agreed that there was a deliberate design to overthrow the balance of the constitution; fewer still agreed with the republican radicals that the Coercive Acts were intended to "enslave America; and the same minister who means to enslave them would, if he had an opportunity, enslave England." Yet Lord Dartmouth felt it necessary to refute that charge specifically, and while it is true, as Christie has explained, that "abundant evidence now available

[7] Horace Walpole, *Memoirs of the Reign of King George the Third* (Denis Le Marchant, ed., London, 1845), I, 10; III, 233; IV, 92; Hansard, *Parliamentary History*, XVI, 842 (cf. Walpole, *Memoirs*, IV, 94); Foord, *His Majesty's Opposition*, p. 314 and n. 2; J. A. Cochrane, *Dr. Johnson's Printer* (Cambridge, 1964), p. 173, n. 3; Harvey C. Mansfield, Jr., *Statesmanship and Party Government* (Chicago, 1965), p. 104; Christie, *Wilkes, Wyvill and Reform*, pp. 35, 11; M. Dorothy George, *English Political Caricature to 1792* (Oxford, 1959), I, 120–121. On the actuality of Bute's influence, see Richard Pares, *King George III and the Politicians* (Oxford, 1953), pp. 104–109.

about the activities of court and government enables historians to dismiss this fear as a chimera," it is nevertheless also true that there was a "contemporary belief in such a threat," a belief that was associated with the American crisis and that proved to be "a powerful stimulus to demands for reform" in English domestic affairs. "The sophisticated members of political society rightly dismissed as rubbish the misconceived but genuine radical fear, that the triumph of British arms and authority in America would be followed by the extinction of British liberties at home," but the fear remained, widespread enough, powerful enough, to force disbelievers to acknowledge it and to confront it. Thus the cool, well-informed, and hard-headed Dr. John Fothergill, the secret negotiator between Franklin and Dartmouth in the winter of 1774–75, felt it necessary to explain that he did "not quite" credit the ministry with "endeavoring to enslave [the colonists] by system. I believe they are very happy if they can find expedients for the present moment." So too Strahan wrote rather desperately to his American correspondent that "I know the *good disposition* of the ministry towards you . . . *I know* there is no disposition, either in the King, the ministry, or the Parliament, to oppress America in any shape." [8]

That this was the issue, for thoughtful and informed people, on which decisions of loyalty to the government turned is nowhere so clearly and sensitively revealed as in the record Peter Van Schaack left of his tormented meditations of January, 1776. A wellborn, scholarly, and articulate New Yorker of 29 who prepared himself for deciding the question of his personal loyalty

[8] John Sawbridge, quoted in Gipson, *British Empire*, XII, 127, 136; Christie, *Wilkes, Wyvill and Reform*, pp. 127, 136, 223, 67; Fothergill to Lt. Col. Ironside, December 22, 1774, in *Bulletin of the Friends Historical Society*, 5 (1913), 5; Strahan to David Hall, August 24, 1770, November 10, 1768, *Pa. Mag.*, XI (1887–88), 351; X (1886), 464. Fothergill admitted, however, that there was a high degree of "national corruption," which he explained not as a result of "the riches of the east" but rather of the sensualism and libertinism generated by slavery that the West India planters brought back to England.

by undertaking in seclusion a critical examination of the works of Locke, Vattel, Montesquieu, Grotius, Beccaria, and Pufendorf, he noted first his fear of the destructive consequences of conceding Parliament's right to bind the colonies in all cases whatsoever. That danger, he wrote, was perfectly clear. "But my difficulty arises from this," he said:

that taking the whole of the acts complained of together, they do not, I think, manifest a system of slavery, but may fairly be imputed to human frailty and the difficulty of the subject. Most of them seem to have sprung out of particular occasions, and are unconnected with each other . . . In short, I think those acts may have been passed without a preconcerted plan of enslaving us, and it appears to me that the more favorable construction ought ever to be put on the conduct of our rulers. I cannot therefore think the government *dissolved;* and as long as the society lasts, the power that every individual gave the society when he entered into it, can never revert to the individual again but will always remain in the community.* [*footnote:*]* Locke.[9]

All of this, however, forms but one side of the role of conspiratorial thinking in the advent of the Revolution. There is an obverse to this that is of great importance, though, since in the end it was not in itself determinative of events, it has of necessity been neglected in the chapter above.

The opponents of the Revolution — the administration itself — were as convinced as were the leaders of the Revolutionary movement that they were themselves the victims of conspiratorial designs. Officials in the colonies, and their superiors in England, were persuaded as the crisis deepened that they were confronted

[9] Henry C. Van Schaack, *The Life of Peter Van Schaack* (New York, 1842), pp. 58, 56–57. So too James Iredell, reconstructing in 1776 the evolution of the policies of the Continental Congress, explained that the starting point for all policy decisions had been a careful estimation of the motivation of the ministry: had Grenville, it was asked, "acted from *principle* and not from any *bad motive*"? Iredell, "Causes Leading up to the American Revolution," in Griffith J. McRee, ed., *Life and Correspondence of James Iredell . . .* (New York, 1857–58), I, 312 ff.

A NOTE ON CONSPIRACY

by an active conspiracy of intriguing men whose professions masked their true intentions. As early as 1760 Governor Bernard of Massachusetts had concluded that a "faction" had organized a conspiracy against the customs administration, and by the end of the decade he and others in similar positions (including that "arch-conspirator" Thomas Hutchinson) had little doubt that at the root of all the trouble in the colonies was the maneuvering of a secret, power-hungry cabal that professed loyalty to England while assiduously working to destroy the bonds of authority and force a rupture between England and her colonies.[10]

The charge was quickly echoed in England. The Massachusetts Convention of 1768 elicited from the House of Lords resolutions based on the belief that "wicked and designing men" in the colonies were "evidently manifesting a design . . . to set up a new and unconstitutional authority independent of the crown of England."[11] Such dangerous charges, tantamount to treason but objectively indistinguishable from faction — which was itself, in eighteenth-century terms, merely the superlative form of party[12] — had been a source of concern in the colonies since the start of the controversy. Under Grenville, Arthur Lee wrote, "every expression of discontent . . . was imputed to a desire in those colonies to dissolve all connection with Britain; every tumult here was inflamed into rebellion." The fear that colonial leaders

[10] Bernard's fear of a conspiratorial faction is the main theme that runs through his extensive correspondence of the 1760's (13 vols., Sparks MSS, Houghton Library, Harvard University, excerpted in *The Barrington-Bernard Correspondence* . . . , Edward Channing and A. C. Coolidge, eds., Cambridge, 1912); see also Gipson, *British Empire*, X, 116; XI, 33–34, 155, 157, 159; Bernard to Earl of Halifax, December 2, 1763, in Josiah Quincy, Jr., *Reports of Cases . . . in the Superior Court of Judicature . . . Between 1761 and 1772 . . .* (Samuel M. Quincy, ed., Boston, 1865), p. 394.

[11] Hansard, *Parliamentary History*, pp. 479, 478 (cf. Gipson, *British Empire*, XI, 234, 244).

[12] "Faction is to party what the superlative is to the positive: party is a political evil, and faction is the worst of all parties." Bolingbroke, "The Idea of a Patriot King," in *Works* . . . (London, 1754), III, 83.

nursed secret ambitions that they masked, with greater or lesser success, by continuing professions of loyalty grew as the crisis deepened. If in 1771 Hutchinson, an equal with his arch-enemies the Adamses in detecting secret purposes behind open professions, could report with relief that "the faction in this province against the government is dying," he still felt it necessary to add "but it dies hard." After the Tea Party such cautious optimism faded, and officials confirmed once and for all their belief that malevolent factions were implacably at work seeking to satisfy hidden ambitions and to destroy the ties to England.[13]

Such charges were commonly heard: among crown officials, at every level; but also in other circles — among Tories, such as those in inland Worcester, Massachusetts, who defied the majority, and the leadership, of the Town Meeting, and published a denunciation of "the artful, crafty, and insidious practices of some evil-minded and ill-disposed persons who . . . intend to reduce all things to a state of tumult, discord, and confusion." The committees of correspondence, they declared, had been the illegal creations of "a junto to serve particular designs and purposes of their own . . . tending directly to sedition, civil war, and rebellion." [14]

Such denunciations of the work of seditious factions seeking private aims masked by professions of loyalty, which abound in the writings of officials and of die-hard Tories, reach the extreme of vilification in Chief Justice Peter Oliver's scurrilous *Origin & Progress of the American Rebellion* and attain the ultimate in respectability in George III's statement to Parliament of October 26, 1775 — a statement that may be taken as the precise obverse of Jefferson's claim, in the Declaration of Independence, that

---

[13] "Monitor IX," *Virginia Gazette* (R), April 21, 1768; Frothingham, *Warren,* p. 158.

[14] William Lincoln, *History of Worcester, Massachusetts . . .* (Worcester, 1837), pp. 87, 88. (I owe this reference to Richard D. Brown.)

there was a "design to reduce [the colonies] under absolute despotism."

> The authors and promoters of this desperate conspiracy [George III informed Parliament] have in the conduct of it derived great advantage from the difference of our intentions and theirs. They meant only to amuse, by vague expressions of attachment to the parent state and the strongest protestations of loyalty to me, whilst they were preparing for a general revolt . . . The rebellious war now levied is . . . manifestly carried on for the purpose of establishing an independent empire.

This charge, emanating from the highest source, could not be left unanswered, and there lies in the records of the Continental Congress an elaborate refutation of the King's accusation — an essay, remarkably verbose and rhetorical, crowded with exclamations and gesticulations yet full of subtle perceptions, that fills no less than thirteen pages in the printed *Journals* of the Congress. Cast in the form of an "Address to the Inhabitants of the Colonies," it was written by a committee headed by John Dickinson and James Wilson, and though it was tabled by the Congress because it seemed unduly apologetic and defensive at the time (February 1776) and, in Madison's phrase, was "evidently short of the subsisting maturity" of opinion then in favor of independence, it nevertheless remains a most revealing exposition of the intellectual, political, and psychological dilemmas created by an escalating mutuality of conspiratorial fears. The Crown's representation of the actions of the Congress as those of "a seditious and unwarrantable combination," Wilson and Dickinson wrote, is malicious and false.

> We are, we presume, the first rebels and conspirators who commenced their conspiracy and rebellion with a system of conduct immediately and directly frustrating every aim which ambition or

rapaciousness could propose. Those whose fortunes are desperate may upon slighted evidence be charged with desperate designs. But how improbable is it that the colonists who have been happy and have known their happiness in the quiet possession of their liberties; who see no situation more to be desired than that in which, till lately, they have been placed; and whose warmest wish is to be re-installed in the enjoyment of that freedom which they claim and are entitled to as men and as British subjects — how improbable is it that *such* would, without any motives that could tempt even the most *profligate* minds to crimes, plunge themselves headlong into all the guilt and danger and distress with which those that endeavor to overturn the constitution of their country are always surrounded and frequently overwhelmed? . . . Whoever gives impartial attention to the facts we have already stated and to the observations we have already made must be fully convinced that all the steps which have been taken by us in this unfortunate struggle can be accounted for as rationally and as satisfactorily by supposing that the defense and re-establishment of their rights were the objects which the colonists and their representatives had in view as by supposing that an inde-pendent empire was their aim. Nay, we may safely go farther and affirm, without the most distant apprehension of being refuted, that many of those steps can be accounted for rationally and satisfactorily only upon the former supposition and cannot be accounted for, in that manner, upon the latter . . . Cannot our whole conduct be reconciled to *principles and views of self-defense?* Whence then the uncandid imputation of *aiming at an independent empire?* Is no regard to be had to the professions and protestations made by us, on so many different occasions, of attachment to Great Britain, of allegiance to His Majesty, and of submission to his government upon the terms on which the constitution points it out as a duty and on which alone a *British sovereign* has a right to demand it? . . . But the nature of this connection, and the principles on which it was originally formed and on which alone it can be maintained seem unhappily to have been misunderstood or disregarded by those who laid and conducted the late destructive plan of colony-adminis-tration.

Their conclusion was resigned: "Let neither our enemies nor our friends make improper inferences from the solicitude which we have discovered to remove the imputation of aiming to establish an independent empire. Though an independent empire is not our *wish,* it may — let your oppressors attend — it may be the fate of our countrymen and ourselves." [15]

By then, in February of 1776, the lines of political division had long since hardened; troops were engaged in hostilities. Yet the accusations of malign purpose continued, culminating on the American side in the enumeration of conspiratorial efforts that forms the substance of the Declaration of Independence, and on the English side in a group of publications refuting those charges. The most interesting, if not the ablest, of these replies is by the ubiquitous Thomas Hutchinson, an exile in England since 1774, and, though consulted by the ministry and honored by Oxford University, still desperately eager to convince the world that his original suspicions had been correct. His *Strictures upon the Declaration of the Congress at Philadelphia* was his penultimate effort (his *History* would be the last) to prove that "if no taxes or duties had been laid upon the colonies, other pretenses would have been found for exception to the authority of Parliament." For the colonies, he explained, had been "easy and quiet" before the famous controversies started; "but there were men in each of the principal colonies who had independence in view before any of those taxes were laid or proposed . . . Their design of independence began soon after the reduction of Canada." Failing to attain their goals by arguments from the natural rights of mankind, they found "some grievances, real or imaginary, were therefore necessary." These they produced simply by seeing to it "that every fresh incident which could be made to serve the purpose . . . should be improved accordingly." Professions of

---

[15] Merrill Jensen, ed., *American Colonial Documents to 1776 (English Historical Documents,* IX, London, 1955), p. 851; *Journals of the Continental Congress, 1774–1789* (W. C. Ford, *et al.,* eds., Washington, D.C., 1904–1937), IV, 146n, 139, 141, 142, 144, 146. Cf. references in Burnett, *Letters,* I, 348, and *American Historical Review,* I (1895–96), 684 ff.

loyalty and concessions were "only intended to amuse the authority in England." No indulgence short of independence could ever have satisfied them, "for this was the object from the beginning." The chiefs of the rebellion in each colony found grounds "to irritate and enflame the minds of the people and dispose them to revolt"; and so it was that "many thousands of people who were before good and loyal subjects have been deluded and by degrees induced to rebel." The design, Hutchinson concluded, after answering one by one every charge in the Declaration, "has too well succeeded." [16]

The accusations of conspiratorial designs did not cease with the pamphlet series touched off by the Declaration, nor even with the American successes in battle. They merely shifted their forms, and began a process of adaptation that has allowed them to survive into our own time. Just as radical pamphleteers in England, patriot historians in America, and such Whig leaders as the younger Pitt continued after the war to blame the Revolution on the deliberate malevolence of the administrations of the 1760's and 1770's, so loyalists like Galloway and Thomas Jones continued to "expose" the Americans' conspiracy; continued to argue that no error had been committed by the government of George III in not conceding more to America since the colonists had been secretly determined from the start to cast off their dependence upon England; continued too to link the rebels with opposition factions in England; and began, in the nadir of military defeat, darkly to suggest that the strangely defeated commander in chief, Sir William Howe, was himself not above

[16] John H. Hazelton, *The Declaration of Independence, Its History* (New York, 1906), pp. 232 ff.; [Thomas Hutchinson], *Strictures* . . . (Malcolm Freiberg, ed., Boston, 1958 [*Old South Leaflets*, no. 227]), pp. 5–7, 9. See also the English government's quasi-official 132-page *Answer to the Declaration of the American Congress* (London, 1776), written, on commission of the Treasury, by John Lind.

suspicion of secret collaboration with the faction that had carried out so successfully the long-planned design of independence.[17]

These wartime and postwar accusations were both an end and a beginning — an end of the main phase of the ideological Revolution and the beginning of its transmutation into historiography. Charges of conspiratorial design settled easily into a structure of historical interpretation, on the one hand by Hutchinson, in the manuscript third volume of his *History of . . . Massachusetts-Bay* (published 1828); by Peter Oliver, in his frenzied *Origin & Progress of the American Rebellion* (1781, published 1961); by Thomas Jones, in his *History of New York during the Revolutionary War* (1780–1790, published 1879); by Jonathan Boucher, in the book-length Introduction of his *View of the Causes and Consequences of the American Revolution* (1797); — and on the other hand by Mercy Otis Warren, in her three-volume *History of the . . . American Revolution* (1805); by David Ramsay, in his *History of the American Revolution* (1789); and by patriot historians of individual states: Belknap, Burk, Trumbull, Ramsay. These are the histories of participants, or near-participants: heroic histories, highly personified and highly moral, in which the conspiratorial arguments propounded during the Revolution are the essential stuff of explanation. These views, caricatured and mythologized in such immortal potboilers as Weems' *Washington,* survived almost unaltered through the next generation — survived, indeed, through the next two generations — to enter in a new guise into the assumptions of twentieth-century scholarship. The "progressive" historians of the early twentieth century and their successors of the post-World War I era adopted un-

---

[17] On the supposed link-up among colonial conspirators, opposition factions in England, and the suspicious conduct of General Howe on the field of battle, see especially Joseph Galloway's *Historical and Political Reflections on the Rise and Progress of the American Rebellion* . . . (London, 1780), and his *A Reply to . . . Sir William Howe* . . . (London, 1780).

knowingly the Tory interpretation in writing off the Revolutionary leaders' professed fears of "slavery" and of conspiratorial designs as what by then had come to be known as propaganda. They implied when they did not state explicitly that these extravagant, seemingly paranoiac fears were deliberately devised for the purpose of controlling the minds of a presumably passive populace in order to accomplish predetermined ends — Independence and in many cases personal advancement — that were not openly professed. No Tory or administration apologist during the Revolution itself ever assumed more casually than did such distinguished modern scholars as Philip Davidson and John C. Miller that the fears expressed by the Revolutionary leadership were factitious instruments deliberately devised to manipulate an otherwise inert public opinion. Conversely, nowhere in the patriot literature of the Revolution proper is there a more elaborate effort to prove that there was in actuality a ministerial conspiracy — a plot of King's friends aimed at victimizing the colonists — than that made by Oliver Dickerson in his *Navigation Acts and the American Revolution* (1951).[18]

But the eighteenth century was an age of ideology; the beliefs and fears expressed on one side of the Revolutionary controversy were as sincere as those expressed on the other. The result, anticipated by Burke as early as 1769, was an "escalation" of distrust toward a disastrous deadlock: "The Americans," Burke said, "have made a discovery, or think they have made one, that we mean to oppress them: we have made a discovery, or think

[18] See especially Philip Davidson, *Propaganda and the American Revolution, 1763–1783* (Chapel Hill, 1941); John C. Miller, *Sam Adams, Pioneer in Propaganda* (Boston, 1936), and his *Origins of the American Revolution* (Boston, 1943). For an excellent account of the process by which the ideological arguments of participants in the Revolution became built into the structure of historical explanation, see Sydney G. Fisher, "The Legendary and Myth-making Process in Histories of the American Revolution," *Proceedings of the American Philosophical Society*, 51 (1912), 53–75.

we have made one, that they intend to rise in rebellion against us . . . we know not how to advance; they know not how to retreat . . . Some party must give way." [19]

---

[19] *Sir Henry Cavendish's Debates of the House of Commons* . . . (John Wright, ed., London, 1841–1843), I, 398–399.

Chapter V
TRANSFORMATION

But what do we mean by the American Revolution? Do we mean the American war? The Revolution was effected before the war commenced. The Revolution was in the minds and hearts of the people; a change in their religious sentiments, of their duties and obligations . . . *This radical change in the principles, opinions, sentiments, and affections of the people was the real American Revolution.*

— John Adams to Hezekiah Niles, 1818

IT WAS an elevating, transforming vision: a new, fresh, vigorous, and above all morally regenerate people rising from obscurity to defend the battlements of liberty and then in triumph standing forth, heartening and sustaining the cause of freedom everywhere. In the light of such a conception everything about the colonies and their controversy with the mother country took on a new appearance. Provincialism was gone: Americans stood side by side with the heroes of historic battles for freedom and with the few remaining champions of liberty in the present. What were once felt to be defects — isolation, institutional simplicity, primitiveness of manners, multiplicity of religions, weakness in the authority of the state — could now be seen as virtues, not only by Americans themselves but by enlightened spokesmen of reform, renewal, and hope wherever they might be — in London coffeehouses, in Parisian *salons,* in the courts of German princes. The mere existence of the colonists suddenly became philosophy teaching by example. Their manners, their morals, their way of life, their physical, social, and political condition were seen to vindicate eternal truths and to demonstrate, as ideas and words never could, the virtues of the heavenly city of the eighteenth-century philosophers.

But the colonists' ideas and words counted too, and not merely because they repeated as ideology the familiar utopian phrases of the Enlightenment and of English libertarianism. What they were saying by 1776 was familiar in a general way to reformers and illuminati everywhere in the Western world; yet it was different. Words and concepts had been reshaped in the colonists' minds in the course of a decade of pounding controversy — strangely reshaped, turned in unfamiliar directions, toward conclusions they could not themselves clearly perceive. They found a new world of political thought as they struggled to work out the implications of their beliefs in the years before Independence. It was a world not easily possessed; often they withdrew in some confusion to more familiar ground. But they touched its boundaries, and, at certain points, probed its interior. Others, later — writing and revising the first state constitutions, drafting and ratifying the federal constitution, and debating in detail, exhaustively, the merits of these efforts — would resume the search for resolutions of the problems the colonists had broached before 1776.

This critical probing of traditional concepts — part of the colonists' effort to express reality as they knew it and to shape it to ideal ends — became the basis for all further discussions of enlightened reform, in Europe as well as in America. The radicalism the Americans conveyed to the world in 1776 was a transformed as well as a transforming force.

1. REPRESENTATION AND CONSENT

The question of representation was the first serious intellectual problem to come between England and the colonies, and while it was not the most important issue involved in the Anglo-American controversy (the whole matter of taxation and representation was "a mere incident," Professor McIlwain has observed, in a much more basic constitutional struggle[1]), it received the earliest and most exhaustive examination and underwent a most revealing transformation. This shift in conception took place rapidly; it began and for all practical purposes concluded in the two years of the Stamp Act controversy. But the intellectual position worked out by the Americans in that brief span of time had deep historical roots; it crystallized, in effect, three generations of political experience. The ideas the colonists put forward, rather than creating a new condition of fact, expressed one that had long existed; they articulated and in so doing generalized, systematized, gave moral sanction to what had emerged haphazardly, incompletely and insensibly, from the chaotic factionalism of colonial politics.

What had taken place in the earlier years of colonial history was the partial re-creation, as a matter of fact and not of theory, of a kind of representation that had flourished in medieval England but that had faded and been superseded by another during the fifteenth and sixteenth centuries. In its original, medieval, form elective representation to Parliament had been a device by which "local men, locally minded, whose business began and ended with the interests of the constituency," were enabled, as attorneys for their electors, to seek redress from the royal court of Parliament, in return for which they were expected to commit their constituents to grants of financial aid. Attendance at Parliament of representatives of the commons was for the most part an obligation unwillingly performed, and local communities bound their representatives to local interests in every way possible: by requiring local residency or the ownership of local

[1] Charles H. McIlwain, "The Historical Background of Federal Government," *Federalism as a Democratic Process* (New Brunswick, N.J., 1942), p. 35.

property as a qualification for election, by closely controlling the payment of wages for official services performed, by instructing representatives minutely as to their powers and the limits of permissible concessions, and by making them strictly accountable for all actions taken in the name of the constituents. As a result, representatives of the commons in the medieval Parliaments did not speak for that estate in general or for any other body or group larger than the specific one that had elected them.[2]

Changing circumstances, however, had drastically altered this form and practice of representation. By the time the institutions of government were taking firm shape in the American colonies, Parliament in England had been transformed. The restrictions that had been placed upon representatives of the commons to make them attorneys of their constituencies fell away; members came to sit "not merely as parochial representatives, but as delegates of all the commons of the land." Symbolically incorporating the state, Parliament in effect had become the nation for purposes of government, and its members virtually if not actually, symbolically if not by sealed orders, spoke for all as well as for the group that had chosen them. They stood for the interest of the realm; for Parliament, in the words by which Edmund Burke immortalized this whole concept of representation, was not "a *congress* of ambassadors from different and hostile interests, which interests each must maintain, as an agent and advocate, against other agents and advocates; but Parliament is a *deliberative* assembly of *one* nation, with *one* interest, that of the whole, where, not local purposes, not local prejudices ought to guide, but the general good, resulting from the general reason of the whole." "Instructions, therefore," Speaker Onslow said, "from particular constituents to their own Members are or can be only

---

[2] *Interim Report . . . on House of Commons Personnel . . .* (London, 1932), quoted in George L. Haskins, *The Growth of English Representative Government* (Philadelphia, 1948), p. 130; also pp. 111, 76–77.

of information, advice, and recommendation . . . but not absolutely binding upon votes and actings and conscience in Parliament." The restrictions once placed upon representatives to make them attorneys of their constituencies fell away.[3]

But the colonists, reproducing English institutions in miniature, had been led by force of circumstance to move in the opposite direction. Starting with seventeenth-century assumptions, out of necessity they drifted backward, as it were, toward the medieval forms of attorneyship in representation. Their surroundings had recreated to a significant extent the conditions that had shaped the earlier experiences of the English people. The colonial towns and counties, like their medieval counterparts, were largely autonomous, and they stood to lose more than they were likely to gain from a loose acquiescence in the action of central government. More often than not they felt themselves to be the benefactors rather than the beneficiaries of central government, provincial or imperial; and when they sought favors from higher authorities they sought local and particular — in effect private — favors. Having little reason to identify their interests with those of the central government, they sought to keep the voices of local interests clear and distinct; and where it seemed necessary, they moved — though with little sense of innovating or taking actions of broad significance, and nowhere comprehensively or systematically — to bind representatives to local interests. The Massachusetts town meetings began the practice of voting instructions to their deputies to the General Court in the first years of settle-

---

[3] S. B. Chrimes, *English Constitutional Ideas in the Fifteenth Century* (Cambridge, England, 1936), p. 131. On the political functioning of this form of representation, see Samuel H. Beer, "The Representation of Interests in British Government: Historical Background," *American Political Science Review,* 51 (1957), 614–628. Burke's statement is from his speech to the electors of Bristol, 1774; for Speaker Onslow's almost identical understanding that "Every Member, as soon as he is chosen, becomes a representative of the whole body of the Commons, without any distinction of the place from whence he is sent to Parliament," see W. C. Costin and J. Steven Watson, eds., *The Law and Working of the Constitution: Documents, 1660–1914* (London, 1952), I, 392.

ment, and they continued to do so whenever it seemed useful throughout the subsequent century and a half. Elsewhere, with variations, it was the same; and elsewhere, as in Massachusetts, it became customary to require representatives to be residents of, as well as property owners in, the localities that elected them, and to check upon their actions as delegates. With the result that disgruntled contemporaries felt justified in condemning Assemblies composed "of plain, illiterate husbandmen, whose views seldom extended farther than to the regulation of highways, the destruction of wolves, wildcats, and foxes, and the advancement of the other little interests of the particular counties which they were chosen to represent." [4]

[4] Kenneth Colegrove, "New England Town Mandates," *Publications of the Colonial Society of Massachusetts*, XXI (*Transactions*, 1919), 411–436; William Smith, *History of the Late Province of New-York, from Its Discovery to . . . 1762*, I (*Collections of the New-York Historical Society* [vol. IV] *for the Year 1829*, New York, 1829), 309; see also, II, 14. Cf. William Douglass's excoriation of the Massachusetts law requiring a representative to be "a resident in the township for which he is elected." A gentleman, he argued, "of good natural interest, and resident in the province, a man of reading, observation, and daily conversant with affairs of policy and commerce, is certainly better qualified for a legislator than a retailer of rum and small beer called a tavern keeper in a poor obscure country town remote from all business." Residence in the province, together with the ownership of property in the constituency, should be quite enough to qualify a representative, he wrote. *A Summary, Historical and Political, of the . . . British Settlements in North-America* (Boston, 1749–1751), I, 506–507. For the argument in Pennsylvania in 1728 that the representative was at best a "creature of the people . . . Here is no *transessentiating* or *transubstantiating* of being from people to representative, no more than there is an absolute transferring of a title in a letter of attorney," see Roy N. Lokken, *David Lloyd* (Seattle, 1959), p. 232. See in general the material assembled in Hubert Phillips, *The Development of a Residential Qualification for Representatives in Colonial Legislatures* (Cincinnati, 1921); for an excellent account in detail, see Richard P. McCormick, *The History of Voting in New Jersey* (New Brunswick, 1953), chap. ii. The pamphlets published in Massachusetts in 1754 over the controversial excise bill of that year are particularly revealing of the tendency of thought on representation before the Revolution. See Evans listings 7176, 7186, 7227, 7296, 7303, 7304, 7312, 7319, 7332, 7418; the last of these, *An Appendix to the Late Total Eclipse of Liberty . . . Thoughts on . . . the Inherent Power of the People . . . Not Given Up to Their Representatives . . .* (Boston, 1756), by the harassed printer Daniel Fowle, was reprinted in 1775.

All of this, together with the associated experience common to all of the colonies of selecting and controlling agents to speak for them in England,[5] formed the background for the discussion of the first great issue of the Anglo-American controversy. For the principal English argument put forward in defense of Parliament's right to pass laws taxing the colonies was that the colonists, like the "nine tenths of the people of Britain" who do not choose representatives to Parliament, were in fact represented there. The power of actually voting for representatives, it was claimed, was an accidental and not a necessary attribute of representation, "for the right of election is annexed to certain species of property, to peculiar franchises, and to inhabitancy in certain places." In what really counted there was no difference between those who happened to live in England and those in America: "none are actually, all are virtually represented in Parliament," for, the argument concluded,

every Member of Parliament sits in the House not as representative of his own constituents but as one of that august assembly by which all the commons of *Great Britain* are represented. Their rights and their interests, however his own borough may be affected by general dispositions, ought to be the great objects of his attention and the only rules for his conduct, and to sacrifice these to a partial advantage in favor of the place where he was chosen would be a departure from his duty.[6]

[5] The colonial agents in England were in fact, though never in theory, closely bound representatives in England of colonial constituencies. The Members of Parliament among them shared keenly at times the feeling of Charles Garth that he was "equally representative of this province of South Carolina and of Devizes in Parliament" (L. B. Namier, "Charles Garth, Agent for South Carolina" *English Historical Review*, 54 [1939], 645). But as the crisis developed it became obvious that conceiving of the agents as in some constitutional sense actual representatives of the colonies in England conceded major principles of the colonial arguments, and the notion was explicitly repudiated.

[6] [Thomas Whately], *The Regulations Lately Made Concerning the Colonies and the Taxes Imposed upon Them, Considered* (London, 1765), p. 109. For a discussion of Whately's pamphlet and others arguing the same point, together

In England the practice of "virtual" representation provided reasonably well for the actual representation of the major interests of the society, and it raised no widespread objection. It was its opposite, the idea of representation as attorneyship, that was seen as "a new sort of political doctrine strenuously enforced by modern malcontents." But in the colonies the situation was reversed. There, where political experience had led to a different expectation of the process of representation and where the workings of virtual representation in the case at hand were seen to be damaging, the English argument was met at once with flat and universal rejection, ultimately with derision. It consists, Daniel Dulany wrote in a comprehensive refutation of the idea, "of facts not true and of conclusions inadmissible." What counts, he said in terms with which almost every writer in America agreed, was the extent to which representation worked to protect the interests of the people against the encroachments of government. From this point of view the analogy between the nonelectors in England and those in America was utterly specious, for the interests of Englishmen who did not vote for members of Parliament were intimately bound up with those who did and with those chosen to sit as representatives. The interests of all three, "the nonelectors, the electors, and the representatives, are individually the same, to say nothing of the connection among the neighbors, friends, and relations. The security of the nonelectors against oppression is that their oppression will fall also upon the electors and the representatives. The one can't be injured and the other indemnified." But no such "intimate and inseparable relation" existed between the electors of Great Britain and the inhabitants of the colonies. The two groups were by no means involved in the same consequences of taxation: "not a single actual elector

with Dulany's reply to them, see Introduction to [Daniel Dulany], *Considerations on the Propriety of Imposing Taxes* (Annapolis, 1765: JHL Pamphlet 13), in Bailyn, *Pamphlets*, I.

in England might be immediately affected by a taxation in America imposed by a statute which would have a general operation and effect upon the properties of the inhabitants of the colonies." [7]

Once a lack of natural identity of interests between representatives and the populace was conceded, the idea of virtual representation lost any force it might have had; for by such a notion, James Otis wrote, you could "as well prove that the British House of Commons in fact represent all the people of the globe as those in America." The idea, in such situations, was "futile" and "absurd" — the work of a "political visionary." It was a notion, Arthur Lee wrote, with supporting quotations from Bolingbroke, Locke, Sidney, Camden, Pulteney, Petyt, Sir Joseph Jekyll, and assorted Parliamentary speakers, that "would, in the days of superstition, have been called witchcraft," for what it means is that while "our privileges are all *virtual,* our sufferings are *real* . . . We might have flattered ourselves that a *virtual obedience* would have exactly corresponded with a *virtual representation,* but it is the ineffable wisdom of Mr. Grenville to reconcile what, to our feeble comprehensions, appeared to be contradictions, and therefore a *real* obedience is required to this *virtual* power." Who, precisely, is the American freeman's virtual representative in England?

[7] William Seal Carpenter, *The Development of American Political Thought* (Princeton, 1930), p. 47n; Dulany, *Considerations* (JHL 13), pp. 7, 10. Thus also, e.g., [Ebenezer Devotion], *The Examiner Examined* . . . (New London, 1766): "There is nothing, say the colonists, that can give a proper representation but the actual choice of a representative, or in failure of this, an obvious sameness of interest in him that represents and the party represented, or at least an interwoven, inseparable interest between the nonelector and him that elects" (p. 16). And see, among the many other refutations of virtual representation, Maurice Moore, *The Justice and Policy of Taxing the American Colonies* . . . (Wilmington, N. C., 1765: JHL Pamphlet 16); Richard Bland, *An Inquiry into the Rights of the British Colonies, Intended as an Answer to* ["]*The Regulations Lately Made*["] . . . (Williamsburg, 1766: JHL Pamphlet 17); *Some Observations of Consequences in Three Parts* . . . ([Philadelphia], 1768), pp. 23 ff.

Does he know us? Or we him? No. Have we any restriction over his conduct? No. Is he bound in duty and interest to preserve our liberty and property? No. Is he acquainted with our circumstances, situation, wants, &c.? No. What then are we to expect from him? Nothing but taxes without end.[8]

But it was not merely the American situation that called into question the idea of virtual representation. Logically one could lead the argument further and say that the whole conception, wherever or however it might be applied, was defective. If it was wrong in America it was wrong in England too, and should be rooted out no less thoroughly in the one place than in the other. "To what purpose," James Otis asked in a celebrated passage, "is it to ring everlasting changes to the colonists on the cases of Manchester, Birmingham, and Sheffield, who return no members? If those now so considerable places are not represented, they ought to be." For, as John Joachim Zubly, the Swiss-born pastor of Savannah, Georgia, wrote in an almost verbatim denial of what Burke five years later would describe as the proper function of representatives,

every representative in Parliament is not a representative for the whole nation, but only for the particular place for which he hath been chosen. If any are chosen for a plurality of places, they can make their election only for one of them . . . no member can represent any but those by whom he hath been elected; if not elected, he cannot represent them, and of course not consent to anything in their behalf . . . representation arises entirely from the free election of the people.

So widely believed, indeed, — such a simple matter of fact — was it that " 'virtual representation' " anywhere, under any conditions, was "too ridiculous to be regarded," that the American

---

[8] [James Otis], *Considerations on Behalf of the Colonists* . . . (London, 1765), p. 9; Benjamin Church, *An Oration Delivered March Fifth 1773* . . . (Boston, 1773), p. 15; [Arthur Lee], "Monitor III," *Virginia Gazette* (R), March 10, 1768.

Tories gladly used it as a basis of protest against the assumed representativeness of the makeshift Provincial and Continental Congresses. For it was not much of an exaggeration of Otis' earlier arguments to claim in New York in 1775 that by the patriots' reasoning "every man, woman, boy, girl, child, infant, cow, horse, hog, dog, and cat who *now* live, or ever *did* live, or ever *shall* live in this province are fully, freely, and sufficiently represented in this present glorious and august Provincial Congress." [9]

But the colonists' discussion of representation did not stop with the refutation of the claims made for virtual representation. The debate broadened into a general consideration of the nature and function of representation — in situations where interests of electors and elected, franchised and disfranchised, coincided as well as where they did not. The virtues of binding representatives by instructions were now explicitly explored. Some approached the question cautiously, arguing that, though the idea "that the constituent can bind his representative by instructions" may in recent years have become "an unfashionable doctrine," nevertheless, "in most cases" the "persuasive influence" if not the "obligatory force" of instructions should be insisted upon: "a representative who should act against the explicit recommendation of his constituents would most deservedly forfeit their regard and all pretension to their future confidence." But the dominant voices were direct and decisive. The right to instruct representatives, Arthur Lee declared in the fourth of his "Monitor" papers, has been denied only "since the system of corruption which is now arrived to so dangerous a heighth began first to predominate in

[9] Otis, *Considerations,* p. 6; [John Joachim Zubly], *An Humble Enquiry into the Nature of the Dependency of the American Colonies* . . . ([Charleston], 1769: JHL Pamphlet 28), p. 17 (see also pp. 11, 16, 22); [John Dickinson], *An Essay on the Constitutional Power of Great-Britain over the Colonies in America* . . . (Philadelphia, 1774), in *Pennsylvania Archives,* 2d ser., III, 594; *The Triumph of the Whigs; or, T'Other Congress Convened* (New York, 1775: JHL Pamphlet 62), p. 8.

our constitution. Then it was that arbitrary ministers and their prostituted dependents began to maintain this doctrine dangerous to our liberty, that the representatives were independent of the people. This was necessary to serve their own tyrannical and selfish purposes." Elected representatives, he stated, "are *trustees for their constituents* to transact for them the business of government . . . and for this *service* they, like all other agents, were paid by their constituents, till they found it more advantageous to sell their voices in Parliament, and then . . . wished to become independent of the people." Defended, he wrote, by all the great authorities from Demosthenes to Coke, its denial condemned by Sir William Wyndham as "the most monstrous, the most slavish doctrine that was ever heard," the right of freemen not merely to choose representatives but to bind them with instructions "must have begun with the constitution," and was "an ancient and unalienable right in the people." The fact that "Mr. Blackstone, in his commentary on the law of England, has asserted the contrary" carried no weight with him. It was enough to point out that Blackstone "founds his opinion on that fiction of a person's being, after he is elected, the representative of the whole kingdom, and not of a particular part. The sophistry of this argument is sufficiently manifest, and has been fully exploded. The British constitution is not to be new modelled by every *court* lawyer. [*footnote:*] *Mr. Blackstone is solicitor to the Queen.*" Constituents, it was agreed, had nothing less than "an inherent right to give instructions to their representatives." For representatives, James Wilson concluded, were properly to be considered the "creatures" of their constituents, and they were to be held strictly "accountable for the use of that power which is delegated unto them." [10]

[10] Dulany, *Considerations* (JHL 13), p. [3]; *Virginia Gazette* (R), March 17, 1768; [Stephen Johnson], *Some Important Observations* . . . (Newport, 1766: JHL Pamphlet 19), p. 32; [James Wilson], *Considerations on the . . . Authority of the British Parliament* (Philadelphia, 1774: JHL Pamphlet 44), p. 9.

But what did that mean? There were far-reaching implications, some of which, first drawn out during this decade of debate, would remain persistent problems until finally resolved in the realization of American democracy in the nineteenth and twentieth centuries. It was seen, even in the 1760's and 1770's, that if a representative were kept to strict accountability, he would in effect be acting "in every respect as the persons who appointed him . . . would do were they present themselves." With the result, it was concluded, that a representative assembly "should be in miniature an exact portrait of the people at large. It should think, feel, reason, and act like them." If the population shifted in composition, so too should the character of the assembly, for "equal interest among the people should have equal interest in it." There might well be, in fact, "some permanent ratio by which the representatives should . . . increase or decrease with the number of inhabitants." [11]

And what if such were the case? The result would be, if not a wholly original contribution to advanced thought, at least a reversion to a radical concept that had long since disappeared from the mainstream of English political theory. For such arguments led to a recovery and elaboration of conceptions of government by the active and continuous consent of the governed that had flourished briefly a century earlier, during the Commonwealth period, and had then faded during the Restoration, persisting subsequently only as arguments of the most extreme

[11] Moore, *Justice and Policy* (JHL 16), p. 7; [John Adams], *Thoughts on Government* . . . (Philadelphia, 1776: JHL Pamphlet 65), pp. 9, 10; *Four Letters on Interesting Subjects* (Philadelphia, 1776: JHL Pamphlets 69), pp. 21–22. See also the importance attached by Jefferson to the crown's denial of an increase of representation in the colonial assemblies to reflect the growth and spread of the population. [Jefferson], *A Summary View of the Rights of British America* . . . (Williamsburg, [1774]: JHL Pamphlet 43), pp. 17, 18. So too Adams felt that a truly representative imperial Parliament would reflect in its size and complexity the variety of peoples represented in it: Adams ("Novanglus"), in *Works*, IV, 101–102.

radicals and of the most vociferous and intransigent leaders of the Parliamentary opposition.[12] The view of representation developing in America implied if it did not state that direct consent of the people in government was not restricted, as Locke would have had it, to those climactic moments when government was overthrown by the people in a last final effort to defend their rights, nor even to those repeated, benign moments when a government was peaceably dissolved and another chosen in its place.[13] Where government was such an accurate mirror of the people, sensitively reflecting their desires and feelings, consent was a continuous, everyday process. In effect the people were present through their representatives, and were themselves, step by step and point by point, acting in the conduct of public affairs. No longer merely an ultimate check on government, they *were* in some sense the government. Government had no separate existence apart from them; it was *by* the people as well as *for* the people; it gained its authority from their continuous consent. The very nature and meaning of law was involved. The traditional sense, proclaimed by Blackstone no less than by Hobbes,

---

[12] On the continuity of radical theories of representation, see Alfred De Grazia, *Public and Republic* (New York, 1951), pp. 21 ff., 45 ff.; Caroline Robbins, *The Eighteenth-Century Commonwealthman* (Cambridge, 1959), pp. 30, 193, 268, 338–339, 364–366, 370–374; Ian R. Christie, *Wilkes, Wyvill and Reform* (London, 1962), *passim*, esp. pp. 36, 43, 48–49, 63, 146–147, 179–184; Gipson, *British Empire*, XI, 194–195, 220–221.

[13] E.g., Locke, *Second Treatise of Government*, xiii, 149. Cf. Otis' discussion of the Glorious Revolution in his *Rights of the British Colonies Asserted and Proved* (Boston, 1764: JHL Pamphlet 7), 15 ff., quoting Locke on the dissolution of government (p. 23). For a forceful invocation of the Lockean notion of active consent at the moment of rebellion, see the argument for the constitutionality of the Continental Congress on the grounds of analogy to "the *assembly of the barons at* RUNNINGMEDE, when MAGNA CHARTA was signed, the *Convention Parliament* that recalled Charles II, and the *Convention of Lords and Commons* that placed King William on the throne," in James Wilson and John Dickinson's "Address to the Inhabitants of the Colonies" (1776), *Journals of the Continental Congress, 1774–1789* (W. C. Ford, *et al.*, eds., Washington, D. C., 1904–1937), IV, 137.

that law was a command "prescribed by source superior and which the inferior is bound to obey" — such a sense of law as the declaration of a person or body existing independently above the subjects of law and imposing its will upon them, was brought into question by the developing notion of representation. Already in these years there were adumbrations of the sweeping repudiation James Wilson and others would make of Blackstone's definition of law, and of the view they would put in its place: the view that the binding power of law flowed from the continuous assent of the subjects of law; the view "that the only reason why a free and independent man was bound by human laws was this — that he bound himself." [14]

These were deep-lying implications of making representation — systematically, in principle as well as in fact — "a substitute for legislation by direct action of the people." They were radical possibilities, glimpsed but not wholly grasped, thrown up in the creative clash of ideas that preceded the Revolution, and drawn into the discussion of the first state constitutions even before Independence was declared. They were perhaps, in these early years, understood most clearly by the more perceptive of the Tories, who stood outside and viewed with apprehension the tendency of events and the drift of theory. "The position," the Anglican minister Samuel Seabury wrote in 1774, "that we are bound by no laws to which we have not consented either by ourselves or our representatives is a novel position unsupported by any authoritative record of the British constitution, ancient or modern.

[14] Wilson on Blackstone, in Andrew C. McLaughlin, *The Foundations of American Constitutionalism* (New York, 1932), pp. 83–84; cf. [Moses Mather], *America's Appeal to the Impartial World* . . . (Hartford, 1775: JHL Pamphlet 59), p. 39. See, in general, on the points involved, Carpenter, *Development of American Political Thought*, pp. 91 ff.; J. W. Gough, *Fundamental Law in English Constitutional History* (Oxford, 1955), pp. 175–176, 120; Charles H. McIlwain, *Constitutionalism and the Changing World* (New York, 1939), pp. 64–65.

It is republican in its very nature, and tends to the utter subversion of the English monarchy." [15]

2. CONSTITUTIONS AND RIGHTS

Certain of the Tories understood also with special clarity the
meaning of changes that were taking place in other areas of
thought. They grasped, and exclaimed against in protest, the
transformation of the notion of what a constitution was and of
the nature of the rights that constitutions existed to protect.
"What is the constitution," Charles Inglis demanded in his an-
guished reply to *Common Sense* — what is "that word so often
used — so little understood — so much perverted? It is, as I conceive — *that assemblage of laws, customs, and institutions which
form the general system according to which the several powers
of the state are distributed and their respective rights are secured
to the different members of the community*." It was still for him,
as it had been traditionally, what John Adams had described a
decade earlier as "a frame, a scheme, a system, a combination
of powers": the existing arrangement of governmental institutions, laws, and customs together with the animating principles,
the *stamina vitae,* that gave them purpose and direction. But so
far toward a different conception of constitutionalism had American thought shifted after 1765 that by 1776 Inglis' quite traditional definition could only be uttered as the *cri de coeur* of one
bypassed by history.[16]

[15] Carpenter, *Development of American Political Thought,* pp. 43, 91; [Samuel
Seabury], *A View of the Controversy* . . . (New York, 1774), in Clarence H.
Vance, ed., *Letters of a Westchester Farmer (1774-1775) (Publications of the
Westchester County Historical Society,* VIII, White Plains, 1930), p. 111.

[16] [Charles Inglis], *The True Interest of America . . . Strictures on a Pam-
phlet Intitled Common Sense* . . . (Philadelphia, 1776), p. 18. Cf. above, Chap.
III, note 12. On the seventeenth-century background in England of the later
American developments, see Corinne C. Weston, *English Constitutional Theory
and the House of Lords, 1556-1832* (London, 1965), pp. 99-100; Gough,
Fundamental Law, pp. 51, 59, 67.

The first suggestions of change came early in the period, the full conclusion only at the very end. At the start what would emerge as the central feature of American constitutionalism was only an emphasis and a peculiarity of tone within an otherwise familiar discourse. While some writers, like Richard Bland, continued to refer to "a legal constitution, that is, a legislature," and others spoke of "the English constitution . . . a nice piece of machinery which has undergone many changes and alterations," most of the writers saw the necessity of emphasizing principles above institutions, and began to grasp the consequences of doing so.[17] The confusions and difficulties inherent in this process are dramatically illustrated in the troubled career of James Otis.[18]

The heart of the problem Otis faced in the early 1760's was the extent to which, indeed the sense in which, the "constitution" could be conceived of as a limitation on the power of lawmaking bodies. In the writs of assistance case in 1761 he had struck a bold and confident note — so bold, indeed, that John Adams later wrote, rather romantically, that "then and there the child Independence was born." On that famous occasion Otis had said not only that an act of Parliament "against the constitution is void" but that it was the duty of the courts to "pass such acts into disuse," for the "reason of the common law [could] control an act of Parliament." But what was the "constitution" which an act of Parliament could not infringe? Was it a set of fixed principles and rules distinguishable from, antecedent to, more fundamental than, and controlling the operating institutions of government?

---

[17] [Richard Bland], *The Colonel Dismounted: Or the Rector Vindicated* . . . (Williamsburg, 1764: JHL Pamphlet 4), p. 22; [William Hicks], *Considerations upon the Rights of the Colonists to the Privileges of British Subjects* . . . (New York, 1766: JHL Pamphlet 18), p. 1.

[18] Otis' constitutional thought is discussed in detail in the Introductions to his *Rights of the British Colonies* (JHL 7) and his *Vindication of the British Colonies* . . . (Boston, 1765: JHL Pamphlet 11) in Bailyn, *Pamphlets*, I. The reader is referred to these essays for full elaboration and documentation of the interpretation that follows.

And was there consequently a "constitutional" limitation on Parliament's actions? Otis' answers were ambiguous, and proved to be politically disastrous. The main authority for his statement in the writs case that an act of Parliament against the constitution was void was Coke, reinforced by later judges expounding the great chief justice's dictum in *Bonham's Case*. But in that pronouncement Coke had not meant, as Professor Thorne has made clear, "that there were superior principles of right and justice which Acts of Parliament might not contravene." Thinking in terms of private law, not constitutional construction, Coke had meant only that the courts would interpret statutes "in such a way as not to conflict with those same accepted principles of reason and justice which . . . were presumed to underlie all law"; and by saying that the courts might "void" a legislative provision that violated the constitution he had meant only that the courts were to construe statutes so as to bring them into conformity with recognized legal principles.[19]

[19] Adams, *Works*, X, 248; Josiah Quincy, Jr., *Reports of Cases . . . in the Superior Court of Judicature . . . Between 1761 and 1772 . . .* (Samuel M. Quincy, ed., Boston, 1865), p. 474; Samuel E. Thorne, "Dr. Bonham's Case," *Law Quarterly Review*, 54 (1938), 545, 549, 551, and the same author's edition of *A Discourse upon the . . . Statutes . . .* (San Marino, 1942), pp. 85–92. Equally suggestive of the complicated anachronism of Otis' thought is his silent, perhaps unconscious, paraphrasing of Grotius, discussed below, p. 205, n. 46. The complete recovery of what Coke and the other early English jurists had meant by "voidance," and hence their easy ability to reconcile absolute Parliamentary supremacy and constitutionalism, seems to have become possible only when the American redefinition of the concept of "constitution" had reached its fulfillment in the early nineteenth century. Thus Chancellor Kent, after quoting Blackstone on the absolute supremacy of Parliament, wrote in his famous *Commentaries:* "When it is said in the [English law] books that a statute contrary to natural equity and reason, or repugnant or impossible to be performed, is void, the cases are understood to mean that the courts are to give the statute a reasonable construction. They will not readily presume, out of respect and duty to the lawgiver, that any very unjust or absurd consequence was within the contemplation of the law. But if it should happen to be too palpable in its direction to admit of but one construction, there is no doubt in the English law as to the binding efficacy of the statute. The will of the legis-

Otis, drawing the language of seventeenth-century law into the constitutional struggle of the eighteenth century, found himself veering toward positions he was neither intellectually nor politically prepared to accept. "If the reasons that can be given against an act are such," he wrote in his *Rights of the British Colonies* in 1764, "as plainly demonstrate that it is against *natural* equity, the executive courts will adjudge such act void." And again, in an Appendix to the same pamphlet, originally written as a memorial to the Massachusetts agent in London, commenting on the statement that "judges will strain hard rather than interpret an act void, *ab initio*," he wrote: *"This is granted, but still [Parliament's] authority is not boundless if subject to the control of judges in any case."* Was this not to limit the power of Parliament by the provisions of a fixed constitution distinct from and superior to the legislature, a constitution interpreted and applied by the courts? Others, in time, would say it was. Indeed, a contemporary authority whom Otis quoted at length in the Appendix to his pamphlet could hardly have said this more clearly. Does the power of legislators extend to fundamental law, and if so may they "change the constitution of the state?" Otis asked in the words of the Swiss theorist Emmerich de Vattel. No, was the answer: "they ought to consider the fundamental laws as sacred if the nation has not in very express terms given them the power to change them. For the constitution of the state ought to be fixed; and since that was first established by the nation, which afterwards trusted certain persons with the legislative power, the fundamental laws are excepted from their commission."

But though Otis quoted this passage from Vattel he did not draw its implications. He ignored them, in fact, in working out

---

lature is the supreme law of the land, and demands perfect obedience." James Kent, *Commentaries on American Law* (New York, 1826), I, 419–420; cf. pp. 420–421, 425 on the American concept of "voidance."

his own view of the constitution and of the limits of Parliament's powers. If an act of Parliament violated natural laws, "which are *immutably* true," he wrote, it would thereby violate "eternal truth, equity, and justice," and would be "consequently void."

. . . and so it would be adjudged by the Parliament itself when convinced of their mistake. Upon this great principle Parliaments repeal such acts as soon as they find they have been mistaken . . . When such mistake is evident and palpable . . . the judges of the executive courts have declared the act "of a whole Parliament void." See here the grandeur of the British constitution! See the wisdom of our ancestors! . . . If the supreme legislative errs, it is informed by the supreme executive in the King's court of law . . . This is government! This is a constitution! to preserve which . . . has cost oceans of blood and treasure in every age; and the blood and the treasure have upon the whole been well spent.

Parliament was thus itself part of the constitution, not a creature of it, and its power was "uncontrollable but by themselves, and we must obey. They only can repeal their own acts . . . let the Parliament lay what burdens they please on us, we must, it is our duty to submit and patiently bear them, till they will be pleased to relieve us." Yet Parliament's enactments against the constitution — against, that is, the whole system of laws, principles, and institutions based on reason and justice of which it was a part — were void, Otis argued; the courts will adjudge them so, and Parliament itself, by the necessity of the system, will repeal them.[20]

It was a strange argument, comprehensible only as an effort to apply seventeenth-century assumptions to eighteenth-century problems. For Otis continued to assume, with Coke, that Parliament was effectively a supreme judicial as well as a supreme legislative body and hence by definition involved in judicial

[20] Otis, *Rights of the British Colonies* (JHL 7), pp. 41, 73n, 47, 39–40.

179

processes. He continued to believe, too, that moral rights and obligations were not "differentiated as they would be today from legal rights and obligations," and that they naturally radiated from, rather than restricted, enacted law.[21] And he expected fundamental, or higher, law to "control" positive acts of government not in the sense of furnishing judges with grounds for declaring them nonexistent because they conflicted with the "constitution" but only in the sense of providing judges with principles of interpretation by which to modify gross inequities and to interpret "unreasonableness" and self-contradiction in ways that would allow traditional qualities of justice to prevail.

But these assumptions were no longer applicable, in the same way, in the eighteenth century. Parliament was in reality no longer a court but an all powerful sovereign body, and the problem at hand concerned the structure and authority of government, not private law. Otis' theory of the constitution that included a self-correcting Parliament sensitive to the principles of justice and responsive to the admonitions of the courts was, insofar as it was realistic at all, an anachronism, and it came under attack by both the administration, which charged him with attempting to restrict the power of Parliament, and by the colonial radicals, who accused him of preaching passive obedience and nonresistance.

Otis had been faithful, in this way, to the seventeenth-century sources of constitutional thought which he, like so many Americans, revered. Others — poorer scholars, perhaps, but better judges of the circumstances that surrounded them — were less faithful, and in the end more creative. The dominant view of the constitution in 1764 was still the traditional one, unencumbered by Otis' complexities. While Otis was quoting Coke together with Vattel without grasping the implications of their conjunction, others were referring to constitutions as "a sort of fundamental laws"; as the common law; as Parliament; and as

[21] Gough, *Fundamental Law*, pp. 45, 35–36.

the whole complex of existing laws and public institutions.[22] The transition to more advanced ground was forced forward by the continuing need, after 1764, to distinguish fundamentals from institutions and from the actions of government so that they might serve as limits and controls. Once its utility was perceived and demonstrated, this process of disengaging principles from institutions and from the positive actions of government and then of conceiving of them as fixed sets of rules and boundaries, went on swiftly.

In 1768 Samuel Adams, accustomed to drawing more extreme conclusions than most of his contemporaries, wrote in a series of letters in behalf of the Massachusetts House of Representatives that "the constitution is fixed; it is from thence that the supreme legislative as well as the supreme executive derives its authority," and he incorporated the same language into the famous Massachusetts Circular Letter of that year. At the same time a Philadelphian, William Hicks, wrote that if one were to concede that statutes were "a part of [the] constitution" simply because they were once promulgated by government, one would have no basis for restraining the actions of any government. There is nothing sacrosanct, he wrote, in the "variant, inconsistent form of government which we have received at different periods of time"; they were accidental in origins, and their defects should be corrected by comparison with ideal models. In 1769 the emerging logic was carried further by Zubly, who flatly distinguished legislatures from the constitution, and declared that the existing Parliament "derives its authority and power from the constitution, and not the constitution from Parliament." The constitution, he wrote, "is permanent and ever the same," and Parliament "can no more make laws which are against the constitution or the unalterable

[22] Andrew Eliot, *A Sermon Preached before His Excellency Francis Bernard* . . . (Boston, 1765: JHL Pamphlet 15), p. 19; [Martin Howard, Jr.,] *A Letter from a Gentleman at Halifax* (Newport, 1765: JHL Pamphlet 10), p. 10; Bland, *Colonel Dismounted* (JHL 4), pp. 27, 29.

privileges of British subjects than it can alter the constitution itself . . . The power of Parliament, and of every branch of it, has its bounds assigned by the constitution." [23]

In 1770 the constitution was said to be "a line which marks out the enclosure"; in 1773 it was "the standing measure of the proceedings of government" of which rulers are "by no means to attempt an alteration . . . without public consent"; in 1774 it was a "model of government"; in 1775 it was "certain great first principles" on whose "certainty and permanency . . . the rights of both the ruler and the subjects depend; nor may they be altered or changed by ruler or people, but [only] by the whole collective body . . . nor may they be touched by the legislator." Finally, in 1776 there came conclusive pronouncements. Two pamphlets of that year, brilliant sparks thrown off by the clash of Revolutionary politics in Pennsylvania, lit up the final steps of the path that led directly to the first constitutions of the American states. "A constitution and a form of government," the author of *Four Letters on Important Subjects* wrote, "are frequently confounded together and spoken of as synonymous things, whereas they are not only different but are established for different purposes." All nations have governments, "but few, or perhaps none, have truly a constitution." The primary function of a constitution was to mark out the boundaries of governmental powers — hence in England, where there was no constitution, there were no limits (save for the effect of trial by jury) to what the legislature might do. In order to confine the ordinary actions of government, the constitution must be grounded in some fundamental source of authority, some "higher authority than the giving out temporary

[23] Samuel Adams, quoted in Randolph G. Adams, *Political Ideas of the American Revolution* (3d ed., New York, 1958), p. 138; the texts of the letters are in Adams' *Writings* (H. A. Cushing, ed., New York, 1904–1908), I, 152 ff. (see esp. p. 156); the Circular Letter is at pp. 184–188. [William Hicks], *The Nature and Extent of Parliamentary Power Considered* . . . (Philadelphia, 1768: JHL Pamphlet 24), p. 31; Zubly, *Humble Enquiry* (JHL 28), p. 5.

laws." This special authority could be gained if the constitution were created by "an act of *all*," and it would acquire permanence if it were embodied "in some written charter." Defects, of course, might be discovered and would have to be repaired: there would have to be some procedure by which to alter the constitution without disturbing its controlling power as fundamental law. For this, the means "are easy":

> some article in the constitution may provide that at the expiration of every seven or any other number of years a *provincial jury* shall be elected to inquire if any inroads have been made in the constitution, and to have power to remove them; but not to make alterations, unless a clear majority of all the inhabitants shall so direct.

Thus created and thus secured, the constitution could effectively designate what "part of their liberty" the people are to sacrifice to the necessity of having government, by furnishing answers to "the two following questions: first, what shall the form of government be? And secondly, what shall be its power?" In addition, "it is the part of a constitution to fix the manner in which the officers of government shall be chosen, and determine the principal outlines of their power, their time of duration, manner of commissioning them, etc." Finally, "all the great rights which man never mean, nor ever ought, to lose should be *guaranteed*, not *granted*, by the constitution, for at the forming a constitution, we ought to have in mind that whatever is left to be secured by law only may be altered by another law." [24]

The same ideas, in some ways even more clearly worked out, appear in the second Pennsylvania pamphlet of 1776, *The Genuine Principles of the Ancient Saxon or English Constitution*, which was largely composed of excerpts from Obadiah Hulme's *An*

[24] Samuel Cooke, *A Sermon Preached at Cambridge* . . . (Boston, 1770), p. 11; Charles Turner, *A Sermon Preached before His Excellency Thomas Hutchinson* (Boston, 1773), pp. 16, 17, 18–19; Peter Whitney, *The Transgressions of a Land* . . . (Boston, 1774), p. 8; Mather, *America's Appeal* (JHL 59), pp. 22–23; *Four Letters on Important Subjects* (JHL 69), pp. 18, 15–16, 19, 22.

Historical Essay on the English Constitution, published in London in 1771, a book both determinative and representative of the historical understanding that lay behind the emerging American constitutionalism. Here too was stated the idea of a constitution as a "*set of fundamental rules* by which even the supreme power of the state shall be governed" and which the legislature is absolutely forbidden to alter. But in this pamphlet there are more explicit explanations of how such documents come into being and of their permanence and importance. They are to be formed "by a convention of the delegates of the people appointed for that express purpose," the pamphlet states, and they are never to be "added to, diminished from, nor altered in any respect by any power besides the power which first framed [them]." They are to remain permanent, and so to have the most profound effect on the lives of people. "Men entrusted with the formation of civil constitutions should remember they are *painting for eternity: that the smallest defect or redundancy in the system they frame may prove the destruction of millions.*" [25]

Accompanying this shift in the understanding of constitutionalism, and part of it, was another change, which also began as a relocation of emphasis and ended as a contribution to the transforming radicalism of the Revolution. The *rights* that constitutions existed to protect were understood in the early years of the period, as we have seen, to be at once the inalienable, indefeasible

[25] *Genuine Principles* (JHL 70), pp. 4, 35, 34; on Hulme and the influence of his *Essay*, see Robbins, *Eighteenth-Century Commonwealthman*, pp. 363–365. Among the many statements of the idea of a fixed constitution published by 1776, see especially those of the Tories; e.g., Seabury, *A View*, in Vance, *Letters of a Westchester Farmer*, p. 123; and [Thomas Bradbury Chandler], *What Think Ye of the Congress Now?* . . . (New York, 1775), p. 44. But for a dramatic illustration of the speed with which Revolutionary ideas were maturing, compare Chandler's and Seabury's understanding with that expressed by the Concord Town Meeting in 1776, in S. E. Morison, ed., *Sources and Documents of the American Revolution* . . . (Oxford, 1923), p. 177.

rights inherent in all people by virtue of their humanity, and the concrete provisions of English law as expressed in statutes, charters, and court decisions; it was assumed that the "constitution" in its normal workings would specify and protect the inalienable rights of man. But what if it did not? What if this sense proved false, and it came to be believed that the force of government threatened rather than protected these rights? And what if, in addition, the protective machinery of rights — the constitution — came to be abstracted from the organs of government and to be seen not as an arrangement of institutions and enactments but as a blueprint for institutions, the ideal against which the actual was to be measured?

These questions were first posed early in the controversy, in the course of one of the most vituperative exchanges of constitutional views of the entire period. It is true, Judge Martin Howard, Jr., of Rhode Island wrote in response to Stephen Hopkins' *Rights of Colonies Examined* (1765), that the common law carries within it and guarantees with special force the "indefeasible" personal rights of men; for Britons it is the common law that makes these natural rights operative. But Parliament's power is no less a part of that same common law. "Can we claim the common law as an inheritance, and at the same time be at liberty to adopt one part of it and reject the other?" If Parliament is rejected, so too must political and even personal rights. If rights are accepted as inextricable parts of laws and institutions, the laws and institutions must be accepted in all their normal workings.[26]

James Otis accepted the challenge. But in his stinging reply — a bitter, sarcastic, half-wild polemic — he again displayed a commitment to tradition that kept him from following through the logic of his own argument; again, he succeeded in dramatizing but not in resolving the issue. The judge's "truly *Filmerian*" performance, he wrote, has "inaccuracies in abundance, declamation

[26] Howard, *Halifax Letter* (JHL 10), p. 11.

and false logic without end . . . and the most indelicate fustian."
His central error is that he "everywhere confounds the terms
rights, liberties, and privileges, which, in legal as well as vulgar
acceptation, denote very different ideas." The source of this confusion, Otis said, was a misreading of Blackstone; from his *Commentaries,* Howard had mistakenly derived the idea that the
rights of natural persons are the same as those of artificial persons:
that is, "bodies politic and corporate." Corporate rights are indeed
"matters of the mere favor and grace of the donor or founder";
but that is not to say that the rights of natural people are too.
Britons are entitled to their "natural absolute personal rights" by
virtue of "the laws of God and nature, as well as by the common
law and the constitution of their country so admirably built on
the principles of the former." Only such a one as Judge Howard,
with his "Filmerian sneer," who "cannot see any difference between power and right, between a blind, slavish submission and
a loyal, generous, and rational obedience" — only such a person
could fail to understand that the origin of "the inherent, indefeasible rights of the subject" lay in "the law of nature and its
author. This law is the grand basis of the common law and of all
other municipal laws that are worth a rush. True it is that every
act of Parliament which names the colonies . . . binds them. But
this is not so, strictly and properly speaking, by the common law
as by the law of nature and by the constitution of a parliament
or sovereign and supreme legislative in a state." [27]

Otis had shifted the emphasis of discussion to the priority of
abstract rights, but he had not attempted to follow through the
implications of his own thought: he continued to assume that the
actual law would express, and naturally protect, the universal
rights of man. But if he did not draw the conclusions implicit in
his own logic, others did: there is in the proliferating discussion
of constitutionalism a steadily increasing emphasis on the uni-

[27] Otis, *Vindication* (JHL 11), pp. 4, 3–4, 8, 9, 13, 14.

versal, inherent, indefeasible qualities of rights. John Dickinson, also a lawyer — indeed, a more professionally trained lawyer than Otis — attacked in a more knowing and thorough way the idea that rights are matters of "favor and grace." True, in 1764 he had vehemently defended the charter of Pennsylvania against the attacks of Joseph Galloway and others, but not because he believed that "the liberties of the subject were mere favors granted by charters from the crown." The liberties of Pennsylvanians, he had proclaimed in a ringing oration in the Pennsylvania Assembly, are "founded on the acknowledged rights of human nature." The value of a charter like that of Pennsylvania was that it stated the true character of such liberties beyond any misunderstanding, and freed them from the entanglements of those ancient, archaic customs "that our ancestors either had not moderation or leisure enough to untwist." Two years later (1766) he elaborated the point significantly. Charters, he wrote in his *Address to the Committee of Correspondence in Barbados,* like all aspects of the law, are *"declarations* but not *gifts* of liberties." Kings and Parliaments cannot give "the *rights essential to happiness."*

We claim them from a higher source — from the King of kings, and Lord of all the earth. They are not annexed to us by parchments and seals. They are created in us by the decrees of Providence, which establish the laws of our nature. They are born with us; exist with us; and cannot be taken from us by any human power without taking our lives. In short, they are founded on the immutable maxims of reason and justice.

Written laws — even the great declarations like Magna Carta — do not create liberties; they "must be considered as only declaratory of our rights, and in affirmance of them." [28]

[28] [John Dickinson], *An Address to the Committee of Correspondence in Barbados* . . . (Philadelphia, 1766), in Paul L. Ford, ed., *Writings of John Dickinson* (*Memoirs of the Historical Society of Pennsylvania,* XIV, Philadelphia, 1895), pp. 261, 262; John Dickinson, *A Speech Delivered* . . . *1764,* in *ibid.,* p. 34; [Silas Downer], *A Discourse Delivered in Providence* . . . *at the Dedication of the Tree of Liberty* (Providence, 1768: JHL Pamphlet 25), p. 6.

Ultimately, the conclusion to be drawn became obvious: the entire legitimacy of positive law and legal rights must be understood to rest on the degree to which they conformed to the abstract universals of natural rights. Not all were willing, even in 1775, to go as far as Alexander Hamilton, who wrote in bold, arresting words that "the sacred rights of mankind are not to be rummaged for among old parchments or musty records. They are written, as with a sunbeam, in the whole *volume* of human nature, by the hand of divinity itself, and can never be erased or obscured by mortal power." But if some found this statement too enthusiastic, few by 1774 — few even of the Tories — disagreed with the calmer formulation of the same idea, by Philip Livingston. Had he understood his antagonist, the Rev. Thomas Bradbury Chandler, correctly? Had Chandler really meant to say "that any right . . . if it be not confirmed by some statute law is not a legal right"? If so, Livingston declared, "in the name of America, I deny it." Legal rights are "those rights which we are entitled to by the eternal laws of right reason"; they exist independent of positive law, and stand as the measure of its legitimacy.[29]

Neither Hamilton nor Livingston, nor any of the other writers who touched on the subject, meant to repudiate the heritage of English common and statutory law. Their claim was only that the source of rights be recognized, in Jefferson's words, as "the laws of nature, and not as the gift of their chief magistrate," and that as a consequence the ideal must be understood to exist before the real and to remain superior to it, controlling it and limiting it. But what was the ideal? What precisely were the ideal rights of man? They were, everyone knew, in some sense Life, Liberty, and Property. But in what sense? Must they not be specified?

[29] [Alexander Hamilton], *The Farmer Refuted* . . . (New York, 1775), in *Papers of Alexander Hamilton* (Harold C. Syrett, et al., eds., New York and London, 1961–), I, 122; [Philip Livingston], *The Other Side of the Question* . . . (New York, 1774: JHL Pamphlet 51), p. 9.

Must not the ideal now be reduced from a radiant presence and a conglomerate legal tradition to specific enumerated provisions? Must not the essential rights of man be specified and codified if they were to serve effectively as limits on the actions of courts and legislatures? In 1765 James Otis had fulminated at the mere suggestion that a document might profitably be drawn up stating the "rights of the colonies with precision and certainty." Insolence, he had called it, pedantry and nonsense; Britons had no need for "codes, pandects, novels, decretals of popes." "The common law is our birthright, and the rights and privileges confirmed and secured to us by the British constitution and by act of Parliament are our best inheritance." But thought had shifted rapidly in the decade that followed, Arthur Lee exhorting his countrymen in 1768 to draw up a petition of rights *and never desist from the solicitation till it be confirmed into a bill of rights,*" and Andrew Eliot a year later despairing of all solutions save that of "an American bill of rights." No voice was raised in objection when in 1776 the idea was proclaimed, and acted upon, that "all the great rights . . . should be *guaranteed*" by the terms of a written constitution.[30]

These closely related changes — in the view of what a constitution was and of the proper emphasis in the understanding of rights — were momentous; they would shape the entire future development of American constitutional thought and practice. Yet they did not seem to be momentous at the time. They were

[30] Jefferson, *Summary View* (JHL 43), p. 22; Otis, *Vindication* (JHL 11), p. 32; *Four Letters on Interesting Subjects* (JHL 69), p. 22; [Arthur Lee], "Monitor III," *Virginia Gazette* (R), March 10, 1768 (see also nos. IV and V where Lee works out further his arguments for "a confirmation of our rights . . . to merit the title of the *Magna Carta Americana*"); Eliot to Hollis, July 10, 1769, in MHS *Colls.*, 4th ser., IV, 442. Later there would be doubts about the value of enumerating rights just as there would be about other of the ideas developing before 1776. See particularly Madison's penetrating analysis in his letter to Jefferson of October 17, 1788, *Papers of Thomas Jefferson* (Julian P. Boyd, ed., Princeton, 1950–), XIV, 18–19, especially arguments 2 and 4.

not generally experienced as intrusive or threatening alterations. They were hardly seen as changes at all: they drifted into consciousness so gradually and easily and were accepted with so little controversy that writers would soon feel called upon to remind Americans that the fundamental principles of their political and constitutional thought were "of recent date, and for [them] the world is indebted to America; for if [the distinction between constitutional law and that of the ordinary legislature] did not originate in this country, it was here that it was first reduced to practice, exemplified, and its utility and practicability first established." [31] For in this area too, as in so many other developments in political and social thought, the way had been paved by the peculiar circumstances of colonial life. Whatever Otis may have thought of the issue when he came to consider it in theoretical terms, the fact was that written constitutions — documents not different essentially from the "codes, pandects, novels" he denounced — had existed, had been acted upon, had been assumed to be proper and necessary, for a century or more. Some, like the charter of the Massachusetts Bay Colony, had originated as commercial charters, concessions of powers by the crown to enterprisers willing to undertake the risks of exploration and settlement. These, in the colonial setting, had quickly changed in character, and "by some metamorphosis or feat of legerdemain had . . . become the frame of government for a state." The Massachusetts Bay charter in particular "approximated a popular constitution," Professor McIlwain has written, "more closely than any other instrument of government in actual use up to that time in America or elsewhere in modern times." It is hardly surprising, he concludes, that the Fundamental Orders of Connecticut of 1639, " 'the first American constitution accepted by the people,' "

[31] Anon., "A Concise View of the Principles of the Constitution and Government of the .United States . . . ," in Jedidiah Morse, comp., *Annals of the American Revolution* . . . (Hartford, 1824), p. 385.

should have been written by men who emigrated from Massachusetts.[32]

Later crown charters, like those of Connecticut and Rhode Island, were designed in the first place to be basic instruments of government; and if the seventeenth-century proprietary grants — those of New York, Maryland, and the Carolinas — were anachronistic in their feudal terminology, they too created "governing powers" and provided for public institutions that were expected to be "incapable of alteration or amendment except by concession from the grantor." Most important of all, because most deliberately "constitutional" in character, were the foundations laid down by William Penn for the establishment of government in New Jersey and Pennsylvania. This remarkable man — courtier and sectarian; saint, schemer, and scholar — whose imaginative grasp of the possibilities of constitution-making led him eventually to propose not only a "Plan of Union for the Colonies" but also a scheme for "The Establishment of a European Diet, Parliament, or Estates," devoted himself enthusiastically to constructing a proper framework of government for the Quaker colonies. In consultation with the leading political theorists of his time, he drew up and published a series of concessions, frames of government, and charters, which were, in effect, blueprints for "civil administration, elections, court procedure, the exercise of justice, fines, penalties, and . . . the duties and obligations of officeholders." These schemes, again and again revised in an effort to adjust soaring idealism to the demands of ordinary human real-

[32] Charles M. Andrews, *The Colonial Period of American History* (New Haven, 1934–1938), I, 440; McIlwain, *Constitutionalism and the Changing World*, p. 241 (cf. Andrews, *Colonial Period*, II, 102 ff.). See, in general, Benjamin F. Wright, Jr., "The Early History of Written Constitutions in America," *Essays . . . in Honor of Charles Howard McIlwain* (Cambridge, 1936), pp. 344–371. For the claim that "to Plymouth belongs the credit for having established what may fairly be described as the first American constitution" (the code of laws of 1636), see George L. Haskins, "The Legacy of Plymouth," *Social Education*, 26 (1962), 9.

ities, could hardly have been more clearly fundamental, more manifestly constituent, in nature.[33]

By the Revolutionary period, the surviving charters, which in origins had been the instruments of the aggressive creation, or legitimation, of power, had become defensive bulwarks against the misuse of power. In Connecticut, Rhode Island, and Massachusetts they were cherished still, as they had been for a century and more, as special confirmations of "the ancient common law of England, and of the common rights of Englishmen." In Pennsylvania, in the years immediately preceding the Stamp Act, the attack launched against the Penn family's tax privileges, which had been written into the original charter, was fended off by impassioned pleas, like that of John Dickinson, to preserve intact, Proprietary tax privileges and all, the "laws and liberties framed and delivered down to us by our careful ancestors . . . Any body of men acting under a charter must surely tread on slippery ground when they take a step that may be deemed a surrender of that charter." Nor were the benefits of these famous compacts "between the sovereign and the first patentees" valued only in the particular provinces in which they had survived. Everywhere in the colonies the existing charters were prized as "evidential of the rights and immunities belonging to all the King's subjects in America." [34]

For some people, in fact, the charters had acquired, in the course

[33] Andrews, *Colonial Period*, II, 137 (cf. 49), 283n; III, 269, 287n–288n, 286. On the Duke's Laws of New York, see A. E. McKinley, "The Transition from Dutch to English Rule in New York," *American Historical Review*, 6 (1900–01), 704 ff.

[34] [Thomas Fitch, *et al.*], *Reasons Why the British Colonies Should Not Be Charged with Internal Taxes* (New Haven, 1764: JHL Pamphlet 6), p. 9; Dickinson, *Speech Delivered . . . 1764*, in Ford, *Writings*, p. 30; Cooke, *Sermon Preached at Cambridge*, p. 33. Dickinson's assumption in 1764 that Pennsylvania's Charter of Privileges of 1701 was in effect unalterable fundamental law is particularly important. See David L. Jacobson, "John Dickinson's Fight against Royal Government, 1764," *W.M.Q.*, 3d ser., 19 (1962), 72–74. For a particularly valuable analysis of the extent to which colonial charters had taken on the characteristics of modern written constitutions before the Revolution, and

of the years, an additional, transcendent sanction. Those who viewed the world in the light of covenant theology could see the colonial charters as valid not merely in the eyes of the law but in the eyes of God as well: "our charter . . . was a solemn *covenant* between [the King] and our *fathers*" — a "sacred" covenant by which the crown had contracted with a morally regenerate people to maintain their "rights, liberties, and privileges . . . inviolably firm and free from the least innovations, in the same manner that King David stood engaged by the covenant of the people." For "the covenant people of God" in particular, these charters, on the eve of the Revolution, were known to contain "the first great principles, or stamina, of their governments . . . prescribing the forms of their several governments, determining and bounding the power of the crown over them within proper limits, and ascertaining and securing their rights, jurisdictions, and liberties." [35]

It took no wrench of mind, no daring leap, to accept, by then, the concept of a fixed, written constitution limiting the ordinary actions of government. Famous examples of the fact had long been present: the explicit idea, following, brought this experience into consciousness, gave it new meaning and propulsive power.

The same, though perhaps less obviously so, was true of the change in emphasis in the meaning of rights. The abstraction of rights from their embodiments in ancient, customary law, and their purposeful compilation and publication were not entirely

at the Revolution in effect *became,* by subtle alterations, actual state constitutions, see Charles R. Erdman, Jr., *The New Jersey Constitution of 1776* (Princeton, 1929).

[35] Samuel Webster, *The Misery and Duty of an Oppressed and Enslav'd People* . . . (Boston, 1774), pp. 10 ff. (the quotation is at 22); Mather, *America's Appeal* (JHL 59), p. 24. See also Johnson, *Some Important Observations* (JHL 19), pp. 42 ff.; and, for a full presentation of this theme and of the political significance of the renewal of "jeremiad" preaching on the eve of the Revolution, Perry Miller, "From the Covenant to the Revival," *The Shaping of American Religion* (James W. Smith and A. Leland Jamison, eds., *Religion in American Life*, I, Princeton, 1961).

new things for the colonists. Experience in such matters was buried deep in the colonial past; the process, and its results, had been familiar a century before it became systematically important in constitutional theory.

Denied the guidance of experts in the law, lacking sure ideas of what precisely the law provided and what rights were theirs, yet passionately devoted to the belief that English laws and English rights *were* theirs if they would but claim them, the first settlers in British America had found it necessary to compile the law they knew, enumerate its provisions, and specify some, at least, of the rights it guaranteed. The process could hardly have begun earlier than in fact it did. The Pilgrims, responding not to theory but to the practical needs of everyday life, drew up a code of law as early as 1636: "it contains," a leading authority on the early history of American law has written, "a rudimentary bill of rights," which, when elaborated and enlarged in the later years of the seventeenth century, became "a recognizably modern bill of rights." The Puritans did the same, also within two decades of settlement. Their *Laws and Liberties* of 1648 was in design an abridgement of the laws they had themselves enacted; but, "the culmination of an extraordinarily creative period" of legal and constitutional thought, it went beyond restating and digesting the laws in force, to define "the just rights and privileges of every freeman." It quickly became famous, and influential, in all the colonies. It proved to be

the fountainhead of Massachusetts law during most of the seventeenth century, and even thereafter, and its provisions were widely copied by other colonies, or used by them as models in framing their own laws. Through such intercolonial borrowing, its influence spread into other parts of New England, beyond to New York and even to Delaware and Pennsylvania.[36]

[36] Haskins, "Legacy of Plymouth," pp. 9–10, 22; Andrews, *Colonial Period,* I, 458; George L. Haskins, *Law and Authority in Early Massachusetts* (New York, 1960), pp. 136 ff., 120.

But the other colonies were not entirely dependent on New England models. Acting independently, in response to needs similar to those that had motivated the Massachusetts codifiers, they too drew up, on various occasions, their own formulations of rights. The ill-fated "Charter of Liberties and Privileges" passed by the first General Assembly of New York in 1683, contained not only "the outlines of a constitution for the province" but a "bill of rights" as well. Even more elaborate, and explicit, were the provisions of the "Rights and Privileges of the Majesty's Subjects" enacted eight years later, in 1691, by the same body. This remarkable statute, objected to in England because of its "large and doubtful expressions" and disallowed there, listed the rights of the individuals in the form of a series of categorical prohibitions on government: the individual was to be free from unlawful arrest and imprisonment, arbitrary taxation, martial law and the support of standing armies in time of peace, feudal dues, and restrictions on freehold tenure; in addition, he was guaranteed due process of law, especially trial by jury, and, if Protestant, full liberty to "enjoy his or their opinion, persuasions, [and] judgments in matters of conscience and religion throughout all this province."[37]

But, again, it was William Penn who saw farthest and accomplished the most. His "Laws, Concessions, and Agreements" for the province of West New Jersey, which he drafted probably in collaboration with Edward Byllynge and published in 1677, provided not only for the distribution of land and the organization of government but also, and in great detail, for "the common laws or fundamental rights and privileges" of the inhabitants. The central purpose of this remarkably enlightened document was, in fact, to state, so that they might be known and be pre-

[37] Andrews, *Colonial Period*, III, 117, 119; *The Colonial Laws of New York* . . . (Charles Z. Lincoln, *et al.*, eds., Albany, 1894–1896), I, 244–248; *Documents Relative to the Colonial History of the State of New-York* . . . (E. B. O'Callaghan and Berthold Fernow, eds., Albany, 1856–1887), IV, 263–264.

served intact in the New World, "such liberties as were guaranteed by law for the good government of a people, in accord with, as near as conveniently might be, 'the primitive, ancient, and fundamental laws of the people of England.'" Most explicit of all were Penn's statements of rights and privileges in the provisions he made for his own province of Pennsylvania. In his original Concessions and in his Frames of Government, but even more in the so-called "Laws Agreed upon in England" and in the Charter of Liberties and the Charter of Privileges, he laid out, point by point, the rights, duties, and proper regulations of "every phase of human life, civil and social." [38]

By no means all of these documents were bills of rights as we know them. Most of them were not thought of as defining rights antecedent to government and law, rights to which government and law must accommodate themselves. The most common assumption behind them was, rather, that these were rights that the law — English law if not colonial — already provided for and that were now being compiled simply to make them better known and more readily available for reference in a wilderness environment. Presumed to be neither "basic" in some special way nor logically comprehensive, they were mainly devoted to eliminating arbitrary procedures in the enactment and execution of laws. But some of them are nevertheless astonishingly modern, containing some of the precise prohibitions on governmental powers and some of the exact guarantees of individual action that would later come to be thought of as necessary parts of fully evolved bills of rights. The eighteenth century would add nothing to the declaration, in the "Concessions . . . or Fundamental

[38] *The Grants, Concessions, and Original Constitutions of the Province of New Jersey* . . . (Aaron Leaming and Jacob Spicer, eds., [Somerville, N.J., 1881]), pp. 382–409; John E. Pomfret, *The Province of West New Jersey, 1609–1702* (Princeton, 1956), pp. 92 ff.; Andrews, *Colonial Period*, III, 273–274 (cf. 167), 286; *The Federal and State Constitutions, Colonial Charters* . . . (F. N. Thorpe, comp., Washington, D. C., 1909), V, 3044 ff.

Rights" of West New Jersey, that "no men nor number of men upon earth hath power or authority to rule over men's conscience in religious matters"; nor would much improvement be made in the clause providing that no one "shall be deprived or condemned of life, limb, liberty, estate, [or] property . . . without a due trial and judgment passed by twelve good and lawful men of his neighborhood." And it is doubtful if James Madison, writing a full century later, would better the statements in New York's *Act Declaring What Are the Rights and Privileges* guaranteeing "due course of law," trial by jury, and freedom from the obligation to quarter troops in peacetime.[39]

All of these codes and declarations — whatever the deliberate assumptions of their authors, and however archaic or modern-sounding their provisions — were, at the very least, efforts to abstract from the deep entanglements of English law and custom certain essentials — obligations, rights, and prohibitions — by which liberty, as it was understood, might be preserved. As English law in America became better known in the eighteenth century through the work of an increasingly professional bar, and as governmental and judicial processes became stabilized in the colonies, the original need that had given rise to these documents faded. Except where they were embedded in, or protected by, crown charters, they tended to drop from prominence — but not from awareness. In some places surviving intact from the settlement period to the Revolution, well remembered in others where they had been eliminated from the statutes, and everywhere understood to be reasonable and beneficent, these documents formed a continuous tradition in colonial American life, and drifted naturally into the thought of the Revolutionary generation. So in 1774 Alexander Hamilton asserted, as a conclusive argument, that New York's "very remarkable" Act of 1691 "confutes all that has been said concerning the novelty of our present

[39] *Grants of New Jersey*, pp. 394, 395; *Colonial Laws of New York*, I, 247.

claims, and proves that the injurious reflections on the [Continental] Congress for having risen in their demands are malicious and repugnant to truth." [40]

3. SOVEREIGNTY

Representation and consent, constitution and rights — these were basic problems, consideration of which led to shifts in thought that helped shape the character of American radicalism. But of all the intellectual problems the colonists faced, one was absolutely crucial: in the last analysis it was over this issue that the Revolution was fought. On the pivotal question of sovereignty, which is the question of the nature and location of the ultimate power in the state, American thinkers attempted to depart sharply from one of the most firmly fixed points in eighteenth-century political thought; and though they failed to gain acceptance for their strange and awkward views, they succeeded nevertheless in opening this fundamental issue to critical discussion, preparing the way for a new departure in the organization of power.

The idea of sovereignty current in the English-speaking world of the 1760's was scarcely more than a century old. It had first emerged during the English Civil War, in the early 1640's, and had been established as a canon of Whig political thought in the Revolution of 1688. It was composed essentially of two elements. The first was the notion that there must reside somewhere in every political unit a single, undivided, final power, higher in legal authority than any other power, subject to no law, a law unto itself. Derived in part from the political theory of classical antiquity, in part from Roman law, and in part from medieval thought, this idea came to England most directly in the sixteenth-century writings, especially those of Jean Bodin, that sought to justify and fortify monarchial supremacy.

[40] Hamilton, *Farmer Refuted,* in Syrett, *Papers,* I, 163.

But in these early writings the concept of sovereignty still retained important limitations derived from its legal, religious, and pre-national origins. By sovereign Bodin had meant supreme, but not arbitrary: not without restrictions or controls, that is; the action of the sovereign state, he assumed, must still "embody the law of nature and of God." Bodin's theory, Professor McIlwain writes, for all its efforts to establish a power beyond appeal, "is a theory of law not of might, the theory of the *Rechtsstaat;* and it is this theory which . . . for two generations after Bodin dominated even English thought." But then, in the mid-seventeenth-century crisis in England, a change came. In the desperate necessity to isolate a reliable source of order, the permeation of might with right ended; a generation of cold-eyed analysts stripped the idea of sovereignty of its moral and legalistic qualities and laid bare the doctrine of naked force. Hobbes and Filmer are the names most obviously associated with this change in English thought; but it was not their work alone. The familiar restrictions had been attacked and undermined, if not eliminated, by earlier defenders of the royal prerogative — Roger Mainwaring and Robert Sibthorpe (whom the colonists would frequently denounce as pre-eminent absolutists), Francis Bacon, and James I himself. Yet it was, nevertheless, Hobbes who, in a series of writings in the mid-seventeenth century, first went beyond the immediate claims of monarchy to argue systematically that the only essential quality of sovereignty as such — whoever or whatever its possessor might be — was the capacity to compel obedience; and it was with his name, and with Filmer's, that the colonists came to associate the conception of the *Machtstaat* in its most blatant form.[41]

---

[41] McIlwain, *Constitutionalism and the Changing World*, pp. 26–29, 52–55, 72 ff.; Gough, *Fundamental Law*, pp. 117 ff.; Margaret A. Judson, *The Crisis of the Constitution* . . . *1603–1645* (New Brunswick, N.J., 1949), chaps. iv, v; George L. Mosse, *The Struggle for Sovereignty in England* (East Lansing, Mich., 1950), chap. iv.

Final, unqualified, indivisible power was, however, only one part of the notion of sovereignty as it was understood by Englishmen on the eve of the American Revolution. The other concerns its location. Who, or what body, was to hold such powers? For the absolutists of James I's time, as later for Filmer, the answer was, of course, the crown. But others who also believed with Hobbes that "the preservation of life itself depended essentially upon power and not upon law" feared that an absolutely unfettered King would become an absolute despot — precisely the sort of ruler that Charles I had sought to become. In the extraordinary outburst of political theorizing that took place in 1642 when the final break with the crown was made, a new conclusion was drawn from the argument that there must necessarily be "an arbitrary power in every state somewhere." If this power fell to "one man or to a few there may be danger in it, but the Parliament is neither one nor few," and as a result "no inconvenience" would follow from placing arbitrary power in Parliament's hands. Parliament is "so equally and geometrically proportionable" in its composition, "and all the [e]states do so orderly contribute their due parts therein" that its absolute, arbitrary power "is not dangerous nor need to be restrained." [42]

The words are those of Henry Parker, taken from the pamphlet of 1642 in which he "worked out for the first time in English history a theory of Parliamentary sovereignty." He, and others with him, developed the idea further under the pressure of attacks that came, on the one hand from extreme Royalists, now defenders of fundamental law as a necessary qualification on sovereignty, and on the other from extreme libertarians, determined to protect the individual against government in any form. Parker's view survived and flourished, and the result, by the Restoration, was a conception of Parliament that would have been inconceivable

[42] Margaret A. Judson, "Henry Parker and the Theory of Parliamentary Sovereignty," *Essays [to] McIlwain*, pp. 152, 144, 150, 151.

a generation earlier: a body absolute and arbitrary in its sovereignty; the creator and interpreter, not the subject, of law; the superior and master of all other rights and powers within the state. It was this conception of Parliamentary sovereignty that triumphed in the Glorious Revolution; and it was this conception, justified in the end by the theory of an ultimate supremacy of the people — a supremacy, that is, normally dormant and exercised only at moments of rebellion against tyrannical government — that was carried on into the eighteenth century and into the debates that preceded the American Revolution.[43]

It had been a gradual development, and it had ended in a significant inversion. The earliest tradition, Professor McIlwain writes in one of his most striking essays, had been that of Hooker and Coke, Eliot and Hale, who

would have repudiated all arbitrary government whatsoever, whether by king or parliament; Filmer had declared that any government in England must be both arbitrary and royal; for Hobbes it must be arbitrary but not necessarily royal; for many Whigs a century later it must be arbitrary and cannot be royal. Thus after 1689, and the revolution settlement which marked the final triumph of the Whigs, the arbitrary power of Hobbes and Filmer was for the first time "engrafted into the English constitution" . . . and vested in the national assembly . . . For the Whigs the only real sovereign must be the Parliament, that is all.

By the mid-eighteenth century this Whig conception of a sovereign Parliament had hardened into orthodoxy. In the year of the Stamp Act, it was given its classic formulation by Blackstone, who wrote in his *Commentaries* that "there is and must be in all [forms of government] a supreme, irresistible, absolute, uncontrolled authority, in which the *jura summi imperii,* or the rights of sovereignty, reside," and that in England this "sovereignty of the British constitution" was lodged in Parliament, the

[43] Judson, "Henry Parker," pp. 153, 163, 164; Gough, *Fundamental Law,* pp. 176 ff.

aggregate body of King, Lords, and Commons, whose actions "no power on earth can undo." [44]

The formula seemed incontrovertible — "its truth is intuitive," Thomas Pownall declared, "and need not be demonstrated" — and it quickly became the foundation of the English claim against America. For there were few who would deny that "a power to tax is a necessary part of every supreme legislative authority." Therefore if Parliament "have not that power over America they have none, and then America is at once a kingdom of itself." The logic of the Declaratory Act, consequently, was impeccable: Parliament "had, hath, and of right ought to have, full power and authority to make laws and statutes of sufficient force and vitality to bind the colonies and people of America . . . in all cases whatsoever." [45]

How to qualify, undermine, or reinterpret this tenet of English political theory was the central intellectual problem that confronted the leaders of the American cause; and there is no more fascinating spectacle in the history of American political thought than the efforts that were made — starting in the struggle with England over the extent of Parliament's power and continuing into the debates on the ratification of the Federal Constitution — to come to terms with this problem. It is a classic instance of the creative adjustment of ideas to reality. For if in England the concept of sovereignty was not only logical but realistic, it was far from that in the colonies. From the beginning of settlement, circumstances in America had run directly counter to the exercise

---

[44] McIlwain, *Constitutionalism and the Changing World,* pp. 63–64; on the complexities of Blackstone's position, see Ernest Barker, *Essays on Government* (Oxford, 1945), pp. 137–138; for Blackstone's application of these ideas to the question of Parliament's control of the colonies, see Lawrence H. Gipson, "The Great Debate . . . on the Stamp Act, 1766, as Reported by Nathaniel Ryder," *Pa. Mag.,* 86 (1962), 17.

[45] T. C. Hansard, *The Parliamentary History of England . . .* (London, 1806–1820), XVI, 612; [Jared Ingersoll], *Mr. Ingersoll's Letters Relating to the Stamp-Act* (New Haven, 1766; JHL Pamphlet 22), p. 13.

of unlimited and undivided sovereignty. Despite the efforts that had been made by the English government in the late seventeenth century to reduce the areas of local jurisdiction in the colonies, local provincial autonomy continued to characterize American life. Never had Parliament or the crown, or both together, operated in actuality as theory indicated sovereign powers should. They had exercised authority, of course. The crown had retained the final power of legalizing or annulling actions of the colonial legislatures and of the colonial courts; it had made appointments to high office; it had laid down rules and policies for its colonial officials to follow; it had held in its own hand major decisions, civil and military, affecting relations with other nations; and it had continued to claim control of, if not actually to control, vast areas of wild land in the west as well as certain settled territories in the east. Similarly, Parliament had created the colonial postal system, regulated naturalization, and laid down rules for certain economic activities in the colonies, of which the laws of trade and navigation were the most important. But these were far from total powers; together they did not constitute governance in depth, nor did they exclude the exercise of real power by lesser bodies or organs of government. They touched only the outer fringes of colonial life; they dealt with matters obviously beyond the competence of any lesser authority; they concerned the final review of actions initiated and sustained by colonial authorities. All other powers were enjoyed, in fact if not in constitutional theory, by local, colonial organs of government. This area of residual authority, constituting the "internal police" of the community, included most of the substance of everyday life.

It had in fact been local American agencies that effectively created and maintained law and order, for there had been no imperial constabulary, and such elements of England's military power as had appeared in America from time to time had acted for purposes that only incidentally involved the daily lives of the colonists. It had in fact been local, common law courts that administered justice in the colonies; the courts associated with the home government had been condemned as "prerogative," their jurisdiction repeatedly challenged and closely restricted. And it had in fact been local bodies — towns and counties in the first instance, ultimately the provincial Assemblies — that laid down the rules for daily life; rules concerning the production and distribution of wealth, personal conduct, the worship of God — most of the ways in which people deal with the world, animate and inanimate, about them. And these same bodies had been the ones accustomed to tax. Moneys had of course been collected by the home authorities; but they had been fees, dues, and rents — charges, for the most part, incidental to the regulation of overseas trade — not taxes. The power of taxing, from the earliest years of settlement, had been exercised by the representative Assemblies of the various colonies, and exercised without competition — indeed with encouragement — from England.

The condition of British America by the end of the Seven Years' War was therefore anomalous: extreme decentralization of authority within an empire presumably ruled by a single, absolute, undivided sovereign. And anomalous it had been known to be at the time. For decades before 1763 the situation had been remarked on, and reforms proposed by officers of the crown in the colonies as well as by administrators and theorists in England. But since, in the age of Walpole and Newcastle, no sustained effort had been made to alter the situation, the colonists found themselves in 1763 faced not merely with new policies but with a challenge to their settled way of life — a way of life that had been familiar in some places for a century or more. The arguments the colonists put forward against Parliament's claims to the right to exercise sovereign power in America were efforts to express in logical form, to state in the language of constitutional theory, the truth of the world they knew. They were at first,

necessarily, fumbling and unsure efforts, for there were no arguments — there was no vocabulary — to resort to: the ideas, the
terminology, had to be invented.

How was this to be done? What arguments, what words,
could be used to elevate to the status of constitutional principle
the division of authority that had for so long existed and which
the colonists associated with the freedom they had enjoyed?
Here again Otis' pronouncements were among the first and most
famous (they are inextricably involved with his statements on
rights and the constitution), and they are also among his most
confused. In this instance as in others, the curiously anachronistic
quality of his thought led him into difficulties he could not resolve and toward conclusions he could not accept. He assumed
the validity of the current concept of sovereignty — "a supreme
legislative and a supreme executive power must be placed *somewhere* in every commonwealth. Where there is no other positive
provision or compact to the contrary, those powers remain in the
whole body of the people." And he agreed also that in England
this power resided in Parliament. "The power of Parliament is
uncontrollable but by themselves, and we must obey. They only
can repeal their own acts. There would be an end of all government if one or a number of subjects or subordinate provinces
should take upon them so far to judge of the justice of an act
of Parliament as to refuse obedience to it." But to say that a
sovereign Parliament is absolute, he added, is not to say that it
is arbitrary. "The Parliament cannot make 2 and 2, 5," he wrote
in a silent paraphrase of Grotius that encapsulates the whole pre-
Hobbesian view of sovereignty; "omnipotency cannot do it." The
pillars of Parliament "are fixed in judgment, righteousness, and
truth." [46]

[46] Otis, *Rights of the British Colonies* (JHL 7), pp. 12, 39, 47, 48. The
passage in Grotius (*De Jure Belli Et Pacis*, I, i, 10, ¶ 5) containing the arith-
metical example Otis used concerns natural law as a logically necessary restriction on omnipotent power, and it is broadly suggestive of the context of

This position, which reverted to a conception of sovereignty that had been realistic at a time when Parliament's legislative authority had not in fact been supreme, could not in the 1760's be maintained as an effective political argument. It could easily be shown to be self-contradictory. Seeking to maintain it — asserting, that is, the absolute power of what was, by definition, a benign authority — Otis found himself weaving back and forth, fending off attacks from both political extremes. Judged by what he had said about constitutional limitations on legislative power in the writs of assistance case in 1761, his assertion in 1765 that — such is the nature of sovereignty — "it is our duty to submit," appeared to leading patriots to constitute an astonishing reversal, and they could only conclude that he had been "corrupted and bought off" by the ministry. Otis reacted more keenly, however, to the opposite charge, leveled at him both in England and America, that his view of the self-defining restrictions of Parliament's power amounted to claiming for the colonies "an independent, uncontrollable, provincial legislative." Never, he replied, had he intended to make such a claim. Everyone knows, he wrote in his *Vindication,* repeating one of the most commonplace phrases of eighteenth-century political theory, that *"imperium in imperio* [is] the greatest of all political solecisms," [47] and that

Otis' thought and of the reasons for his ultimate dilemma: "Natural law," Grotius wrote, "is so immutable that it cannot be changed by God himself. For though the power of God be immense, there are some things to which it does not extend: because if we speak of those things being done, the words are mere words, and have no meaning, being self-contradictory. Thus God himself cannot make twice two not be four; and in like manner, he cannot make that which is intrinsically bad, not be bad." See, in general on Otis' constitutional arguments the Introductions to his *Rights of the British Colonies* and to his *Vindication of the British Colonies* (JHL 11), in Bailyn, *Pamphlets,* I.

[47] Thus, e.g., Bolingbroke had used the phrase in condemning Walpole's "Robinocracy": such a ministerial government "may properly be called . . . *imperium in imperio,* which hath been always treated as a solæcism in politics by the best writers upon government . . ." *The Craftsman,* no. 172 (October 18, 1728), as republished, vol. V (London, 1731), p. 153. So also in *The Votes and Proceedings of the Freeholders . . . of . . . Boston . . .* (Boston, [1772]: JHL Pam-

there is, consequently, no limit to Parliament's power of legislation or taxation. England "justly asserts the right and authority to bind her colonies where she really thinks the good of the whole requires it; and of this she remains the supreme judge, from whose final determination there is no appeal" — though, of course, he added, from this it does not follow "that 'tis always expedient and in all circumstances equitable for the supreme and sovereign legislative" to use its power.

By 1776 Otis' argument, grossly distended by the pressures placed upon it, was blatantly self-contradictory. By then he was beseeching his readers to believe that he had never intended so much as to hint at limitations on the "unlimited authority of Parliament over the colonies," apologizing to them if he had inadvertently given a different impression, and proclaiming himself in basic agreement with the Grenville ministry. But simultaneously he lashed out at that "contaminated knot of thieves, beggars and transports" in Newport responsible for such "evil work" as Judge Howard's *Halifax Letter,* which stated essentially the same position he was defending.[48]

It was a bewildering performance, and it is little wonder that he was denounced as a "double-faced Jacobite-Whig." [49] His political judgment, on this occasion as on others, was obviously

---

phlet 36), p. 4, Catholics are condemned as introducing "that solecism in politics, *imperium in imperio,* leading directly to the worst anarchy and confusion, civil discord, war and bloodshed"; *"imperium in imperio,"* Daniel Leonard wrote, is "the heighth of political absurdity." *The Origin of the American Contest with Great-Britain* . . . (New York, 1775: JHL Pamphlet 56), p. 56. For the explicit repudiation of the formula, see Iredell's remarks, quoted below, pp. 224–225.

[48] *Rights of the British Colonies,* p. 40; Adams, *Works,* X, 296–297; Otis, *Vindication* (JHL 11), pp. 4, 14, 5; [Otis], *Brief Remarks on the Defence of the Halifax Libel* . . . (Boston, 1765), pp. 22, 5. On the political embarrassment of Otis' ambiguity, see Governor Bernard's statement of 1770, quoted in Gipson, *British Empire,* XII, 39.

[49] Ellen E. Brennan, "James Otis: Recreant and Patriot," *New England Quarterly,* 12 (1939), 722.

erratic. But his troubles mainly stemmed, here as in his arguments on other constitutional issues, from his peculiar application of early seventeenth-century ideas and assumptions to eighteenth-century problems. Failing to recognize that the idea of sovereignty had long since acquired as an essential characteristic arbitrariness as well as absolutism, he saw no danger in allowing Parliament to exercise sovereign authority, and to exercise it not only over the nation proper but over distant colonies as well. Parliament might make occasional mistakes, he admitted, but in the end — such was the wonder of the British constitution — it would necessarily act justly and wisely. If the Stamp Act was in fact wrong, Parliament would repeal it.

The repeal, when it came, was too late to vindicate Otis' position. By then, leading colonial writers were attacking the problem of sovereignty in a different way — a more realistic and pragmatic way. Tacitly acknowledging that by accepted definition sovereignty was both absolute and arbitrary, but convinced nevertheless that there were things that Parliament could not rightly do, they set out, silent on the metaphysics of the problem, to locate pragmatically a line of separation between powers of Parliament that were valid when exercised in America and those that were not. It was only later and gradually, when challenged by informed and articulate opponents, that they faced up to the implications of what they had been doing, and acknowledged that they were in effect calling "sovereignty itself into question" and attempting to reconceive the basic principles of state authority.[50]

The path the colonists took away from the accepted eighteenth-

[50] "If, intemperately, unwisely, fatally," Edmund Burke predicted in his Speech on American Taxation, "you sophisticate and poison the very source of government by urging subtle deductions . . . from the unlimited and illimitable nature of supreme sovereignty, you will teach them by these means to call that sovereignty itself in question. When you drive him hard, the boar will surely turn upon the hunters. If that sovereignty and their freedom cannot be reconciled, which will they take? They will cast your sovereignty in your face. Nobody will be argued into slavery."

century notions of sovereignty appears now, in retrospect, to have been so clear that it is surprising that it was not seen sooner than it was by the colonists themselves. For, as Otis made abundantly evident, any effort to restrict Parliament's power assumed that sovereignty was in some sense divisible; and to search deliberately for the actual seams along which the fabric of power might be divided was to grope toward a political order in which "powers of government are separated and distinguished and in which these powers are distributed among governments, each government having its quota of authority and each its distinct sphere of activity."[51] But the awareness of this fact was slow in developing: the discussion began at the level of specific distinctions in the powers of Parliament, and it progressed to more general grounds only after it was shown that these distinctions could not be maintained.

The first distinction advanced in the effort to express in constitutional language the limitations on Parliament's power familiar to the colonists, was extemporized casually by the simple expedient of applying to this constitutional problem one of the most common pairs of antonyms in the English language. No distinction could be more obvious or more fundamental than that between things "internal" and things "external." Not only did it appear to separate out conveniently the powers that had been exercised for so long by the colonists' own Assemblies and those that had been exercised by Parliament, but it did so echoing the

[51] Andrew C. McLaughlin, "The Background of American Federalism," *American Political Science Review,* 12 (1918), 215. The interpretation in the pages that follow owes much to this essay which argues "that the essential qualities of American federal organization were largely the product of the practices of the old British empire as it existed before 1764" and that "the discussions of the generation from the French and Indian war to the adoption of the federal Constitution, and more particularly, the discussions in the ten or twelve years before independence" were devoted to the problems of this kind of organization. See also McLaughlin, *Foundations of American Constitutionalism,* chap. vi; McIlwain, "Historical Background of Federal Government."

words of some of the most respected authorities on questions of government.[52] An ordinary distinction already drawn into theoretical discussions, used in all sorts of ways in everyday speech, it quickly drifted into the discussion of Anglo-American relations. It was used loosely throughout the pre-Revolutionary years, applied generally to spheres of government, and it was specified by some to the problem of taxation.

Thus in 1764 Richard Bland, searching for a principle by which to assign exclusive powers to colonial governments and yet retain the colonies' dependency on England, found the distinction between things internal and things external to be essential to his purpose. If Virginians are freemen, he argued, they must have a representative assembly capable of enacting "laws for the INTERNAL government of the colony" — "internal" being defined so as to exclude "all power derogatory to their dependence upon the mother kingdom . . . In every instance, therefore, of

[52] Thus Burlamaqui in his *Principles of Natural and Politic Law* (1747; first complete English trans., 1752) argued that "there are two sorts of obligations, one internal and the other external. By internal obligation I understand that which is produced only by our own reason, considered as the primitive rule of conduct, and in consequence of the good or evil the action in itself contains. By external obligation we mean that which arises from the will of a being on whom we allow ourselves dependent and who commands or prohibits some particular things under a commination of punishment" (I, vi, 13; see also I, x, 8–10). Similarly, Vattel, arguing that nations, like men, are naturally "free and independent of each other" except where a bonded obligation has been incurred, pointed out that such an obligation "and the right correspondent to it . . . is distinguished into *external* and *internal*. The obligation is *internal*, as it binds the conscience, and as it comprehends the rules of our duty; it is *external*, as it is considered relatively to other men, and as it produces some right between them." He then discussed the freedom of action permissible to nations in the light of internal and external obligations. *Law of Nations* (London, 1759: the edition used by both Otis and Bland), I, Introduction, secs. 16–17, 20, 27 (pp. 5–7). For an example of the direct use of Burlamaqui's distinction between internal and external obligations in the discussion of Parliament's powers in America, see Samuel Cooper to Thomas Pownall, March 25, 1773, in *American Historical Review*, 8 (1902–03), 328. For the importance of the distinction in Harrington's thought, see Charles Blitzer, *An Immortal Commonwealth* (New Haven, 1960), pp. 111 ff.

our EXTERNAL government we are and must be subject to the authority of the British Parliament, but in no others; for if the Parliament should impose laws upon us merely relative to our INTERNAL government, it deprives us, as far as those laws extend, of the most valuable part of our birthright as Englishmen . . ." And if Parliament is limited in its legislative power over the colonies to external matters, "then any tax respecting our IN-TERNAL polity which may hereafter be imposed on us by act of Parliament is arbitrary, as depriving us of our rights, and may be opposed."

When the Stamp Act controversy exploded, the distinction naturally became part of the discussion of the rights involved. Stephen Hopkins, writing for the colony of Rhode Island, began by defining stamp duties as internal taxes and hence properly within the jurisdiction of the separate colonial legislatures, which had responsibility for the "internal government" of the colonies. The colonial jurisdiction of Parliament, he wrote, was quite different. Its proper power was over

things of a more general nature, quite out of the reach of these particular legislatures . . . One of this kind is the commerce of the whole British empire, taken collectively, and that of each kingdom and colony in it as it makes a part of that whole. Indeed, everything that concerns the proper interest and fit government of the whole commonwealth, of keeping the peace, and subordination of all the parts towards the whole and one among another, must be considered in this light.

For all such "matters of general nature" there must be some "supreme and overruling authority" to make laws and "compel their execution," and such a supreme power, everyone knows, Hopkins wrote, lies in "that grand and august legislative body," Parliament. He did not at this point develop the idea that if "internal" taxes were denied Parliament, "external" taxes might not be; he was not attempting to distinguish among types of taxes but to deal with the broader issue of spheres of authority within which taxation fell.[53]

Others, however, would make this distinction — casually, almost inadvertently, and not with the sense that it was exclusive, comprehensive, or rigorously logical. Thus Connecticut's protest, published under the title *Reasons Why the British Colonies in America Should Not Be Charged with Internal Taxes,* in effect defined all taxation as "internal" taxation, and though it denied Parliament all right to tax the colonies, conceded to it the right to raise revenue through duties on trade, since such commercial fees, as distinct from taxes, fell properly within the sphere of "external" government. Others agreed, especially when it was understood, as Dulany explained, that the essential difference between internal taxes and trade duties was that the former were levied *"for the single purpose of revenue"* and the latter only "for the regulation of trade." [54]

But discriminating among the intentions of lawmakers was both difficult and dangerous; trade duties — whether called "external taxes" or not — could be as onerous as excise taxes. "They may find duties on trade enough," Thomas Hutchinson warned, "to drain us so thoroughly that it will not be possible to pay internal taxes as a revenue to them or even to support government within ourselves." It was obviously to the benefit of the administration to consolidate the advantage this presumed concession appeared to bestow, no matter how "nonsensical" informed people believed distinctions in revenue-raising powers to be. By 1765 English opponents of American claims were imputing to

[53] Bland, *Colonel Dismounted* (JHL 4), p. 22; [Stephen Hopkins], *The Rights of Colonies Examined* (Providence, 1765: JHL Pamphlet 9), pp. 10, 11. For Hopkins' later distinction between taxing the colonies in their "interior police" and in their "foreign importations," see Bailyn, *Pamphlets,* I, 504.
[54] On Connecticut's pamphlet and the issues involved, see Introduction to Pamphlet 6 in Bailyn, *Pamphlets,* I, and the documents cited there; Dulany, *Considerations* (JHL 13), p. 33.

the distinction between "internal" and "external" taxation, said to be commonly drawn in the colonies (it was the opinion "of most people" in Boston, according to Hutchinson), an importance and a rigor that had never been intended for it and that made it vulnerable to attacks no one had expected it to have to withstand. That the usage took on this importance and became the subject of powerful attacks was to a considerable extent the result of the stress placed on it by Benjamin Franklin in the course of his famous three-hour testimony before the House of Commons in February 1766.[55]

No one could have been better informed on the state of American thinking and on the armory of weapons the colonists had devised to attack Parliamentary taxation than Franklin. Having

[55] Hutchinson to Ebenezer Silliman, Boston, November 9, 1764, quoted in Edmund S. Morgan and Helen M. Morgan, *The Stamp Act Crisis* (Chapel Hill, 1953), p. 216; Thomas Whately to John Temple, May 2, 1767, in MHS *Colls.*, 6th ser., IX, 83. Cf. Edmund S. Morgan, "Colonial Ideas of Parliamentary Power, 1764–1766," *W.M.Q.*, 3d ser., 5 (1948), 311–341, where it is argued that the colonists never admitted Parliament's right to levy external taxes, the presumed concession being an attribution to the colonists by writers and debaters in England, and that the colonists' arguments against Parliamentary taxation appeared fully developed in the Stamp Act crisis. The present interpretation, which owes much to Morgan's, differs from it not so much on whether or not this concession was ever made by the colonists (I find that it was, though uncommonly and, in the ways indicated, indeliberately) but on the more basic question of the development of the colonists' constitutional ideas. In the perspective of the fundamental problem of sovereignty, whether the colonists did or did not admit Parliament's right to impose "external" taxes is less important than that they universally thought in terms of "internal" and "external" spheres of government, and that this distinction, of which the taxing issue was a specification, provided them with the means of discriminating among and qualifying the sovereign powers of Parliament. (On this point, see, in addition, the citations in note 65 below.) For an example of the colonists' admission of external taxation, see, besides those cited in Bailyn, *Pamphlets*, I, Charles Carroll's explanation of the propriety of Parliament's taxing the colonies by "disallowing drawbacks and imposing duties on our imports and exports," in his letter to Henry Graves, September 15, 1765, *Unpublished Letters of Charles Carroll of Carrollton* . . . (Thomas M. Field, ed., New York, 1902), p. 90. Cf., more generally, James Iredell's "Causes Leading up to the American Revolution," in Griffith J. McRee, *Life and Correspondence of James Iredell* (New York, 1857–58), I, 287 ff.

left America well after the discussion of the Stamp Act had begun, and having kept in continuous communication with the colonists and with the other agents in London since his arrival there, he knew the official and unofficial literature of opposition thoroughly. In his blandly confident, adroit, and hardheaded testimony covering the whole range of issues in the controversy, the "internal"–"external" distinction became crucial. Since it allowed him to evade the question of whether or not his countrymen were in principle denying Parliament's right to tax them, he referred to it frequently and was forced to defend it. The colonists were not, he said, denying Parliament's right to collect moneys from them. They had long acknowledged Parliament's right "of laying duties to regulate commerce." What they were objecting to as "unconstitutional and unjust" was Parliament's effort "to lay internal taxes," for such a right "was never supposed to be in Parliament, as we are not represented there." His interrogators pressed him: Did he really believe that such a distinction was valid? Yes, Franklin assured them, he did; the difference between "external" and "internal" taxing was "very great."

An external tax is a duty laid on commodities imported; that duty is added to the first cost and other charges on the commodity, and, when it is offered to sale, makes a part of the price. If the people do not like it at that price, they refuse it; they are not obliged to pay it. But an internal tax is forced from the people without their consent, if not laid by their own representatives.

But may not the colonists "by the same interpretation object to Parliament's right of external taxation?" Franklin's reply was shrewdly evasive:

Many arguments have been lately used here to show them that there is no difference, and that if you have no right to tax them internally, you have none to tax them externally, or make any other law to bind them. At present they do not reason so; but in time they may possibly be convinced by these arguments.[56]

Some, in the colonies, were in fact already approaching such conclusions. Dulany's pamphlet, published only a few months before Franklin spoke, had done more than sophisticate the meaning of "internal" taxation. It had broadened the discussion, and led it to a higher plane of generality. For, Dulany had argued, if there were, as he believed, powers that inferior bodies might exercise "without control or compulsion" — if there were areas where "the authority of the superior can't properly interpose" — does it not follow that the superior authority is actually limited in what it can do "by the powers vested in the inferior"?[57] In the light of such a possibility, and in the light of the approaching Townshend Duties — aimed as obviously as the Stamp Act at raising a revenue yet "external" by the colonists' own definition — the inadequacy of the much overstrained distinction between "internal" and "external" taxation for marking the limits of Parliament's power over the colonies became obvious. John Dickinson, in his *Farmer's Letters* (1767–68), flatly and formally repudiated it, and, examining the problem of Parliament's power with greater acuity than any writer had shown before, went on to a new stage in the exploration of the idea of sovereignty.

All taxation, Dickinson wrote in his famous pamphlet, being an "imposition to raise money," is essentially the same, and so there is no difference between "external" and "internal" taxation. Parliament has no right to levy taxes on Americans for any purpose whatsoever: that much was clear. What was not so clear,

---

[56] Albert H. Smyth, ed., *The Writings of Benjamin Franklin* (New York, 1905–1907), IV, 421, 424, 445, 446. On Franklin's constitutional ideas, see Verner W. Crane, ed., *Benjamin Franklin's Letters to the Press, 1758–1775* (Chapel Hill, 1950), pp. xxxvii–xlvi, 60–61, and documents cited there.

[57] Dulany, *Considerations* (JHL 13), p. 15.

what needed discussion, and what he followed out in his thought boldly and imaginatively, was the proper role of a central government in a truly imperial constitution. The legislature of an empire, he said, was different from the legislature of a nation. Though the two might exist in the same body, they had different functions and powers as organs of government. Over the American colonies Parliament must have all the power, but only the power, necessary to maintain the essential connections of empire, and this meant the power to regulate commerce and other aspects of the economy "in such a manner as [England] thought most conducive to their mutual advantage and her own welfare." The duties imposed in the course of such regulation, he made clear, would be legitimate, for such "external impositions" do not grant property away but only prevent its acquisition. England's other imperial powers were quite specific, and inhered not in Parliament but in the crown: the power to repeal colonial legislation, to exercise "the *executive* authority of government," and to sit in appeal "from all judgments in the administration of justice." [58]

In admitting that Parliament had such regulatory authority but yet no taxing powers whatever over America, Dickinson was approaching a conception of sovereignty different in essence from what had been accepted hitherto. For in assuming an empire to be basically different from a unitary nation, he was saying now explicitly that its sovereign body need not be supreme everywhere and in all matters in the territory it controlled, but only on some issues and in some ways, and that other, lesser bodies might exercise absolute and arbitrary powers — sovereign powers in effect — within spheres specifically allotted to them.

Once the discussion had reached this level, a maturing of views took place rapidly. For the reiterated assertions that were soon heard to the effect that even "the boldest advocates for the

[58] [John Dickinson], *Letters from a Farmer in Pennsylvania* . . . (Philadelphia, 1768: JHL Pamphlet 23), pp. 20, 24.

power of Parliament cannot, at this day, without blushing, assert that it is sovereign and supreme *in every respect whatsoever"* — such assertions required a fuller rationalization and a more cogent explanation of principle than even Dickinson had given them if they were to be kept from degenerating into the more extreme claims, already being heard in 1768, that Parliament "cannot pass *any* laws to bind us." Such a notion, the Reverend John Joachim Zubly stated in 1769, must contain "some fallacy couched under an otherwise specious appearance." For it is not a matter of all or nothing. There are, he wrote in his fumbling yet original and penetrating *Enquiry,* significant gradations in the authority of Parliament derived from the variety of separate national entities it rules. The British "EMPIRE" is a more "extensive word" than the "kingdom" of Great Britain; it refers to "England, Scotland, Ireland, the Islands of Man, Jersey, Guernsey, Gibraltar, and Minorca, etc., in the Mediterranean; Senegal, etc., in Africa; Bombay, etc., in the East Indies; and the islands and colonies in North America, etc." The peoples of these extensive domains are not to be equally affected by Parliament's power. With regard to trade, yes: "the power of making it most beneficial to the head and every branch of the empire is vested in the British Parliament"; and with regard to rights, yes: Parliament must guarantee that "all the British subjects everywhere have a right to be ruled by the known principles of their common constitution." But otherwise, the various peoples of the empire are ruled unequally by Parliament; the "nature and degree of [their] dependence" upon Parliament "is not exactly alike," and Parliamentary laws affect them only in cases where they are specifically named, and to the extent of the specification.[59]

[59] Hickes, *Nature and Extent of Parliamentary Power* (JHL 24), p. xiii (see also, p. 23: "while the power of the British Parliament is acknowledged *sovereign and supreme in every respect whatsoever,* the liberty of America is no more than a flattering dream, and her privileges delusive shadows"); Downer, *Discourse* (JHL 25), p. 7; Zubly, *Humble Enquiry* (JHL 28), pp. 2–4, 6, 9.

By then the departure from the traditional understanding of sovereignty had gone far enough to make a sharp recall to orthodoxy advisable on the part of spokesmen for England. The most notable statement of this sort was written in 1769 by William Knox, a Grenvillite, who the following year would be appointed undersecretary of state for the colonies. Knox, setting a pattern for subsequent opponents of American claims, began by ridiculing what he understood to have been the shifting American positions on what Parliament could and could not do in regard to the colonies. First, he said, the colonists had attempted to distinguish "internal" taxation from "external"; then, when Parliament "seemed to adopt the distinction" and introduced just such "external" taxing, they changed their minds and decided to distinguish taxation for the purpose of regulating trade from taxation for the purpose of creating a revenue — a distinction, Knox wrote, "of all absurdities the most ridiculous that ever was contended for." Finally, they had rejected taxation altogether and admitted only commercial regulation. There was no logic or law behind such gyrations. What Americans were really objecting to had nothing to do with constitutional principles. Their objection was not to Parliament's constitutional right to levy certain kinds of taxes as opposed to certain others, but to its effort to collect any. Their theoretical position was worthless:

For if the authority of the legislative be not in one instance equally supreme over the colonies as it is over the people of England, then are not the colonies of the same community with the people of England. All distinctions destroy this union; and if it can be shown in any particular to be dissolved, it must be so in all instances whatever. There is no alternative: either the colonies are a part of the community of Great Britain or they are in a state of nature with respect to her, and in no case can be subject to the jurisdiction of that legislative power which represents her community, which is the British Parliament.[60]

[60] [William Knox], *The Controversy Between Great Britain and Her Colonies Reviewed* . . . (London, 1769), as reprinted in *Old South Leaflets,* no. 210

TRANSFORMATION

It was a rebuttal not so much of the pragmatic efforts that had been made in America to limit the power of Parliament as of attempts like that of Zubly to devise a theoretical justification for dividing sovereign power in any way at all. This abstract problem was at the heart of the controversy between England and the colonies, and once directly confronted, it could not be evaded. As a consequence the major constitutional issue in debate shifted permanently after 1769 from the specific questions of taxes and the administration of government to the correct definition of a concept of political science. While defenders of England's policies followed Knox in insisting on the indivisibility of Parliament's sovereignty, American leaders, gingerly choosing among the alternatives open to them, felt their way toward new conclusions.

The structure of this critical problem of theory is perhaps best revealed in the remarkable series of exchanges between Lieutenant Governor Thomas Hutchinson of Massachusetts and the two Houses of Assembly of that colony in 1773. Smarting under the publication late in 1772 of the belligerent *Votes and Proceedings* of the Boston Town Meeting, Hutchinson on January 6, 1773, launched a formal debate with the legislature on the central question involved.[61] His opening speech was characteristically

(S. E. Morison, ed.), pp. 8–9, 10–11 (pp. 34–35, 44, 50 in the original edition). Cf. [John Mein], *Sagittarius's Letters and Political Speculations* . . . (Boston, 1775), p. 12; [Jonathan Boucher], *A Letter from a Virginian* . . . ([New York], 1774: JHL Pamphlet 46), pp. 20, 23; Leonard ("Massachusettensis"), *Origin of the American Contest* (JHL 56), pp. 62–63.

[61] The entire debate was published by order of the House in a 126-page pamphlet entitled *The Speeches of His Excellency Governor Hutchinson to the General Assembly . . . 1773. With the Answers of His Majesty's Council and the House of Representatives Respectively* . . . (Boston, 1773: JHL Pamphlet 37). The same documents, with the exception of the governor's concluding speech of March 6, are reprinted in [Alden Bradford, ed.], *Speeches of the Governors of Massachusetts, from 1765 to 1775* . . . (Boston, 1818), pp. 336–396. The passages quoted in the paragraphs that follow are from pp. 5, 7, 11, 13, 18, 19, 20, 31, 35, 56–57, 60, 61, 81, 115, of the pamphlet, corresponding to pp. 337, 338, 340, 342, 344, 345, 351, 353, 364, 368, 369, 379 in Bradford's *Speeches*.

temperate and lucid. Assuming that "from the nature of government there must be one supreme authority" and that for Britons everywhere it was lodged in Parliament, "of which the King is a constituent part," he explained that the Boston *Votes* were subversive in that some of them deny "the supreme authority of Parliament" and others "speak of this supreme authority . . . in such terms as have a direct tendency to alienate the affections of the people from their sovereign." Methodically, he took up the arguments of the Town Meeting, arguments based in turn on reason, on the charter, on the rights of Englishmen, and on natural rights. He concluded that there was "no line that can be drawn between the supreme authority of Parliament and the total independence of the colonies: it is impossible there should be two independent legislatures in one and the same state for . . . two legislative bodies will make two governments as distinct as the kingdoms of England and Scotland before the Union." He ended in the same spirit of reason in which he had begun, requesting the two Houses, since "independence I may not allow myself to think that you can possibly have in contemplation," to communicate their sentiments to him "with the same freedom and unreservedness as I have communicated mine to you" so that he might be convinced of his error "if I am wrong in my principles of government or in the inference which I have drawn from them."

The two Houses lost no time in replying. The Council, confessing certain doubts about some of the Boston Resolves but vehemently defending the town's right to issue such declarations, pointed out that if in insisting that Parliament's indivisible authority was "supreme" Hutchinson had meant to imply that it was "unlimited," he should realize that he was in effect offering the colonies only the choice between slavery (except for the liberties that might be granted them by "the mere grace and favor of their governors") and "a declaration of total independence." The councilors denied that the choice was properly so narrow. There is no such thing, they wrote, as total, absolute authority: "supreme or unlimited authority can with fitness belong only to the sovereign of the universe"; the supreme authority in all human governments, including that of Parliament, is by its very nature limited. The real question is how to state those limitations and thus to define other alternatives than those Hutchinson had offered. To fix "with precision" the limits of Parliament's authority, "to determine the exact lines of right and wrong," was, they admitted, a most difficult task which ordinarily they would not attempt; but the governor's speech having "made it absolutely necessary" for them to do so, they proceeded to review the essential parts of the constitution that demonstrated the illegality of Parliament's taxing the people of Massachusetts.

The House leaders too confessed that "it is difficult to draw a line of distinction between the universal authority of Parliament over the colonies and no authority at all," but they declared that if they were forced to make a choice between all or nothing they would certainly choose the latter, for "there is more reason to dread the consequences of absolute uncontrolled supreme power, whether of a nation or a monarch, than those of total independence." But why this choice? What if, as Hutchinson said, two independent legislatures *did* make two separate governments? If they were "united in one head and common sovereign" and did not interfere with each other, could they not "live happily in that connection and mutually support and protect each other"?

Hutchinson retorted sharply to the Council, informing them that their efforts to separate out permissible from forbidden powers in a sovereign body "rather tend to evince the impracticability of drawing such a line." Logically, what they were saying was that two supreme authorities could act simultaneously over the same people; but this, he insisted, was simply impossible. The claims of the House he could not so easily dismiss, for he understood the importance of the legal arguments that could be mobilized to defend the idea that two absolute legislatures might coexist within an empire if they came into contact only in the person of the King. It took this accomplished lawyer, scholar, and politician twenty-two pages of closely wrought and learned prose to state his reasons for believing that the chartered authority of the Massachusetts government derived and depended not from the King but from "the *crown* of England" and was "consequently subject to the supreme authority of England," that is, to Parliament.

The debate went on in exchanges of messages for two months, until it exhausted the knowledge, ingenuity, and patience of all involved. The final statement was Hutchinson's, and it was prophetic. You believe, he said in his recapitulation, that "a *subordinate* power in government . . . , whilst it keeps within its limits, is not subject to the control of the *supreme* power." This is illogical, for how can there be "a *subordinate* power without a power *superior* to it? Must it not, so far as it is without control, be itself supreme?"

It is essential to the being of government that a power should always exist which no other power within such government can have right to withstand and control. Therefore, when the word *power* relates to the supreme authority of government it must be understood *absolute* and *unlimited*.

The future looked dark, he said, for "no sensible writer upon government has before denied" the principles he was restating, and if the members of the Massachusetts General Court

are still of opinion that two jurisdictions, each of them having a share in the supreme power, are compatible in the same state, it can be to no purpose to reason or argue . . . It's enough to observe that this disagreement in our principles will have its influence upon all the deductions which are made from them.

And so it did. The powerful influence of "this disagreement in our principles" was felt generally in the two years that followed. Leading Americans like John Dickinson continued to insist — though now with increasing desperation — that "the sovereignty over the colonies must be limited," that "a line there must be," in principle as well as in fact, setting off Parliament's powers from those of the colonial legislatures, and that this line gave to the English government control of the commerce and foreign affairs of the colonies and to the colonial Assemblies "exclusive right of internal legislation," including taxing. But the response was as adamant, as rigidly secured to the traditional conception of sovereignty as Hutchinson's had been. By the middle of October 1774, when Dickinson's view was adopted as the official American position by the first Continental Congress, its ineffectiveness was widely conceded. Spokesmen for England repeated, with what appears to have been an almost obsessive and ritualistic regularity, that if the colonial legislatures were not in principle "subordinate to the supreme sovereign authority of the nation . . . there is *imperium in imperio:* two sovereign authorities in the same state; which is a contradiction." Arguments to the contrary, Joseph Galloway wrote, were nothing but "unintelligible jargon and horrid nonsense"; an independent unit of government within the territory of the principal state, he explained, "is a *monster, a thing out of nature*"; what the Revolutionaries had taken into their *"learned* heads, philosophers-like," to do was to "conceive that the supreme legislative authority, which is indivisible in its nature, was, like matter, divisible *ad infinitum;* and under this profound mistake, you began with splitting and dividing it, until by one slice after another, you have hacked and pared it away to less than an atom." [62]

There was little point, in the face of such inflexibility, in con-

---

[62] Dickinson, *Essay on the Constitutional Power of Great-Britain,* in *Pennsylvania Archives,* 2d ser., III, 603, 569–589. Cf. article 4 of the Declaration and Resolves of the first Continental Congress. Seabury, *A View,* in Vance, *Letters of a Westchester Farmer,* p. 119; [Joseph Galloway], *A Reply to an Address to . . . a Candid Examination . . .* (New York, 1775), pp. 17, 26, 20.

tinuing to press for a formal classification and division of Parliament's powers. Defenders of American claims were forced to move on to the politically more extreme position that the Massachusetts House had maintained. Acknowledging the impossibility of convincing the authorities in England that Parliament's sovereignty might be divisible, they pursued, with careful logic and a wealth of legal learning, the idea of an imperial federation of sovereign states sharing and establishing unity in a single monarch. If, Moses Mather argued, two supreme powers within a single state are really "the height of political absurdity" then let Parliament's power be totally excluded from the colonies. But the exclusion of Parliament's authority would not necessarily mean the total elimination of all links to England. For, he explained, a "state" was, after all, only "a country or body of people that are connected and united under one and the same constitution of civil government," and there was therefore no contradiction in conceiving of two such entities sharing the same king. George III derived his authority as "King of the American colonies" from a source different from that which empowers his rule as King of Great Britain. And since, "when several rights or capacities meet and are vested in one and the same person they remain entire and as distinct as though they were vested in different persons," the King's role as the first of the three estates in Parliament in no way means that the authority of that body extends to America.[63]

Others arrived by other routes at this total rejection of Parliamentary authority in favor of what would become the modern notion of Commonwealth relations. James Iredell condemned the "beautiful theory" of sovereignty as "narrow and pedantic," "calculated to sacrifice to a *point of speculation* the happiness of millions," and developed the argument from the inapplicability of the idea of sovereignty — "the great solecism of an *imperium*

[63] Mather, *America's Appeal* (JHL 59), pp. 44, 47, 34, 46.

in imperio" — "to the case of several *distinct* and *independent legislatures* each engaged within a *separate* scale and employed about *different* objects. The *imperium in imperio* argument is, therefore, not at all applicable to our case, though it has been so vainly and confidently relied on." The most powerful presentations were based on legal precedents, especially *Calvin's Case* (1608), which, it was claimed, proved on the authority of Coke and Bacon that subjects of the King are by no means necessarily subjects of Parliament. One of the most notable pamphlets that developed the details of this claim, James Wilson's *Considerations on the Nature and the Extent of the Legislative Authority of the British Parliament* (1774), opened with a revealing confession. The maturing of his thought, Wilson wrote in his Preface, had been an unwilling progression. He had begun, only a few years earlier, with the

expectation of being able to trace some constitutional line between those cases in which we ought, and those in which we ought not, to acknowledge the power of Parliament over us. In the prosecution of [my] enquiries, [I] became fully convinced that such a line does not exist, and that there can be no medium between *acknowledging* and *denying* that power in all cases.

Under the pressure of insistent declarations that sovereignty was indivisible he had followed out the "principles of reason, of liberty, and of law," to their natural conclusion, which was that "the only dependency which [the colonies] ought to acknowledge is a dependency on the crown." [64]

But the position that Wilson and others had given up — that Parliament's sovereignty did extend to America but was consti-

[64] James Iredell, *Address to the Inhabitants of Great Britain* (n.p., 1774), in McRee, *Iredell*, I, 206, 207, 217, 219; Wilson, *Considerations* (JHL 44), pp. [iii], 31. On Calvin's Case and the legal-historical argument, see Bailyn, *Pamphlets*, I, 709–710 (note 25) and documents cited there. See also Hutchinson's arguments, *Speeches*, pp. 62–83; and, in general, Adams, *Political Ideas*, chaps. iii, v.

tutionally limited by the powers reserved to the colonial legislatures — had not been forgotten. The movement of thought had
been so rapid, however, that this argument, radical for the mid-
1760's, had by 1775 become a conservative bastion; it was defended not only in point of theory by authentic leaders of the
American cause who, like John Dickinson, hesitated to proceed
to the more extreme position, but also by outspoken Tories who,
continuing to ridicule the theory of divided sovereignty, accepted
it in practice as they sought to establish some measure of rapport
with the new forces of American life. To "disavow the authority
of Parliament" and still claim allegiance to the King, the New
York Tory leader Samuel Seabury wrote in 1774, "is another
piece of Whiggish nonsense"; and he cited Pitt's speeches in
Parliament and Dickinson's *Farmer's Letters* to defend the argument, now comfortably old-fashioned, that the line to be drawn
— in fact if not in theory — between "the supremacy of Great
Britain and the dependency of the colonies" should leave "all
internal taxation . . . in our own legislatures, and the right of
regulating trade . . . [and] enacting all general laws for the
good of the colonies" in Parliament. So also, with minor variations, wrote the English traveler John Lind; so too wrote Daniel
Leonard in Massachusetts; so too Joseph Galloway in Pennsylvania; so too Thomas Bradbury Chandler in New York; and
so too, in the end — though still ambiguously and much too late
— did the government of George III.[65]

[65] Seabury, *A View*, in Vance, *Letters of a Westchester Farmer*, pp. 112, 125;
[John Lind?], *An Englishman's Answer, to the Address, from the Delegates
. . .* (New York, 1775), pp. 14–16; Leonard ("Massachusettensis"), in *Novan-
glus and Massachusettensis . . .* (Boston, 1819), pp. 202–203 (also *Massachusetts
Gazette*, February 20–27, 1775) Galloway's Plan of Union, 1774, in Morison,
Sources and Documents, pp. 116–118; [Chandler], *What Think Ye of the
Congress Now?* p. 44. The distinction between fact and theory in accepting a
division of sovereignty between internal and external jurisdictions was drawn
with particular clarity by Thomas Pownall, replying to Dickinson's *Essay*, in the
1774 edition of his *Administration of the British Colonies*, II, 89–111. Pownall,
a former governor of Massachusetts and in general sympathetic to the colonies

TRANSFORMATION

Through all these years of crisis, when American thought had moved steadily from Otis' archaisms and confusions to Wilson's advanced speculations on imperial federalism, the British ministry, fortified by fresh, militant assertions such as Dr. Johnson's that "in sovereignty there are no gradations," had remained adamant in its refusal even to consider infringing the Declaratory Act. Its final, pre-Independence proposals for reconciliation did not compromise the point. Only in 1778 — after Independence had invoked the ultimate sovereignty of the people; after most of the states had organized their own governments, and the Articles of Confederation of the new nation had been drawn up and submitted to the states for ratification; and only under the pressure of the catastrophe at Saratoga and of France's entrance into the war — only then, in the instructions to the ill-fated Carlisle Commission, did the North administration relent sufficiently to endorse, though still not in theory, the position that Dickinson had advanced so long ago in the *Farmer's Letters.*

Such a grudging concession was by then grotesquely irrelevant to the realities of the situation. The idea that Americans would at that late date be willing, as the instructions to the Carlisle Commission put it, "to return to their condition of 1763" and to

---

(see Introduction to Dulany's *Considerations,* in Bailyn, *Pamphlets,* I), conceded that "in the ordinary exercise" of government, Parliament would respect the line Dickinson described, but "that *in the intendment and remembrance of law,* the power of Parliament, as *a supreme censorial or remedial power,* must be supposed to have a right to go to all cases whatsoever." Similarly, though England has "given up forever" the levying of internal taxes on the colonies, she would never allow herself to suffer the "open test of humiliation" involved in formally renouncing that right (pp. 95–96). Pownall's discussion in this 23-page "Postscript" on Dickinson's *Essay* (and also in his book proper, chapter v and vol. II, 32 ff.) follows Dickinson's in focusing sharply on the distinction between internal and external spheres of jurisdiction. Independence did not put an end to the discussion of this mode of distinguishing spheres of jurisdiction; it carried over into the debate on federalism in the early national period, as, e.g., in R. H. Lee's "Federal Farmer" letters of 1787, as reprinted in Forrest McDonald, ed., *Empire and Nation* (Englewood Cliffs, N. J., 1962), pp. 110–111, 120.

do so in such a way that "the sovereignty of the mother country should not be infringed" was unthinkable.[66] The course of intellectual, as well as of political and military, events had brought into question the entire concept of a unitary, concentrated, and absolute governmental sovereignty. It had been challenged, implicitly or explicitly, by all those who had sought constitutional grounds for limiting Parliament's power in America. In its place had come the sense, premised on the assumption that the ultimate sovereignty — ultimate yet still real and effective — rested with the people, that it was not only conceivable but in certain circumstances salutary to divide and distribute the attributes of governmental sovereignty among different levels of institutions. The notion had proved unacceptable as a solution of the problem of Anglo-American relations, but it was acted upon immediately and instinctively in forming the new union of sovereign states. The problems, intellectual and political, inherent in such an arrangement would persist; some were scarcely glimpsed when the nation was formed. The belief that *"imperium in imperio"* was a solecism and the assumption that the "sovereignty of the people" and the sovereignty of an organ of government were of the same order of things would remain to haunt the efforts of those who would struggle to build a stable system of federal government. But the initial challenges to the traditional eighteenth-century notion of sovereignty had been made. Later analysts, starting where the colonists had left off before Independence and habituated to think in terms of "qualified sovereignty," "lesser sovereignties," "the divisibility of sovereignty," would continue the effort to make federalism a logical as well as a practical system of government.[67]

[66] Royal Instructions to the Peace Commission of 1778, in Morison, *Sources and Documents*, pp. 192, 200.

[67] On the history of the debate on sovereignty in the later eighteenth century and early nineteenth century, see, e.g., Adams, *Political Ideas*, chaps. vii, viii; *Records of the Federal Convention of 1787* (Max Farrand, ed., New Haven,

TRANSFORMATION

They would not entirely succeed; the task would be a continuing one, never fully completed. Generations later there would still be those, states rightists and nationalists, who would repudiate this legacy of the Revolution and reinvoke in different contexts the theories of Hobbes and Blackstone, of Hutchinson and Knox. But the federalist tradition, born in the colonists' efforts to state in constitutional language the qualification of Parliament's authority they had known — to comprehend, systematize, and generalize the unplanned circumstance of colonial life — nevertheless survived, and remains, to justify the distribution of absolute power among governments no one of which can claim to be total, and so to keep the central government from amassing "a degree of energy, in order to sustain itself, dangerous to the liberties of the people." [68]

1911–1937), I, 27, 323, 328, 331–332, 467; II, 347, 584; *The Federalist*, nos. 9, 15, 20, 31, 32, 39, 40, 44, 45, 62, 81; Jackson T. Main, *The Antifederalists* (Chapel Hill, 1961), pp. 120–125; Charles E. Merriam, *A History of American Political Theories* (New York, 1936), pp. 254 ff.; and above all, Madison's private speculations, written to Jefferson in 1787, on "the due partition of power between the general and local governments," in Boyd, *Jefferson Papers*, XII, 273–279, and his public statement of 1792, in *Writings* (G. Hunt, ed., New York, 1900–1910), VI, 91–93.

[68] Anon., "Concise View," in Morse, *Annals*, p. 394.

Chapter VI

THE CONTAGION OF LIBERTY

The American war is over: but this is far from being the case with the American revolution. On the contrary, nothing but the first act of the great drama is closed. It remains yet to establish and perfect our new forms of government, and to prepare the principles, morals, and manners of our citizens for these forms of government after they are established and brought to perfection.

— Benjamin Rush, 1787

O N SUCH fundamental issues — representation and consent, the nature of constitutions and of rights, the meaning of sovereignty — and in such basic ways, did the colonists probe and alter their inheritance of thought concerning liberty and its preservation. To conceive of legislative assemblies as mirrors of society and their voices as mechanically exact expressions of the people; to assume, and act upon the assumption, that human rights exist above the law and stand as the measure of the law's validity; to understand constitutions to be ideal designs of government, and fixed, limiting definitions of its permissible sphere of action; and to consider the possibility that absolute sovereignty in government need not be the monopoly of a single all-engrossing agency but (*imperium in imperio*) the shared possession of several agencies each limited by the boundaries of the others but all-powerful within its own — to think in these ways, as Americans were doing before Independence, was to reconceive the fundamentals of government and of society's relation to government.

These were, to be sure, probings, speculations, theories, by which a generation convinced of the importance of ideas in politics attempted to deal with the problems they faced. But they were not mere mental gymnastics. Not only did they provide the rational grounds of resistance to the authority of Parliament but by 1776 they had become matters of the most immediate, local urgency, for by then the colonies — independent states in all but name — had begun their extraordinary work of constitution writing. Up and down the still sparsely settled coast of British North America, groups of men — intellectuals and farmers, scholars and merchants, the learned and the ignorant — gathered for the purpose of constructing enlightened governments. During the single year 1776 eight states drafted and adopted constitutions (two did so even before Independence). Everywhere there were discussions of the ideal nature of government; everywhere principles of politics were examined, institutions weighed, and practices considered. And these debates — which were but forerunners of discussions that would continue well into the nineteenth century, until the political and social meaning of the American Revolution would be more fully realized — were direct continuations of the discussions that had preceded Independence. The same issues and the same terms were involved. Indeed, some of the most original pamphlets written in the entire Revolutionary period appeared in the transition years 1775 and 1776, and treat simultaneously, as if they were a single undifferentiated set of problems, the constitutional questions of imperial relations and of the organization of the internal governments of the new states.

The originality of these discussions of the nature of government and the uses of power was self-intensifying. Thinkers at each stage, impelled by a spirit at once quizzically pragmatic and loftily idealistic, built upon the conclusions of their predecessors and grasped implications only vaguely sensed before. The movement of thought was rapid, irreversible, and irresistible. It swept past boundaries few had set out to cross, into regions few had wished to enter.

How infectious this spirit of pragmatic idealism was, how powerful — and dangerous — the intellectual dynamism within it, and how difficult it was to plot in advance the direction of its spread, had become clear well before Independence. Institutions were brought into question and condemned that appeared to have little if any direct bearing on the immediate issues of the Anglo-American struggle. New, and difficult, problems, beyond the range of any yet considered, unexpectedly appeared.

I. SLAVERY

No one had set out to question the institution of chattel slavery, but by 1776 it had come under severe attack by writers following out the logic of Revolutionary thought. The connection, for those who chose to see it, was obvious. "Slavery" was a central concept in eighteenth-century political discourse. As the absolute political evil, it appears in every statement of political principle, in every discussion of constitutionalism or legal rights, in every exhortation to resistance. Can any power in this province, a Massachusetts polemicist asked in 1754, "make slaves of any part of the [British] nation?" Who would not choose "to dine upon a turnip, with old *Fabricus,* and be a freeman, rather than flow in luxury, and be a slave?" It was the loss of attachment to a free constitution that had plunged Rome from the summit of her glory "into the black gulf of infamy and slavery." Tyrannical governments reduce people to "a kind of slaves to the ministers of state." An ambitious ministry must be taught "that any attempt to enslave us would be as fruitless as it would be impolitic." "*Those* who are *taxed* without their own consent expressed by themselves or their representatives," John Dickinson wrote, with supporting quotations from Pitt and Camden, "are *slaves. We are taxed without our consent expressed by ourselves or our representatives. We* are therefore — SLAVES." Yes, Josiah Quincy concluded in 1774, "I speak it with grief — I speak it with anguish — Britons are our oppressors: I speak it with shame — I speak it with in-dignation — *we are slaves"* — "the most abject sort of slaves," said John Adams.[1]

This was not simply lurid rhetoric. Slavery as a political con-cept had specific meaning which a later generation would lose. To eighteenth-century Americans it meant, as a newspaper writer put it in 1747, "a force put upon humane nature, by which a man is obliged to act, or not to act, according to the arbitrary will and pleasure of another"; it meant, a later pamphleteer wrote, "being wholly under the power and control of another as to our actions and properties." [2] It meant the inability to maintain one's just property in material things and abstract rights, rights and things which a proper constitution guaranteed a free people. Both symptom and consequence of disease in the body politic, it was the condition that followed the loss of freedom, when corruption, classically, had destroyed the desire and capacity of the people to retain their independence: most commonly, when the elements of power had destroyed — by bribery, intimidation,

---

[1] *The Eclipse* ([Boston], 1754), p. 7; Joseph Warren, *An Oration* . . . (Boston, 1772: JHL Pamphlet 35), p. 6; [John Allen], *The American Alarm . . . for the Rights, and Liberties, of the People* . . . (Boston, 1773: JHL Pamphlet 39), 1st sec., p. 9; *A Serious Address to . . . New-York* . . . (New York, 1774: JHL Pamphlet 42), p. 5; [John Dickinson], *Letters from a Farmer in Pennsylvania* . . . (Philadelphia, 1768: JHL Pamphlet 23), p. 38; Josiah Quincy, Jr., *Observations on the . . . Boston Port-Bill; with Thoughts on . . . Standing Armies* . . . (Boston, 1774), in Josiah Quincy, *Memoir of the Life of Josiah Quincy Jun.* . . . (Boston, 1825), p. 451; John Adams ("Novanglus"), in *Works*, IV, 28. Curiously, Dickinson's phrase in the original, newspaper ver-sion of the *Farmer's Letters* was almost identical with Quincy's: "We are there-fore — I speak it with grief — I speak it with indignation — we are SLAVES."
[2] *New York Evening Post*, November 16, 1747; [Moses Mather], *America's Appeal to the Impartial World* . . . (Hartford, 1775: JHL Pamphlet 59), p. 48.

or more subtle means — the independence of the "democratical" elements of the constitution.

"Slavery" in this sense, far from being mere exclamation and hyperbole, was a term referring to a specific political condition, a condition characteristic of the lives of contemporary Frenchmen, Danes, and Swedes as well as of Turks, Russians, and Poles. And it applied equally to the black plantation laborers in the American colonies, for their condition was only a more dramatic, more bizarre variation of the condition of all who had lost the power of self-determination. The subjects of governments "under the absolute and arbitrary direction of one man," the newspaper writer of 1747 commented,

are all *slaves,* for he that is obliged to act or not to act according to the arbitrary will and pleasure of a governor, or his director, is as much a *slave* as he who is obliged to act or not according to the arbitrary will and pleasure of a master or his overseer. And indeed, I never see anything of the kind but it gives me a lively idea of an overseer directing a plantation of Negroes in the West Indies; the only difference I know is that the slaves of the latter deserve highly to be pitied, the slaves of the former to be held in the utmost contempt.

The degradation of chattel slaves — painfully visible and unambiguously established in law — was only the final realization of what the loss of freedom could mean everywhere; for there was no such thing "as *partial* liberty": he who has authority "to restrain and control my conduct in any instance without my consent hath in all." From this point of view it made little difference whether one's bondage was private or public, civil or political, or even whether one was treated poorly or well. Anyone "who is bound to obey the will of another," Stephen Hopkins wrote, is "as really a slave though he may have a good master as if he had a bad one; and this is stronger in politic bodies than in natural ones, as the former have perpetual succession and remain the same; and although they may have a very good master at one time, they may have a very bad one at another."[3]

The presence of an enslaved Negro population in America inevitably became a political issue where slavery had this general meaning. The contrast between what political leaders in the colonies sought for themselves and what they imposed on, or at least tolerated in, others became too glaring to be ignored and could not be lightened by appeals to the Lockean justification of slavery as the favorable fate of people who "by some act that deserves death" had forfeited their lives and had been spared by the generosity of their captors.[4] The reality of plantation life was too harsh for such fictions. The identification between the cause of the colonies and the cause of the Negroes bound in chattel slavery — an identification built into the very language of politics — became inescapable.

It was not grasped by all at once, nor did it become effective evenly through the colonies. But gradually the contradiction between the proclaimed principles of freedom and the facts of life in America became generally recognized. How embarrassing this obvious discrepancy could be to enthusiastic libertarians was revealed early in the period. What could the Colonel (Richard Bland) mean, the Reverend John Camm demanded to know, by asserting that under an English government "all *men* are *born free"?* Does he mean

that *Virginia* is not an *English government,* or that Negroes are not under it *born slaves,* or that the said slaves are not men? Whichever

---

[3] *New York Evening Post,* November 16, 1747 (cf. *Boston Gazette,* May 10, 1756); [Richard Wells], *A Few Political Reflections* . . . (Philadelphia, 1774), p. 82; Mather, *America's Appeal* (JHL 59), p. 48; [Stephen Hopkins], *The Rights of Colonies Examined* (Providence, 1765: JHL Pamphlet 9), p. 16.

[4] Locke, *Second Treatise of Government,* iv, 23.

of these confident assertions he undertakes to maintain, and one of them he must maintain, he will find insuperable difficulties to oppose him as soon as he is able to cast an eye on the situation of *Virginia,* the map of America, or on the condition and rational conduct of his own domestics.[5]

It was an unanswerable argument — but Camm did not choose to pursue it. Few in the South did; for while everyone believed in liberty and everyone knew that slavery was its denial, everyone knew also, as a South Carolinian wrote in 1774, that the abolition of slavery would "complete the ruin of many American provinces, as well as the West India islands." Few even of the most enlightened Virginians were willing to declare, as Jefferson did in the instructions he wrote for his colony's delegation to the first Continental Congress, that "the rights of human nature [are] deeply wounded by this infamous practice" and that "the abolition of domestic slavery is the great object of desire in those colonies where it was unhappily introduced in their infant state"; fewer still lent active support to the developing antislavery movement, however logically it followed from the principles of the Revolution. But though Patrick Henry, like the majority of his neighbors, felt that "the general inconvenience of living here without them" rendered the freeing of slaves in the south impractical, nevertheless he could not ignore the contradiction involved in maintaining slavery "at a time when the rights of humanity are defined and understood with precision in a country above all others fond of liberty"; and, confessing his own guilt and inconsistency, he wrote that he looked forward to the time "when an opportunity will be offered to abolish this lamentable evil." Even in the South the contagion of liberty spread to the institution of chattel slavery in no way directly involved in the

[5] [John Camm], *Critical Remarks on a Letter Ascribed to Common Sense* . . . (Williamsburg, 1765), p. 19.

236

controversy with England; even in the South there would be efforts, as a result, in some degree to control it.[6]

It was in the northern and middle colonies, however, that arguments against slavery explicitly associated with the Anglo-American political controversy were heard throughout the period, increased steadily in number and intensity, and resulted in material alterations. At first the relevance of chattel slavery to libertarian ideals was noted only in individual passages of isolated pamphlets. While Boston merchants in 1764 were still content to speak in a matter-of-fact way of the economics of the slave trade, James Otis, following out the idea that "by the law of nature" all men are "free born" concluded that by "all men" was meant all human beings "white or black," and he launched forthwith a brief but characteristically fierce attack upon the whole institution of slavery.

Does it follow that 'tis right to enslave a man because he is black? Will short curled hair like wool instead of Christian hair . . . help the argument? Can any logical inference in favor of slavery be drawn from a flat nose, a long or short face? Nothing better can be said in favor of a trade that is the most shocking violation of the law of nature, has a direct tendency to diminish the idea of the inestimable value of liberty, and makes every dealer in it a tyrant . . .

So corrupting is the evil, he concluded, that "those who every day barter away other men's liberty will soon care little for their own" — which explains, he added, the "ferocity, cruelty, and brutal barbarity that has long marked the general character of the sugar islanders." The only idea of government such people can have is

[6] *Some Fugitive Thoughts on a Letter Signed Freeman* . . . ([Charleston], 1774), p. 25; [Thomas Jefferson], *A Summary View of the Rights of British America* . . . (Williamsburg, [1774]: JHL Pamphlet 43), pp. 16–17; J. Franklin Jameson, *The American Revolution Considered as a Social Movement* (Princeton, 1926), pp. 32–33. On the successful opposition to the clause condemning the slave trade in the first draft of the Declaration of Independence, see Carl Becker, *The Declaration of Independence* (New York, 1922), pp. 212–213; and Benjamin Quarles, *The Negro in the American Revolution* (Chapel Hill, 1961), pp. 42–43.

that which they see "exercised over ten thousand of their fellow men, born with the same right to freedom and the sweet enjoyments of liberty and life as their unrelenting task-masters, the overseers and planters." [7]

At this point, however, the argument, though logical, was still a digression in the Anglo-American debate; the explicit association of the political claims of the colonists with attacks on chattel slavery was not as yet automatically made even in the North. So, in 1765, the Reverend Stephen Johnson of Lyme, Connecticut, preaching on "the general nature and consequences of enslaving measures" and dilating on the iniquity of slavery and on its "shocking ill effects and terrible consequences" to both enslavers and enslaved, drew his illustrations from the Bible, from ancient history, "the oppression of Holland," and the histories of France and of England under "former popish reigns" but not from the life around him; he confined his "application" of these principles and illustrations to "the impending calamities which threaten us": he did not mention the enslavement of Negroes in America. Similarly, John Dickinson, having defined taxation without representation as "a state of the most abject slavery," declared that he could not conceive of "an idea of a slavery more *complete,* more *miserable,* more *disgraceful,* than that of a people where *justice is administered, government exercised,* and a *standing army maintained* AT THE EXPENSE OF THE PEOPLE, and yet WITHOUT THE LEAST DEPENDENCE UPON THEM" — an opinion Arthur Lee echoed, also without making the connection between politics and social institutions. [8]

[7] *Considerations upon the Act of Parliament* (Boston, 1764: JHL Pamphlet 5), pp. 15–16; James Otis, *Rights of the British Colonies* (Boston, 1764: JHL Pamphlet 7), p. 29.

[8] [Stephen Johnson], *Some Important Observations . . .* (Newport, 1766: JHL Pamphlet 19), pp. 5, 7, 8, 9, 52; Dickinson, *Farmer's Letters* (JHL 23), p. 48; Lee's "Monitor" letters, nos. II, IV, VI, *Virginia Gazette* (R), March 3, 17, 31, 1768. See also [Silas Downer], *A Discourse Delivered in Providence . . .* (Provi-

But increasingly the connection was made. Samuel Cooke, in his Massachusetts election sermon of 1770, argued that in tolerating Negro slavery "we, the patrons of liberty, have dishonored the Christian name, and degraded human nature nearly to a level with the beasts that perish," and he devoted most of his text to "the cause of our African slaves." Pointing out that God "is no respecter of persons," he begged the assembled leaders of Massachusetts to take the initiative in this cause of the oppressed so relevant to their own more immediate cause. And Benjamin Rush, in a sweeping condemnation of slavery, "On Slave-Keeping" (1773), begged "Ye advocates for American liberty" to rouse themselves and "espouse the cause of humanity and general liberty." Bear a testimony, he wrote in the language of the Quakers, "against a vice which degrades human nature . . . The plant of liberty is of so tender a nature that it cannot thrive long in the neighborhood of slavery. Remember, the eyes of all Europe are fixed upon you, to preserve an asylum for freedom in this country after the last pillars of it are fallen in every other quarter of the globe." [9]

By 1774 this cry had become a commonplace in the pamphlet literature of the northern and middle colonies. How can we "reconcile the exercise of SLAVERY with our *professions of freedom*," Richard Wells, "a citizen of Philadelphia," demanded to know. There was no possible justification for the institution, he said. If, as some claimed, the slaves were bought from those who had a right to sell them, where are the titles to prove it? Even a convict who clearly "has *forfeited his life* to the laws of his country and is respited for transportation" has papers that

---

dence, 1768: JHL Pamphlet 25), pp. 10, 12; and the citation of Dr. Johnson's definition of slavery in the *Boston Evening Post*, 1767, quoted in Gipson, *British Empire*, XI, 144.

[9] Samuel Cooke, *A Sermon Preached at Cambridge . . .* (Boston, 1770), pp. 42, 41; Dagobert D. Runes, ed., *The Selected Writings of Benjamin Rush* (New York, 1947), p. 17.

show his just condemnation. And if the claim that we are inflicting just punishment on Africans for crimes committed in their native lands ("which is the last wretched argument . . . advocates for slavery insist on") could be substantiated, what would it prove except that the colonists had become *"executioners* [for] an Ethiopian savage government"? The only claim the Americans had over the Africans is the claim of *"force* and *power"*; and that being the case, "what arguments can we advance in *their* favor which will not militate against ourselves, whilst England remains superior by land and by sea?" A remonstrance against the slave trade by the forthcoming Continental Congress and a pledge by the colonists not to import or buy slaves, would, he declared, "breathe such an independent spirit of liberty, and so corroborate our own claims that I should dare to hope for an intervening arm of Providence to be extended in our favor." He concluded by reviewing the laws of manumission passed in Pennsylvania, Maryland, and New Jersey.

Even more vigorous and more harshly abusive of the hypocrisy of colonial claims in the face of domestic slavery was the Baptist preacher and pamphleteer, John Allen. The "iniquitous and disgraceful practice of keeping African slaves," he wrote in *The Watchman's Alarm,* was a total abomination; it violated God's laws, the charter of Massachusetts, the natural and inalienable rights of mankind, and the laws of society and humanity.

Blush ye pretended votaries for freedom! ye trifling patriots! who are making a vain parade of being advocates for the liberties of mankind, who are thus making a mockery of your profession by trampling on the sacred natural rights and privileges of Africans; for while you are fasting, praying, nonimporting, nonexporting, remonstrating, resolving, and pleading for a restoration of your charter rights, you at the same time are continuing this lawless, cruel, inhuman, and abominable practice of enslaving your fellow creatures . . .

It would not be surprising, he warned, if the Africans too took heart from the Biblical injunction to "loose the bands of wickedness, undo the heavy burdens, let the oppressed go free." They had far greater reason than their masters to do so, for "what is a trifling three-penny duty on tea compared to the inestimable blessings of liberty to one captive?" Joyfully he celebrated those "sincere friends to the rights and liberties of mankind" who were known to have freed their slaves.

As the crisis deepened and Americans elaborated their love of liberty and their hatred of slavery, the problem posed by the bondage tolerated in their midst became more and more difficult to evade. What were they to say to the Englishmen who told them flatly to "put away the accursed thing (that horrid oppression) from among them, before they presumed to implore the interposition of divine justice: for, whilst they retain their brethren . . . in the most shameful involuntary servitude, it is profane in them to look up to the merciful Lord of all, and call Him father!" And what reply could Bostonians give to the Loyalist printer John Mein who denounced their hypocrisy in "ground-[ing] their rebellions on the 'immutable laws of nature'" and yet ("It cannot be! It is nevertheless very true") themselves owned two thousand Negro slaves? Some found at least a partial excuse in pointing out, with Jefferson, that repeated attempts by certain colonies to ban the slave trade or tax it out of existence had met resounding vetoes in England so that the good of the colonies and the rights of human nature had been sacrificed to "the immediate advantages of a few African corsairs." [10]

[10] Wells, *A Few Political Reflections,* pp. 79–80, 81, 82, 83: [John Allen], *The Watchman's Alarm to Lord N---h* . . . (Salem. 1774), pp. 25, 27, 28; Granville Sharp, *A Declaration of the People's Natural Right to Share in the Legislature* . . . (New York, 1774), p. 14n; [John Mein], *Sagittarius's Letters and Political Speculations* . . . (Boston, 1775), pp. 38–39; Jefferson, *Summary View* (JHL 43), pp. 16–17. Sharp's pamphlet, originally published in London in 1774, was reprinted four times in the colonies before the year was out (Thomas R. Adams, *American Independence . . . A Bibliographical Study* . . . , Providence, 1965, entries 139e-h). On the original, English context of Sharp's pamphlet, see Frank J. Klingberg, *The Anti-Slavery Movement in England* (New Haven, 1926), chap. ii.

But the excuse was weak, and in any case something more than excuses was needed. Action was called for to restrict "the cruel and barbarous slave trade" and to alleviate the sufferings of the "oppressed and injured Africans." And something even more than that was called for by preachers in the North devoted to the covenant theology: repentance, expiation, for sins so long committed. It was on this note, and with the explicit refutation of Locke's justification of slavery as a proper alternative to condemning criminals to death, that the pre-Revolutionary discussion of chattel slavery in the context of Revolutionary ideology climaxed and concluded. Two powerful pamphlets entirely devoted to the subject of slavery, written by two close friends in the Congregational ministry, presented a broad range of antislavery arguments explicitly associated with Revolutionary ideology and centered on key doctrines of neo-Puritan theology. The first originated as a sermon delivered in Farmington, Connecticut, in 1774 on the eve of the meeting of the first Continental Congress. The preacher, Levi Hart, of the village of Griswold, prefaced his remarks by explaining that his aim was "to treat the subject only in a moral and religious view"; he would not pretend to pronounce on politics. But his sermon was a jeremiad in form typical of the sulphurous denunciations and exhortations by which the Puritan clergy had sought, since the end of the seventeenth century, to keep its version of orthodoxy relevant to the vital public affairs of the society.

He began by sharply contrasting liberty and slavery and by offering a variety of definitions of liberty, from which he concluded that any society that permits its members to deprive innocent people of their liberty or property was guilty of tyranny and oppression. Consider then the crime, the sin, involved in the toleration of and connivance in *"the horrible slave trade"* by the public in the British colonies. If facts did not compel him to, he said, he "could never believe that British Americans would be guilty of such a crime." It had no justification whatever. The idea that slavery was a just and generous substitute for a deserved death penalty was irrelevant to the American situation, whatever its merits as a theory might be. "What have the unhappy Africans committed against the inhabitants of the British colonies and islands in the West Indies to authorize *us* to seize them, or bribe them to seize one another, and transport them a thousand leagues into a strange land, and enslave them for life?" It was now "high time for this colony to wake up and put an effectual stop to the cruel business of stealing and selling our fellow men." For how, when the colonists themselves "are the tyrants," could they plead for freedom? "What inconsistence and self-contradiction is this! . . . When, O when shall the happy day come, that Americans shall be *consistently* engaged in the cause of liberty?" Only on that day will American liberties be established on a lasting foundation, for only on that day will "the hard bondage of sin and satan" be thrown off and "the most perfect liberty" be enjoyed. Christ alone is "the giver and supporter of original, perfect freedom." So, then, be wise in season,

bid adieu to the kingdom of darkness, the cause of tyranny and oppression, enlist under the captain of the Lord's host, fight under his banner, you may be sure of victory, and liberty shall be your lasting reward, for whom the Son maketh *free* shall be *free indeed*.[11]

But it was left to Hart's friend and mentor, Samuel Hopkins, student of Jonathan Edwards, rigorous theologian and powerful advocate of his own, "Hopkinsian," version of predestinarian Calvinism, to make the final statement, and to link most securely the religious and secular underpinnings of antislavery. Hopkins' interest in the cause of the Negro had been kindled much earlier, when he had first come to see the social meaning of his doctrines of "disinterested benevolence" and "general atonement." For sev-

[11] Levi Hart, *Liberty Described and Recommended* . . . (Hartford, 1775), pp. v, 9 ff., 15, 16, 20, 22, 23.

eral years after his arrival in Newport, Rhode Island, he worked to free the slaves of masters near at hand; in 1770 he undertook the training of Negro missionaries to be sent to Africa as part of a scheme of colonization he promoted with his friend Ezra Stiles. The crisis of American affairs demanded a full clarification of his ideas, for he believed the cause of the colonies and the cause of emancipation to be indissolubly united. Hopkins' explanation came in 1776 in a sixty-three page pamphlet entitled *A Dialogue Concerning the Slavery of Africans; Shewing It To Be the Duty and Interest of the American Colonies To Emancipate All the African Slaves . . .*

He painted a vivid and affecting picture of the reality of Negro slavery; the viciousness of the slave trade, corrupting to both slavers and enslaved; the horrors of the transportation and marketing of the Negroes; and their treatment on the American plantations. Methodically he examined the common arguments in defense of the practice, rejecting as nonsense both the idea that slavery was a means of bringing Christianity to the heathens, and the notion that a "forfeiture" was somehow involved in their bondage. The Negroes, he said, have "never forfeited their liberty or given anyone the right to enslave and sell them." Yet they are held in bondage by those whose own struggle for liberty they daily witness and whose heroic pronouncements that slavery is worse than death they must continuously hear. "Oh, the shocking, the intolerable inconsistence! . . . This gross, barefaced, practiced inconsistence." The slavery we complain of "is lighter than a feather compared to their heavy doom, and may be called liberty and happiness when contrasted with the most abject slavery and inutterable wretchedness to which they are subjected." Our so-called Sons of Liberty: what are they but oppressors of thousands "who have as good a claim to liberty as themselves, [and] are shocked with the glaring inconsistence"? For such a sin, he concluded, multiplied in its evil by the indifference that surrounds it, we are under divine judgment. In such a state, only calamities will attend our efforts. Our cause will never triumph until the evil is expunged, until repentance and restitution are truly made. For the struggle for liberty in America can prosper only under God's protection, and that will never fully be granted while the enslavement of the Negroes continues. If we persist, Hopkins warned, the vengeance of God will be upon us: He will withdraw from us such protection as He has so far given, and "punish us seven times more." The guilt was universal; let repentance be so too.[12]

Such ideas were weapons. By July of 1776 much had already been done to extend the reign of liberty to the enslaved Negroes. In Massachusetts, efforts had been made as early as 1767 to abolish the slave trade, and in 1771 and 1774 the legislature voted conclusively to do so but was rebuffed by the governor's veto. In the same year the Continental Congress pledged itself to discontinue the slave trade everywhere, while Rhode Island, acknowledging that "those who are desirous of enjoying all the advantages of liberty themselves should be willing to extend personal liberty to others," ruled that slaves imported into the colony would thereafter automatically become free. Connecticut did the same; Delaware prohibited importation; and Pennsylvania taxed the trade out of existence. There, too, in 1775, the Quakers, long the most outspoken advocates of emancipation though not leaders in the Revolutionary movement, formed the first antislavery society in the Western world. In the South there was at least a general acquiescence in the Congress' inclusion of the slave trade in the nonimportation program and satisfaction on the part of many when in April 1776 Congress fulfilled its earlier pledge and

[12] Quarles, *Negro in the American Revolution*, pp. 33–35; [Samuel Hopkins], *A Dialogue* . . . (Norwich, 1776), pp. 12, 15, 23, 24, 50, 30, 52, 54.

voted "that no slaves be imported into any of the thirteen colonies." [13]

The institution of chattel slavery was not dead, even in the North, nor would it be for many years to come; critics of the Declaration of Independence would continue to join with Thomas Hutchinson in condemning the apparent hypocrisy of a people who declared that all men were created equal, endowed with inalienable rights, and yet deprived "more than an hundred thousand Africans of their rights to liberty and *the pursuit of happiness,* and in some degree to their lives." But it had been subjected to severe pressure as a result of the extension of Revolutionary ideas, and it bore the marks ever after. As long as the institution of slavery lasted, the burden of proof would lie with its advocates to show why the statement "all men are created equal" did not mean precisely what it said: *all* men, "white or black." [14]

2. ESTABLISHMENT OF RELIGION

Whatever one's views of sin and retribution, in strictly secular terms the "shocking, the intolerable inconsistence" of chattel slavery could not be denied: in many minds the cause of emancipation came naturally and logically to be associated with the defense of American liberty against the encroachments of the English government. Yet nothing shows the protean, uncon-

[13] Quarles, *Negro in the American Revolution,* pp. 40–41; Thomas E. Drake, *Quakers and Slavery in America* (New Haven, 1950), pp. 85–90; W. E. B. DuBois, *The Suppression of the African Slave-Trade . . .* (New York, 1896), pp. 42–47.

[14] [Thomas Hutchinson], *Strictures upon the Declaration of the Congress at Philadelphia . . .* (London, 1776), as reprinted in *Old South Leaflets,* no. 227 (Malcolm Freiberg, ed., Boston, 1958), p. 11; Quarles, *Negro in the American Revolution,* p. 43. On the carry-over of the antislavery arguments of the Revolutionary period to the debates of the ante-bellum era, see Philip F. Detweiler, "Congressional Debate on Slavery and the Declaration of Independence, 1819–1821," *American Historical Review,* 63 (1957–58), 598–616.

trollable character of the Revolutionary movement more clearly than the position in which certain of the spokesmen for anti-slavery found themselves in regard to another issue which also took fire in the heat of the Revolution. For if Otis and Cooke, Hart and Hopkins were fervent in the struggle against chattel slavery, they were members, if not leaders, of churches in some degree established, and these, to others, were as inconsistent as slavery with the logic of Revolutionary thought, *"Freedom from Civil and Ecclesiastical Slavery"* being both, one pamphlet proclaimed in its title, *"the Purchase of Christ."* [15]

The establishment of religion had been a problem for Americans almost from the first years of settlement. Though most of the early settlers had carried with them traditional assumptions concerning the state's responsibility for supervising and enforcing orthodox religious institutions, and though most of the original communities had sought to recreate ecclesiastical establishments, there had been difficulties from the start. In some places, as in Virginia, trouble was created by the physical circumstances of the situation: the scattering of population and the distance from ecclesiastical centers in Europe. Elsewhere, as in Massachusetts, where the physical circumstances were favorable, the very intensity of religious motivation and the desire to specify and enforce a letter-perfect orthodoxy led to schismatic challenges to the establishment. Still elsewhere, as in New York, the sheer diversity of religious persuasions in the population made the establishment of any one church problematic.

Only rarely in the settlement period, however, were difficulties created by anti-establishment principles, and only in one colony, Pennsylvania, did systematic, principled opposition to establishments survive to shape the character of instituted religion in the eighteenth century. Elsewhere the pattern of establishments in

[15] Jonathan Parsons' Massacre Day sermon, 1774 (Newburyport, [1774]).

religion, like that of so many other areas of life in the colonies, was the result of unsystematic, incomplete, pragmatic modifications of a traditional model. By the 1750's so irregular, so ill-defined, and so quickly shifting were the religious establishments in the various colonies that they defy a simple summary. In the Virginia of Jefferson's youth, the Church of England was established; but the law requiring nonconformist organizations to register with the government was often ignored, especially in the western counties where the settlement of dissenters was actively promoted by the government; nonconformists were not barred from their own worship nor penalized for failure to attend the Anglican communion, and they were commonly exempted from parish taxes. Dissent within Protestantism excluded no one from voting or from holding public office: even Roman Catholics were known to occupy government posts despite the laws that excluded them. And Virginia's was one of the more conservative establishments. The effective privileges of the Church of England were at least as weak in South Carolina and Georgia; they hardly existed in North Carolina. There was scarcely a vestige of them in the middle colonies, and where they had survived in law, as in four counties of New York, they were either ignored or had become embattled by violent opposition well before the Revolution. And in Massachusetts and Connecticut, where the establishment, being nonconformist according to English law, was legally tenuous to begin with, tolerance in worship and relief from church taxation had been extended to the major dissenting groups early in the century, resulting well before the Revolution in what John Adams described as "the most mild and equitable establishment of religion that was known in the world, if indeed [it] could be called an establishment."[16] And this had been further weakened

---

[16] *Diary and Autobiography*, III, 312. That the Congregational establishments in New England were severe was a commonplace, however, especially among the Anglican opponents of the Revolutionary movement. See, e.g., [James Chalmers], *Plain Truth* . . . (Philadelphia, 1776: JHL Pamphlet 64), p. 64:

by the splintering effect of the Great Awakening. Almost everywhere the Church of England, the established church of the highest state authority, was defensive, driven to rely more and more on its missionary arm, the Society for the Propagation of the Gospel, to sustain it against the cohorts of dissent.

That establishments of such irregularity and weakness should have come under fire at all is a measure of the contagiousness of Revolutionary thought. There had been deliberate opposition to establishments before the Revolution, but it had been scattered and ineffective. In Virginia, challenges had been made as early as the 1740's by itinerant New Light Presbyterian preachers who shaped a spontaneous, formless outpouring of evangelical fervor into articulate defiance of ecclesiastical law. In Connecticut and Massachusetts the religious awakening of the mid-century had spawned uncontrollable groups of "Separates," strict Congregationalists who believed their evangelicalism to be the only true orthodoxy and who therefore refused to accept the legal benefits available to officially recognized dissenters; they had attacked the establishment with all the arguments they could muster: arguments from "the Bible, natural law, the rights of Englishmen, covenants, charters, and statutes." Claiming liberty of conscience to be an "unalienable right of every rational creature," they had often preferred to suffer imprisonment and loss of property rather than to pay taxes in support of a church not their own; some had ended by advocating explicitly the complete separation of church and state.[17]

". . . it were folly supreme, madness, to expect angelic toleration from New England, where she has constantly been detested, persecuted, and execrated"; in matters of toleration the people of New England were "not yet arrived in the seventeenth or eighteenth century."

[17] Wesley M. Gewehr, *The Great Awakening in Virginia, 1740–1790* (Durham, N.C., 1930), pp. 49 ff.; George M. Brydon, *Virginia's Mother Church . . .* (Richmond and Philadelphia, 1947–1952), II, 159 ff.; Alice M. Baldwin, *The New England Clergy and the American Revolution* (Durham, N.C., 1928), pp. 65, 76, 77, 79. For a descriptive account of the Separates, see C. C. Goen, *Revivalism and Separatism in New England, 1740–1800* (New Haven, 1962).

This final, extreme conclusion had been argued most forcefully, however, not in New England and not by such humble people as the Congregational Separates, but in New York, by a group of sophisticated lawyers in the course of a campaign against the privileges of the Church of England which in 1752 and 1753 they had carried on in the pages of the *Independent Reflector*. The immediate issue had been the founding, with the financial support of the provincial government, of an Anglican college in New York; but to William Livingston and the other opposition pamphleteers the controversy spilled over into the general question of the establishment of religion. Before the battle was over, Livingston and his collaborators had brought into question the right of any one religious group to claim for itself exclusive privileges of public support, and had advanced for the first time in American history the conception that public institutions, because they were "public," should be if not secular at least nondenominational.[18]

All of these episodes form an important background to the attack on establishments of religion that developed in the Revolutionary years. Yet episodes they remained: uncoordinated, for the most part short-lived, and differing in underlying assumptions. Their conclusions were felt to be deviations from what was normal and proper, not advances toward it. They lacked the legitimacy that flows from broad popular approbation, from long familiarity, or from complete and irrefutable logic; they did not spread beyond the situation of their origins, and they quickly faded from prominence. The open hostility of the Virginia evangelicals to the established church — an hostility so little grounded in doctrine that its professors had not known what to call themselves when asked to state "their creed and name" ("Lutherans," they decided when one of them happened to remember favorably

---

[18] William Livingston, *et al.*, *The Independent Reflector* . . . (Milton M. Klein, ed., Cambridge, 1963), papers 17–22.

Luther's Commentary on Galatians)[19] — their deliberate opposition to the Church of England had dissolved quickly with the
arrival in Virginia in 1748 of Samuel Davies, an astute politician
as well as preacher, who channeled their fervor into a decorous
Presbyterianism well within the boundaries of official dissent. In
New England the intensity of Separatist agitations and claims
had eased by the 1760's, and the groups themselves were beginning to disappear, either by absorption into the major denomina-
tions or as a result of the disintegrating effect of successive splin-
terings. And in New York, once the government had succeeded
in silencing the *Reflector*, the group and the ideas that had sustained it fell victim to the unruly politics of the province and lost
their identity in the tumbling chaos of factional disputes.

These were scattered, uncoordinated, and deviant episodes, fad-
ing in the permissive atmosphere of the colonies. But then in the
decades of the sixties and seventies they were recalled with new
relevance. Acquiring in the context of Revolutionary thought a
higher justification, a breadth, generality, and intensity they had
not had before, they merged into the broad movement, mingling
sectarianism and secular reform, that would result, ultimately, in
the disestablishment of religion in the states and in the United
States of America.

Anti-establishment sentiment and constitutional arguments
against Parliamentary power were intimately mingled from the
very earliest pre-Revolutionary years; but the relationship at the
start was in a significant way the obverse of what it would become. Two powerful explosions, one in Virginia and one in
Massachusetts, overlapping in time and in doctrine with the first

---

[19] They were ultimately convinced by "an old Scot" who offered them hos-
pitality one night that they were really Presbyterians. Brydon, *Virginia's Mother
Church*, II, 157.

major constitutional disputes, brought the issue of church-state relations vividly to public attention.

In Virginia the Two-Penny Act of 1759 ignited the colonists' smoldering anticlericalism. The clergy's protest against what they claimed was an illegal devaluation of their salaries succeeded not only in forcing the disallowance of the act in England but in eliciting from the Bishop of London a letter denouncing the people of Virginia for disrespect to the Church of England, laxness in dealing with dissenters, and a desire "to lessen the influence of the crown and the maintenance of the clergy." In their slashing defense of the Assembly and its act, Richard Bland and Landon Carter turned in fury not only against the leader of the clerical "cabal," the Reverend John Camm, but against the clergy in general and against the Bishop of London as well. Whose fault is it, Bland demanded to know, if, as the Bishop charged, the clergy in Virginia were not accorded the respect due the ministers of an established church? The respect they receive is the respect they earn, for they "stand upon the same level with other men, and are not superior to them, as I know of, in station or learning." Obviously an established church was of great importance in any state, and the clergy should be held in high esteem; but there would be limits to that even if none of the clergy were a disgrace to their calling, as in fact so many in Virginia were; for "the preservation of the community is to be preferred even to them."

The issue could not be contained. If the Anglican clergy were under attack, Camm wrote, echoing the Bishop of London, so too was the prerogative of the crown, and if that were reduced "to a mere shadow, to something that has no *weight* . . . we should only hereby sap one of the strongest batteries erected for the defense of liberty and property." Bland did not deny that "the royal prerogative is, without doubt, of great weight and power in a dependent and subordinate government," but the overriding consideration must be the good of the people: *"salus populi est suprema lex* . . . every consideration must give place to it" — even royal instructions when they conflict with it, a fact that is surely "evident to reason" and a "clear and fundamental . . . rule in the English constitution."

But the last, and most famous, word in this controversy was neither Bland's nor Camm's. It belonged to a rising young lawyer, Patrick Henry, who, in one of the Parsons' Cause cases, defended a parish sued by its rector for wages lost through the Two-Penny Act. That act, Henry said in the hour-long harangue to the jury that made his reputation and became one of the most renowned, as it was one of the most extravagant, statements of the early Revolutionary years — that act had been passed for the good of the people; the King who disallowed it "from being the father of his people degenerated into a tyrant, and forfeits all rights to his subjects' obedience." As for the ministers of the Church of England, they had been described by their lawyer as benevolent and full of holy zeal; but they were in fact the opposite: rapacious harpies who would, "were their powers equal to their will, snatch from the hearth of their honest parishioner his last hoecake, from the widow and her orphan children their last milch cow! the last bed, nay, the last blanket from the lying-in woman!" In opposing the Two-Penny Act they had acted with characteristic disregard for the public good and thus violated the principle upon which established churches must rest: "the only use of an established church and clergy in society is to enforce obedience to civil sanctions, and . . . when a clergy cease to answer these ends, the community have no further need of their ministry, and may justly strip them of their appointments." For their behavior in the present case "instead of useful members of the state, they ought to be considered as enemies of the community, and . . . very justly deserved to be punished with signal severity." [20]

In Massachusetts the attack on the evil of an over-all establishment of religion was a response of the efforts of the Church of England to extend its influence into the heartland of American dissent.[21] In 1759 the Church had established in Cambridge, on the very doorstep of Harvard College, a mission of its Society for the Propagation of the Gospel. Assignment to this Anglican outpost would have been dangerous even for the wisest and most diplomatic of missionaries; but the person appointed to the position, East Apthorp, was inexperienced, contentious, and supercilious. Inevitably he blundered. He blundered in building for himself a house "more in the fashion of a bishop's palace than that of a simple missionary," and he blundered, also, in the way in which he replied — indeed, in replying at all — to a series of newspaper articles ridiculing the efforts the Society for the Propagation of the Gospel had been making to rescue the *"natives, Africans,* and *heathens"* of Massachusetts from the "barbarism" of their nonconformity. The burden of his argument — that the original charter of the Society for the Propagation of the Gospel had not confined its mandate "to the conversion of heathens" but had empowered it to maintain episcopal ministers "among the *English* subjects in . . . the most populous and settled parts of the continent" — was both weak, and, to the majority of New Englanders, obnoxious. And its offensiveness was magnified by a number of incidental touches: Apthorp's insistent identification

---

[20] William S. Perry, ed., *Historical Collections of the American Colonial Church: Volume I, Virginia* ([Hartford], 1870), p. 461; Richard Bland, *A Letter to the Clergy of Virginia* . . . (Williamsburg, 1760), pp. 4, 19, 18; John Camm, *A Single and Distinct View* . . . (Annapolis, 1763), p. 24; Richard L. Morton, *Colonial Virginia* (Chapel Hill, 1960), II, 811; William Wirt Henry, *Patrick Henry* (New York, 1891), I, 41.

[21] On the Mayhew-Apthorp controversy, see above, pp. 96–97, and Bailyn, *Pamphlets,* I, Introduction to Pamphlet 3; and on Mayhew's earlier career, see Introduction to Pamphlet 1.

of Christian orthodoxy with episcopacy; his equating of New England nonconformity not only with superstition, fanaticism, hypocrisy, and persecution but with "popery or Mohammedanism" as well; and the arrogance of his assertion that the Society was "above censure" and "incapable of wrong motives in the application of its liberality." Above all else, however, Apthorp's pamphlet played into the profound fears felt by non-Anglicans everywhere in the colonies, and especially in New England, that an American episcopate was about to be established. It was to this deep-lying anxiety, acutely inflamed in 1763 by the known, and even more by the suspected, maneuvers of the Archbishop of Canterbury, that Jonathan Mayhew, pastor of Boston's West Church and long famous for his advanced views in both politics and theology, addressed himself in his pamphlet attacks on Apthorp and the Society for the Propagation of the Gospel.[22]

In the course of his overwhelming reply, *Observations on the Charter and Conduct of the Society,* Mayhew argued that by "orthodox" the founders of the Society had meant not only Anglicans but all Protestants,[23] and that it had not been intended that the Society's funds would go to support episcopal clergymen in places "where a competent provision was already made for a clergy of the congregational or presbyterian persuasion." The sending of missionaries to places like Cambridge was a violation of the Society's charter, and it resulted only in "setting altar against altar" in the hope that one day nonconformists in New England would submit to the establishment of the Church of England. Such a prospect was frightening to Mayhew. The essen-

---

[22] Wendell D. Garrett, *Apthorp House, 1760–1960* (Cambridge, 1960), pp. 12, 13; [East Apthorp], *Considerations on the Institution and Conduct of the Society* . . . (Boston, 1763), pp. 7, 10–11, 17, 14, 23.

[23] Significantly, "the etymology of the word *orthodox*" played an important role in the arguments of the Baptists ten years later, disputing not a threatened Anglican establishment but the actual Congregational establishment in Massachusetts of which Mayhew, formally at least, had been a member. Allen, *American Alarm* (JHL 39), 4th sec., p. 11.

tial character of the Church of England was only too well known, he wrote: a mode of worship completely alien "from the simplicity of the Gospel and the apostolic times"; an "enormous hierarchy [that ascended] by various gradations from the dirt to the skies"; and a leadership that, historically, included those "mitred, lordly SUCCESSORS *of the fishermen of Galilee*" who had driven the colonists' ancestors from "the fair cities, villages, and delightful fields of Britain" into the "arms of savages and barbarians" as punishment for their nonconformity. If the Church of England were ever established in New England, he warned, religious oaths would be demanded as they were in England "and all of us [would] be taxed for the support of *bishops* and their *underlings*." Such an over-all establishment could only be created by act of Parliament or by fiat of the crown; but neither Parliament nor crown had the right to extend the ecclesiastical laws of England to America, or, indeed, to reach in any other way into the internal affairs of the colonies.

It was this association of religious with secular life in the colonies that in the end dominated the controversy. The point, implicit throughout, was made explicit by Mayhew himself:

if bishops were speedily to be sent to America, it seems not wholly improbable, from what we hear of the *unusual* tenor of some late Parliamentary acts and bills for raising money on the poor colonies *without their consent,* that provisions might be made for the support of these bishops, if not of all the Church clergy also, in the *same way.*

John Adams, among contemporaries, passed the final verdict on the affair. The Mayhew-Apthorp controversy, he recollected fifty-four years later,

spread an universal alarm against the authority of Parliament. It excited a general and just apprehension that bishops, and dioceses, and churches, and priests, and tithes, were to be imposed on us by Parliament. It was known that neither King, nor ministry, nor arch-

bishops could appoint bishops in America without an Act of Parliament; and if Parliament could tax us, they could establish the Church
of England with all its creeds, articles, tests, ceremonies, and tithes,
and prohibit all other churches, as conventicles and schism shops.[24]

These two famous episodes — the Two-Penny Act and the
Parsons' Cause in Virginia, and the Mayhew-Apthorp controversy
in Massachusetts — dramatized popular resentments against real
or potential religious establishments and brought together the
issues of civil and ecclesiastical oppression just at the time when
the first constitutional arguments against the extension of Parliament's power in America were being worked out. But the local
leaders in both these cases soon discovered that their arguments
were two-edged swords, and that they themselves were at least
as vulnerable as their opponents. For much of what they had
alleged against the home authorities was soon used against them
with even greater force by dissenters in their own midst who
stood to them as they had stood to Camm, to Apthorp, and to
the establishment behind them, and who, arguing against the
privileges of the locally dominant churches, found in the vocabulary Bland and Mayhew were using in their constitutional claims
against England a powerful reinforcement.

The burden of this internal opposition was borne by the radical
sectarians: New Light Presbyterians, Separate Baptists, and Strict
Congregationalists; with the result that the most advanced pre-
Revolutionary arguments for disestablishment — arguments that
would eventually bear fruit in all the governments of the new
nation — were unstable compounds of narrow denominationalism
and broad libertarianism. In Virginia a new influx of radical dissenters overturned the ecclesiastical stability of the 1750's. Waves
of Separate Baptists, violently hostile to coercion in any form,
uninhibited New Light Presbyterians, and finally, after 1770,

[24] Mayhew, *Observations* . . . (Boston, 1763), pp. 20–21, 26, 155–156;
Richard J. Hooker, "The Mayhew Controversy," *Church History*, 5 (1936),
254; Adams, *Works*, X, 288.

Methodists, all clamoring for full freedom of religion, put almost insupportable pressures on the hitherto benign establishment. To deal with these increasingly belligerent claims, the Burgesses appointed in 1769 a Committee for Religion, and instructed it to draw up a new, comprehensive act of toleration. It was a powerful committee that included among other leading liberal politicians Camm's old enemy Richard Bland, who in these years confided to a friend that though he considered himself "a sincere son of the established church" he nevertheless embraced "her doctrines without approving of her hierarchy, which I know to be a relic of the papal encroachments upon the common law," and argued that the creation of an American episcopate would produce "greater convulsions than anything that has ever, as yet, happened in this part of the globe." Yet the bill the committee submitted in 1772 reflected more concern for guaranteeing social stability in a situation of increasing religious controversy than for easing the intensity of anti-establishment feeling. It proposed to write into law new limitations on the freedom of local nonconformists to worship as they pleased. Dissenters would be required to meet only during daylight hours, in licensed meetinghouses with unlocked doors; baptizing and even preaching to slaves was to be prohibited, and dissenters suspected of disloyalty could be forced to take the test oath and to swear to the articles of the Church of England.[25]

A storm of protest followed the publication of the bill. Petitions were received from nonconformists throughout the colony demanding for themselves "and other Protestant dissenting ministers liberty to preach in all places and at all seasons without restraint." The language of these protests at first remained pragmatic, premised on the continuation of a religious establishment in Virginia and aimed at warding off specific disabilities. But

[25] Brydon, *Virginia's Mother Church*, II, 249 ff., 367 ff.; Gewehr, *Great Awakening*, chap. v, pp. 146–147; *Virginia Magazine of History and Biography*, 6 (1898–1899), 132, 131.

gradually these demands were extended and their bearing on the political claims of the colonies made clear. The Presbyterians of Hanover County led the effective opposition, claiming full freedom of "preaching or teaching at any time or place in this colony," and pointing out that such freedom "in civil affairs . . . has long been so friendly to the cause of liberty." "The interest of American liberty," they concluded, is "certainly most deeply concerned in the matter." Similar, more belligerent, claims were made by the Baptists, and it became clear that the passage of the proposed bill, fortifying the establishment in Virginia, would create the same convulsion in that one colony that Bland had feared for all the colonies.[26]

The bill was dropped, and in the confusion of 1774 and 1775 the issue was momentarily lost sight of. But as Independence approached and the need to draft plans for a new state government became urgent, the discussion was revived. Petitions and protests flooded the Assembly, and in the atmosphere of impending revolution they acquired a powerful new appeal. They appeared now not as deviant claims against what was proper and normal but as legitimate and persuasive proposals, appropriately part of a general effort to realize more fully, and universalize, the natural tendencies of colonial life.[27] The unstable union of sectarian par-

---

[26] Brydon, *Virginia's Mother Church*, II, 378–380, 381, 555, 556, 557.

[27] Thus, for example, the militia and freeholders of Augusta County instructed their representatives not to forget, in their efforts to establish American rights and privileges, "the illiberal treatment which a difference in religious sentiments . . . has produced," and ordered them to work for a declaration "that no religious sect whatever be established in this commonwealth." In a reply to this, published in Purdy's *Gazette*, a writer who proposed to speak for the established church had to admit that "it seems somewhat hard and repugnant to liberty to oblige men to pay towards the support of a church to which they do not belong"; his support for the establishment was defensive, based only on the ground that if such an institution was for the general good those who opposed it must concede to it "in consideration of the many advantages they may be supposed to derive from the state." "The Sentiments of the Several Companies of Militia and Freeholders of Augusta, in Virginia . . . ," Peter Force, ed., *American Archives . . .* (Washington, D.C., 1837–1853), 5th ser., II, cols. 815, 816.

ticularism and political idealism was consummated. The famous clause of the Virginia Declaration of Rights, passed in June of 1776, stating that religion "can be directed only by reason and conviction" and that "all men are equally entitled to the free exercise of religion according to the dictates of conscience," was written, in its crucial phrases, by James Madison, confessedly influenced by the claims of the Presbyterians and the "persecuted Baptists" as well as by enlightenment ideals. A delegation of dissenters from three counties pointed out that now that the government was to be "new-modeled," considerations of justice, of good policy, and of the need for unity in the military struggle for "our liberty, our ALL," urged the granting of "equal privilege" — in religion as in civil affairs — to all: it would be a "great injustice" if one denomination were to be established among people "worshiping the same God, and all struggling in the same common cause." In Prince Edward County, dissenters rejoiced that the Bill of Rights had delivered them "from a long night of ecclesiastical bondage," and they requested the House "to raise religious as well as civil liberty to the zenith of glory, and . . . that without delay all church establishments might be pulled down, and every tax upon conscience and private judgment abolished." Others declared "that their hopes have been raised and confirmed by the declarations of this House with regard to equal liberty," and prayed that "the burden of an ecclesiastical establishment . . . as well as every other yoke may be broken, and that the oppressed may go free." Still others condemned establishments as "inconsistent with the spirit of taxation which supposes those on whom impositions are laid to be benefited thereby." And finally, Hanover County's Presbyterians, professing themselves to be "governed by the same sentiments which have inspired the United States of America," pointed out that now that the "yoke of tyranny" had been cast off and government was about to be reconstituted on "equitable and liberal foundations," the House should keep in mind "that every argument for civil liberty gains additional strength when applied to liberty in the concerns of religion." Asking for "no ecclesiastical establishments" in their own behalf, they stated their absolute opposition to permitting any other group to enjoy "exclusive or separate emoluments or privileges . . . to the common reproach and injury of every other denomination." The only just, reasonable, and effective solution was to abolish "all partial and invidious distinctions" at once and for all time.[28]

In the end, a decade later, in Jefferson's great Act for Establishing Religious Freedom and the disestablishing legislation that surrounded it, this goal, sought jointly by spokesmen for minority denominationalism and enlightened reform, was attained in the state of Virginia. In Massachusetts and Connecticut the same conclusion was reached with greater difficulty and after a struggle that lasted into the nineteenth century. But there, paradoxically, the pre-Revolutionary opposition to the internal establishment had been even fiercer than in Virginia, and the contagion of Revolutionary thought more virulent.

The leadership in the fight against the internal establishments in New England in the 1760's and 1770's was taken by the Separate Baptists, "the most radical of the despised and illegal Separates." These doctrinally self-conscious predestinarian evangelists of the eighteenth century, like Jehovah's Witnesses in the twentieth, were fiercely belligerent, acutely sensitive to slights, and indefatigable in righting every wrong done them; they became, however limited and parochial their intended goals, spearheads in the drive toward a fuller realization of equality. Inheriting in the mid-1760's the social views of the earlier Strict Congregationalists, reinforced by large increases in membership, and

[28] William T. Hutchinson, et al., eds., Papers of James Madison (Chicago, 1962–), I, 112, 170–175; Brydon, Virginia's Mother Church, II, 562–563, 564, 565, 566; Journal of the House of Delegates of Virginia. Anno Domini, 1776. (Richmond, 1828), pp. 25, 7, 15, 35, 48, 24–25.

strengthened by a newly perfected group organization and by the leadership of the fantastically energetic proselytizer and pamphleteer Isaac Backus, they threw themselves into the fight for equal rights.[29]

Their work was cut out for them. Complacent leaders of the favored church declared that "liberty is the *fundamental* principle of our establishment" since each congregation was free to organize itself, pick its own minister, and, once it certified itself as a unit of a legitimate dissenting denomination, gain exemption from "ministerial taxes." How much better off, they said, was true Christianity here than in England. Abroad there was discrimination against dissenters and limitations of speech and inquiry; but at home in New England there was "liberty of conscience, the rights of private judgment and [an acknowledgment of] the absurdity of advancing the kingdom of Christ by penal laws." Superior human authority was disdained: "We regard neither pope nor prince as head of the church; nor acknowledge that any Parliaments have power to enact articles of doctrine or forms of discipline or modes of worship or terms of church communion." [30]

But popes and parliaments were hardly the point. Everyone conceded that freedom abounded in America, in religious affairs, at this level even in Massachusetts. What was galling to the Baptists and to others who resented having to receive freedoms as favors from those with the right to choose the beneficiaries, was the extent to which the local civil authorities, rejoicing in the advocacy of civil liberty, themselves exercised the very powers they refused to allow others to exercise over them. The toleration they permitted was not freedom or equality; they retained, and used, the power to say what was "regular" enough to be tolerated,

[29] Goen, *Revivalism and Separatism*, pp. 269, 208 ff., 273 ff.; on Backus, see pp. 215-224.
[30] Amos Adams, *Religious Liberty an Invaluable Blessing . . .* (Boston, 1768), pp. 39, 32.

and to tie up in humiliating administrative detail what they could not deny in principle. The established church of Massachusetts, Backus wrote, "has declared the Baptists to be irregular, therefore the secular power still *force* them to support the worship which they conscientiously dissent from." This is not liberty, but hypocrisy: "many who are filling the nation with the cry of LIBERTY and against *oppressors* are at the same time themselves violating that dearest of all rights, LIBERTY of CONSCIENCE." The same persons who protest "year after year against being taxed without their consent and against the scheme of imposing episcopacy upon them . . . impose cruelly upon their neighbors, and force large sums from them to uphold a worship which they conscientiously dissent from." Let those who claim liberty for themselves in one sphere grant it to others in another.

The note was sounded again and again. Suppose episcopacy were established here, Backus argued in one of a series of pamphlets supporting the claims of the Baptists, and suppose the Congregational church were permitted to exist only on sufferance and within an elaborate machinery of certification and approval. What kind of liberty would those presently in power consider this to be? How astonishing, he wrote, "that any of the same men should at the same time show worse treatment to the fellow subjects here than what they complain of from the higher powers!" They protest against taxation without representation; but the representation they are denied is at least possible: "what must it be to deprive them of a right that never can be conveyed to any representative!" They call themselves *"Sons of* LIBERTY, but they treat me like *sons of* VIOLENCE." [31]

The establishment was shocked; disbelieving. "Our Baptist brethren," the libertarian Andrew Eliot wrote Thomas Hollis in

---

[31] [Isaac Backus], *A Seasonable Plea for Liberty of Conscience, Against Some Late Oppressive Proceedings* . . . (Boston, 1770), pp. 8, 3, 14; Isaac Backus, *A Letter to a Gentleman in the Massachusetts General Assembly, Concerning Taxes To Support Religious Worship* ([Boston], 1771), pp. 10 ff., 20, 21, 18.

1771, "all at once complain of grievous persecutions in the Massachusetts! These complaints were never heard of till we saw them in the public prints. It was a great surprise when we saw them, as we had not heard that the laws in force were not satisfactory." He was himself, of course, for full religious freedom: "I do not like anything that looks like an establishment." But what precisely did the Baptists have to complain about? As soon as a group of them "produce a certificate that they are Baptists, they are excused from all ministerial taxes." And the arrangement is prejudiced in their favor: "The certificate is to be given by persons of their own denomination, who are hereby made the only judges, and who it is to be supposed (like all others) will be fond of increasing their own party." The present trouble, he reflected, is probably the result of agitation carried on by a mischievous "young Baptist minister from Pennsylvania" working in collaboration with bishop-loving Anglicans. For if in the past there were

some particular acts of hardship and injustice . . . they must have proceeded from some accidental cause. There is nothing in the present complexion of this country that looks like persecution. Both magistrates and ministers are as free from it as they ever were in any age or country. If it were not so, I should detest New England as much as now I love it, and if possible would leave it . . . I hate every species of persecution, and cannot bear that a people should be accused of it that in my conscience I believe are free from it.[32]

But even Eliot could not altogether ignore the force of the argument associating Baptists' claims with the principles the colonists were advocating in their complaints against Parliament. "I wish," he admitted, "our fathers had contrived some other way for the maintenance of ministers than by a tax. Thank God we have none in Boston." The reasonableness of the association

[32] Eliot to Hollis, Boston, January 29, 1771, MHS *Colls.*, 4th ser., IV, 455, 456, 457.

was undeniable, and as the Anglo-American controversy deepened in the seventies so too did the frequency and intensity of the arguments that applied the logic of secular liberty to the condition of religion and the churches. In town after town in Massachusetts — Ashfield, Berwick, Bolton, Hadley, Haverhill, Montague — embattled Baptists fortified their pleas for full freedom of religion with language borrowed from the larger controversy. The most famous episode took place in Ashfield, a hamlet of some five hundred souls in the western hills of Massachusetts. The Baptists of that obscure village, claiming they had settled the town in the first place and under the worst of wartime conditions, had refused to pay taxes to support the church of "men of a contrary persuasion" (Congregationalists) who had subsequently invaded the place and outvoted them in the town meeting. As a result their property was confiscated. Their adversaries justified the action on the grounds that the Baptists were not a denomination worthy of toleration at all, but only a group of wild schismatics too "fluctuating and unstable" to remain peaceably within any respectable organization, and forming in their so-called church only "a sink for some of the filth of Christianity in this part of the country." The *"natural rights"* the Baptists claim, it was said, threaten anarchy; they would create a situation in which everyone could exempt themselves "from the payment of public taxes if they should happen not to be inclined to pay them." Like everyone else, they must be bound within their civil obligations and not released "to a state of nature." The General Court must deal firmly with them, for just as it is the duty of the legislature to protect "all regular religious societies of Protestants," so too must it cast off those who "cannot, in any tolerable sense, answer the valuable ends of religion to the community."

To such charges the Baptists replied in a campaign of indignant protest and petition that did not cease even after the issue had been taken to London and decided in their favor by no less an authority than the King in Council. The Ashfield remonstrants explained to the General Court in detail the "distressed circumstances which we think cries aloud for some pity to be showed upon us." They pointed out that the local authorities "say they will not favor us because we are of a different opinion in religion from them." Yet they took encouragement "in this our address, from the consideration of the rights of mankind having been *so well* defined in the votes of this honorable House, by which we are taught to think 'that no taxation can be equitable where such restraint is laid upon the taxed as takes from him the liberty of GIVING his *own money freely.*' " [33]

But the heart of the problem, in Ashfield as elsewhere, was the assumption of a justifiable tie between church and state. It was against this that the Ashfield remonstrants particularly directed their case, and it was this that Backus primarily attacked in his comprehensive *Appeal to the Public for Religious Liberty,* published in 1773. Notice, he pointed out, the implications of the axiom that "religious liberty is so blended with civil that if one falls it is not to be expected that the other will continue." The legislature can compel acceptance of its own definition of proper religious practice; and so orthodoxy in effect is decided by majority vote, though God himself said that only a *"few* find the narrow way, while *many* go in the broad way." Yes, some minorities are tolerated in Massachusetts; but some are not, and the procedure of deciding which are and which are not worthy of this privilege gives to a group of civil magistrates — a body which, since each man must speak for himself before God, cannot in the nature of things represent anyone in matters of religion — the power of passing judgment on "the *springs* of their neighbors' actions." You are condemned, he told the Massachu-

[33] *Ibid.,* 455; *The Acts and Resolves, Public and Private, of the Province of the Massachusetts Bay* . . . (Boston, 1869–1922), IV, 1036, 1040, 1038.

setts magistrates, out of your own mouths, for you say that England cannot in right tax beyond her own domain: "have we not as good right to say you do the *same thing*, and so that wherein you judge others you condemn yourselves?" Just as "the present contest between Great Britain and America, is not so much about the greatness of the taxes already laid as about submission to their taxing power, so . . . our greatest difficulty at present concerns the submitting to a taxing power in ecclesiastical affairs." The two campaigns for liberty are logically and morally one. The success of one is dependent on the other: how can anyone reasonably expect that God "will turn the heart of our earthly sovereign to hear the pleas for liberty of those who will not hear the cries of their fellow subjects under their oppressions?" [34]

The point by this time was too obvious to be ignored, and other forceful pamphleteers hammered it home. John Allen, in his florid declamation, *The American Alarm, or the Bostonian Plea, for the Rights and Liberties of the People,* informed the members of the General Court that they had pleaded "like men — like stewards, like gods, for the natural rights and liberties of the people . . . And yet will you dare to make or enforce any law to take away by force and power the properties of your brethren not only contrary to their consent but contrary to their own consciences, because they will not worship the golden image which you have set up?" A true son of liberty, he said, seeks to protect "the sacred liberties of the conscience of mankind as well as to plead for and preserve their civil liberties and properties." You have no more right either by the word of God or by the law of nature to tax the Baptists, or any other minority group, and force them to support a religious worship not their own than you have to tax the angels or allow one man to cut another's throat.

[34] Charles Turner, *A Sermon Preached before His Excellency Thomas Hutchinson* . . . (Boston, 1773), p. 39; Isaac Backus, *An Appeal* . . . (Boston, 1773), pp. 16 ff., 23, 28, 30 ff., 43–44, 54, 55, 52.

You tell your governor that the Parliament of England have no right to tax the Americans . . . because they are not the representatives of America; and will you dare to tax the Baptists for a religion they deny? Are you gentlemen their representatives before GOD, to answer for their souls and consciences any more than the representatives of England are the representatives of America? . . . if it be just in the General Court to take away my sacred and spiritual rights and liberties of conscience and my property with it, then it is surely right and just in the British Parliament to take away by power and force my civil rights and property without my consent; this reasoning, gentlemen, I think is plain.[35]

Yet still not plain enough; and it was to dramatize what was to many, by 1774, the manifestly logical extension into ecclesiastical affairs of the claims Americans were making in civil matters, that the Baptists undertook their invasion of the first Continental Congress in Philadelphia.[36]

It was an extraordinary episode, demonstrating vividly the mutual reinforcement that took place in the Revolution between the struggles for civil and religious liberty. On the evening of October 14, 1774, the Massachusetts delegates were invited to Carpenter's Hall by a group of Philadelphians to do "a little business." When they arrived they found themselves faced by "a great number of Quakers seated at the long table with their broad brimmed beavers on their heads" together with a conclave of Baptists and local Philadelphia dignitaries. The assemblage had gathered to confront the Massachusetts delegates with the discrepancy between the way "in which liberty in general is now beheld" and the way the Baptists were treated in Massachusetts. Our colony and her delegates, John Adams, one of the delegates, later recalled, had thus been summoned "before a self-created tribunal, which was neither legal nor constitutional." The

---

[35] Allen, *American Alarm* (JHL 39), 4th sec., pp. 2, 3, 7, 8, 9.

[36] The three paragraphs that follow are derived from Adams, *Diary and Autobiography*, III, 311, 312; and Alvah Hovey, *A Memoir of the Life and Times of the Rev. Isaac Backus, A.M.* (Boston, 1858), pp. 205, 210, 220–221.

THE CONTAGION OF LIBERTY

lengthy condemnation of Massachusetts for retaining, inconsistently with her professed desire for civil liberty, an oppressive establishment of religion, was read out by the Reverend James Manning, president of the College of Rhode Island, and it was supported by the Quaker leaders as well as by Backus and other Baptists. The charge concluded with the hope that the Massachusetts delegates would assure the conference, in the name of the liberty they had come to Philadelphia to preserve, that the offensive laws would be repealed and things in Massachusetts placed "as they were in Pennsylvania."

The Massachusetts delegates were astonished and acutely embarrassed. Years later Adams reconstructed the main points of the groping speech he extemporized for the occasion. In the first place, he said, we delegates cannot bind our constituents, and so there is no point in our giving assurances of any kind: further, the establishment of religion in Massachusetts is so mild that it can hardly be called an establishment at all; and finally, the people of Massachusetts were as conscientious as those of Pennsylvania: they too were acting in accordance with their consciences, and therefore "the very liberty of conscience" sought by the Baptists demanded, by extension, that the laws in question be retained. It was a shabby performance. To the last point the Quaker leader Isaac Pemberton could only exclaim with disgust "Oh! sir, pray don't urge liberty of conscience in favor of such laws!" The conference lasted five hours, and it so upset Adams' equanimity that thirty years later, when he came to write his autobiography, he still felt it necessary to explain the whole thing away by concluding that it had been a plot hatched by that "artful Jesuit" Pemberton in order "to break up the Congress, or at least to withdraw the Quakers and the governing part of Pennsylvania from us."

But if such a rationalization was effective in later years, it was not at the time. The Massachusetts delegates returned home to

269

face still another challenge by the Baptists, this one addressed to the Provincial Congress and hurled with even more painful accuracy. A tax of three pence a pound on tea has made a great noise in the world: "but your law of last June laid a tax of the same sum every year upon the Baptists in each parish . . . All America are alarmed at the tea tax, though, if they please, they can avoid it by not buying the tea; but we have no such liberty." These taxes we are determined not to pay "not only upon your principle of not being taxed where we are not represented, but also because we dare not render that homage to any earthly power which [we] . . . are fully convinced belongs only to God."

The same charge came from other sources. To the Baptists' clamor was added in 1774 a Presbyterian voice at least as sharp and shrill as theirs. In his *Freedom from Civil and Ecclesiastical Slavery, the Purchase of Christ,* Jonathan Parsons, the dour, eloquent, fiercely predestinarian New Light preacher of Newburyport, turned a sermon commemorating the Boston Massacre into a memorable plea for religious freedom. He spoke in defense of those "true" Calvinists, of whom he was a leader, believed to be heterodox by the establishment but known among themselves to be the only truly orthodox. They had refused to take refuge within the official categories of dissent, and consequently had been taxed for the support of an establishment not of their own choosing. "If this is not enslaving men in their most important interests, in the name of wonder, what is?" Was it not a shocking inconsistency "that a *province* which holds an *ecclesiastical tyranny* beyond all her sister colonies should be foremost in her attempts for *civil* liberty"? The evil must be expunged if any hope is to be held for success in the cause of civil liberty, "for while we plead for liberty on one hand and promote slavery on the other, our principles are too contracted and corrupt; and if we regard oppression in our hearts the Lord will not hear us." The church as well as the state "must be founded on principles of justice, benevolence, and moderation, or there can be no peace . . . O that court and country may break through the prejudices and selfishness of the age!" [37]

The pressure was powerful; and though the politics of the later Revolutionary years would permit a partial establishment of religion to persist in Massachusetts, the ultimate conclusion everywhere was clear. The disestablishment of religion was neither an original goal nor completely a product of the Revolution. Its roots lay deep in the colonial past, in circumstances that Jonathan Parsons described as a "random way of settling ministers and churches, together with a vile contempt of creeds and confessions . . . all seem to jumble together, and make mere *hodgepodge.*" These unplanned, unexpected conditions, lacking in completeness and justification, were touched by the magic of Revolutionary thought, and were transformed. Our ancestors learned through their own suffering and the example of England, Samuel Williams wrote in his prophetic *Discourse on the Love of Our Country* (1775),

what must be the effect of endeavoring to enforce *uniformity* in doctrine or discipline. This, with the gradual improvement of the human mind that has since taken place, has been leading these colonies into that truly righteous and catholic principle, *universal toleration and liberty of conscience;* which, if not already perfect, we are in the sure path to.

No doubt "the fierce and bigoted" of every denomination will remain inflamed with a desire to establish themselves at the expense of others. But their efforts will never succeed. "The different parties among us will subsist, and grow up into more large

---

[37] Parsons, *Freedom*, pp. 8–9n, 7, 9–10, 14, 15.

and respectable bodies. And the mutual interests and wisdom of all cannot fail to perfect that universal toleration and liberty of conscience which is so generally and well begun." [38]

3. THE DEMOCRACY UNLEASHED

If some were elevated and invigorated by the support given to antislavery and disestablishment sentiment by the extension of the colonists' constitutional arguments, others were dismayed and felt threatened. Slaveholders were generally alarmed, and sought to check when they could not simply ignore such disturbing ramifications of thought. Anglicans in Virginia and Congregationalists in Massachusetts found fields other than religion in which to follow out the implications of their views on civil liberty. Yet the threat in both cases was limited, for the ultimate consequences were known, and the possibility of standing fast — for the present at least — remained. But there was another area — an area more directly relevant to the central constitutional questions of the Revolution than either of these — in which such limitations did not exist: where the possibility of standing fast did not remain; where the ultimate resolution of thought could not easily be seen; where the familiar meaning of ideas and words faded away into confusion, and leaders felt themselves peering into a haze, seeking to bring shifting conceptions somehow into focus.

"You and I, my dear friend," John Adams wrote in 1776, "have been sent into life at a time when the greatest lawgivers of antiquity would have wished to live. How few of the human race have ever enjoyed an opportunity of making an election of government . . . When! before the present epocha, had three millions of people full power and a fair opportunity to form and

---

[38] Parsons, *Freedom*, pp. 8–9n; Samuel Williams, *A Discourse on the Love of Our Country . . .* (Salem, 1775: JHL Pamphlet 55), p. 15.

establish the wisest and happiest government that human wisdom can contrive?" [39] But how fair in fact was the opportunity? Everyone knew the basic prescription for a wise and just government. It was so to balance the contending powers in society that no one power could overwhelm the others and, unchecked, destroy the liberties that belonged to all. The problem was how to arrange the institutions of government so that this balance could be achieved.

For Americans the ideal solution had been England's "mixed" government, in which major elements of society formed a self-balancing equilibrium of governmental institutions. The question that emerged with unanticipated urgency after 1775 was how this solution could apply in the new governments of the American states. For the primary assumptions that had been made concerning the nature of the basic social forces in the state could no longer be maintained. Factions, interests, pressure groups of course existed in eighteenth-century America as they do in the twentieth century. But these, to eighteenth-century minds, were the burdensome impedimenta, the unfortunate but more or less less inevitable details of public life which must be borne but need scarcely be dignified by a place in formal political thought; only occasionally were they included, except by way of denunciation, in political and constitutional theory. The categories within which the colonists thought about the social foundations of politics were inheritances from classical antiquity, reshaped by seventeenth-century English thought. The primary units of politics, they believed, were the three basic orders of

---

[39] [John Adams], *Thoughts on Government* . . . (Philadelphia, 1776: JHL Pamphlet 65), p. 27. The sentiment was widely shared. Thus the contemporary historian David Ramsay wrote in his *History of the American Revolution* (Philadelphia, 1789), I, 356: "In no age before, and in no other country, did man ever possess an election of the kind of government under which he would choose to live. The constituent parts of the ancient free governments were thrown together by accident. The freedom of modern European governments was, for the most part, obtained by the concessions or liberality of monarchs or military leaders. In America alone, reason and liberty concurred in the formation of constitutions."

society corresponding to the three basic forms of government: royalty, the nobility, and the commons. These formal strata were distinct in composition and interests. Royalty was unique in its sanctity and prerogative power; it stood for order and authority, and it symbolized and unified the state. The commons had the power of numbers and of productivity; it was unique in promoting liberty and individual expression. The nobility, centrally important to the constitution, had a stalwart independence guaranteed by inherited wealth and status which enabled it to mediate the powerful conflicts generated above and below; it acted as a balance wheel, preventing the commons, on the one hand, from turning society into a licentious mob, and the crown, on the other, from becoming tyrannical. Each was essential, and equally essential, in achieving the equilibrium in government that brings tranquility and happiness to all; but any of them, released from the counter-pressures of the others, would degenerate — into a tyranny, or into a self-aggrandizing oligarchy, or into an anarchic democracy destructive, in the end, to liberty as well as to property. Somehow, through great historic struggles, these social forces had been brought into the English government in a perfect balance, and it was this that accounted, it was believed, for the political stability that nation enjoyed.[40]

This constitutional miracle the colonists felt they shared, for they too lived within the jurisdiction of the British government. But they lived also within their own immediate governments, and therein lay a problem that many had recognized from the earliest years but that became acute only after 1763 when the foundations of government in America came under intense scrutiny. It had long been known that the balance of social forces in the colonial polities were peculiarly skewed, for one of the basic components did not exist in proper form. The commons

---

[40] On the derivation and development of this classical theory of the English constitution and the ambiguities within it, see above, Chap. III, pp. 67–76, and notes 15, 16.

was obviously and vigorously present; and so too was the crown in the person of the King's vicegerent, the governor; but the nobility was not. Who could qualify? It was generally agreed that the members of the House of Lords were "peers of England and not of America," and while a few noblemen had lived in the colonies from time to time, these individuals could scarcely be mistaken for an order of American society: even if their numbers had been sufficient, their status and political role in the colonies would not have been.[41] Nowhere in eighteenth-century America had the legal attributes of nobility been recognized or perpetuated. The law made no provision for hereditary privileges; no office of government had been guaranteed by birth. Indeed, the situation was almost exactly the reverse of the traditional, for the group closest to a privileged order in the colonies were the councilors, the governors' advisors and members of the upper chambers of the legislatures, but their identity as a social group was the creation, rather than the creator, of their role in government. In a number of colonies a few families had tended to dominate the Councils; but they had less legal right to do so than certain royal officials who, though hardly members of an American nobility, sat on the Councils by virtue of their offices. Councilors could be and were removed by simple political maneuver. Council seats were filled either by appointment or election: when appointive, they were vulnerable to political pressure in England; when elective, to the vagaries of public opinion at home. As there were no special privileges, no peculiar group possessions, manners, or attitudes to distinguish councilors from other affluent Americans, so there were no separate political interests expressed in the Councils as such.

Yet these were the bodies expected to maintain, by their inde-

---

[41] Allen, *American Alarm* (JHL 39), 1st sec., p. 12; Warren, *Oration* (JHL 35), pp. 9–10. For a general discussion of this problem in the earlier eighteenth century, see Bernard Bailyn, *The Origins of American Politics* (New York, 1968), chap. iii.

pendence from pressures generated above and below, the balance of the whole. The fact that they could not do so had been considered a major failing of colonial government from the early years of the century, though precisely in what way differed according to the colony examined and the point of view of the examiner. In the colonies in which the Councils were appointed by the crown, the results were deplored with particular vehemence by those who stood on the side of the commons. Richard Henry Lee's description of the situation in Virginia was typical. The constitution of Virginia, he explained to his brother Arthur Lee in 1766, was modeled on the excellent pattern of England's. "But unhappily for us, my brother, it is an exterior semblance only; when you examine separately the parts that compose this government, essential variations appear between it and the happily poised English constitution." In Britain, the King, with his executive powers, and the Commons, "representing the democratic interest," are prevented from overextending their claims

by a powerful body of nobles, independent in the material circumstances of hereditary succession to their titles and seats in the second bench of the legislature . . . With us, the legislative power is lodged in a governor, Council, and House of Burgesses. The two first [are] appointed by the crown, and their places held by the precarious tenure of pleasure [of the crown] only. That security therefore which the constitution derives in Britain from the House of Lords is here entirely wanting, and the just equilibrium totally destroyed by two parts out of three of the legislature being in the same hands.[42]

The analysis was a commonplace of the time, and so too was the conclusion. Councilors of the royal colonies, one pamphleteer wrote in the same year, being "proud of the dignity annexed to their office and fond of maintaining such a flattering superiority . . . naturally become tools of that ministry upon whose favor their very existence depends, since the same power which raised

[42] James C. Ballagh, ed., *Letters of Richard Henry Lee* (New York, 1912–1914), I, 19.

them to their exalted rank can, for a single act of disobedience, sink them into their original obscurity." The result, it was widely agreed, was that in the royal colonies where the councilors "are the meanest creatures and tools in the political creation, dependent every moment for their existence on the tainted breath of a prime minister . . . the crown has really two branches of our legislature in its power," a situation, which, if it ever became universal and fully exploited, would result in the death of liberty in America. But the complaints in the royal colonies came not only from representatives of "the democracy." Royal officials also objected when they discovered that in order to run their governments at all they had to appoint to their Councils local leaders whose interests proved to be indistinguishable from those of the lower House.[43]

Such complaints by crown officials were as nothing, however, next to those that emanated from Massachusetts, where the Council was elected by the Assembly. From Francis Bernard, governor of the Bay Colony during the Stamp Act troubles, and others in his administration, came a stream of bitter denunciations of "the constitutional imbecility of the Council." With such a perverted middle chamber, Bernard wrote after an electoral purge of the Council, good government could not possibly exist. If councilors continued "to be turned out of their places whenever they exercise[d] the dictates of their own judgments in contravention to the fury of a seditious demagogue," the result would be anarchy.[44]

[43] [William Hicks], *Considerations upon the Rights of the Colonists to the Privileges of British Subjects* . . . (New York, 1766: JHL Pamphlet 18), pp. 12–13; Adams ("Novanglus"), *Works*, IV, 117; Bernard Bailyn, "Politics and Social Structure in Virginia," James M. Smith, ed., *Seventeenth-Century America* (Chapel Hill, 1959), p. 113.

[44] *Letters to the Ministry from Governor Bernard, General Gage, and Commodore Hood* . . . (Boston, 1769 [Evans 11176]), p. 12; *Copies of Letters from Governor Bernard, &c. to the Earl of Hillsborough* [Boston, 1769], p. 9. See also Edward Channing and Archibald C. Coolidge, eds., *The Barrington-Bernard Correspondence* . . . (Cambridge, 1912), pp. 198, 256–258.

As the Anglo-American troubles multiplied and greater control over government was sought by officialdom on the one hand and popular leaders on the other, more and more thought was given to the means by which "an independent and honest middle branch of legislature" might be created capable of resisting both "the exuberances of popular liberty and . . . the stretches of the government party when . . . either advanced beyond the constitutional line of propriety." Remedies were sought for this constitutional weakness, and proposals were made that reached into the roots of American society. A number of writers came to the conclusion that the only solution was the creation of a privileged social order from which the members of the Council could be chosen. Ideally, Governor Bernard wrote, a hereditary nobility should be created in the colonies. And though he acknowledged that America was not yet "(and probably will not be for many years to come) ripe enough for an hereditary *nobility*," he saw no reason why "a *nobility* for life" could not be established at once. A life peerage "would probably give strength and stability to the American governments as effectually as an hereditary *nobility* does to that of *Great Britain*." It was a logical idea, which others too came to believe was the solution to a crucial problem of government. In New York the scurrilous attacker of Alexander McDougall, the pseudo-Wilkes, attributed much of the current troubles to the fact that England's "AUGUST PEERAGE . . . does not obtain, with its due weight, in the royal colonies." Its pale imitation, the Council, is "equal in legislative and judicial authority; but in influence, privileges and stability, vastly inferior." No one, surely, unless his principles were *"verging to democracy"* — ("God forbid that we should ever be so miserable as to sink into a republic!") — would wish anything but strength for this "essential though imperfect branch of the mixed monarchy." Let us hope that "with the increase of numbers and opulence" the colonies will achieve "a perfect *copy* of that *bright original* which is the envy and admiration of the world!" And the one thing, above all others, that would advance the progress toward that goal would be the vesting of the councilors "with their offices for life."[45]

Andrew Oliver, the provincial secretary of Massachusetts and a close political ally of Bernard, in less rhetorical language, went further. In one of the letters whose publication as a pamphlet in 1773 so inflamed public opinion in Massachusetts he stated that the necessary independence of the middle branch could never be achieved under the present circumstances. A way must be found "to put a man of fortune above the common level and exempt him from being chosen by the people into the lower offices" where he might be subject to popular intimidation. The best solution, as he saw it, was to create "an order of patricians or esquires . . . to be all men of fortune or good landed estates" appointed to that rank for life by act of the governor and Council; from among this social order members of the Council would be chosen, and on them would be bestowed "a title one degree above that of esquire."

Many, of course, disagreed with such proposals. John Adams believed that arguments in favor of creating an American life peerage were part of the general plot against liberty hatched in the corrupt centers of power in England and America. But ideas in favor of creating some kind of social basis for constitutional balance were widespread, even among those who opposed the strengthening of English power in America. William Drayton, who knew well enough that the colonies did "not yet desire dignities, lordships, and dukedoms," believed that the main constitutional difficulty in the colonies lay in the appointment to Council

[45] [William H. Drayton], *A Letter from Freeman of South-Carolina . . .* (Charleston, 1774: JHL Pamphlet 45), p. 4: *Select Letters on the Trade and Government of America . . . by Governor Bernard . . .* (2d ed., London, 1774), p. 83; *No. 3. The Dougliad. On Liberty . . .* [New York, 1770: JHL Pamphlet 33], pp. 2-3.

seats of "more strangers from England than men of rank in the colony," and urged that councilors be appointed for life from among those qualified not only by local birth and residence but by local property in sufficient quantity to distinguish them in an unmistakable way from the population at large and make them independent of pressures and temptations from any source.[46]

The idea that constitutional liberty was bound up with the mediating political power of a privileged social order persisted into the turmoil of the Revolutionary crisis,[47] but it came under new pressures and was challenged by the more advanced thinkers of the time. If America breaks free of English control, it was asked, what would become of the liberty-preserving balance? What elements would there be to be balanced? Monarchy as a social order would obviously be gone. The commons, on the other hand, would most certainly and substantially be there. And that great guarantor of liberty, the middle order?

The idea that the newly independent American states, con-

---

[46] *Copy of Letters Sent to Great-Britain by His Excellency Thomas Hutchinson . . . and Several Other Persons . . .* (Boston, 1773: JHL Pamphlet 40), p. 31; Adams ("Novanglus"), *Works*, IV, 25, 27, 28; Drayton, *Letter from Freeman*, pp. 32, 18 (cf. 12). Adams' opponent "Massachusettensis" (Daniel Leonard), who in the end advocated nothing more drastic than filling all the Council seats in the colonies by crown appointment, favored that solution because it was at least an approximation of the proper arrangement which was ruled out because "the infant state of the colonies does not admit of a peerage." *Novanglus and Massachusettensis . . .* (Boston, 1819), p. 194. For Adams' "Sixth principle of revolution . . . *the necessity of resisting the introduction of a royal or Parliamentary nobility or aristocracy into the country*," see MHS *Colls.*, 5th ser., IV, 344.

[47] Nor did it disappear after Independence. The idea in its original form continued to be advocated, retrospectively for the thirteen colonies, prospectively for Canada, not only by exiled loyalists like Joseph Galloway and William Smith, Jr., but also by leading English officials like the younger Pitt, who attributed the loss of the colonies to "the want of more resemblance in their constitution with that of Great Britain." The result was the Constitutional Act of 1791 which authorized for Canada the creation of life peers to sit in the legislative councils of the provinces. Corinne C. Weston, *English Constitutional Theory and the House of Lords, 1556–1832* (London, 1965), pp. 160 ff.

ceived in the spirit of equal rights and privileges and formed out of a remarkably equalitarian tradition, would deliberately create a privileged order was unthinkable. It was even ludicrous, as the Tory author of *What Think Ye of the Congress Now?* exuberantly pointed out in analyzing the Continental Congress's activities. "An American *House of Lords* is in agitation," he wrote, to be composed of hereditary "orders of the American nobility."

I am ravished and transported at the foresight of the American grandeur . . . Oh! how we shall shine with dukes in America! There will be no less than fifty-three of them . . . The Committees of Correspondence will furnish us with marquises; and the Committees of Observation, with earls. The viscounts may consist of heroes that are famed for their exploits in *tarring and feathering;* and the barons, or lowest order, of those whose merit has been signalized in burning such pamphlets as they were unable to answer.

No one seriously proposed to create a new social basis for the middle level of government. But what would the result be? Republican states, of course. This in itself — in view of the Commonwealth derivation of some of the colonists' most cherished ideas, in view also of the high esteem in which successful republics were held, and in view of the "genius of the Americans, their republican habits and sentiments" — was a matter, for most Americans, of satisfaction. But it was a matter also of concern, for while the condition of life in America and the moral qualities of the people made the creation of republics peculiarly feasible, other circumstances made their survival problematic.[48]

Republics had always been known to be delicate polities, peculiarly susceptible to inner convulsions and outer pressures. And the larger the state the greater the danger. Monarchy, it was

[48] [Thomas Bradbury Chandler], *What Think Ye of the Congress Now?* . . . (New York, 1775), pp. 34–35; Ramsay, *History*, I, 350. On the "quick transition from monarchy to republic in form and belief," see Cecelia M. Kenyon, "Republicanism and Radicalism in the American Revolution . . . ," *W.M.Q.*, 3d ser., 19 (1962), 165–166; *Papers of Thomas Jefferson* (Julian P. Boyd, ed., Princeton, 1950–), II, 26.

generally agreed, was best suited to extensive domains, popular government to small territories. The great and glorious republics of the past — "the ancient republics — Rome, Carthage, Athens, etc.," and more recently Switzerland and Holland — had all been small in size compared with the united colonies, compared even with most of the individual states. Republican government "may do well enough for a single city or small territory, but would be utterly improper for such a continent as this. America is too unwieldy for the feeble, dilatory administration of democracy." [49]

"Democracy" — this was the point. "Republic" and "democracy" were words closely associated in the colonists' minds; often they were used synonymously; and they evoked a mixed response of enthusiasm and foreboding. For if "republic" conjured up for many the positive features of the Commonwealth era and marked the triumph of virtue and reason, "democracy" — a word that denoted the lowest order of society as well as the form of government in which the commons ruled — was generally associated with the threat of civil disorder and the early assumption of power by a dictator.[50] Throughout the colonial period, and in-

[49] [Charles Inglis], *The True Interest of America . . . Strictures on a Pamphlet Intitled Common Sense . . .* (Philadelphia, 1776), pp. 17, 49 ff.; Jonathan Boucher, *A View of the Causes and Consequences of the American Revolution . . .* (London, 1797), p. lxix.

[50] Rev. Samuel Johnson to the Archbishop of Canterbury, July 13, 1760, quoted in Oscar Zeichner, *Connecticut's Years of Controversy* (Chapel Hill, 1949), p. 28; Madison to Jefferson, October 24, 1787, Boyd, *Jefferson Papers*, XII, 276–277; *The Federalist*, no. 14; Roy N. Lokken, "The Concept of Democracy in Colonial Political Thought," *W.M.Q.*, 3d ser., 16 (1959), 570–580. Cf. Robert R. Palmer, "Notes on the Use of the Word 'Democracy,' 1789–1799," *Political Science Quarterly*, 68 (1953), 203–226. For a characteristic description of how democracies succumb to demagogues, see [James Chalmers], *Additions to Plain Truth . . .* (Philadelphia, 1776), pp. 128–129. For John Adams' frantic efforts to keep the distinction between a democracy and a republic clear ("I was always for a free republic, not a democracy, which is as arbitrary, tyrannical, bloody, cruel, and intolerable a government as that of Phalaris with his bull is represented to have been. Robespierre is a perfect exemplification of the character of the first bellwether in a democracy"), and for his bewildering attempts to define republicanism so as to accommodate the balance of the English constitution without "either an hereditary king or an hereditary nobility," see his letters to Mercy

creasingly in the early Revolutionary years, the dangers of "demo-cratical despotism" preyed on the minds not merely of crown officials and other defenders of prerogative but of all enlightened thinkers: clerics like Andrew Eliot, who pointed out the "many inconveniencies which would attend frequent popular elections"; and lawyers like John Dickinson, who believed that "a people does not reform with moderation," or like William Drayton, who stated forthrightly that he was as desirous of checking "the exuberances of popular liberty" as he was the excesses of preroga-tive. The leaders of the Revolutionary movement were radicals — but they were eighteenth-century radicals concerned, like the eighteenth-century English radicals, not with the need to recast the social order nor with the problems of economic inequality and the injustices of stratified societies but with the need to purify a corrupt constitution and fight off the apparent growth of prerogative power.[51] To them it did not seem reasonable to

Warren, 1807, in MHS *Colls.*, 5th ser., IV, 394, 325, 353, 473. His conclusion that he "never understood" what a republican government was ("and I believe no other man ever did or ever will") appears to be well substantiated by his subsequent statement that "to speak technically, or scientifically, if you will, there are monarchical, aristocratical, and democratical republics" (*Works*, X, 378). Throughout, however, he was grappling with the problem of recreating the "equipoised" balance of the English constitution in the circumstances of the American states. Cf. Robert R. Palmer, *The Age of the Democratic Revolution . . . The Challenge* (Princeton, 1959), pp. 58–59, 267–276.

[51] Thus Ian Christie's description of the extreme English radicals of the Revolu-tionary period: "They were no democrats . . . their ideal was a broad, propertied oligarchy, in which the lower orders should clearly know and accept their place — Hollis [Mayhew's and Eliot's mentor in libertarianism] even advocated keep-ing the masses illiterate." *Wilkes, Wyvill and Reform* (London, 1962), pp. 15–16. See also Christie's emphasis in his general conclusions, pp. 222 ff., on the contrast between the reforming radicalism of the 1760's, concerned primarily with the threat to constitutional liberties in England and America, and the later, work-ing-class radicalism "which could be described in the words of the Chartist, Rayner Stephens, as 'a knife and fork question.' " Note the parallel interpretation in Weston, *English Constitutional Theory*, pp. 143 ff. Christie's description of the radicals of the 1760's holds equally well for most of the commonwealthmen and coffeehouse radicals of the early eighteenth century, whose views became so influential in America. Trenchard and Gordon, for example, refused to consider any alteration in the property structure of England (*Cato's Letters*, no. 85); ob-

"collect and assemble together the tailors and the cobblers and the ploughmen and the shepherds" of a vast domain and expect them to "treat and resolve about matters of the highest importance of state." They would not know enough, they would not be skilled enough in government, they would not be sufficiently disinterested or independent of pressures to manage a government properly. Surely tradition and the lessons of history indicated that without an economically independent, educated, leisured order of society standing securely and permanently above the petty selfishness of multitudes of ordinary men scattered through half a continent, nothing would be expressed in government but "infinite diversity or particular interests [and] dissonant opinions"; and the result might well be chaos.[52]

How then, in a society where "no distinction of ranks existed . . . and none were entitled to any rights but such as were common to all," and where the government could by definition express only the will of "the democracy" could the liberty-saving balance be preserved? What, indeed, were the elements to be balanced, and by what organs of government should their inter-

---

jected not to inequality as such but only to artificial inequality (no. 45); were anti-majoritarian (no. 62); and were vehemently opposed to charity schools, which, they said, "take the lowest dregs of the people from the plough and labor to make them tradesmen, and by consequence drive the children of tradesmen to the plough, to beg, to rob, or to starve . . . there are few instances in which the public has suffered more than in breeding up beggars to be what are called scholars . . . What benefit can accrue to the public by taking the dregs of the people out of the kennels and throwing their betters into them?" (no. 133)

[53] *Copies of Letters from Governor Bernard,* p. 16; [John Randolph], *Considerations on the Present State of Virginia* ([Williamsburg], 1774), in Earl G. Swem edition (New York, 1919), pp. 15, 17; Andrew Eliot, *A Sermon Preached before His Excellency Francis Bernard* . . . (Boston, 1765: JHL Pamphlet 15), p. 49; Dickinson, *Farmer's Letters* (JHL 23), p. 58; Drayton, *Letter from Freeman* (JHL 45), p. 4; Inglis, *True Interest of America,* pp. 24, 53; [John Lind?], *An Englishman's Answer to the Address from the Delegates* . . . (New York, 1775), p. 19; Edward Barnard, *A Sermon Preached before His Excellency Francis Bernard* . . . (Boston, 1766), p. 13.

ests be expressed?[53] The discussion of these crucial questions —
questions upon which the future character of public life in America would depend — began when the burning public issue was
still the colonies' relation to England and ended a decade or more
later in the revisions of the first state constitutions. Between the
two points was a continuous, unbroken line of intellectual development and political experience. It bridged two intellectual
worlds: the mid-eighteenth-century world, still vitally concerned
with a set of ideas derived ultimately from classical antiquity —
from Aristotelian, Polybian, Machiavellian, and seventeenth-century English sources, and the quite different world of Madison
and Tocqueville. Between the two was not so much a transition
of ideas as a transformation of problems, the ultimate characteristics of which may be seen emerging indeliberately and unsurely
in the passionate debate touched off by Paine's *Common Sense.*

For the intellectual core of that brilliant pamphlet advocating
the independence of the colonies was its attack on the traditional
conception of balance as a prerequisite for liberty. The assumption of the admirers of "the so much boasted constitution of England" that the balance of socio-constitutional forces was liberty-
preserving, Paine proclaimed, was a fallacy. "The more simple
anything is," he argued, "the less liable it is to be disordered, and
the easier repaired when disordered." The constitution of England is "so exceedingly complex" that its evils can scarcely be
diagnosed. What it consists of, really, is "the base remains of two
ancient tyrannies" — "monarchical tyranny in the person of the
King . . . [and] aristocratical tyranny in the persons of the
peers" — thinly overlaid with "new republican materials in the
persons of the commons, on whose virtue depends the freedom

[53] The majority in all the states, Ramsay wrote, "saw and acknowledged the
propriety of a compounded legislature, yet the mode of creating two branches out
of a homogeneous mass of people was a matter of difficulty." Ramsay, *History,*
I, 351.

of England." The famous notion "that the constitution of England is a *union* of three powers reciprocally *checking* each other is farcical," and he proceeded to specify its emptiness and self-contradiction. What liberty there was in England was *"wholly owing to the constitution of the people, and not to the constitution of the government."* In America, where the character of the people was ideal for the attainment of liberty, institutions should be devised that conformed not to inherited prejudices and the accidents of history but to the true principles of human liberty. Let the American colonies cast off the chains that tie them to England and its corrupt monarchy, and as independent states create unicameral assemblies chosen annually by a "more equal" system of representation than heretofore and presided over by "a president only." And let "a CONTINENTAL CHARTER or charter of the United Colonies (answering to what is called the Magna Carta of England)" be framed to provide for a unicameral assembly for the nation as well, selected by the same electorate and also presided over by a president, chosen from the various states in rotation. "But where, says some, is the King of America? I'll tell you, friend, he reigns above, and doth not make havoc of mankind like the Royal Brute of Great Britain." [54]

It was a superbly rhetorical and iconoclastic pamphlet whose slashing attack upon the English monarchy — the one remaining link, in early 1776, between England and the colonies — and upon the concept of balance in the constitution made it an immediate sensation. But if Paine was with the exception of Marx "the most influential pamphleteer of all time," [55] he was also one of the most controversial. *Common Sense* had scarcely been published when it came under strong attack, not only by loyalists but by some of the most ardent patriots who feared the tendencies of

[54] [Thomas Paine], *Common Sense* . . . (Philadelphia, 1776: JHL Pamphlet 63), pp. 6, 7, 8, 11, 54, 56, 57.
[55] Harold Laski, quoted in Harry H. Clark, ed., *Thomas Paine* (New York, 1961), p. cl.

Paine's constitutional ideas as much as they approved his plea for Independence.

The Tories' attack began with James Chalmers' ponderous *Plain Truth,* which condemned Paine's views of society and human nature, and defended the English constitution "which with all its imperfections is, and ever will be, the pride and envy of mankind." All the well-known elements of "this beautiful system" were necessary for freedom: without the crown "our constitution would immediately degenerate into democracy" — a plausible enough kind of state no doubt, but one much favored by demagogues who well know that it, above all other forms of government, was susceptible to absolute corruption. "If we examine the republics of Greece and Rome, we ever find them in a state of war, domestic or foreign." Holland, which survived only because of England's support, had participated "in wars the most expensive and bloody ever waged by mankind." Even Switzerland had fared badly: its "bleak and barren mountains" had not preserved its constitution from assault by "ambition, sedition, and anarchy." The "quixotic system" of government proposed by Paine was "really an insult to our understanding" and would soon give way "to government imposed on us by some Cromwell of our armies," for when popular legislatures presumed to create armies they soon became their victims, unless like Holland they somehow managed "to drown [their] garrisons." Even if dictatorship were avoided, Paine's Congress would become the center of controversies that would conclude in "all the misery of anarchy and intestine war." [56]

[56] Chalmers, *Plain Truth* (JHL 64), pp. 3, 4, 8, 11, 10, 62, 63, 65. "Rationalis," in an essay published as an Appendix to *Plain Truth,* continued the defense of the English constitution, claiming that the trouble with England was not its constitution but the use made of it by corrupt politicians. "The infinite distractions and mischiefs which have happened in the ancient and modern republics" were only too well known: lacking balance and control, these governments bred factions one of which in each case triumphed over the others, and turned itself into "a many-headed monster, a tyranny of many." "Scenes of blood and devasta-

A more sophisticated Tory attack on Paine's constitutional ideas, Charles Inglis' *True Interest of America,* was less influential since the entire first printing of the pamphlet was destroyed by a Whig mob; by the time a new edition was prepared independence had been declared and the pamphlet was largely ignored. Yet it is in some ways more revealing than *Plain Truth,* for while Inglis too could fulminate and fume, he understood Paine thoroughly, and analyzed with notable clarity the logic and evidence of his views. In the end Inglis endorsed the traditional idea that monarchy alone is suited to the government of an extensive domain and that popular governments can survive only in small territories where the inhabitants form a homogeneous community with a unified economic interest.[57]

Paine's most influential opponents, however, were not Tories but those who agreed with him on the question of independence but who disagreed with his constitutional proposals. John Adams, who distrusted him from the instant he laid eyes on him (or so he said in later years) and called him "a *star of disaster*" whose constitutional ideas flowed either from "honest ignorance or foolish superstition on one hand or from willful sophistry and knavish hypocrisy on the other," denounced Paine's advocacy of unicameral assemblies in both states and nation, and, fearing the effect "so popular a pamphlet might have among the people," set about to put things right.

What bothered Adams most about *Common Sense* was that its plan of government "was so democratical, without any re-

---

tion . . . the fury of one party encountering the rage of another . . . [men] as fierce and savage as wolves and tigers . . . terrible disorders, outrage, and confusion . . . arbitrary power" — these were the fruits of governments dominated by the democracy, in Greece, in Carthage, in Rome, in Holland, and even in England when Cromwell seized the power from the Commonwealth and ruled "with absolute sway" (pp. 71, 75–78).

[57] Inglis, *True Interest,* p. 17. On the printing history of the pamphlet, which was originally entitled *The Deceiver Unmasked* . . . , see Adams, *Bibliographical Study,* entries 219a–c.

straint or even an attempt at any equilibrium or counterpoise, that it must produce confusion and every evil work." The premise of his own plan, sketched in his *Thoughts on Government,* which circulated among the constitution-makers of several states in manuscript in the spring of 1776, was that it was possible to devise republican governments, by definition lacking the first and second orders of society, with inner balances as effective as those of a mixed monarchy. It was possible because a republic was, by proper definition, only "an empire of laws, and not of men," and this permitted "an inexhaustible variety" of institutional forms "because the possible combinations of the powers of society are capable of innumerable variations." In an extensive country, direct assembly of the whole population was out of the question, and so the first step was "to depute power from the many to a few of the most wise and good" who should form in their assembly "an exact portrait of the people at large . . . equal interest among the people should have equal interest in it." Yet however representative of the interests of society this single assembly might be, it should not be given control of all the branches of government, for it was the nature of popular assemblies to be fickle, "productive of hasty results and absurd judgments," avaricious, and ambitious. Difficult for the electorate to control, an unchecked representative assembly would quickly make itself permanent, exempt itself from the burdens it laid on its constituents, and pass and execute laws for its own benefit. And in any case popular assemblies were unsuited to exercise certain of the powers of government: they were too open and inefficient to act as an executive, and too slow in procedure and ignorant of the law to act as a judiciary. The organization of government "ought to be more complex" than a single unicameral assembly. Even separating the executive from the legislative power and placing it in the hands of an organ of government other than the assembly would not be sufficient, for "these two powers will oppose and enervate upon each other until the contest shall end in war." There would have to be also an additional assembly "as a mediator between these two extreme branches." Chosen by the representative assembly, it "should have a free and independent exercise of its judgment, and consequently a negative voice in the legislature." Let the two houses together choose annually an executive capable of exercising independent judgment to the extent of vetoing acts of the legislature. Distinct from all of this should be the judiciary, composed of men of learning, legal experience, and wisdom. "Their minds should not be distracted with jarring interests," and they should be guaranteed independence by life tenures. Such a republican system, expressing but yet controlling and refining the will of the people, would create an "arcadia or elysium" compared with all other governments "whether monarchical or aristocratical." [58]

The proposal was necessarily conjectural — alternative possibilities were suggested throughout — and it was crowded with ambiguities and paradoxes. What was there in the character of the middle branch — the second assembly — that distinguished its members from the population in general? What did it represent? How could it retain its independence if it were elected annually by a body extremely sensitive to public opinion? Its

---

[58] Adams, *Diary and Autobiography*, III, 330, 331, 333; Adams, *Thoughts on Government* (JHL 65), pp. 8, 9, 10, 11–12, 13, 14, 15, 21, 26. Cf. Adams' autobiographical summary under the date 1775, which illustrates particularly well the complex shift that took place in conceiving of balance in government, from a balance of formal socio-constitutional orders to the separation of functioning powers of government: "But what plan of a government would you advise? [he was asked at the Continental Congress.] A plan as nearly resembling the governments under which we were born and have lived as the circumstances of the country will admit. Kings we never had among us, nobles we never had. Nothing hereditary ever existed in the country: nor will the country require or admit of any such thing: but governors and councils we have always had, as well as representatives. A legislature in three branches ought to be preserved, and independent judges. Where and how will you get your governors and councils? By elections. How, who shall elect? The representatives of the people in a convention will be the best qualified to contrive a mode." *Diary and Autobiography*, III, 356.

similarities to the middle bodies of other governments were superficial, for it could not be thought of as embodying a separate order or interest in a society that consisted of only one order. And it could not constitute a distinct function of government, for those — the legislative, executive, and judicial — were otherwise provided for. What was clear throughout, however, was that Adams was seeking to perpetuate that "balance between . . . contending powers" that had been the glory of England's uncorrupted constitution.

The point was widely endorsed, and in other pamphlets of 1776 more fully explored. In Virginia, Adams' pamphlet arrived amid the "welter of proposed drafts of constitutions" then before the legislature, and it elicited a mixed reaction. Patrick Henry gave it his highest accolade by saying that its ideas were "precisely the same [as those] I have long since taken up," and wrote that he hoped it would help influence those "opulent families" known to be working for the establishment of aristocratic rather than republican forms of government. What precisely these counter-revolutionary anti-republicans had in mind, and the extent of their agreement with Adams on the key point of the anomalous middle chamber, was made clear in what Henry called a "silly thing" and Richard Henry Lee described as a "contemptible little tract," Carter Braxton's *Address to the Convention of . . . Virginia,* written for the specific purpose of refuting Adams' *Thoughts on Government.*

Braxton's "anti-republicanism," it developed, was the result of his effort to recreate artificially the traditional socio-constitutional basis of governmental balance. The present tyranny of the British government, he wrote, is not as Paine had said, intrinsic to its structure but the result of "a monied interest" having usurped the power of the crown and destroyed "those barriers which the constitution had assigned to each branch" of the government. Let not the whole be condemned for the momentary corruption of a part. Let Virginia, in principle at least, "adopt and perfect that system which England has suffered to be so grossly abused and the experience of the ages has taught us to venerate." Restore the independence of the branches lost in England. Let there be a popular assembly from which the blood-sucking adherents of the moneyed interests would be excluded and the system of representation made "equal and adequate" so that the prerogative would not be able to corrupt it. Let the house of representatives choose a governor to serve for life and a council of state to constitute "a distinct or intermediate branch of the legislature, and hold their places for life in order that they might possess all the weight, stability, and dignity due to the importance of their office" as well as the time and means for the reflective study of policies and laws. Only such an independent, superior "second branch of the legislature" would be able to "mediate and adjust" the differences that might arise between the governor and the house, "investigate the propriety of laws, and often propose such as may be of public utility." Such a government might have certain failings, but it would at least avoid the evils of popular governments, "fraught with all the tumult and riot incident to simple democracy," that some were now advocating. "Democratical" governments have rarely succeeded, for the mass of the people have only rarely had the power of self-denial, the disdain of riches, of luxury, and of dominance over others necessary to sustain such governments. They have survived only in small countries "so sterile by nature" that men, of necessity equally poor, had no temptation to seek and use power in defense of their interests. The very promise of life in America argued against the stability of democratic governments.[59]

Others in Virginia, including some of those who were striving

[59] Boyd, *Jefferson Papers*, I, 333, 335; Henry to Adams, Williamsburg, May 20, 1776, in Adams, *Works*, IV, 201; [Carter Braxton], *An Address to . . . Virginia; on the Subject of Government* . . . (Philadelphia, 1776: JHL Pamphlet 66), pp. 10, 13, 11, 22, 20, 23, 15–16, 18.

deliberately to establish a government "very much of the democratic kind," agreed that a "second branch of legislation" was
necessary, though they differed in the degree to which they conceived of this branch as a function of government rather than as
an embodiment of a social order. Jefferson, whose draft constitution for his state was a far more "radical departure" than could
possibly be accepted, not only provided for a "senate" but so
devised the election of its members that they would be, once
chosen, "perfectly independent of their electors"; and though he
felt that his device — election of the senators by the representatives for a nonrenewable term of nine years — would provide the
necessary independence, he said that he "could submit, though
not so willingly, to an appointment [of senators] for life or to
anything rather than a mere creation by and dependence on the
people." And the plan George Mason prepared for the state's
official drafting committee provided for the election of the upper
house not by the people but by a separate group of specifically
elected "deputies or sub-electors" whose sole function it would be
to choose members of the upper house from among those pos-
sessing "an estate of inheritance of lands in *Virginia* of at least
two thousand pounds value." [60]

There were almost as many variations in these constitutional
programs attempting somehow to restrain the force of "the
democracy" within a republican system as there were writers, for
all proposals had to be extemporized from unevenly applicable
models in circumstances imperfectly understood. Braxton was
alarmed at the "democratical" tendencies of Adams' thought,
and Adams was horrified by the same drift in Paine's. There
were depths below depths, and at the very bottom of the descent
from a mixed monarchy *manqué* to a total repudiation of complexity and balance in society and government was an ill-written

[60] *Letters of Richard Henry Lee*, I, 203; Boyd, *Jefferson Papers*, I, 334, 504,
366.

pamphlet of thirteen pages published, probably in New England, without identification of author, printer, or place of publication.

Dedicated "to the honest *farmer* and *citizen*," *The People the Best Governors* developed, incompletely yet repetitiously, the theme stated in its title. "The people know best their own wants and necessities, and therefore are best able to rule themselves." They must themselves directly control all branches of government, and if the dispersal of population makes representation necessary, safeguards must immediately be erected against any effort of the representatives to act independently of the people. It must be firmly established that the power of representatives "ought never to extend any farther than barely the making of laws," and that they were never to create by their own determination additional organs of government. They might appoint a Council, but only for purposes of advice: "for the representatives to appoint a Council with a negative authority is to give away that power which they have no right to do, because they themselves derived it from the people." It would amount to the creation of an independent upper chamber of the legislature: but what, or whom, could such a body represent? It too would be "virtually the representatives of the people," and as such could not be empowered by any other body than the electorate.[61]

But it was in Pennsylvania in 1776 that the full range of possibilities in devising governmental institutions proper for a society lacking the traditional orders of men was most fully explored and most lucidly explained, and it was there that the transformation of the framework within which all this thought proceeded could be most clearly seen.

Some in Pennsylvania, accepting forthrightly the radical implications of the revolutionary situation but still thinking in

[61] *The People the Best Governors: Or, a Plan of Government Founded on the Just Principles of Natural Freedom* ([Hartford?], 1776: JHL Pamphlet 68), pp. [3]-6.

traditional terms, concluded that in the American situation "a well-regulated democracy," of all forms of government, "is most equitable." How could it be otherwise? The constitution of Pennsylvania could scarcely make provision for "a representative of a king, for we have none; nor can there be need of a council to represent the house of lords, for we have not, and hope never shall have, a hereditary nobility different from the body of the people." To make "places of power" a prerogative of birth was poor policy indeed, for "wisdom is not a birthright"; nor was life tenure in office advisable since "men's abilities and manners may change." The fact that other governments have "something, a senate, a council, or upper house," was no reason for Pennsylvania to have one too. "Free government can better, much better, subsist without it. Different branches of legislature cause much needless expense, two ways: first, as there are more persons to maintain; and second, as they waste time and prolong a session by their contentions." If Rome had been a "true democracy, without a senate," it would have lasted longer, and now if Americans were to "admit different branches of legislature" the result might well be just the sort of civic degeneration that has taken place in England. The direction thought should take in the present transactions in America ("the most important . . . in any nation for some centuries past") was toward a "truly popular government" where rotation in office would be mandatory and continuous, and where officeholders would be held to strict accountability. Above all, let the organization of government be simple. At present we have no estate of hereditary privilege. If, nevertheless, we create an organ of government modeled on those that elsewhere have served the political interests of privileged orders, there will soon be some here who will learn how to maintain control of such an institution, and in time become used to thinking of it as somehow peculiarly their own. In the end, therefore, Pennsylvanians may discover that they have artificially created what fate had mercifully spared them.[62]

Another writer, sharing the same assumptions, went to the opposite extreme, proposing an elaborate system of "three different bodies," an assembly, a senate, and a council, all of which were to have initiating and vetoing powers in legislation.[63] But the future lay with two other Pennsylvania writers, one of whom expressed clearly what was becoming a general agreement concerning the character of the second chamber in an American republic, an agreement which constitution writers would struggle to express adequately in institutions in the years that followed, and the other of whom pointed directly to what, evolving logically from the breakdown of traditional notions of the social basis of English constitutionalism, would become the fundamental conception of a new theory of politics.

The first writer, observing that the colony had "but one order of freemen in it," argued historically, with evidence quoted wholesale from a book published five years earlier in England, that "the best model that human wisdom, improved by experience, has left them to copy" was "the old Saxon form of government" which had been transferred from "the German woods . . . into England about the year four hundred and fifty." At that time England had been a society of "small republics" within

---

[62] "The Interest of America," in Force, *American Archives*, 4th ser., VI, cols. 841–843.

[63] The assembly was to be popularly elected; the senate was to be chosen by specially elected deputies from among themselves; and the council, together with the governor and lieutenant governor, was to be chosen by the assembly and senate together from among those who had served as senators. The main duty of the council was to serve as a plural executive but it was to participate also in the legislative process as a third house. The triple-headed complexity of the whole, it was explained, would give "maturity and wisdom to acts of legislation, as also stability to the state, by preventing measures from being too much influenced by sudden passions." *An Essay of a Frame of Government for Pennsylvania* (Philadelphia, 1776), pp. [3], 5 ff., 10, 11 ff.

which the entire population, "being all equally interested in every question," had met often in council for full and equal discussion, and from which deputies had been sent to "a national Council and legislative authority." Let Pennsylvania's government be the same as this "beautiful system." Let there be extreme decentralization of political power, frequent elections by secret ballot, open debates in assemblies, popularly elected and moderately paid judges and local officers, and militia armies with elected field commanders. As for the perplexing question of "the respective powers of the several branches of the legislature," the most judicious arrangement would be to have, in addition to a representative assembly, a council composed of men distinguished by their "superior degree of acquaintance with the history, laws, and manners of mankind, and by that means they will be more likely to foresee the mischievous consequences that might follow a proceeding which at first view did not appear to have anything dangerous in it." And it would also be a good idea to have, in addition, a "small privy council" to advise and assist the governor in the execution of his duties. The possibility that the members of the upper house would *"inveterate* themselves" could be eliminated by having them elected at short intervals, for that would give the ultimate decision to the people at large, who surely have not forgotten, nor will fail to guard against, "the mischiefs which have overspread the world, from the days of Sylla to the present bloody period, from the same tyrannic source." [64]

The substitution of knowledge, wisdom, and judgment for hereditary privileges as the necessary qualifications for membership in the second chamber of the legislature was only the beginning of a solution to the problem, however, for there was as yet no sense of how these qualities could be recognized publicly,

[64] *The Genuine Principles of the Ancient Saxon, or English Constitution* . . . (Philadelphia, 1776: JHL Pamphlet 70), pp. 17, 4, 16, 13, 18–19, 23, 36, 37.

isolated, and recruited into a particular branch of government. Nor was it clear that such a solution avoided the perpetuation of a quasi-traditional aristocracy and hence was free of inconsistency with basic Revolutionary principles, for it was difficult to throw off the assumption that superiority was unitary, that "gentlemen of education,.... leisure, ... wisdom, learning, and a firmness and consistency of character" were also gentlemen of "fortune." [65] But it was a solution of sorts that pressed against the boundaries of traditional ideas even if it did not penetrate much beyond them. The adumbration of a truly new configuration of ideas became visible at the same time, however, in another pamphlet dealing with the same problem, the remarkably original and cogent *Four Letters on Interesting Subjects*.

The entire discussion of the effects of divisions among and within the branches of government, the author declared, had been clouded by myths and misunderstandings. Arguments against the simplest forms of government are based on the idea that a number of houses check each other to the general advantage of all. But in fact the notion "has but little weight." For, in the first place, such checking "tends to embarrass and prolong business"; in the second place, it may injure collective "honor and tempers, and thereby produce petulances and ill-will which a more simple form of government would have prevented"; and in the third place, "the more houses, the more parties": different houses may serve only to institutionalize and sharpen conflicts of interests that otherwise might be reconciled. Suppose, the writer went on, "the landed interest would get into one house, and the commercial interest into the other." The result would be that

a perpetual and dangerous opposition would be kept up, and no business be got through. Whereas, were there a large, equal and annual representation in one house *only,* the different parties, by

[65] "Essex Result," in Theophilus Parsons, *Memoir of Theophilus Parsons* . . . (Boston, 1859), p. 370.

being thus blended together, would hear each others' arguments; which advantage they cannot have if they sit in different houses. To say there ought to be two houses because there are two sorts of interest is the very reason why there ought to be but one, and *that one* to consist of every sort.[66]

Here quietly but profoundly the ground of political thought had shifted. The writer was not a "Sidney . . . the 'classical' republican *par excellence,* with no feeling whatever for the shifting possibilities of political life," and his essay was not, like the classical sources all eighteenth-century Americans venerated, "concerned with *forms* of government rather than with their institutions." [67] The essential units participating in the constitution were no longer abstract categories, formal orders of society derived from the assumptions of classical antiquity; they were interests, which, organized for political action, became factions and parties. Their constitutional role was not to manipulate independently a separate institution of government but to join in conflict within a single institution and "blend" themselves together into a general consensus. "Balance" was still involved, but with the repudiation of monarchy and nobility and the confinement of society to "the democracy," the notion of what the social powers were that must be balanced and controlled was changing. What were now seen, though still only vaguely, were the shifting, transitory competitive groupings into which men of the eighteenth century actually organized themselves in the search for wealth, prestige, and power. And the concern with balance in government was shifting from a concern with social orders to that of functioning branches of government.

This shift in ways of thinking about the social basis of politics was part of a more general turn toward realism in political and

[66] *Four Letters on Interesting Subjects* (Philadelphia, 1776: JHL Pamphlet 69), pp. 19–20.
[67] Felix Raab, *The English Face of Machiavelli* (London, 1964), pp. 221, 216.

constitutional thought. By the time the debates on the first state constitutions had been concluded, the sense that public affairs were basically struggles among formal orders of society had begun to fade and with it the whole elaborate paradigm that lay at the heart of eighteenth-century political thought. To be sure, the ancient formulations that had been so deeply engraved on the eighteenth-century mind still continued to be used; Americans of 1776 still referred to the crown, the aristocracy, and the democracy as social categories basic to politics and observed that each had its own fundamental principle or spirit in government: for monarchy, fear; for aristocracy, honor; for democracy, virtue. And it was still found natural to assume that the ultimate goal of politics was a motionless equilibrium among these entities, and that public controversy deliberately undertaken was essentially malign or aberrant. But the actual problems of government the American faced were now so urgent, so new, and so comprehensive that attention was beginning to concentrate on the visible and real rather than on the traditional and theoretical. The ancient classifications remained in the back of people's minds; but the problems posed by those disreputable and dangerous elements — factions, interests, and parties — and by the need to redefine the functions of the branches of government were more immediate and obtrusive. A republican constitution, to be successful, must somehow cope with the fact that the larger the unit of government the greater the number of contending factions and the smaller the chance that a republican government could control them. How could they be mastered or confined? What would prevent them from tearing a government to pieces? Contention as such must be understood; the struggles of men, in whatever groupings they might form, rather than in fixed social categories, must be taken into account, and the functioning of the organs of government in controlling them more fully explored. Politics in its "vague and vulgar acceptation, . . . referring to the wrangling debates of modern assemblies, debates which far too often turn entirely on the narrow, selfish, and servile views of party" — politics in this humble sense rather than in the traditional, "more dignified sense" must be comprehended and dealt with, not explained away as a series of momentary instabilities and aberrations in an otherwise poised and symmetrical system.[68]

Constitutional thought, concentrating on the pressing need to create republican governments that would survive, tended to draw away from the effort to refine further the ancient, traditional systems, and to move toward a fresh, direct comprehension of political reality. Denied, by the urgency of new problems, the satisfactions of elaborating familiar abstractions, Americans edged toward that hard, clear realism in political thought that would reach fulfillment a decade later in the formation of the national government and achieve its classic expression in *The Federalist*. In the process the modern American doctrine of the separation of functioning powers would be created, and the concept of "democracy" transformed.

4. "WHETHER SOME DEGREE OF RESPECT BE NOT ALWAYS DUE FROM INFERIORS TO SUPERIORS"

Yet none of this — not the changes in the concepts of representation and consent, of constitutions and rights, or of sovereignty, nor the unexpected challenge to such a deeply embedded institution as slavery, nor the unplanned defiance of orthodoxy and establishment in religion, nor the tendency to forsake the traditional assumptions concerning the social basis of politics and the constitutional arrangements that followed from these assump-

---

[68] Boucher, "On Civil Liberty, Passive Obedience, and Nonresistance," *A View of the Causes and Consequences*, p. 499n.

tions — none of these developments measure fully the transforming effect of the Revolutionary movement in America, even at
its inception. Beyond these specific changes were others: subtler,
vaguer, and ultimately, perhaps, even more important.

In no obvious sense was the American Revolution undertaken
as a social revolution. No one, that is, deliberately worked for
the destruction or even the substantial alteration of the order of
society as it had been known. Yet it was transformed as a result
of the Revolution, and not merely because Loyalist property was
confiscated and redistributed, or because the resulting war destroyed the economic bases of some people's lives and created
opportunities for others that would not otherwise have existed.
Seizure of Loyalist property and displacements in the economy
did in fact take place, and the latter if not the former does
account for a spurt in social mobility that led earlier arrivés to
remark, "When the pot boils, the scum will rise." Yet these were
superficial changes; they affected a small part of the population
only, and they did not alter the organization of society.

What did now affect the essentials of social organization —
what in time would help permanently to transform them — were
changes in the realm of belief and attitude. The views men held
toward the relationships that bound them to each other — the
discipline and pattern of society — moved in a new direction in
the decade before Independence.

Americans of 1760 continued to assume, as had their predecessors for generations before, that a healthy society was a hierarchical society, in which it was natural for some to be rich and some
poor, some honored and some obscure, some powerful and some
weak. And it was believed that superiority was unitary, that the
attributes of the favored — wealth, wisdom, power — had a natural affinity to each other, and hence that political leadership
would naturally rest in the hands of the social leaders. Movement,

of course, there would be: some would fall and some would rise; but manifest, external differences among men, reflecting the principle of hierarchical order, were necessary and proper, and would remain; they were intrinsic to the nature of things.

Circumstances had pressed harshly against such assumptions. The wilderness environment from the beginning had threatened the maintenance of elaborate social distinctions; many of them in the passage of time had in fact been worn away. Puritanism, in addition, and the epidemic evangelicalism of the mid-eighteenth century, had created challenges to the traditional notions of social stratification by generating the conviction that the ultimate quality of men was to be found elsewhere than in their external condition, and that a cosmic achievement lay within each man's grasp. And the peculiar configuration of colonial politics — a constant broil of petty factions struggling almost formlessly, with little discipline or control, for the benefits of public authority — had tended to erode the respect traditionally accorded the institutions and officers of the state.[60]

Yet nowhere, at any time in the colonial years, were the implications of these circumstances articulated or justified. The assumption remained that society, in its maturity if not in its confused infancy, would conform to the pattern of the past; that authority would continue to exist without challenge, and that those in superior positions would be responsible and wise, and those beneath them respectful and content. These premises and expectations were deeply lodged; they were not easily or quickly

[60] Horace Walpole, like so many other European writers of the eighteenth century, noted the fact, recording in his *Memoirs* the story making the rounds in London at the time the colonists were seeking affiliation with the crown to the exclusion of Parliament, "that a wealthy merchant in one of the provinces had said, 'They say King George is a very honest fellow; I should like to smoke a pipe with him,' so little conception had they in that part of the world, of the majesty of an European monarch!" *Memoirs of the Reign of King George the Third* (Denis Le Marchant, ed., London, 1845), II, 72n.

displaced. But the Revolution brought with it arguments and attitudes bred of arguments endlessly repeated, that undermined these premises of the *ancien régime*.

For a decade or more defiance to the highest constituted powers poured from the colonial presses and was hurled from half the pulpits of the land. The right, the need, the absolute obligation to disobey legally constituted authority had become the universal cry. Cautions and qualifications became ritualistic: formal exercises in ancient pieties. One might preface one's charge to disobedience with homilies on the inevitable imperfections of all governments and the necessity to bear "some injuries" patiently and peaceably. But what needed and received demonstration and defense was not the caution, but the injunction: the argument that when injuries touched on "fundamental rights" (and who could say when they did not?) then nothing less than "duty to God and religion, to themselves, to the community, and to unborn posterity require such to assert and defend their rights by all lawful, most prudent, and effectual means in their power." Obedience as a principle was only too well known; disobedience as a doctrine was not. It was therefore asserted again and again that resistance to constituted authority was "a doctrine according to godliness — the doctrine of the English nation . . . by which our rights and constitution have often been defended and repeatedly rescued out of the hands of encroaching tyranny . . . This is the doctrine and grand pillar of the ever memorable and glorious Revolution, and upon which our gracious sovereign GEORGE III holds the crown of the British empire." What better credentials could there be? How lame to add that obedience too "is an eminent part of Christian duty without which government must disband and dreadful anarchy and confusion (with all its horrors) take place and reign without control" — how lame, especially in view of the fact that one could easily mistake this "Christian obedience" for that "blind, enslaving obedience which is no part of the Christian institution but is highly injurious to religion, to every free government, and to the good of mankind, and is the stirrup of tyranny, and grand engine of slavery." [70]

Defiance to constituted authority leaped like a spark from one flammable area to another, growing in heat as it went. Its greatest intensification took place in the explosive atmosphere of local religious dissent. Isaac Backus spoke only for certain of the Baptists and Congregational Separates and against the presumptive authority of ministers, when, in the course of an attack on the religious establishment in Massachusetts, he warned that

we are not to obey and follow [ministers] in an implicit or customary way, but each one must consider and follow others no further than they see that the end of their conversation is Jesus Christ the same yesterday, and today, and forever more . . . People are so far from being under obligation to follow teachers who don't lead in this way they incur guilt by such a following of them.

It took little imagination on the part of Backus' readers and listeners to find in this a general injunction against uncritical obedience to authority in any form. Others were even more explicit. The Baptist preacher who questioned not merely the authority of the local orthodox church but the very "etymology of the word [orthodoxy]" assured the world that the colonists

have as just a right, before GOD and man, to oppose King, ministry, Lords, and Commons of England when they violate their rights as Americans as they have to oppose any foreign enemy; and that this is no more, according to the law of nature, to be deemed rebellion than it would be to oppose the King of France, supposing him now present invading the land.

But what to the Baptists was the establishment, to Anglicans was dissent. From the establishment in New England, ever fearful of ecclesiastical impositions from without, came as strong a current of anti-authoritarianism as from the farthest left-wing

[70] Johnson, *Some Important Observations* (JHL 19), pp. 27–28.

sect. It was a pillar of the temple, a scion of the church, and an apologist for New England's standing order who sweepingly disclaimed "all human authority in matters of faith and worship. We regard neither pope nor prince as head of the church, nor acknowledge that any Parliaments have power to enact articles of doctrine or forms of discipline or modes of worship or terms of church communion," and, declaring that "we are accountable to none but *Christ*" — words that had struck at the heart of every establishment, civil and religious, since the fall of Rome — concluded with the apparent paradox that "*liberty* is the *fundamental* principle of our establishment."[71]

In such declarations a political argument became a moral imperative. The principle of justifiable disobedience and the instinct to question public authority before accepting it acquired a new sanction and a new vigor. Originally, of course, the doctrine of resistance was applied to Parliament, a nonrepresentative assembly 3,000 miles away. But the composition and location of the institution had not been as crucial in creating opposition as had the character of the actions Parliament had taken. Were provincial assemblies, simply because they were local and representative, exempt from scrutiny and resistance? Were they any less susceptible than Parliament to the rule that when their authority is extended beyond "the bounds of the law of God and the free constitution . . . 'their acts are, *ipso facto*, void, and cannot oblige any to obedience' "? There could be no doubt of the answer. Any legislature, wherever located or however composed, deserved only the obedience it could command by the justice and wisdom of its proceedings. Representative or not, local or not, any agency of the state could be defied. The freeholders of Augusta, Virginia, could not have been more explicit

[71] Isaac Backus, *A Fish Caught in His Own Net* . . . (Boston, 1768), p. 61; Allen, *American Alarm* (JHL 39), 4th sec., p. 11; 1st sec., p. 15; Adams, *Religious Liberty*, pp. 38, 39.

in applying to local government in 1776 the defiance learned in the struggle with Parliament. They wrote their delegates to Virginia's Provincial Congress that

should the future conduct of our legislative body prove to you that our opinion of their wisdom and justice is ill-grounded, then tell them that your constituents are neither guided nor will ever be influenced by that slavish maxim in politics, "that whatever is enacted by that body of men in whom the supreme power of the state is vested must in all cases be obeyed," and that they firmly believe attempts to repeal an unjust law can be vindicated beyond a simple remonstrance addressed to the legislators.[72]

But such threats as these were only the most obvious ways in which traditional notions of authority came into question. Others were more subtly subversive, silently sapping the traditional foundations of social orders and discipline.

"Rights" obviously lay at the heart of the Anglo-American controversy: the rights of Englishmen, the rights of mankind, chartered rights. But *"rights,"* wrote Richard Bland — that least egalitarian of Revolutionary leaders — "imply *equality* in the instances to which they belong and must be treated without respect to the dignity of the persons concerned in them." This was by no means simply a worn cliché, for while "equality before the law" was a commonplace of the time, "equality without respect to the dignity of the persons concerned" was not; its emphasis on social equivalence was significant, and though in its immediate context the remark was directed to the invidious distinctions believed to have been drawn between Englishmen and Americans its broader applicability was apparent. Others seized upon it, and developed it, especially in the fluid years of transition when new forms of government were being sought to replace those believed to have proved fatal to liberty. "An affectation of

---

[72] Johnson, *Some Important Observations* (JHL 19), p. 22; "Sentiments of the Several Companies," Force, *American Archives*, 5th ser., II, col. 817.

rank" and "the assumed distinction of 'men of consequence'" had been the blight of the Proprietary party, a Pennsylvania pamphleteer wrote in 1776. Riches in a new country like America signified nothing more than the accident of prior settlement. The accumulation of wealth had been "unavoidable to the descendants of the early settlers" since the land, originally cheap, had appreciated naturally with the growth of settlement.

Perhaps it is owing to this accidental manner of becoming rich that wealth does not obtain the same degree of influence here which it does in old countries. Rank, at present, in America is derived more from qualification than property; a sound moral character, amiable manners, and firmness in principle constitute the first class, and will continue to do so till the origin of families be forgotten, and the proud follies of the old world overrun the simplicity of the new.

Therefore, under the new dispensation, "no reflection ought to be made on any man on account of birth, provided that his manners rises decently with his circumstances, and that he affects not to forget the level he came from." [73]

The idea was, in its very nature, corrosive to the traditional authority of magistrates and of established institutions. And it activated other, similar thoughts whose potential threat to stability lay till then inert. There was no more familiar notion in eighteenth-century political thought — it was propounded in every tract on government and every ministerial exhortation to the civil magistracy — than that those who wield power were "servants of society" as well as "ministers of God," and as such had to be specially qualified: they must be acquainted with the affairs of men; they must have wisdom, knowledge, prudence; and they must be men of virtue and true religion.[74] But how

[73] Richard Bland, *An Inquiry into the Rights of the British Colonies . . .* (Williamsburg, 1766: JHL Pamphlet 17), p. 25; *Four Letters on Interesting Subjects* (JHL 69), pp. 2–3.

[74] E.g., Eliot, *Sermon* (JHL 15), pp. 12–30; Turner, *Sermon*, p. 30.

far should one go with this idea? The doctrine that the qualifications for magistracy were moral, spiritual, and intellectual could lead to conflict with the expectation that public leaders would be people of external dignity and social superiority; it could be dangerous to the establishment in any settled society. For the ancient notion that leadership must devolve on men whose "personal authority and greatness," whose "eminence or nobility," were such that "every man subordinate is ready to yield a willing submission without contempt or repining" — ordinary people not easily conceding to an authority "conferred upon a mean man . . . no better than selected out of their own rank" — this traditional notion had never been repudiated, was still honored and repeated. But now, in the heated atmosphere of incipient rebellion, the idea of leaders as servants of the people was pushed to its logical extreme, and its subversive potentialities revealed. By 1774 it followed from the belief that "lawful rulers are the servants of the people" that they were "exalted above their brethren not for their own sakes, but for the benefit of the people; and submission is yielded, not on account of their persons considered exclusively on the authority they are clothed with, but of those laws which in the exercise of this authority are made by them conformably to the laws of nature and equity." In the distribution of offices, it was said in 1770, "merit only in the candidate" should count — not birth, or wealth, or loyalty to the great; but merit only. Even a deliberately judicious statement of this theme rang with defiance to traditional forms of authority: "It is not wealth — it is not family — it is not either of these alone, nor both of them together, though I readily allow neither is to be disregarded, that will qualify men for important seats in government, unless they are rich and honorable in other and more important respects." Indeed, one could make a complete inversion and claim that, properly, the external affluence of

309

magistrates should be the consequence of, not the prior qualification for, the judicious exercise of public authority over others.[75]

Where would it end? Two generations earlier, in the fertile
seedtime of what would become the Revolutionary ideology, the
ultimate subversiveness of the arguments advanced by "the men
of the rights" had already been glimpsed. "The sum of the matter
betwixt Mr. Hoadly and me," the Jacobite, High Church polemicist Charles Leslie had written in 1711, is this:

> I think it most natural that *authority* should *descend,* that is, be
> *derived* from a *superior* to an *inferior,* from *God* to *fathers* and
> *kings,* and from *kings* and *fathers* to *sons* and *servants.* But Mr.
> Hoadly would have it *ascend* from *sons* to *fathers* and from *subjects*
> to *sovereigns,* nay to *God* himself, whose *kingship* the men of the
> *rights* say is *derived* to *Him* from the *people!* And the *argument*
> does naturally carry it all that *way.* For if *authority* does *ascend,* it
> must *ascend* to the *height.*[76]

By 1774 it seemed undeniable to many, uninvolved in or hostile
to the Revolutionary effort, that declarations "before GOD . . .
that it is no rebellion to oppose any king, ministry, or governor
[who] destroys by any violence or authority whatever the rights
of the people" threatened the most elemental principles of order
and discipline in society.[77] A group of writers, opposed not
merely to the politics of resistance but to the effect it would have
on the primary linkages of society — on that patterning of human
relations that distinguishes a civilized community from a primitive mob — attempted to recall to the colonists the lessons of the

---

[75] Bailyn, "Politics and Social Structure in Virginia," p. 94n15; Gad Hitchcock,
A Sermon Preached Before . . . Gage . . . (Boston, 1774), pp. 27–28; Cooke,
Sermon, p. 16; Jason Haven, *A Sermon Preached Before . . . Bernard . . .*
(Boston, 1769), pp. 46–47; Peter Whitney, *The Transgressions of a Land . . .*
(Boston, 1774), p. 16.

[76] [Charles Leslie], *The Finishing Stroke. Being a Vindication of the Patriarchal
Scheme of Government . . .* (London, 1711), p. 87. (I owe this reference to
Mr. John Dunn.)

[77] [John Allen], *An Oration upon the Beauties of Liberty . . .* (Boston, 1773:
JHL Pamphlet 38), p. 28.

past, the wisdom, as they thought of it, of the ages. Citing adages and principles that once had guided men's thoughts on the structure of society; equating all communities, and England's empire in particular, with families; quoting generously from Filmer if not from Leslie; and explaining that anarchy results when social inferiors claim political authority, they argued, with increasing anxiety, that the essence of social stability was being threatened by the political agitation of the time. Their warnings, full of nostalgia for ancient certainties, were largely ignored. But in the very extremism of their reaction to the events of the time there lies a measure of the distance Revolutionary thought had moved from an old to a very new world.

One of the earliest such warnings was written by a young Barbadian, Isaac Hunt, only recently graduated from the College of Philadelphia but already an expert in scurrilous pamphleteering. Opening his *Political Family,* an essay published in 1775 though written for a prize competition in 1766, with a discourse on the necessary reciprocity of parts in the body politic he developed as his central point the idea that "in the *body politic* all inferior jurisdictions should flow from *one superior fountain* . . . a due subordination of the less parts to the greater is . . . necessary to the *existence* of BOTH." Colonies were the children and inferiors of the mother country; let them show the gratitude and obedience due to parents, and so let the principle of order through subordination prevail in the greater as in the lesser spheres of life.[78]

This, in the context of the widespread belief in equal rights and the compact theory of government, was anachronistic. But it expressed the fears of many as political opposition turned into revolutionary fervor. Arguments such as Hunt's were enlarged and progressively dramatized, gaining in vituperation with suc-

[78] Isaac Hunt, *The Political Family, or a Discourse Pointing Out the Reciprocal Advantages Which Flow from an Uninterrupted Union Between Great-Britain and Her American Colonies* . . . (Philadelphia, 1775), pp. 6, 7, 29–30.

cessive publications until by 1774 they were bitter, shrill, and full of despair. Three Anglican clergymen wrote wrathful epitaphs to this ancient, honorable, and moribund philosophy.

Samuel Seabury — Hamilton's anonymous opponent in the pamphlet wars and the future first bishop of the Episcopal Church in America — wrote desperately of the larger, permanent dangers of civil disobedience. The legal, established authorities in New York — the courts of justice, above all — have been overthrown, he wrote, and in their places there were now "delegates, congresses, committees, riots, mobs, insurrections, associations." Who comprised the self-constituted Committee of Safety of New York that had the power to brand innocent people outlaws and deliver them over "to the vengeance of a lawless, outrageous mob, to be *tarred, feathered, hanged, drawn, quartered, and burnt*"? A parcel of upstarts "chosen by the weak, foolish, turbulent part of the country people" — "half a dozen fools in your neighborhood." Was the slavery imposed by their riotous wills to be preferred to the tyranny of a king? No: "If I must be devoured, let me be devoured by the jaws of a lion, and not *gnawed* to death by rats and vermin." If the upstart, pretentious committeemen triumph, order and peace will be at an end, and anarchy will result.

Government was intended for the security of those who live under it — to protect the weak against the strong — the good against the bad — to preserve order and decency among men, preventing every one from injuring his neighbor. Every person, then, owes obedience to the laws of the government under which he lives, and is obliged in honor and duty to support them. Because if *one* has a right to disregard the laws of the society to which he belongs, *all* have the *same* right; and *then* government is at an end.[79]

[79] [Samuel Seabury], *Free Thoughts on the Proceedings of the Continental Congress Held at Philadelphia September 5, 1774* . . . ([New York], 1774), in Clarence H. Vance, ed., *Letters of a Westchester Farmer (1774–1775)* (*Publications of the Westchester County Historical Society*, VIII, White Plains, 1930), pp. 59, 61, 62; [Seabury], *The Congress Canvassed* . . . ([New York], 1774: JHL Pamphlet 49), p. 20.

His colleague, the elegant, scholarly Thomas Bradbury Chandler, was at once cleverer, more thoughtful, and, for those who heeded arguments, more likely to have been convincing. Two of his pamphlets published in 1774 stated with peculiar force the traditional case for authority in the state, in society, and in the ultimate source and ancient archetype of all authority, the family. His *American Querist,* that extraordinary list of one hundred rhetorical questions, put the point obliquely. It asked:

Whether some degree of respect be not always due from inferiors to superiors, and especially from children to parents; and whether the refusal of this on any occasion be not a violation of the general laws of society, to say nothing here of the obligations of religion and morality?

And is not Great Britain in the same relation to the colonies as a parent to children? If so, how can such "disrespectful and abusive treatment from children" be tolerated? God has given no dispensation to people under any government "to refuse *honor* or *custom* or *tribute* to whom they are *due;* to contract habits of thinking and *speaking evil of dignities,* and to weaken the natural principle of respect for those in authority." God's command is clear: his will is that we *"submit to every ordinance of man for the Lord's sake;* and require[s] us on pain of *damnation* to be duly *subject to the higher powers,* and *not to resist* their lawful authority."

Chandler's *Friendly Address to All Reasonable Americans* was more direct. It touched the central theme of authority at the start, and immediately spelled out the implications of resistance. The effort "to disturb or threaten an established government by popular insurrections and tumults has always been considered and treated, in every age and nation of the world, as an unpardonable crime." Did not an Apostle, "who had a due regard for the rights and liberties of mankind," order submission even to that cruelest of all despots, Nero? And properly so: "The bands of society would be dissolved, the harmony of the world confounded, and the order of nature subverted, if reverence, respect, and obedience might be refused to those whom the constitution has vested with the highest authority." [80]

The insistence, the violence of language, increased in the heightening crisis. "Rebellion," Daniel Leonard wrote flatly in 1775, "is the most atrocious offense that can be perpetrated by man," except those committed directly against God. "It dissolves the social band, annihilates the security resulting from law and government; introduces fraud, violence, rapine, murder, sacrilege, and the long train of evils that riot uncontrolled in a state of nature." But the end was near. By the spring of 1775 such sentiments, fulminous and despairing, were being driven underground.

Jonathan Boucher's sermon "On Civil Liberty, Passive Obedience, and Nonresistance" had been written in 1775 "with a view to publication," and though it had been delivered publicly enough in Queen Anne's Parish, Maryland, it was promptly thereafter suppressed; "the press," Boucher later wrote, "was shut to every publication of the kind." Its publication twenty-two years afterward in a volume of Boucher's sermons entitled *A View of the Causes and Consequences of the American Revolution* was the result of the French Revolution's reawakening in the author, long since safely established in England, the fears of incipient anarchy and social incoherence that had agitated him two decades before. It was a fortunate result, for the sermon is a classic of its kind. It sums up, as no other essay of the period, the threat to the traditional ordering of human relations implicit in Revolutionary thought.

Boucher sought, first and foremost, to establish the divine

[80] [Thomas B. Chandler], *The American Querist: Or, Some Questions Proposed* . . . ([New York], 1774: JHL Pamphlet 47), pp. 4, 5, 30; [Thomas B. Chandler], *A Friendly Address to All Reasonable Americans* . . . (New York, 1774: JHL Pamphlet 50), p. 5.

origins of the doctrine of obedience to constituted authority —
a necessity, he felt, not merely in view of the arguments of the
Reverend Jacob Duché whom he was ostensibly refuting, but,
more important, in view of the gross misinterpretation rebellious
Americans had for years been making of that suggestive verse of
Galatians v,1: "Stand fast, therefore, in the liberty wherewith
Christ hath made us free." What had been meant by "liberty"
in that passage, he said, was simply and unambiguously freedom
from sin, for "every sinner is, literally, a slave . . . the only true
liberty is the liberty of being the servants of God." Yet the Gospel
does speak to the question of public obligations, and its command
could hardly be more unmistakable: it orders, always, "obedience
to the laws of every country, in every kind or form of government." The rumor promoted in the infancy of Christianity "that
the Gospel was designed to undermine kingdoms and commonwealths" had probably been the work of Judas, and patently
mixed up the purpose of the First Coming with that of the
Second. Submission to the higher powers is what the Gospel
intends for man: "obedience to government is every man's duty
because it is every man's interest; but it is particularly incumbent
on Christians, because . . . it is enjoined by the positive commands of God."

So much was scriptural, and could be buttressed by such authorities as Edmund Burke, Bishop Butler, "the learned Mr. Selden,"
and Lancelot Andrewes, whose Biblical exegesis of 1650 was
quoted to the effect that "princes receive their power only from
God, and are by him constituted and entrusted with government
of others chiefly for his own glory and honor, as his deputies
and vicegerents upon earth." More complicated was the application of this central thesis to the associated questions of the origins
and aims of government and of the equality of men. As for the
former, the idea that the aim of government is "the common
good of mankind" is in itself questionable; but even if it were

315

correct, it would not follow that government should rest on consent, for common consent can only mean common feeling, and this a "vague and loose" thing not susceptible to proof. Mankind has never yet agreed on what the common good is, and so, there being no "common feeling" that can clearly designate the "common good," one can scarcely argue that government is, or should be, instituted by "common consent."

Similarly popular, dangerous, and fallacious to Boucher was the notion "that the whole human race is born equal; and that no man is naturally inferior, or in any respect subjected to another, and that he can be made subject to another only by his own consent." This argument, he wrote, is "ill-founded and false both in its premises and conclusions." It is hard to see how it could conceivably be true in any sense. "Man differs from man in everything that can be supposed to lead to supremacy and subjection, *as one star differs from another star in glory.*" God intended man to be a social animal; but society requires government, and "without some relative inferiority and superiority" there can be no government.

A musical instrument composed of chords, keys, or pipes all perfectly equal in size and power might as well be expected to produce harmony as a society composed of members all perfectly equal to be productive of order and peace . . . On the principle of equality, neither his parents nor even the vote of a majority of the society . . . can have . . . authority over any man . . . Even an implicit consent can bind a man no longer than he chooses to be bound. The same principle of equality . . . clearly entitles him to recall and resume that consent whenever he sees fit, and he alone has a right to judge when and for what reasons it may be resumed.

A social and political system based on the principles of consent and equality would be "fantastic"; it would result in "the whole business of social life" being reduced to confusion and futility.

316

People would first express and then withdraw their consent to an endless succession of schemes of government. "Governments, though always forming, would never be completely formed, for the majority today might be the minority tomorrow, and, of course, that which is now fixed might and would be soon unfixed."

Consent, equality — these were "particularly loose and dangerous" ideas, Boucher wrote; illogical, unrealistic, and lacking in scriptural sanction. There need be no mystery about the origins of government. Government was created by God. "As soon as there were some to be governed, there were also some to govern; and the first man, by virtue of that paternal claim on which all subsequent governments have been founded, was first invested with the power of government . . . The first father was the first king: and . . . it was thus that all government originated; and monarchy is its most ancient form." From this origin it follows directly that resistance to constituted authority is a sin, and that mankind is "commanded to *be subject to the higher powers.*" True, "kings and princes . . . were doubtless created and appointed not so much for their own sakes as for the sake of the people committed to their charge: yet they are not, therefore, the creatures of the people. So far from deriving their authority from any supposed consent or suffrage of men, they receive their commission from Heaven; they receive it from God, the source and original of all power." The judgment of Jesus Christ is evident: the most essential duty of subjects with respect to government is simply "(in the phraseology of a prophet) *to be quiet, and to sit still.*"

How simple but yet how demanding an injunction, for men are ever "*prone* to be presumptuous and self-willed, always disposed and ready to despise *dominion,* and *to speak evil of dignities.*" And how necessary to be obeyed in the present circumstance.

Sedition has already penetrated deeply; it tears at the vitals of social order. It threatens far more than "the persons invested with the supreme power either legislative or executive"; "the resistance which your political counselors urge you to practice [is exerted] clearly and literally against *authority* . . . you are encouraged to resist not only all authority over us as it now exists, but any and all that it is possible to constitute." [81]

This was the ultimate concern. What Boucher, Leonard, Chandler, and other articulate defenders of the *status quo* saw as the final threat was not so much the replacement of one set of rulers by another as the triumph of ideas and attitudes incompatible with the stability of any standing order, any establishment — incompatible with society itself, as it had been traditionally known. Their fears were in a sense justified, for in the context of eighteenth-century social thought it was difficult to see how any harmonious, stable social order could be constructed from such materials. To argue that all men were equal would not make them so; it would only help justify and perpetuate that spirit of defiance, that refusal to concede to authority whose ultimate resolution could only be anarchy, demagoguery, and tyranny. If such ideas prevailed year after year, generation after generation, the "latent spark" in the breasts of even the most humble of men would be kindled again and again by entrepreneurs of discontent who would remind the people "of the elevated rank they hold in the universe, as men; that all men by nature are equal; that kings are but the ministers of the people; that their authority is delegated to them by the people for their good, and they have a right to resume it, and place it in other hands, or keep it themselves, whenever it is made use of

[81] Leonard ("Massachusettensis"), in *Novanglus and Massachusettensis*, pp. 187–188; Boucher, "On Civil Liberty, Passive Obedience, and Nonresistance," *A View of the Causes and Consequences*, pp. lxxxiv, 504, 506, 507–508, 513n, 512n, 512–516, 511, 524, 525, 534, 535, 548, 552–553.

to oppress them." [82] Seeds of sedition would thus constantly be sown, and harvests of licentiousness reaped.

How else could it end? What reasonable social and political order could conceivably be built and maintained where authority was questioned before it was obeyed, where social differences were considered to be incidental rather than essential to community order, and where superiority, suspect in principle, was not allowed to concentrate in the hands of a few but was scattered broadly through the populace? No one could clearly say. But some, caught up in a vision of the future in which the peculiarities of American life became the marks of a chosen people, found in the defiance of traditional order the firmest of all grounds for their hope for a freer life. The details of this new world were not as yet clearly depicted; but faith ran high that a better world than any that had ever been known could be built where authority was distrusted and held in constant scrutiny; where the status of men flowed from their achievements and from their personal qualities, not from distinctions ascribed to them at birth; and where the use of power over the lives of men was jealously guarded and severely restricted. It was only where there was this defiance, this refusal to truckle, this distrust of all authority, political or social, that institutions would express human aspirations, not crush them.

[82] [Daniel Leonard] ("Massachusettensis"), *The Origin of the American Contest with Great-Britain* . . . (New York, 1775: JHL Pamphlet 56), p. 24 (in *Novanglus and Massachusettensis*, p. 152)

Postscript
FULFILLMENT: A COMMENTARY ON THE CONSTITUTION

Whatever veneration might be entertained for the body of men who formed our Constitution, the sense of that body could never be regarded as the oracular guide in expounding the Constitution. As the instrument came from them it was nothing more than a draft of a plan, nothing but a dead letter, until life and validity were breathed into it by the voice of the people, speaking through the several State Conventions. If we were to look, therefore, for the meaning of the instrument beyond the face of the instrument, we must look for it, not in the General Convention, which proposed, but in the State Conventions, which accepted and ratified the Constitution.

— James Madison, 1796

THE AMERICAN Constitution is the final and climactic expression of the ideology of the American Revolution. As such, in the two centuries of its existence, it has become the subject of more elaborate and detailed scrutiny and commentary than has been given to any document except the Bible. No one has mastered all the useful writings on the Constitution; no one ever will. There is too much; there is movement in too many directions at once; too many disparate issues are alive and flourishing quite independently of each other. Yet there will never be enough. The subject matters too much — matters in the sense of shaping the way we live, what we may do, and how the government may act. We must get the two-hundred-year-old story straight, in some way, in order to make sense of our own world. The Constitution, in all its aspects and ramifications, is profoundly relevant.

But it is more than that. The writing and ratifying of the Constitution, and the original debate over its meaning, are, quite simply, fascinating. The issues are subtle, the details are often puzzling and intriguing, the movement of events complex. And the actors are remarkable. On one side, Madison, Wilson, Ellsworth, Hamilton, Jay, Iredell, the Morrises, Sherman; on the other, the junta of immensely articulate Pennsylvania antifederalists and their counterparts north and south — Melancton Smith, Luther Martin, James Winthrop, George Mason, Patrick Henry, Elbridge Gerry — the list of truly interesting actors in this drama seems endless. Part of the fascination comes from seeing these minds at work, formulating and reformulating, shifting, dodging, lunging.

There can be no ordinary historical characterization of the complicated interplay between the maturing of Revolutionary ideas and ideals and the involvements of everyday life, which is the essence of the history of the Constitution period. Perhaps the most subtle and penetrating depiction of the inner character of the drafting of, and the original debate on, the Constitution is not a historical discourse but a poem, a short poem, by Richard Wilbur. It is called "Mind."

> Mind in its purest play is like some bat
> That beats about in caverns all alone,
> Contriving by a kind of senseless wit
> Not to conclude against a wall of stone.
>
> It has no need to falter or explore;
> Darkly it knows what obstacles are there,
> And so may weave and flitter, dip and soar
> In perfect courses through the blackest air.
>
> And has this simile a like perfection?
> The mind is like a bat. Precisely. Save
> That in the very happiest intellection
> A graceful error may correct the cave.[1]

[1] The poem appeared first in *Things of This World* (1956) and is reprinted here with the kind permission of the publisher, Harcourt Brace Jovanovich, Inc.

FULFILLMENT

They did indeed weave and flitter, dip and soar, and they did indeed correct the cave of their ideological origins. But how?

I

The ideological history of the American Revolution developed in three distinct phases. Each has a voluminous documentation, and each has a distinctive focus and emphasis. The first was the years of struggle with Britain before 1776 when, under the pressure of events and the necessity to justify resistance to constituted authority, the colonists developed from their complex heritage of political thought the set of ideas, already in scattered ways familiar to them, that was most illuminating and most appropriate to their needs. Centered on the fear of centralized power and rooted in the belief that free states are fragile and degenerate easily into tyrannies unless vigilantly protected by a free, knowledgeable, and uncorrupted electorate working through institutions that balance and distribute rather than concentrate power, their ideas were critical of, and challenging to, the legal authority they had lived under. The writings of this early period drew together the basic ideas which would flow through all subsequent stages of American political thought, and provide the permanent foundation of the nation's political beliefs.[2]

---

[2] See, besides the chapters above, Bernard Bailyn, ed., *Pamphlets of the American Revolution, 1750–1776* (Cambridge, 1965–), I; idem, *The Ordeal of Thomas Hutchinson* (Cambridge, 1974), chaps. iii, vi; idem, *Faces of Revolution* (New York, 1990); idem, ed.,

The second phase saw the constructive application of these ideas and the exploration of their implications, limits, and possibilities in the writing and rewriting of the first state constitutions, from 1776 through the 1780's. Obliged now to construct their own governments at the state level, American leaders were forced to think through the fundamentals of their beliefs, and establish republican polities that expressed the principles they had earlier endorsed. They did not work from clean slates. Constrained by institutions that had long existed and by entrenched leadership groups, they were revisers, amenders, elaborators, and conceptualizers, as they applied fresh ideas to existing structures and brought them as close as possible to their ideal. So they explored the nature of written constitutions and of constituent power; worked through the problems of separating functioning powers of government to form balances within single-order societies; and probed the nature of representation, the operative meaning of sovereignty of the people, and individual rights. Few of their conclusions were applied uniformly or in absolute and complete form. But everywhere the institutional problems of republican government at the state level and the principles on which it was based were probed in this constructive phase of the ideological revolution.[3]

The third phase — the writing, debating, ratifying, and amending of the national constitution — resembles the second phase in that it was constructive and concentrated on constitution writing; many of the ideas that had been developed in the writing and discussion of the state constitutions were applied to the national constitution and further refined and developed. But in its essence this phase was distinct. For in the 1780's, under the pressure of rising social tensions, economic confusion pointing to

---

"A Dialogue between an American and a European Englishman (1768)," *Perspectives in American History*, 9 (1975), 343–410.

[3] Gordon S. Wood, *The Creation of the American Republic, 1776–1787* (Chapel Hill, 1969), esp. parts 2 and 3.

the possible collapse of public credit, frustration in international affairs, and the threat of dissolution of the weak Confederation, the central task was reversed. Now the goal of the initiators of change was the creation, not the destruction, of national power — the construction of what could properly be seen, and feared, as a *Machtstaat,* a central national power that involved armed force, the aggressive management of international relations, and, potentially at least, the regulation of vital aspects of everyday life by a government dominant over all other, lesser governments. The background experiences of constitution writing in the states were informative — they were constantly referred to in the Philadelphia convention and in the ratifying debates — but the central issue of 1787–88 was different in its nature from the main issues in the forming of the state governments, and diametrically opposite to the goals of the pre-Revolutionary years. Yet the pre-Revolutionary ideology was fundamental to all their beliefs. How could it be reconciled with present needs?

The Founders certainly did not leave the confinement — the cave — of their own intellectual world and depart for some other. That debate and struggle with Britain was only a decade in the past. How were the original commitments to be reconciled with the radically new needs and proposals?

What follows is not an account of the ratification debate as a whole, but a commentary on this limited but basic question.[4]

---

[4]For a survey of some of the issues involved, concentrating on the uses made of the Revolution "as a rhetorical strategy" in the ratifying debate, each side attempting thereby to influence public opinion in its favor, see Frederick R. Black, "The American Revolution as 'Yardstick' in the Debates on the Constitution, 1787–1788," *Proceedings of the American Philosophical Society,* 117 (June 15, 1973), 162–185. In this Postscript I do not consider the debate on the Constitution as rhetoric, but as reality; I concentrate on the conceptual problems that framed the Founders' understanding; and I stress the continuities in the basic ideology of the Revolution. For an excellent presentation of a similar view carried into the decade after the Constitution, see Lance Banning, "Republican Ideology and the Triumph of the Constitution, 1789–1793," *William and Mary Quarterly,* 31 (April 1974), 167–188, and also Banning's fuller treatment in his *Jeffersonian Persua-*

Until recently the bulk of the available documentation on the ratification debate had been quite small: four volumes of formal debates in the state ratifying conventions published by Jonathan Elliot in 1836, two volumes of pamphlets and essays published by P. L. Ford in the 1890s, and, above all, the *Federalist* papers, which have engrossed attention at least since the appearance of Beard's *Economic Interpretation* in 1913, together with a few well-known antifederalist publications, chiefly the *Federal Farmer* series.[5] Additions were made to the available antifederalist publications, first in Cecelia Kenyon's collection and more comprehensively in Herbert Storing's five volumes of documents, which include antifederalist papers from almost all of the states, and ephemera as well as systematic writings. But it was not until the appearance of the first of the projected twenty volumes of *The Documentary History of the Ratification of the Constitution* that it became possible to grasp the full dimensions of the outpouring of 1787–1789. The completed letterpress volumes of *The Documentary History* will total well over 10,000 pages — upwards of five million words — and microfiche addenda will greatly increase that total. In addition the editors have traced and identify in their annotation the *reprints,* whole or in part, of every published document, thus providing an index of the circulation of the writings, hence their popularity or importance as judged by contemporaries.[6]

sion (Ithaca, 1978) and his careful updating of the issues in *Reviews in American History,* 17 (June 1989), 199–204.

[5] Jonathan Elliot, ed., *The Debates in the Several State Conventions, on the Adoption of the Federal Constitution* . . . (2d ed.; 4 vols., Washington, D.C., 1836); Paul L. Ford, ed., *Essays on the Constitution of the United States* . . . *1787–1788* (Brooklyn, 1892); idem, ed., *Pamphlets on the Constitution of the United States* . . . *1787–1788* (Brooklyn, 1888); Walter H. Bennett, ed., *Letters from the Federal Farmer to the Republican* (University, Ala., 1978). Of the many reprintings of the complete *Federalist* papers, the edition by Jacob E. Cooke (Middletown, 1961) is technically the most useful and will be the edition quoted in references to the last ten papers (LXXVI–LXXXV). Papers I–LXXV appear among the other commentaries on the Constitution so far published in the *Documentary History* series cited in note 6 and will be quoted from that edition.

[6] Cecelia M. Kenyon, ed., *The Antifederalists* (Indianapolis, 1966); Herbert J. Storing,

FULFILLMENT

In reading through this immensity of writings, ranging from lampooning squibs and jingle-jangle verses to scholarly treatises and brilliant polemical exchanges, one easily loses track of any patterns or themes. The sheer bulk is overwhelming, for, as Henry Knox wrote at the time, "The new constitution! the new constitution is the general cry this way. Much paper is spoiled on the subject, and many essays are written which perhaps are not read by either side."[7] Storing's edition of antifederalist writings, said to be complete, turns out in fact to include only about 15 percent of the total available antifederalist material.[8] And the mass of federalist writings reveals the great range and variety of thinking on that side of the struggle, by no means all represented in the *Federalist* papers.[9] In fact, in the full context of the political writings of 1787–88 the importance of the *Federalist* papers seems diminished. Some contemporaries, of course, immediately saw the merits of that long series (more than quadruple the length of any other). George Washington, a close ally of the authors, wrote prophetically to Hamilton that "when the transient circumstances and fugitive performances which attended this *crisis* shall have disappeared, that work will merit the notice of posterity, because in it are candidly discussed the principles of freedom." Noah Webster thought the series "one of the most complete dissertations on government that

---

ed., *The Complete Anti-Federalist* (Chicago, 1981); Merrill Jensen, John P. Kaminski, and Gaspare J, Saladino, eds., *The Documentary History of the Ratification of the Constitution* (Madison, 1976–). An essay in the front matter of the first volume reviews the earlier publishing history of the sources of the ratification controversy. Four volumes to date (XIII–XVI) of the series contain Commentaries on the Constitution, public and private, as distinct from the debates and other materials directly related to the ratifying conventions. These documents are numbered in a single sequence and will be referred to below as CC followed by the number in the sequence. Thus James Wilson's speech of October 6, 1787, will be identified as such, followed by: *Doc. Hist.*, XIII, CC 134.

[7] Knox to John Sullivan, New York, January 19, 1788, *Doc. Hist.*, XV, CC 461.

[8] John P. Kaminski, "Antifederalism and the Perils of Homogenized History: A Review Essay," *Rhode Island History*, 42 (1983), 35.

[9] Herbert J. Storing, "The 'Other' Federalist Papers: A Preliminary Sketch," *Political Science Reviewer*, 6 (1976), 216–247.

ever has appeared in America, perhaps in Europe." And James Iredell, one of the most penetrating minds among the federalists, called *The Federalist*'s treatment of standing armies "masterly" and hoped the whole work "will soon be in every body's hands."[10]

But in the "transient circumstances" of the time it was not so much the *Federalist* papers that captured most people's imaginations as James Wilson's speech of October 6, 1787, the most famous, to some the most notorious, federalist statement of the time. To this early, brief, and luminous pronouncement there were floods of refutations, confirmations, and miscellaneous responses.[11] Comments on the *Federalist* papers, on the other hand, were few, usually scholarly and technical, and politically unremarkable. Rufus King thought Oliver Ellsworth's "Landholder" essays more effective than the *Federalist* (they are indeed remarkably original pieces), and the federalist Judge A. C. Hanson, formerly Washington's private secretary and soon to be the chancellor of the state of Maryland, while acknowledging that the *Federalist* papers display deep penetration and are ingenious and elaborate, found them sophistical in some places, painfully obvious in others, and throughout prolix and tiresome. He could not get through them, he said: they do not "force the attention, rouze the passions, or thrill the nerves." His own short pamphlet, *Remarks on the Proposed Plan,* dedicated to Washington, might be inferior to the *Federalist* as an abstract treatise on government, he said, but "as an occasional pamphlet" he was confident it was "superiour" and "more serviceable."[12]

---

[10] Washington to Hamilton, August 28, 1788, in Harold C. Syrett and Jacob E. Cooke, eds., *Papers of Alexander Hamilton* (New York, 1961–1979), V, 207; Webster, review of *The Federalist,* quoted in *Doc. Hist.,* XVI, 451n; "Marcus" [Iredell], IV, *ibid.,* CC 616.

[11] For the text of Wilson's speech and references to the controversy that followed, see *ibid.,* XIII, CC 134.

[12] King to Jeremiah Wadsworth, New York, December 23, 1787, *ibid.,* XV, CC 368; for Hanson's comments, see *ibid.,* pp. 521–522. Criticism like Hanson's must have been widespread since the antifederalists thought it useful to develop it into an elaborate spoof. In a letter purportedly written in confidence by Benjamin Rush to Hamilton,

FULFILLMENT

Hanson was at least right in thinking that for all their remarkable qualities the *Federalist* papers were not altogether original. Oliver Ellsworth wrote more clearly and fully on judicial review than did the *Federalist* authors, and both he and James Wilson recognized the central importance of that topic before they did. Twenty days before the appearance of *Federalist* X the New Jersey lawyer John Stevens, Jr., anticipated Madison's central argument on republicanism, national size, and self-interest in the first of his "Americanus" essays, an analysis that was independently developed also by an anonymous Connecticut writer seventeen days later. Others went beyond Madison in locating the sources of the problem discussed in *Federalist* X in blockages of thought they discovered in the received tradi-

---

Rush first congratulates Hamilton on their success in bribing the printers to suppress all antifederalist writings, and then adds: "I wish, Sir, I could prevail on Publius not to be so prolix; if his pieces were shorter, they would answer much better; besides, they want that spirit of declamation necessary to excite the public attention. Most people here say (and, I am sorry, with too much justice) that the pieces contain nothing but plagiarisms from history and British politics, and general sentiments that apply more forcibly against the constitution than for it. My dear sir, let me entreat you to have the plan changed." *Newport* (R.I.) *Mercury,* March 24, 1788, p. 4. For other antifederalist abuse of the more heavy-handed *Federalist* papers which "would jade the brain of any poor sinner," see Robert A. Rutland, "The First Great Newspaper Debate . . . 1787–88," *Proceedings of the American Antiquarian Society,* 97, part 1 (April 1987), 53, and *Doc. Hist.,* XIII, 493n.

The enormous importance accorded the *Federalist* papers is largely a twentieth-century phenomenon (though on the uses made of them in the antebellum period, see Rakove's essay in Kessler, ed., *Saving the Republic,* cited fully below). Recognized now as this country's most distinguished work of political theory, it provides abundant material for a large academic industry. The endless outpouring of scholarly writing on the series inundates everything written on the history of the Constitution and on American political thought. A complete bibliography would include hundreds, perhaps thousands, of items. These studies, growing ever more sophisticated, approach now an exquisite refinement of analysis that would have amazed the harried authors, who wrote polemically, to help win a political battle. Among the more notable studies are Morton White's technical philosophical analysis, *Philosophy, The Federalist, and the Constitution* (New York and Oxford, 1987); Daniel W. Howe's psychological analysis, "The Political Psychology of *The Federalist,*" *William and Mary Quarterly,* 44 (July 1987); the fourteen essays in Charles R. Kesler, ed., *Saving the Revolution: The Federalist Papers and the American Founding* (New York and London, 1987); and David Epstein's *The Political Theory of the Federalist* (Chicago, 1984).

tion, inherited ideas that hitherto had been axiomatic but were now revealed to be anachronistic, distorted, or irrelevant.[13]

For the federalists were obliged to work at that basic level if they were to succeed in their central task. They had no choice if they were to justify the creation of a new nation-state potentially as powerful as any other. The old beliefs of '76 which had served to destroy an imperial power had somehow to be reconciled with nationalist needs. Yet it was obvious that the ideological origins of the American Revolution had been rooted not merely in a general fear of power but specifically in the belief that liberty could not survive where corruptible men wielded the apparatus of a powerful national state. Again and again both federalist and antifederalist commentators on the Constitution thought back to the 1760's and 1770's, the federalists to make progress toward justifying a national power system that would be safe for the people's liberties, the antifederalists to show that such a project could never succeed, that it involved a profound self-contradiction, and that the Constitution, if adopted, would plunge the country into precisely the misery that the received

[13] Ellsworth, speech in the Connecticut convention (January 7, 1788), *Doc. Hist.*, III, 553 (the speech appears also in *ibid.*, XV, CC 420, and in Elliot, *Debates*, II, 190–197); Wilson's speeches in the Pennsylvania convention (December 1, 7, 1787), *ibid.*, II, 450–451, 517. Stevens' "Americanus" papers and the federalists' struggle with the received tradition are discussed below, section 3. By the end of January 1788 the question of judicial review had become a prominent and controversial issue, as it had not been in the Philadelphia convention. The Supreme Court's power to define "the sense of every article of the Constitution" and its freedom from "any fixed or established rules" or from correction by any superior power were savagely and brilliantly attacked — in words that would be repeated in every generation thereafter — by "Brutus" in seven of his sixteen essays published in New York, January 31–March 20, 1788. *Ibid.*, XV, CC 489; XVI, CC 510, 530, 551, 576, 598, 632. (On the disputed authorship of the "Brutus" essays, see *ibid.*, XIII, CC 178.) *The Federalist*'s replies, by Hamilton, who as a New York lawyer had earlier presumed the power of judicial review in arguing a case in that state's courts, came late, in LXXVIII, LXXXI, and LXXXII (May 28, 1788), though Hamilton had anticipated some of his later arguments in XXII (December 14, 1787). "Americanus" too preceded *The Federalist*'s arguments in his clear and forceful statement of judicial review published on January 21 (paper VII, cited below, n. 43). For Hanson's feeble responses to "Brutus," in his *Remarks on the Proposed Plan* . . . (Annapolis, 1788), see *Doc. Hist.*, XV, CC 490 (p. 536).

wisdom had always predicted for any powerful centralized regime.

2

The antifederalists have been called "men of little faith" in that they lacked faith in the safe future that the federalists foresaw under the Constitution.[14] But in the context of the great mass of ratification documents, the antifederalists emerge as the ones who *kept* the faith — the ancient faith so fundamental a part of the ideological origins of the Revolution, from which, they argued, the Constitution departed. The antifederalist Judge Thomas Tredwell of New York recalled the old days despairingly: in '76, he declared, "the spirit of liberty ran high, and danger put a curb on ambition . . . Sir, in this Constitution we have not only neglected — we have done worse — we have openly violated, our faith — that is, our public faith." Still emotionally and intellectually involved in the original struggle against an imperial government that had claimed total power over the American people, the antifederalists were haunted by the dangers that had then been foreseen. Now, faced with what seemed a similar threat, they summoned up the ghosts of those passionate years — and in the most specific, literal terms. The identity between antifederalist thought and that of the most fervent ideologists of '76 is at times astonishing.[15]

Mercy Otis Warren could never clear her mind of the dark vision of her ancient enemy, Thomas Hutchinson, who she never ceased believing had been a tool of absolutism and a willing servant of his despotic patron, the Earl of Hillsborough.

---

[14] Cecelia M. Kenyon, "Men of Little Faith: The Anti-Federalists on the Nature of Representative Government," *W.M.Q.*, 3d ser., 12 (1955), 3–43.

[15] Tredwell's forceful speech, prepared for the July 2, 1788, session of the New York ratifying convention but apparently not delivered, appears in Elliot, *Debates*, II, 396–406, quotations at p. 401. For a similar interpretation of the antifederalists' thought, in the context of the transit of generations, see Pauline Maier, *The Old Revolutionaries* (New York, 1980), pp. 282 ff.

Her widely circulated *Observations on the Constitution* (February 1788) is a boiling polemic, not simply against the federalists but also — and simultaneously — against the long-dead governor, that "great champion for arbitrary power [with his] machinations to subvert the liberties of this country" and his design to bring down on America "the infernal darkness of Asiatic slavery." The same threat, she believed, had been renewed by the federalists, and her task, she felt, was to rekindle the dying embers of the patriotism and the love of freedom that had burned so brightly in '76, and to demonstrate the direct connection — the political descent — between the loyalists of '76, with their program of arbitrary power, and James Wilson and his neo-Hutchinsonians, with their "many-headed monster," the Constitution. For her, little but the personnel had changed over the years. The dangers were the same. In 1788 as in 1768 she saw the "deep-laid plots, the secret intrigues, [and] the bold effrontery of . . . interested and avaricious adventurers for place, who, intoxicated with the ideas of distinction and preferment, have prostrated every worthy principle beneath the shrine of ambition." She, and other ardent antifederalists, could see a direct line from the loyalists and the wartime profiteers to the federalists; and she was convinced that once again America faced "*dark, secret* and *profound intrigues* of . . . the statesman long practiced in the purlieus of despotism." Just as Hutchinson had urged his master Hillsborough to eliminate annual elections in Massachusetts in favor of triennial, so the Constitution would make Congressional elections biennial.[16]

---

[16] "A Columbian Patriot" [Mercy Otis Warren], *Observations on the Constitution,* in *Doc. Hist.,* XVI, CC 581 (282, 283, 284, 276, 277). The genealogy of parties, linking present opponents to the enemies of '76, could be argued on both sides. Thus a federalist squib in Pennsylvania identified seven characteristics shared by the anti-federalists and the Tories of '76, among which were: denunciations of conventions and town meetings as mere mob actions; insistence that they, the antifederalists, alone understood the true principles of government; and harping on imaginary grievances. "It is to be hoped the Antifederalists will end their career as some of the Tories, whom they resemble in so many particulars, have done, viz. — in poverty — in exile." *Doc. Hist.,* II, 157.

FULFILLMENT

The fear of a conspiracy against the fragile structure of freedom, the same fear that had lain at the heart of the resistance movement before 1776, pervaded the thought of the antifederalists. No writer of the pre-Revolutionary period was more convinced that he was struggling with a secret plot against liberty than Luther Martin, whose rambling account of the Philadelphia convention, *The Genuine Information,* if extracted from its context, would seem an expression of extreme paranoia. Similarly, Samuel Bryan's eighteen-part "Centinel" series in the *Philadelphia Independent Gazetteer* is a foaming diatribe against those "harpies of power," the criminal conspirators against liberty who shield their secret intentions with "the virtues of a Washington," blatantly lie to the public, and shackle the press to suppress opposition — in fact do anything, no matter how foul and vicious, to fob off on the people "the most odious system of tyranny that was ever projected [the Constitution], a many headed hydra of despotism, whose complicated and various evils would be infinitely more oppressive and afflictive than the scourge of any single tyrant." Precisely who the instigators of this "deep laid scheme to enslave us" were, Bryan was not sure (another Philadelphian was quite certain that the Society of the Cincinnati was responsible and that Rufus King had inadvertently confessed as much in the Massachusetts convention). But it seemed obvious to Bryan that at the very least Franklin had hoodwinked the innocent Washington "by inducing him to acquiesce in a system of despotism and villainy, at which enlightened patriotism shudders."[17]

---

[17] Luther Martin's *The Genuine Information* is an expansion of his speech in the Maryland Assembly, November 29, 1787, justifying his behavior in the Philadelphia convention (*Doc. Hist.,* XIV, CC 304B). The quotations from Bryan's "Centinel" are from no. XII (*Doc. Hist.,* XV, CC 470), where he explicitly defends his characterization of the federalists as *"conspirators."* The term, he writes, "was not, as has been alledged, rashly or inconsiderately adopted; it is the language of dispassionate and deliberate reason, influenced by the purest patriotism. The consideration of the nature and construction of the new constitution naturally suggests the epithet; its justness is strikingly illustrated by the conduct of the patrons of this plan of government." And he goes on

333

But at least Bryan included some reasoned arguments against specific provisions of the Constitution, something Benjamin Workman, an Irish immigrant of 1784, never managed to do in his twelve "Philadelphiensis" papers. There is nothing in the ratification writings to match the violent rhetoric of those feverish diatribes. The federalists, Workman wrote, were "demagogues despising every sense of order and decency"; they were the "meanest traitors that ever dishonoured the human character," and as "the haughty lordlings of the convention" they were engaged in a "conspiracy against the freedom of America both deep and dangerous," a conspiracy that could only end in "one *despotic monarchy*." "Ah my friends," Workman wrote, "the days of a cruel Nero approach fast; the language of a monster, of a Caligula, could not be more imperious" than that of the federalist plotters who "now openly browbeat you with their insolence, and assume majesty."[18]

No doubt Workman, in Tench Coxe's phrase, was simply "bellowing and braying like a wild asses colt,"[19] but calmer minds too saw in the federalists' efforts a renewal of the hidden dangers Americans had faced in the years before 1776. They declared again and again — in a great outpouring of newspaper squibs, carefully reasoned essays, and convention speeches — that the old struggle had been renewed, and that the ancient issues confronted them once more.

---

to say — in a perfect paradigm of conspiratorial psychology — that if there had been any doubt that there was a conspiracy on foot the federalists' "uneasiness" at the charge would clearly prove it: "innocence would have nothing to dread from such a stigma." Bryan continued his "unmasking" of the federalists' conspiracy in later numbers of the "Centinel." The climax came with the attack on Franklin in no. XVII, where he declares himself finally satisfied that he has fully revealed the federalists' "insidious design of enslaving and robbing their fellow-citizens, of establishing those odious distinctions between the well born and the great body of the people, of degrading the latter to the level of slaves and elevating the former to the rank of nobility." *Doc. Hist.*, XVI, CC 642. For Rufus King and the Cincinnati, see *ibid.*, p. 528. Cf. above, pp. 144–159.

[18] Conflated from "Philadelphiensis," V, IX, XI (*ibid.*, XV, CC 356; XVI, CC 507, 609).

[19] *Ibid.*, XVI, 475.

Examination of the Constitution revealed, they believed, a taxing power in the hands of the proposed national government that would prove to be as unqualified by the restraints of the states as Parliament's had been by the colonial assemblies. With such limitless taxing power, Patrick Henry declared in one of his vast speeches in the Virginia convention — one of those heaving oceans of antifederalist passion whose thundering waves threatened to drown Madison's small, tight cogencies — the Senate would live in splendor and a "great and mighty President" would "be supported in extravagant magnificence, so that the whole of our property may be taken by this American government, by laying what taxes they please, giving themselves what salaries they please, and suspending our laws at their pleasure." The New York antifederalist "Brutus" could see an even greater danger, in the federal government's power to "borrow money on the credit of the United States." With this power "the Congress may mortgage any or all the revenues of the union . . . [and] may borrow of foreign nations a principal sum, the interest of which will be equal to the annual revenues of the country. By this means, they may create a national debt so large as to exceed the ability of the country ever to sink. I can scarcely contemplate a greater calamity that could befal this country than to be loaded with a debt exceeding their ability ever to discharge."[20]

The notion that lesser governmental bodies — the states — could effectively share sovereignty with a central power (the principle of federalism) made no more sense to the antifederalists in 1788 than it had when the colonists had fruitlessly proposed it in the years before 1776 and people like Galloway and

[20] "Brutus," VII, *ibid.,* XV, CC 411. Henry's speeches in the Virginia convention, Elliot, *Debates,* III, 56, 386. The former — June 5 — speech, printed, though with omissions, on pp. 43–64 of Elliot's *Debates,* was one of Henry's shorter orations, but it must have taken well over an hour to deliver. For the speech he delivered a short time later, which stretched over the better part of two days of the convention's time, see pp. 137–176. On the national debt: "Brutus," VIII, *Doc. Hist.,* XV, CC 437.

Hutchinson had effectively ridiculed its logic. So once again the antifederalists rang the changes on the famous "solecism," *imperium in imperio,* explaining in endless iteration that, as George Mason put it, "two concurrent powers cannot exist long together; the one will destroy the other." "There is a spirit of rivalship in power," "An Old Whig" of Pennsylvania wrote, "which will not suffer two suns to shine in the same firmament; one will speedily darken the other, and the individual states will be as totally eclipsed as the stars in the meridian blaze of the sun." A "mutual concurrence of powers," Patrick Henry declared, "will carry you into endless absurdity."[21]

The federal government, like the British government before 1776, "Brutus" wrote in two of his finest papers, empowered by the "necessary and proper" and the "supreme law of the land" clauses, "would totally destroy all the powers of the individual states," for no "two men, or bodies of men, [can] have unlimited power respecting the same object." It contradicts logic, scripture, even the principles of mechanics. "The legislature of the United States will have a right to exhaust every source of revenue in every state, and to annul all laws of the states which may stand in the way of effecting it." In the end, the national government, through its taxing power, "Brutus" then wrote in a florid peroration that conjures up the horrors of totalitarian states,

exercised without limitation, will introduce itself into every corner of the city and country. It [the national government] will wait upon the ladies at their toilett, and will not leave them in any of their domestic concerns; it will accompany them to the ball, the play, and the assembly; it will go with them when they visit, and will, on all occasions, sit beside them in their carriages, nor will it desert them even at

---

[21] Mason's remarks on federalism, which he amplified on various occasions, appear in Elliot, *Debates,* III, 29. "An Old Whig" [George Bryan?], VI, *Doc. Hist.,* XIV, CC 292. For the earlier Tory denunciation of pre-Revolutionary dual-sovereignty notions, indistinguishable from the antifederalists' attacks on the Constitution's federalism, see above, pp. 219–223.

church; it will enter the house of every gentleman, watch over his cellar, wait upon his cook in the kitchen, follow the servants into the parlour, preside over the table, and note down all he eats or drinks; it will attend him to his bed-chamber, and watch him while he sleeps; it will take cognizance of the professional man in his office or his study; it will watch the merchant in the counting-house or in his store; it will follow the mechanic to his shop and in his work, and will haunt him in his family and in his bed; it will be a constant companion of the industrious farmer in all his labour, it will be with him in the house and in the field, observe the toil of his hands and the sweat of his brow; it will penetrate into the most obscure cottage; and finally, it will light upon the head of every person in the United States. To all these different classes of people and in all these circumstances in which it will attend them, the language in which it will address them will be, GIVE! GIVE!

The only solution, which was endorsed by other antifederalists, was to go back to the distinction between external and internal taxes and external and internal spheres of power, which had flourished during the Stamp Act struggle twenty-three years earlier and had been endorsed by Franklin in his testimony before Parliament, only to be repudiated in John Dickinson's *Farmer's Letters* and thereafter dropped from serious discussion.[22]

---

[22] "Brutus," V, VI, continued in VII, *Doc. Hist.*, XIV, CC 343; XV, CC 384 (the florid passage), and CC 411. Judge Hanson later commented on this peroration, calling it "the mere phrenzy of declamation, the ridiculous conjuration of spectres and hobgobblins!" *Ibid.*, XV, CC 490A (545). Almost every leading antifederalist at one time or another elaborated on the impossibility of maintaining concurrent, federal powers for any length of time, and predicted that "the state governments must be annihilated, or continue to exist for no purpose." E.g., "Federal Farmer," II, *Doc. Hist.*, XIV, CC 242, quotation at 29. So too did fence straddlers like Samuel Adams, unsure of what position to take and considering both sides carefully (Adams to R. H. Lee, December 3, 1787, *ibid.*, CC 315). For other antifederalist endorsements of the old, and long since repudiated, belief that external and internal spheres of power could be effectively distinguished, see "An Old Whig," VI, *ibid.*, CC 292 (218); and "Brutus," V, *ibid.*, CC 343 (427). For Hamilton's criticism of the idea, see *Federalist* XXX; for Wilson's, arguing against William Findley's invocation of the colonists' arguments against Parliament's efforts to impose "internal taxes or excises," see his summation in the Pennsylvania convention, December 11, 1787, *Doc. Hist.*, II, 557–558. Cf. above, pp. 212 ff.

Thus the antifederalists, impelled by the fear of power, saw ancient issues in modern problems. Just as the king in Parliament once had absolute power over the selection of representatives who collectively might protect the people against excessive exactions by a central power, so, they pointed out, the Constitution, in Article I, Section 4 — one of the most hotly debated clauses in the entire ratification struggle — gave Congress the right to alter the times and manner of holding elections for senators and representatives. And more than that, Patrick Henry declared, representation in Congress will be not actual but virtual. "We contended with the British about representation," he reminded the Virginia ratifying convention. "They offered us such a representation as Congress now does. They called it a virtual representation. If you look at that paper [the Constitution] you will find it so there . . . Representation is not, therefore, the vital principle of this government. So far it is wrong" — and so far "the tyranny of Philadelphia [the federal convention] may be like the tyranny of George III."[23]

Representation was a basic issue, in 1788 as in 1776; but nothing excited antifederalist passions more than Congress' power, under Article I, Section 8, "to raise and support armies," the curse of which, for most antifederalists, was in no way diminished by the two-year limit on military appropriations. (Britain's Parliament, they immediately pointed out, was limited to *annual* funding; and what would keep Congress from continuing appropriations indefinitely?) There is simply no way to measure the volume and fervor of the antifederalists' denunciation of this provision, which revived for them not simply a general fear of military power but the specific danger of "standing armies," a peculiar and distinctive threat to liberty that had been formulated for all time, they believed, in England in the 1690s, and had been carried forward intact to the colonies.

[23] Charles Turner, speech in the Massachusetts convention, Elliot, *Debates,* II, 30–32; Henry, speech in the Virginia convention, *ibid.,* III, 324, 314.

There the danger had been fully realized in 1768, when the first British troops were stationed in peaceful Boston and a predictable "massacre" resulted.[24]

"Standing armies" were not national guards, protecting the people. They were janissary troops, palace guards, predatory mercenaries loyal to the power source — the Crown, the executive, the President, anyone in authority to whom they were loyal or who would pay them. So it had been said in the 1690's; so it had been said in 1768; and so it was said two decades later. The good people of South Carolina, a speaker in that state's ratifying convention warned, will certainly resist the despotism of the Constitution, as threatening to liberty as Archbishop Laud's doctrine of "non-resistance" had been. And what will result? "Your standing army, like Turkish janizaries enforcing despotic laws, must ram it down their throats with the points of bayonets." Surely, a Pennsylvanian "Democratic Federalist" wrote in one of the most powerful replies to Wilson's October 6 speech, surely

the experience of past ages and the . . . most celebrated patriots have taught us to dread a standing army above all earthly evils. Are we then to go over all the thread-bare, common place arguments that have been used without success by the advocates of tyranny, and which have been for a long time past so gloriously refuted! Read the excellent *Burgh* in his political disquisitions on this hackneyed subject, and then say whether you think that a standing army is necessary in a free country.

Even the *"aristocratical"* David Hume, the writer stated, believed that a standing army was *"a mortal distemper in a government."* Wilson's "thread-bare, hackneyed argument" for a standing army, the writer concluded, "has been answered over and over in different ages, and does not deserve even the smallest consideration." One scarcely needed to argue the issue, the dan-

---

[24] "Federal Farmer," III, *Doc. Hist.*, XIV, CC 242 (38–39); and above, pp. 61–63, 112–119.

gers were so obvious and well known. "Brutus" contented himself simply with quoting at great length the famous, often reprinted speech on reducing the army that William Pulteney had delivered to the House of Commons in 1732.

As for the supposed safeguard of the state militias, to the antifederalists the idea made a mockery of reason. Not only did the Constitution specifically allow Congress to nationalize the state troops, hence absorb them into the standing army, but there was nothing to prevent the President from using them as if they *were* standing armies, since he had the power to deploy them anywhere: Virginia's troops could be shipped off to Massachusetts to put down political opposition there, Rhode Island's to Pennsylvania — or for that matter to Cuba or Timbuctoo — wherever the President's adventures might lead him. Even worse: the national government, George Mason said, referring specifically to events in Pennsylvania forty years earlier, might cunningly neglect the state militias, fail to arm them, or otherwise immobilize them, so that in time, when the people felt the need for military protection, they would throw themselves on the mercy of the national government and cry out, " 'Give us a standing army!' " A fantasy? "Those things which *can* be," the Presbyterian preacher David Caldwell said in the North Carolina convention, "*may* be." "I do not . . . say Congress *will* do" the evil he feared, Abraham Holmes of Plymouth County declared in the Massachusetts convention, "but, sir, I undertake to say that Congress . . . *may* do it; and if they do not, it will be owing *entirely* — I repeat it, it will be owing *entirely* — to the goodness of the men, and not in the *least degree* owing to the goodness of the Constitution." And the goodness of men being a hopelessly frail reed, evil possibilities must be eliminated at the start. A standing army, once established, will be uncontrollable.[25]

[25] "A Columbian Patriot" [Warren], *Observations, Doc. Hist.*, XVI, CC 581 (280); Mason, speech in the Virginia convention, Elliot, *Debates*, III, 378–381 (for the full

FULFILLMENT

Limitless taxation, corrupted representation, a specious sharing of sovereignty that would end in absolutism, standing armies — these were not new issues, but ancient issues that had been fought over a generation earlier in precisely the same terms and that had resulted in revolution. Similarly familiar — notorious — was the omission, in Article III, of jury trials in civil cases, a repudiation, it seemed to the antifederalists, of the central safeguard of common law procedure, reminiscent of the Crown's advancement of prerogative courts in its effort, in the 1760's and 1770's, to assert its power over the colonies. Familiar too was the issue of Congressmen paying their own salaries: "Before the Revolution," Dr. John Taylor told the Massachusetts convention, "it was considered as a grievance that the governors, etc., received their pay from Great Britain. They could not, in that case, feel their dependence on the people, when they received their appointments and salaries from the crown." Rawlins Lowndes, in South Carolina, objecting to the lack of popular control over Congressional salaries, had a vivid memory of the precedent, recalling "what a flame was raised in Massachusetts, on account of Great Britain assuming the payment of salaries to judges and other state officers; and that this conduct was considered as originating in a design to destroy the independence of their government."[26]

The fear of "secret services" money dispensed in covert operations by the executive through hidden slush funds — one of the Crown's most dangerous practices — was also revived, along

---

documentation of Mason's view of standing armies and the threat to militia troops, see Robert A. Rutland, ed., *Papers of George Mason, 1725–1792* [Chapel Hill, 1970], III, 1073–1081); Patrick Dollard, speech in the South Carolina convention, Elliot, *Debates,* IV, 338; "A Democratic Federalist," *Doc. Hist.,* XIII, CC 167 (390) — on Burgh, see above, p. 41 and references there; "Brutus," VIII, *Doc. Hist.,* XV, CC 437 (337–338); "Federal Farmer," III, *ibid.,* XIV, CC 242 (39); Caldwell, speech in the North Carolina convention, Elliot, *Debates,* IV, 62 (emphasis added); Holmes, speech in the Massachusetts convention, *ibid.,* II, 111 (emphasis in original).

[26] Taylor, speech in the Massachusetts convention, *ibid.,* II, 53; Lowndes, speech in the South Carolina convention, *ibid.,* IV, 289.

with the sense that the President's pardoning power was a legal re-creation of the ancient precept that the king can do no wrong. Like the King, the President, under Article II, Section 2, was empowered to pardon anyone "for offenses against the United States, except in cases of impeachment." So the President, George Mason wrote, could "screen from punishment those whom he had secretly instigated to commit the crime, and thereby prevent a discovery of his own guilt," a maneuver that would be the less dangerous for him since — Luther Martin pointed out — trials of Presidential impeachments were to be conducted by the Senate, "a privy council to the President" whose "leading and influential members may have advised or concurred in the very measures for which he may be impeached" — senators who would, in addition, still be hopeful of lucrative Presidential appointments. Such trials, moreover, were to be presided over by a chief justice nominated by the President "probably . . . not so much for his eminence in legal knowledge and for his integrity, as from favouritism and influence, since the President, knowing that in case of impeachment the chief justice is to preside at his trial, will naturally wish to fill that office with a person of whose voice and influence he shall consider himself secure."[27]

[27] William Symmes, Jr., to Peter Osgood, Jr., Andover, Mass., November 15, 1787, *Doc. Hist.*, XIV, CC 262, at 111; "Brutus," III, *ibid.*, CC 264 (123–124); Mason, "Objections to the Constitution," *ibid.*, CC 276A (151); Martin, *Genuine Information*, IX, *ibid.*, XV, CC 484 (496–497). Suppose, wrote "Cincinnatus" in his fifth essay (*ibid.*, XIV, CC 307), the Privy Council in England, the official advisory body to the king, "were vested with the sole power of trying impeachments. Would any man say that this would not render that body absolute, and impeachment, to all popular purposes, nugatory?" The most elaborate reply to Mason's and Martin's specific charges against the pardoning power was Iredell's "Marcus" III essay (*ibid.*, XVI, CC 596), in which he concedes that it is *possible* a President would pardon a co-conspirator to "prevent a discovery of his own guilt," but not probable, if only because the pardoned accomplice would then be free to testify against the President with no fear of retribution. Further, the President would be more, not less, exposed if he pardoned his accomplice than if he let the law take its course. In any case, against any possible danger the pardoning power might have, Iredell argued, must be put the necessity of protecting the nation's secret agents when revealed as collaborators by the enemy in time of war and subject to popular fury

FULFILLMENT

So the antifederalists' vision of the dangers they faced was deeply colored by their recollections of the past. "The same causes produces [sic] the same effects," a Massachusetts debater argued, recalling the Boston Massacre in a discussion of standing armies. Like Patrick Henry, they feared the anticipated creation of federal customs officers: "the experience of the mother country leads me to detest them." Like James Winthrop, in his eighteen-part "Agrippa" series, they recalled that at the heart of the disaster of British rule had been Parliament's effort to impose uniformity on the great variety of life in this distant periphery, an effort that would have to be repeated, catastrophically, by Congress and by the federal courts if the national government were in any degree to rule the diverse nation effectively. Artificial uniformity of any kind *would* be, just as it *had been,* disastrous: a uniform trade policy would destroy the successes of regional enterprise; a uniform naturalization law would violate the need either of some states to import people rapidly or of others "to keep their blood pure." And in the end any such effort would require the imposition of armed might, which would lead inevitably — as it always had in the past — to turmoil and civil war.[28]

It was all a familiar story, with a predictable outcome to people who had been through it all before. Amos Singletary — referred to affectionately as our "Honourable Old Daddy" by his colleagues in the Massachusetts ratifying convention — reminded the delegates that he had been "on the stage in the beginning of our troubles, in the year 1775," and *he* recalled,

---

for their apparent treason. No one else — neither the courts nor the juries — could rescue such a "useful but dishonourable character"; for him, the "prerogative of mercy in the chief magistrate of a great country ought to be at hand." See also "Impartial Citizen," V, *Doc. Hist.,* VIII, 428–430; *Federalist* LXIX and LXXIV [Hamilton], *ibid.,* XVI, CC 617, 644.

[28] Samuel Nasson, speech in the Massachusetts convention, Elliot, *Debates,* II, 137; Henry, speech in the Virginia convention, *ibid.,* III, 147; "Agrippa" [Winthrop], IV, V, and esp. VI and VII, in Ford, *Essays,* pp. 63 ff., quotation from IX, 79.

even if no one else did, precisely what had happened. If, at that time, he declared, "any body had proposed such a constitution as this . . . it would have been thrown away at once. It would not have been looked at." For could not Congress under the Constitution do precisely what people like himself had gone to war to prevent — assert a limitless right to tax and to "bind us in all cases whatever"? So they cited leading documents of the pre-Revolutionary debates. They quoted Stephen Hopkins' *Rights of Colonies Examined,* John Dickinson's *Farmer's Letters,* James Burgh's *Political Disquisitions,* Hutchinson's debates with the Massachusetts Assembly; and they invoked the ancient deities — Hampden, Sidney, Pym, Wilkes — and denounced the ancient villains — Hutchinson, Hillsborough, Bute, even those fabled apologists of "passive obedience and non-resistance" in the time of Charles I, Robert Sibthorpe and Roger Mainwaring.[29]

But the historical dimension of the antifederalists' condemnation of the Constitution had a subtler and more powerful element. One unquestionably fundamental belief in the received tradition which had been brought into focus during the pre-Revolutionary struggle with Britain was the conviction that the only truly free states were republics, where people ruled themselves through freely elected representatives; that republics, necessarily delicate structures, could survive only in small units since they required uniformity of opinion, or at least a rough consensus, force being necessary to control clangorous diversity; and that the animating principle of republics was virtue. The ultimate sources of these ideas they rarely cited. Their chief

---

[29] Singletary, speech in the Massachusetts convention, Elliot, *Debates,* II, 101; *United States Chronicle* (Providence, R.I.), August 5, 1788 (quoting Hopkins); "An Old Whig," III (referring to "the publications of the years 1774, 1775, 1776, and 1777"), *Doc. Hist.,* XIII, CC 181; "Centinel," II, III, *ibid.,* CC 190; XIV, CC 243; Robert Whitehill, speech in the Pennsylvania convention, *ibid.,* II, 527; on Burgh, n. 25 above; Henry, speeches in the Virginia convention, Elliot, *Debates,* III, 396, 411; "A Columbian Patriot" [Warren], *Doc. Hist.,* XVI, CC 581 (esp. 281–282). Cf. above, pp. 28–29, 53.

authority, insofar as they needed any authority to document what seemed to them such obvious ideas, was Montesquieu, whose name recurs far more often than that of any other authority in all of the vast literature on the Constitution. He was the fountainhead, the ultimate arbiter of belief, his ideas the standard by which all others were set. They reverted to his authority at every turn, and through his eyes saw the moral impossibility of creating a massive republic.

For the antifederalists, no less than the federalists, had a thoroughly realistic sense of human nature, and never deluded themselves that any people could be entirely virtuous or that any political population could be principally animated by public spirit. Patrick Henry, the most ardent of the antifederalist spokesmen, based his philosophy of government on the universal force and moral validity of what he called "self-love." It is the heart of his most passionate and eloquent oration, which lasted for two days in the Virginia convention — a speech that must have been electrifying when Henry reached his peroration: "Must I give my soul, my lungs, to Congress? Congress must have our souls; the state must have our souls. This is dishonorable and disgraceful."

The devil in it all, he declared, was the *implied* powers of the "necessary and proper" clause combined with the innate evil of human nature. "Implication is dangerous because it is unbounded: if it be admitted at all, and no limits be prescribed, it admits of the utmost extension" because the lust for power, the passion for dominance, will exploit every possibility. Constitutional checks and balances cannot possibly eliminate or even effectively constrain the evil of human nature. The only counterforce that counts, Henry said, is "self-love."

Tell me not of checks on paper; but tell me of checks founded on self-love . . . fair, disinterested patriotism and professions of attachment to rectitude have never been solely trusted to by an enlightened, free people. If you depend on your President's and Senators' patriotism, you are gone . . . The real rock of political salvation is self-love, perpetuated from age to age in every human breast and manifested in every action. If they can stand the temptations of human nature, you are safe . . . there is no danger. But can this be expected from human nature? Without real checks, it will not suffice that some of them are good . . . the wicked will be continually watching: consequently you will be undone . . . I dread the depravity of human nature . . . I will never depend on so slender a protection as the possibility of being represented by virtuous men.

Britain's freedom has survived, Henry concluded, not because of the people's virtue but because the monarch's "self-love, [his] self-interest," coincides with the advancement of the nation's prosperity. The monarch remains monarch for life, and his narrowest self-interest is therefore nourished by the nation's successes and good fortune. But "the President and Senators have nothing to lose. They have not that interest in the preservation of the government that the kings and lords have in England. They will, therefore, be regardless of the interests of the people."[30]

Henry's language was peculiarly his own, but his belief that "man is a fallen creature, a fallible being" was universal among the antifederalists. His colleague Mason, "considering the natural lust of power so inherent in man," feared above all that "the thirst of power will prevail to oppress the people." In North Carolina, one antifederalist said "the depravity of mankind" militates against any confidence that the people's representatives would have sufficient virtue and wisdom to regulate affairs properly, another that "it is the nature of mankind to be tyrannical" and hence he feared "the depravity of human nature, the predominant thirst for power which is in the breast of everyone." And in New York the pseudonymous "Cato" wrote that

[30] Henry, speech in the Virginia convention, Elliot, *Debates,* III, 148, 149, 164, 165, 327. For another antifederalist's similar view of "the principle of self-love," see "Brutus," IV, *Doc. Hist.,* XIV, CC 306; for a federalist's version, see "A Countryman" [Roger Sherman], II, *Doc. Hist.,* XIV, CC 284.

"ambition and voluptuousness aided by flattery will teach magistrates . . . to have separate and distinct interests from the people," a sentiment stated with even greater force by other antifederalists in that state, in Massachusetts, and in South Carolina.[31]

It was because of their fear of human depravity, of mankind's selfish neglect of the public good and passionate devotion to the narrowest self-interest, that the antifederalists were certain that an extended republic, of continental dimensions, could never survive as a free state and would end either as a military dictatorship or as a junta of ruthless aristocrats. The logic of this process was variously expounded, variously phrased, but the conclusion was everywhere the same and always derived from the same received tradition of pre-Revolutionary thought. For most, it was largely a matter of citing what "Brutus," in the first of his notable series to the people of New York, called "the opinion of the greatest and wisest men who have ever thought or wrote on the science of government," principally Montesquieu, whose classic formulation in *The Spirit of the Laws* he quoted:

"It is natural to a republic to have only a small territory, otherwise it cannot long subsist. In a large republic there are men of large fortunes, and consequently of less moderation . . . he has interest of his own; he soon begins to think that he may be happy, great and glorious by oppressing his fellow citizens, and that he may raise himself to grandeur on the ruins of his country. In a large republic, the public good is sacrificed to a thousand views . . . In a small one, the interest of the public is easier perceived, better understood, and more within the reach of every citizen; abuses are of less extent, and of course are less protected."

[31] Mason, speech in the Virginia convention, Elliot, *Debates,* III, 32; speeches of Joseph McDowell and William Lenoir in the North Carolina convention, *ibid.,* IV, 150, 203–204; "Cato," V, *Doc. Hist.,* XIV, CC 286; Charles Turner, speech in the Massachusetts convention, Elliot, *Debates,* II, 30–32; Patrick Dollard, speech in the South Carolina convention, *ibid.,* IV, 337. Cf. Paine, *Common Sense,* quoted above, p. 143, and "A Georgian," *Doc. Hist.,* III, 236.

A sentiment, "Brutus" said, concurred in by Beccaria, exemplified by Greek and Roman history, and simply self-evident. It was perfectly, palpably, logical. A free republic, he patiently explained, must be ruled by laws written by the representatives of the people.

> Now, in a large extended country it is impossible to have a representation possessing the sentiments . . . to declare the minds of the people without having it so numerous and unwieldly as to be subject in great measure to the inconveniency of a democratic government. The territory of the United States is of vast extent . . . Is it practicable for a country so large and so numerous as they will soon become to elect a representation that will speak their sentiments without their becoming so numerous as to be incapable of transacting public business? It certainly is not.

And he went on to discourse on the varieties of climate, economic interests, religion, manners, and habits of the vast and scattered American population which might, he thought, one day far in the future, reach a total of 30 million souls.[32]

Others developed variations on this basic theme. For "Cato," who quoted the same passage of *The Spirit of the Laws* and cited the same examples from classical antiquity (examples helpfully furnished by Montesquieu), agreed with "Brutus," but added that factionalism in an extended republic would lead inevitably to a standing army. For factionalism would produce the threat of secession, and that in turn would require the creation of "a permanent force, to be kept on foot" in order to preserve the state, a necessity created also by the difficulty of executing revenue laws, always the source of opposition to a government, "on the extremes" of the extended realm. Where a military force ruled, "will not political security, and even the opinion of it, be extinguished? Can mildness and moderation exist in a government where the primary incident in its exercise must be force?

---

[32] "Brutus," I, *ibid.*, XIII, CC 178, quotations at 417, 418. For an identical argument, see "Agrippa" [Winthrop], IV, in Ford, *Essays,* pp. 63–65.

Will not violence destroy confidence . . . ?" The "Federal Farmer" had more dramatic apprehensions. In a huge republic, the legislative body would be an uncontrollable mob, and the effectiveness of the sprawling court system would dissipate on the far-flung frontier, so that the rule of law would survive inversely with the distance from the seat of government. The result? "Either neglected laws, or a military execution of them . . . Neglected laws must first lead to anarchy and confusion; and a military execution of laws is only a shorter way to the same point — despotic government." For James Winthrop the issue came down to the inevitable violation of local interests by a nation-state of continental size. And for George Mason it was simply a matter of recorded history. In the whole of history, he declared, "there never was a government over a very extensive country without destroying the liberties of the people . . . popular governments can only exist in small territories. Is there a single example on the face of the earth to support a contrary opinion?"[33]

Upon all of this, rooted in fears formulated in the pre-Revolutionary past, the antifederalists mounted their assault on the Constitution. The newspapers teemed with their condemnations of a constitution that would legalize vast governmental powers, and failed even to include a bill of rights that might stand as a protector of the individual liberties that had been won in the Revolution and that the national government was now being empowered to destroy. Nothing was more unaccountable to them than the absence of a bill of rights in a constitution known to be a design for a government potentially far more powerful than any the American people had ever known before. The federalists' argument that *all* rights were

[33] "Cato," III, *Doc. Hist.*, XIII, CC 195; "Federal Farmer," II, *ibid.*, XIV, CC 244, quotation at 29; "Agrippa" [Winthrop], esp. VII, in Ford, *Essays*, p. 73; Mason, speech in the Virginia convention, Elliot, *Debates*, III, 30. For the use of Montesquieu as the great authority on such matters, see Paul M. Spurlin, *Montesquieu in America, 1760–1801* (University, La., 1940), chap. vi.

reserved to the people because government would have only specified powers made little impression on them. Nor did the claim that if you enumerate rights you limit them to those you happen to list, or the argument that "parchment barriers," a few words on a piece of paper, had never yet prevented anyone in authority from exercising undue power. The antifederalists continued to believe that government *would,* inevitably, infringe on personal rights, that if rights were not specified but simply assumed to exist, in the end it would be up to someone in government to say, in any given situation, what precisely the rights were that should be protected; and that would mean that those who controlled the government could constitutionally silence anyone who disagreed simply by refusing to recognize the rights they claimed.

Did no one know history? Patrick Henry asked. Did no one recall that in Britain the people and the Crown had struggled for a century over the uncertainties of *implied* rights until the matter had finally been settled in the acceptance of an *explicit* bill of rights — and that that had been precisely the first thing that the American people had thought of when they were faced with the necessity of protecting themselves against Parliament's power? Given the powers accorded the new national government in the Constitution, it was said time after time, unless there were a bill of rights,

we are totally insecure in all of them; and no man can promise himself with any degree of certainty that his posterity will enjoy the inestimable blessings of liberty of conscience, of freedom of speech and of writing and publishing their thoughts on public matters, of trial by jury, of holding themselves, their houses and papers free from seizure and search upon general suspicion or general warrants; or in short that they will be secured in the enjoyment of life, liberty and property without depending on the will and pleasure of their rulers.

The whole system, the "Federal Farmer" insisted — and with him almost every other antifederalist — should be "bottomed" on a bill of rights that declared the people's "unalienable and fundamental rights" in such a way as to set limits to the power of government and to serve as an alarm when legislators and rulers overreached their proper bounds.[34]

3

Such was the challenge that faced the federalist leaders in the ratification struggle. Their task was complex. They had, first, to convince doubters that the existing situation under the Articles of Confederation was disastrous, verging on chaos, and that only a radical strengthening of the powers of the central government would solve the nation's problems. They had, next, to explain the details of the proposed government and show how it met the current needs without destroying the liberties America had fought for, and without injuring local interests, at least in the long run. Somehow, too, they had to prove that in the mechanics of government the new nation-state would not absorb or otherwise destroy the state governments, which were seen as the protectors of the people's liberties.

But beyond all of that they had an overriding problem. They had to reach back into the sources of the received tradition, confront the ancient, traditional fears that had lain at the heart of the ideological origins of the Revolution, and identify and reexamine the ancient formulations that stood in the way of the present necessities: take these ideas and apprehensions apart and where necessary rephrase them, reinterpret them — not reject them in favor of a new paradigm, a new structure of thought, but reapply them and bring them up to date. They did not leave the cave, they corrected it. They would have been astonished to hear that they were initiating a change from something scholars would later call "civic humanism" or "classical republicanism"

[34] Henry, speech in the Virginia convention, *ibid.*, p. 150; "An Old Whig," V, *Doc. Hist.*, XIII, CC 224; "Federal Farmer," II, *ibid.*, XIV, CC 242, quotation at 27.

to another, something that would be called "liberalism," or that they were chiefly interested in preserving patrician rule derived from the older tradition. They were neither more nor less determined to protect private property as a foundation of personal freedom and to advance economic enterprise than their predecessors and opponents, and they were no less committed to the need for disinterested "virtue" in government. Both they and their opponents were working within the broad pattern of political thought inherited from the early days of the Revolution, but the urgencies the federalists felt led them to reassess the impediments to the creation of a national state which they found embedded in that enveloping tradition.

This could not easily be done. Aside from the intellectual demands of thinking through the ancient formulations, the task required imagination, boldness, freedom from fear. One of the most revealing themes that runs through the voluminous writings of the federalists is the exhortation to rise to the extraordinary occasion before them by thinking freshly and fearlessly about the problems they faced, and above all not to brood on groundless fears, not to view every change as the stroke of doom and imagine catastrophe around every corner. Catastrophe will be found everywhere, Timothy Pickering warned, "if we give a loose to our imaginations." "Where in the name of common sense," Hamilton wrote,

are our fears to end if we may not trust our sons, our brothers, our neighbours, our fellow-citizens? What shadow of danger can there be from men who are daily mingling with the rest of their countrymen and who participate with them in the same feelings, sentiments, habits, and interests? . . . In reading many of the publications against the Constitution a man is apt to imagine that he is perusing some ill written tale or romance which, instead of natural and agreeable images, exhibits to the mind nothing but frightful and distorted shapes — gorgons, hydras, and chimeras dire — discoloring and disfiguring whatever it represents and transforming every thing it touches into a monster.

"Events merely possible," Hamilton said on another occasion, "have been magnified by distempered imagination into inevitable realities, and the most distant and doubtful conjectures have been formed into a serious and infallible prediction." Stop thinking in extremes, he warned; don't abandon a wise government for "a fantastical Utopia." And don't argue "against a measure from a remote possibility of its being abused. Human sagacity cannot devise any law but what, in its operations, may in some instances bear hard." But it was not easy to purge the antifederalists of what Judge Hanson called their "trumpery of fictions" and what Hamilton insisted was their hopeless infatuation with "halcyon scenes of the poetic or fabulous age." A mind like R. H. Lee's, a writer in Virginia declared, "which delights . . . to indulge itself in *political reveries,* is capable of conceiving any idea, however absurd, and being startled by any danger, however visionary." Madison, as always, spoke soberly and succinctly: "We must limit our apprehensions," he said quietly in the Virginia debates, "to certain degrees of probabil ity," and then in a passage of what was for him extreme rhetoric, he sought to switch the role of the imagination from stirring up morbid fantasies of impending doom to assisting in the construction of "a government for posterity." "Hearken not," he wrote in one of the early *Federalist* papers,

to the voice which petulantly tells you that the form of government recommended for your adoption is a novelty in the political world . . . shut your ears against this unhallowed language. Shut your hearts against the poison which it conveys . . . Is it not the glory of the people of America that whilst they have paid a decent regard to the opinions of former times and other nations, they have not suffered a blind veneration for antiquity, for custom, or for names to overrule the suggestions of their own good sense, the knowledge of their own situation, and the lessons of their own experience?

. . . Had no important step been taken by the leaders of the Revolution for which a precedent could not be discovered, no government established of which an exact model did not present itself, the people of the United States might, at this moment, have been numbered among the melancholy victims of misguided councils, must at best have been labouring under the weight of some of those forms which have crushed the liberties of the rest of mankind.[35]

It was with these injunctions in mind — to dismiss morbid fears of impending doom and to think ahead imaginatively but also realistically — that the federalists turned to the major problems their inheritance had created for them. Some of the problems were blatant, glaring. They were creating a national army, distinct from the state militias. But would these national troops not be, as the antifederalists claimed, the bloodthirsty, venal janissaries, the dreaded palace guards that Americans had been endlessly warned of and which they believed they had themselves confronted in the Revolutionary War? The question had to be answered.

For Noah Webster, commissioned publicist of the federalist cause, the question was simply unreal: "the principles and habits of the Americans are directly opposed to standing armies; and there is as little necessity to guard against them by positive constitutions as to prohibit the establishment of the Mahometan religion." Is Mahometanism prohibited in the state constitutions? No. And is Christianity in danger as a consequence? Do the states outlaw standing armies? No (with a couple of exceptions). And is civilian government in the states threatened by military coups d'état?

But the venerable arguments could not simply be dismissed out of hand. The issue had to be carefully considered. All national, peacetime armies, Tench Coxe explained a month after

---

[35] Pickering to Charles Tillinghast, Philadelphia, December 24, 1787, *ibid.*, CC 288C (197); *Federalist* XXIX [Hamilton], *ibid.*, XV, CC 429; Hamilton, speech in the New York convention, Elliot, *Debates*, II, 262–263, 320; "Impartial Citizen," V, *Doc. Hist.*, VIII, 428; "Aristides" [Hanson], *Remarks, ibid.*, XV, CC 490A (536); *Federalist* XXX [Hamilton], *ibid.*, CC 391 (164); "Cassius," in *Virginia Independent Chronicle*, April 2, 1788; Madison, speech in the Virginia convention, Elliot, *Debates*, III, 433; *Federalist* XIV [Madison], *Doc. Hist.*, XIV, CC 310.

the Constitution had been unveiled, are *not* "standing armies." The American army would have no existence aside from the people's will, since military appropriations were to last for only two years and to be made by the House of Representatives, *"the immediate delegates of the people."* Further, the army would have no monopoly of military force. The state militias would not only "form a *powerful check* upon the regular troops, and will generally be sufficient *to overawe them"* but will make a large national army unnecessary — which would be so in any case because of America's *"detached* situation" geographically. Finally, he said, there is all the difference in the world "between the troops of such a commonwealth as ours, *founded on equal and unalterable principles,* and those of a regal government, where ambition and oppression are *the profession of the king."* In a free state a military officer is simply *"the occasional servant of the people, employed for their defence";* in a monarchy he is always the instrument of the schemes of oppression or conquest which obsess the mind of his royal master.[36]

These were the main themes, but other writers sought to focus more sharply on the crux. "The fallacy lies here," Timothy Pickering wrote: in Europe large standing armies exist to maintain the power of absolute and hereditary monarchs and therefore by definition "are instruments to keep the people in slavery." An army in America would serve only to protect the people who themselves maintain it through representatives who would share in any suffering such troops might create. In Britain "the armies are *his* [the King's] *armies,* and their direction is solely by him without any control . . . Here the army, when raised, is the army of the people." Judge Hanson, who condemned the "clamour against standing armies" as "a mere pretext for terrifying you, like children, with spectres and hobgob-

---

[36] [Noah Webster], *An Examination into the Leading Principles of the Federal Constitution . . . by a Citizen of America* (Philadelphia, [1787]), in Ford, *Pamphlets,* p. 52; "An American Citizen" [Coxe], IV, *Doc. Hist.,* XIII, CC 183A.

blins," touched on another, more pragmatic point which became a standard federalist argument. If there were no standby national army, one would have to be created overnight in the case of sudden invasion or other emergencies, and it might well prove to be too little and too late. If the only armed force were the militia, Francis Corbin elaborated in the Virginia convention, the results would be either a disastrous neglect of farming or a fatal ignorance and incompetence in arms. But the militia would be *part* of the nation's armed might, and that mixture of a citizen militia and a professional national army was vital. Either alone, Wilson Nicholas argued in the Virginia convention, would be a danger: an unemployed standing army would be a public menace, a militia would in itself be wholly incapable of stopping an invasion by a "powerful, disciplined army." Further, a militia army would favor the rich, who could buy substitutes for personal service, and burden the poor, who could not. So let the rich bear the burden of financing the professional army, and the poor the burden of services when needed. The result of such a mixed military establishment will be military competence and no danger, the ideal situation which the Constitution had designed.[37]

It is in the context of this wide-ranging reexamination of the ancient threat of standing armies that Hamilton's discussion of the subject in a series of well-known *Federalist* papers can best be understood. It is clear at once that much of what he wrote was commonplace. He too stressed America's physical isolation, which would not necessitate a large army, any more than Britain's island situation had required one. And he too stressed the concurrent and yet competitive role that the state militias would have. But his writing on this subject is nevertheless unique.

[37] Pickering to Tillinghast, *ibid.,* XIV, CC 288C (203); Samuel Holden Parsons to William Cushing, Middletown, Conn., January 11, 1788, *ibid.,* III, 570; "Aristides" [Hanson], *Remarks, ibid.,* XV, CC 490A (532); "Marcus" [Iredell], IV, *ibid.,* XVI, CC 616 (385); Corbin and Nicholas, speeches in the Virginia convention, Elliot, *Debates,* III, 112–113, 389–390.

Cutting through the visionary fears, the "gorgons, hydras, and chimeras dire," he analyzed the real, operative process by which military power, in the projected constitutional system, could become a threat.

How, he asked, could a danger actually — not theoretically — arise? Suppose a President were determined to build a janissary army to suppress liberty. How could it be done? Short of a complete coup d'état, such an army could be created only "by progressive augmentations" of Congressional appropriations, which would take time and would require that a conspiracy between executive and legislature be sustained through successive transformations in the representative body. Now, can one realistically believe that that could happen? Would an incoming Congressman instantly "commence a traitor to his constituents and to his country"? Would no one be shrewd enough "to detect so attrocious a conspiracy, or bold or honest enough to apprise his constituents of their danger"? If that were really the case, one should forget about representation and live under governments no larger than counties. And beyond all that, how could such a plot, developed over years, be concealed? What benign excuse could be convincingly given for such a visible buildup? None would make sense. In fact the people would not be deceived, and the project and its projectors would be quickly destroyed.

Hamilton, and other federalists following him, did not dismiss the danger of standing armies — the ancient fear persisted: "I am a mortal enemy to standing armies," one of the federalists' most fervent defenders of the armed forces clauses of the Constitution concluded, "in time of peace particularly." Their aim was to show, by close analysis, that while a national army was necessary, the *regular* army of the United States would not — could not — be a *"standing"* army in the traditional sense. If it ever became that, freedom would already — for other, deeper reasons — have been destroyed: at that point "there will not be a particle of virtue in the people; they will be ripe for the most corrupt government."[38]

This hardheaded realism was the essence of the federalists' response to the opposition. Point by point they took on the objections based on inherited notions and probed their applicability in the American situation.

The key doctrine of federalism could survive criticism only to the extent that it could somehow be distinguished from the ancient belief that *imperium in imperio* was an illogical and unresolvable solecism. So they reexamined that old formula, took it apart, and showed, not its falsity, but its irrelevance in the American situation. The antifederalists, Hamilton wrote, obsessed with "artificial distinctions and syllogistic subtleties," reiterated the ancient maxim that *imperium in imperio* is a "political monster." But in operation, he wrote, the states and the national governments would not clash. The "supreme law of the land" clause would have the effect of linking the states' officers, no less than the nation's officers, to the enforcement of federal law and hence lead to a functional merger of — not conflict between — the two levels of authority. There would be no fatal clash, as "Brutus" feared, between the taxing powers of states and nation. The nation's taxing power is specified, and under Article I, Section 10, the states retained all other taxing powers. The two governments would intersect only where they exercised *concurrent* powers, and *concurrence* is not the *repugnancy* that lay at the heart of the ancient precept. Simple prudence and "reciprocal forbearances" would permit a harmonious relationship, and if the national government invaded areas of taxation reserved to the states, such action would be void, and the people would make this clear.[39]

[38] *Federalist* VIII and XXVI [Hamilton], *Doc. Hist.*, XIV, CC 274; XV, CC 366; "An Impartial Citizen," VI, *ibid.*, VIII, 498.
[39] *Federalist* XXII, XV, XXVII, XXXII–XXXIII [Hamilton], *ibid.*, XIV, CC 347, 312; XV, CC 378, 405.

FULFILLMENT

Oliver Ellsworth, the future chief justice, cut deeper into the problem and, in the course of a remarkable address in the Connecticut ratifying convention, explained the essential role of judicial review in resolving the ancient problem. It is said, Ellsworth declared, that Congress and the states cannot coexist in legislative powers. "I ask, *why* can they not? It is not enough to *say* that they cannot. I wish for some reason." There is no more reason for them to conflict than there is for New York City's laws to conflict with those of New York State or London's with Britain's. But, he then said, in a classic statement of judicial review,

if the general legislature should at any time overleap their limits, the judicial department is a constitutional check. If the United States go beyond their powers, if they make a law which the Constitution does not authorize, it is void; and the judicial power, the national judges, who to secure their impartiality are to be made independent, will declare it to be void. On the other hand, if the states go beyond their limits, if they make a law which is an usurpation upon the general government, the law is void, and upright independent judges will declare it to be so.

And all the federalists agreed that the law would be enforced not against states (that would be civil war and would involve the innocent along with the guilty) but against individual people, who collectively were the very source of the authority under which the government would be acting. If that were not the case, Madison wrote at the end of a learned discourse on the political miseries of the United Netherlands, then you would indeed have the hopeless situation of "a sovereignty over sovereigns, a government over governments, a legislation for communities as contradistinguished from individuals" which, just "as it is a solecism in theory, so in practice it is subversive of the order and ends of civil polity, by substituting *violence* in place of *law,* or the destructive *coertion* of the *sword* in place of the mild and salutary *coertion* of the *magistracy*." The ancient pre-

359

cept was not wrong; it did not apply. The Constitution simply avoided the dangers of dual sovereignties, real as they were.[40]

But federalism as a solution to the venerable problem of dual sovereignties was part of a larger issue: the theoretical problem of creating a republic of large, potentially continental size. To the vehement antifederalist insistence, drawn directly from the received tradition, that almost every authority and the entire experience of mankind proved that republics could survive only as small-scale polities, the federalists countered, first, that the national government had only limited and specified powers; the states, which retained all the rest, remained republics of small dimensions; and it would be the states that would continue to regulate the affairs of everyday life. But they themselves recognized the limits of this argument: national law would be supreme where it applied and therefore the national government would have effective power over the use of coercive force, over justice, and over the economy. So they turned to the ancient precept itself, probed its logic and validity, and ended by demonstrating its irrelevance for the American system.

Their mood was typified by Edmund Randolph's remark in the Virginia convention that he was not impressed "that some of the most illustrious and distinguished authors" said that republicanism is impractical in a country of large extent: "I reply, that authority has no weight with me till I am convinced that, not the dignity of names but the force of reasoning, gains my assent." The famous examples and analogies — Switzerland, particularly — did not apply.

---

[40] Ellsworth, speech in the Connecticut convention, *ibid.*, XV, CC 420 (278–279, emphasis added) — cf. above, n. 13; *Federalist* XX [Madison], *ibid.*, XIV, CC 340. Madison's view of federalism as a fulfillment and resolution of the ancient fear of dual sovereignty was a commonplace in federalist thought. Thus the Connecticut lawyer Samuel Holden Parsons, writing a month after the publication of *Federalist* XX, expressed the same idea in similar words, explaining that dual sovereignty is a political absurdity only when both powers are "coextensive in their objects." Towns, surely, or counties have legislative powers *for some purposes:* does that mean a state cannot exist and legislate too? Parsons to Cushing, January 11, 1788 (above, n. 37), p. 573.

The extent and situation of that country [Switzerland] is totally different from ours; their country is surrounded by powerful, ambitious,
and reciprocally jealous nations; their territory small, and soil not very
fertile.

He was convinced that if American laws were made with integrity and executed with wisdom, the extent of the country would
be no problem. Francis Corbin too, in the same debate, rejected
what he called the "old worn-out idea that a republican government is best calculated for a small territory . . . How small
must a country be to suit the genius of republicanism? In what
particular extent of country can a republican government exist? . . . Too small an extent will render a republic weak, vulnerable, and contemptible. Liberty, in such a petty state, must be
on a precarious footing; its existence must depend on the philan-
thropy and good nature of its neighbors." He believed that the
centralized national government would tend to concentrate and
conciliate conflicting opinions within a single forum, better organized and disciplined than thirteen scattered policy-making
bodies attempting to fuse their formulated views into a national
policy. And yet the heterogeneity would guarantee that a majority would never concur sufficiently to oppress a minority. Hamilton too asked how small a country must be to satisfy Montesquieu's prescription. If you think about it carefully, Hamilton
said, the dimensions Montesquieu must have had in mind were
far short of those of the present states. Did the antifederalists
now propose, accordingly, to split up the states "into an infinity
of little jealous, clashing, tumultuous commonwealths, the
wretched nurseries of unceasing discord and the miserable objects of universal pity or contempt"? What an "infatuated policy" that would be — what "a desperate expedient."[41]

But these were general and vague approaches to a problem
that required much more specific formulations. The American

---

[41] Randolph and Corbin, speeches in the Virginia convention, Elliot, *Debates,* III, 85,
69, 107, 108; *Federalist* IX, *Doc. Hist.,* XIV, CC 277 (160).

nation, it was quickly pointed out, would not be a singular but a compound entity, a *confederate* republic, each unit of which (the states) would be relatively small yet the whole large enough to protect itself and serve the society's common needs. True, as James Wilson said, creating a "confederate republic . . . left us almost without precedent or guide, and consequently without the benefit of that instruction which in many cases may be derived from the constitution and history and experience of other nations." For the Swiss and Dutch examples, he agreed, were irrelevant; so too were the examples of classical antiquity. But the *theory,* at least, of confederate republics was not unknown. Montesquieu himself, Hamilton pointed out early in the debate, had developed the idea as a way of "extending the sphere of popular government and reconciling the advantages of monarchy with those of republicanism." And he had also suggested an example of " 'an excellent confederate republic,' " namely, the Lycian (c. second century B.C.), whose central body had in fact had "the most delicate species of interference in [the individual states'] internal administration." That strange conglomeration of cities and republics was, however, a very strained example or parallel; nevertheless, the theory of confederate republics was valid — for reasons the ancients and Montesquieu could never have conceived of. For America alone had developed fully the "vital principle" of representation — "the chain of communication between the people and those to whom they had committed the exercise of the powers of government." And that principle rendered all earlier considerations of size irrelevant. Representation made possible a perfect compromise: a confederated state large enough to protect itself but small enough to retain the freedoms of a republic.[42]

[42] Wilson, speech in the Pennsylvania convention, *ibid.,* II, 352–353, 355; *Federalist* IX [Hamilton], *ibid.,* XIV, CC 277; see also Bowdoin, speech in the Massachusetts convention, Elliot, *Debates,* II, 128. For more on Montesquieu's concept of a confederated republic as a possible solution to the problem of size, see Spurlin, *Montesquieu,* pp. 196–200.

These were singular notes in a developing harmony of opinion. The great crescendo was eventually sounded at a higher level by Madison and Hamilton in several of their most famous *Federalist* papers — but they were preceded by John Stevens' premonitory "Americanus" papers. Stevens, a New Jersey lawyer who would later frame the first patent laws and attain fame as an engineer and developer of steam transport, attacked the insistence that "the axioms of Montesquieu, Locke, etc., in the science of politics are as irrefragable as any in Euclid," and ridiculed the idea of hunting for precedents in Europe. It would be "downright madness to shackle ourselves with maxims and principles which are clearly inapplicable to the nature of our political institutions. The path we are pursuing is new, and has never before been trodden by man." It was the venerated ancient theorists, the systematizers, who posed the most difficult problems. To concede to their "maxims and principles . . . would be an unpardonable indiscretion." What mattered most was America's unique historical experience. Montesquieu's ideas, after all, had been formed in the Old World: "Had he been an American, and now living, I would stake my life on it, he would have formed different principles."

In the new nation, Stevens explained, representation — "the hinge on which all republican governments must move" — will obviate the confusions of democracy in a state of large size, and bicameralism and the "revisory power" of the executive and judiciary will further inhibit the development of the "turbulent spirit." But there were deeper reasons for seeing the large size of a republican nation as a positive advantage. "The gusts of passion," Stevens wrote, twenty days before the publication of Madison's *Federalist* X, destructive in a small territory, dissipate in a large state. Small republics

ever have been, and, from the nature of man, ever will be, liable to be torn to pieces by faction. When the citizens are confined within a narrow compass, as was the case of Sparta, Rome, etc., it is within the power of a factious demagogue to scatter sedition and discontent instantaneously thro' every part of the state.

But in an extensive federal system like that of the United States, factions lose their force before they reach the seat of government. "The different powers are so modified and distributed as to form mutual checks upon each other," thus preventing a plebiscitarian upheaval. The people at large will not need to maintain eternal vigilance. Their representatives and the internal checks of the system itself will do the job for them, and therefore all that is required of the people is to participate in frequent elections and attend closely to their own personal interests. The American government, for its success, will require

nothing more of its subjects than that they should study and pursue merely their own true interest and happiness . . . A government thus founded on the broad basis of human nature, like a tree which is suffered to retain its native shape, will flourish for ages with little care or attention.

In this vein Stevens' ideas developed, fructified, in complex ways. Feeling his way through venerable Old World precedents that he felt obliged to reconsider — to think through, test, and where necessary reformulate — he ridiculed the idea that analogies between Britain and America were useful except insofar as both nations' histories prove that "it is impossible to subjugate a numerous and free people spread over a wide extent of country without the intervention and concurrence of adventitious and extrinsic causes." He condemned again and again the "faction, instability, and frequent revolutions" inherent in small republics and argued that large republics can contain and control insurrections better than small ones, and thereafter can create reconciliation more readily. He denied that there were more abrasive interests in large states than in small and declared that an "infinite number and variety of distinct and jarring interests . . . necessarily prevail among the individuals of a society in a state of civilization." If the government does not serve to reconcile these clashing interests, "I say there is an end of every thing . . . we must then relinquish all our ideas of the efficiency of government as mere chimeras."[43]

Stevens, of course, was no Madison or Hamilton. But like both of them he pounded away at the necessity of reconsidering inherited formulations, testing them for their applicability in the American setting, and excoriated utopianism and self-validating theorizing. His one favorable citation of Montesquieu is a passage in which the Frenchman disparaged Harrington, whom Stevens himself attacked directly together with Plato and Thomas More for having "amused themselves with forming visionary schemes of perfected governments . . . no better than romances." Hamilton, equally blistering on abstract, systematic speculation, pointed out that the tiny republics of classical antiquity were in fact scenes of constant and often fatal squabbling; only the larger confederacies had any stability. And as for the fear that law and order would be unenforceable on America's far borderlands, that, he said, was "a palpable illusion of the imagination." People on the borderlands will be equally well represented in the central government, will be equally well informed on the effectiveness of their representatives in serving their interests, and in addition their interests will be vigilantly protected by the state governments, if only "from the rivalship of power." But beyond all that, Hamilton wrote, there is the simple fact that distance will not create different interests in kind:

the citizens who inhabit the country at and near the seat of government will, in all questions that affect the general liberty and prosperity, have the same interest with those who are at a distance; and . . . will

[43] Stevens' seven "Americanus" essays, not yet included in the *Doc. Hist.* series, were published in the *New York Daily Advertiser,* November 2, 23, 30; December 5–6, 12, 1787; and January 12, 21, 1788. The quotations and specific citations in the text are from nos. I–IV, VI.

stand ready to sound the alarm when necessary, and to point out the actors in any pernicious project. The public papers will be expeditious messengers of intelligence to the most remote inhabitants of the union.[44]

But it was left to Madison — first in his extraordinary letter to Jefferson (October 24, 1787) and then in two of his finest *Federalist* papers (X and LI) — to give this whole line of argument its ultimate range, depth, and intellectual elegance.[45] He did not simply assume faction and interest; most commentators, antifederalists as well as federalists, did that.[46] He defined them, and showed that they were "sown in the nature of man," manifested particularly in the inescapable inequalities in the distribution of property. Then he logically reduced the possibility of coping with faction to controlling its effects, and demonstrated that this would be possible only in extended republics. This was so, he argued, partly because America's unique electoral system would tend to produce local representatives of "most attractive merit and the most . . . established characters" capable of grasping and pursuing "great and national objects," but principally because "the greater number of citizens and extent of territory" in a large republic would reduce the possibility that any one faction would become dominant and hence be in a position to oppress the rest.

[44] *Federalist* LXXXIV [Hamilton], Cooke ed., pp. 582, 583. Cf. n. 5 above.

[45] Madison to Jefferson, October 24, 1787, in Robert A. Rutland *et al.*, eds., *Papers of James Madison* (Chicago and Charlottesville, 1973–), X, 205–220; *Federalist* X, LI, *Doc. Hist.* XIV, CC 285; XVI, CC 503. The famous passage quoted at length below is from CC 285, at 181.

[46] For the passionate antifederalist James Winthrop's defense of state sovereignty in terms of protecting local interest groups, see "Agrippa," VII, in Ford, *Essays*, p. 73: "It is only by protecting local concerns that the interest of the whole is preserved. No man when he enters society does it from a view to promote the good of others, but he does it for his own good. All men having the same view are bound equally to promote the welfare of the whole." For a federalist's view of "interest," published three days before the appearance of *Federalist* X, see "Philanthrop," *Doc. Hist.*, III, 468–470 ("surely real true self interest, considered on a large extensive scale, is public good").

Extend the sphere, and you take in a greater variety of parties and interests; you make it less probable that a majority of the whole will have a common motive to invade the rights of other citizens; or if such a common motive exists, it will be more difficult for all who feel it to discover their own strength, and to act in unison with each other.

And he went on to illustrate the moderating effect of distance and numbers on inflammatory religious sects and on "a rage for paper money, for an abolition of debts, for an equal division of property, or for any other improper or wicked project."

It is surprising that there should ever have been any confusion about what Madison was saying and meaning in his most famous *Federalist* paper. Nothing he said about factionalism or its material basis was new or controversial. Antifederalist as well as federalist assumed the same. Nor was he introducing any shift in basic ideology or anticipating something modern scholars would call liberalism or interest-group politics; and he was neither opposing "civic humanism" nor exalting it.[47] He was

[47] It is worth noting that *Federalist* X, far from constituting a sudden new theory of politics, was the expansion of ideas Madison had long been considering. It was in his pre-convention memorandum "Vices of the Political System of the United States" (April 1787) that he had first recorded his concern for "the insecurity of private rights" in majoritarian republics and argued that the larger the sphere of the republic, the greater the probability that factions would check and neutralize each other and the less likely that any one of them would be a threat to the preservation of private rights. When he came to deal with the operational mechanics of the Constitution, he used the idea of extended spheres in a more specific way, to justify his proposal, which the convention rejected, of a Congressional veto over state legislation deemed to be in conflict with the Constitution, federal laws and regulations, and individual rights. Why would Congress not itself be factious, partial, unfair, even exploitative in using such a veto? Why would it be impartial? When, in his letter to Jefferson of October 24, he came to answer that question and hence to justify his advocacy of a Congressional veto, he explained that the multitude of interests and factions in America's extended republic would guarantee Congress' impartiality. No one group would be able fully to control Congress, hence no one group would be in a position to use Congress' veto for its own, selfish purposes. Madison thought so highly of this justification of his defeated idea of a Congressional veto that he excerpted that entire section of the letter in his own hand, apparently for later use. He did not wait long to reuse it. Within a month he took over this passage, written to Jefferson to justify the Congressional veto, and developed it along the lines of his earlier, more general "Vices," simply to argue, in *Federalist* X (November 22), that an extended republic reduced rather than increased the dangers of factionalism;

doing what John Stevens had been doing before him, what James Wilson and Alexander Hamilton were doing too, and what many other, lesser figures — Edmund Randolph, Francis Corbin, James Bowdoin, Charles Pinckney — were also doing, namely, showing the inapplicability in America of the inherited notion that republics can survive only on a small scale. For all of the federalists who commented at length on the problem of size, the safety of republican government lay in extension, not contraction; all of them believed that in a system like America's the greater the numbers and the extent of territory, the more solidly based and the safer free government would become. None of this had to be learned from Madison. The difference between Madison and the other federalist writers who tackled the problem of size lay not in the point of the arguments but in the style and quality of argumentation. No other writer had Madison's cogency, penetration, knowledge, and range.

Nor did they need him to show them the way on the larger and engrossing question of virtue and republicanism. Federalists and antifederalists both agreed that man in his deepest nature was selfish and corrupt; that blind ambition most often overcomes even the most clear-eyed rationality; and that the lust for power was so overwhelming that no one should ever be entrusted with unqualified authority. The difference between the two parties lay in the conclusion they reached with respect to the extent and power of a central government. Because the antifederalists saw corruption and the lust for power everywhere, they argued that the weaker the power available, the less harm the manipulation of power could do. The federalists argued that the problem in the American situation had been

---

and he used it again, similarly, in *Federalist* LI (February 6, 1788). Madison would have been surprised to learn that these familiar ideas, of factionalism and its relation to extended spheres, would at one point, generations later, be hailed as the advent of a new political science, at another as the justification for patrician rule. Cf. *Papers of James Madison*, X, 205–206; excerpted passage at 209–214.

exaggerated. Yes, people were innately evil and self-seeking, and yes, no one could be trusted with unconfined power. That was as true in America as anywhere else. But under the Constitution's checks and balances power would be far from unconfined, and for such a self-limiting system there would be virtue enough for success.

Madison had begun his statements on this question in *Federalist* LV and LVI, published in mid-February 1788: "As there is a degree of depravity in mankind," he then wrote, "which requires a certain degree of circumspection and distrust, so there are other qualities in human nature which justify a certain portion of esteem and confidence." Four months later he elaborated the point in what was for him a remarkable outburst. It was touched off by Mason's insistence, in the Virginia ratifying convention, that legislators will do everything mischievous they can think of and fail to do anything good. Why is it not as reasonable, Madison replied, to assume that they will as readily do good as evil? — not that one should "place unlimited confidence in them, and expect nothing but the most exalted integrity and sublime virtue." And then followed this statement of his basic philosophy:

I go on this great republican principle, that the people will have virtue and intelligence to select men of virtue and wisdom. Is there no virtue among us? If there be not we are in a wretched situation. No theoretical checks, no form of government, can render us secure. To suppose that any form of government will secure liberty or happiness without any virtue in the people is a chimerical idea.[48]

Other federalists, equally convinced of the power of self-interest, greed, and corruption, said the same. Washington wrote Lafayette that the guarantee that the American government would never degenerate into despotism lay in the ultimate virtue of

---

[48] *Federalist* LV, *ibid.,* XVI, CC 525 (114–115); Madison, speech in the Virginia convention, Elliot, *Debates,* III, 536–537.

the American people. John Dickinson asked, "will a virtuous and sensible people choose villains or fools for their officers? Or, if they should choose men of wisdom and integrity, will these lose both or either, by taking their seats? If they should, will not their places be quickly supplied by another choice? Is the like derangement again, and again, and again, to be expected? Can any man believe that such astonishing phenomena are to be looked for?" Similarly, the federalist Reverend Samuel West in the Massachusetts convention demanded to know whether it was likely that people would "choose men to ruin us . . . May we not rationally conclude that the persons we shall choose to administer [the Constitution] will be, in general, good men?" — a sentiment that astonished his adversary, General Samuel Thompson, who thought it "quite contrary to the common language of the clergy, who are continually representing mankind as reprobate and deceitful, and that we really grow worse and worse day after day." Even the archconservative Fisher Ames, ever fearful of the destructiveness of pure democracy, conceded, in justifying republicanism, that "the people always mean right; and, if time is allowed for reflection and information, they will do right." But it was Hamilton — clear in his belief that in the proportion that riches and luxury prevail, virtue will tend to become a mere "graceful appendage of wealth, and the tendency of things will be to depart from the republican standard" — who nevertheless most strongly reinforced Madison's balanced view of human nature: "The supposition of universal venality in human nature," he wrote in *Federalist* LXXVI, "is little less an error in political reasoning than the supposition of universal rectitude. The institution of delegated power implies that there is a portion of virtue and honor among mankind, which may be a reasonable foundation of confidence. And experience justifies the theory."[49]

[49] Washington to the Marquis de Lafayette, Mount Vernon, February 7, 1788, *Doc. Hist.,* XVI, CC 509; "Fabius" [Dickinson], IX, in Ford, *Pamphlets,* p. 215; West, Thomp-

So, the federalists argued, virtue existed sufficient for the purposes of a government of checks and balances — in fact, *must* exist, as Madison said, in "any form of government" that secured liberty and happiness. It followed, therefore, that the peculiar identification of virtue with republicanism — the hitherto unquestioned precept whose authority could be traced back to classical antiquity — was simplistic: not wrong, but misapplied. Without virtue *"no* form of government can render us secure." But the critique of the received tradition could go much deeper. A few — not many — of the federalists went beyond the standard federalist formulation, which assumed the existence of basic virtue, and probed more deeply the logic and presuppositions of the ancient formulation.

This deeper critique had begun from a peculiar angle even before the Constitution was written. In 1784–85 a twenty-four-year-old American law student in London, William Vans Murray, wrote six essays in defense of the American state governments which appeared in pamphlet form in Philadelphia while the convention was still at work and were then reprinted in the *American Museum* at about the time the Constitution was published. Their purpose was to examine what Murray called the "false theory," the "hackneyed assertion," that "democratic forms required a tone of manners unattainable and unpreservable in a society where commerce, luxury, and the arts have disposed the public mind to the gratifications of refinement" — the error, in other words, that "what is usually understood by the term virtue, as fancifully displayed by Montesquieu, is the root of democracy" and that "the progress of luxury" de-

---

son, and Ames speeches in the Massachusetts convention, Elliot, *Debates,* II, 32–33, 33–34, 10; Winfred E. A. Bernhard, *Fisher Ames* (Chapel Hill, 1965), pp. 6, 73; Gerald Stourzh, *Alexander Hamilton and the Idea of Republican Government* (Stanford, 1970), pp. 70–74, quotation at 71; *Federalist* LXXVI, Cooke ed., pp. 513–514. Cf. Hamilton's earlier statement (*Federalist* XXII, *Doc. Hist.,* XIV, CC 347) that only "minds animated and guided by superior virtue" can overcome the natural corruptibility of ordinary people suddenly elevated to positions of power in a republic, and on such minds, protected and favored by a proper constitution, the survival of freedom will depend.

stroys it. The American situation, Murray wrote, defies such "system mongers," and he devoted his entire second essay — a discourse of well over 4,000 words — to demonstrating the falseness of the belief that virtue was incompatible with wealth and luxury or peculiarly necessary for a free state in an advanced civilization.

It all went back to Montesquieu, Murray wrote, and the trouble with Montesquieu is that he had "never studied a free democracy." If he had, he would have realized that "a greater share of virtue is not [more] necessary to a democratic than to a monarchial form." It wasn't really a question of virtue: virtue was necessary for both forms. But spartan asceticism, being based on a "love of poverty . . . [which] could operate but in very small societies of men," is not the only form of virtue. In fact, in the growing affluence of democratic America, not only has freedom flourished but the development of the human race has advanced, giving the lie to the idea that the spirit of a "simple age, uncultivated and rude, was essential to that very form which . . . is best adapted to the plenitude of human felicity." "Liberty and . . . the fullest dispersion of luxury through every vein of the body politic are in all degrees and respects compatible with each other." Montesquieu had simply not probed deeply enough: "great as he was and venerable as he will ever be, [he] was too fond of hypothesis . . . He was too mechanical, too geometrical"; his writing shows the "ingenuity of a great mind which fritters away its powers in conceit."[50]

---

[50] Murray, "Political Sketches," *American Museum*, II, no. 3 (September 1787), 220, 227, 228, 230, 231, 232. Cf. Alexander deConde, "William Vans Murray's *Political Sketches*: A Defense of the American Experiment," *Mississippi Valley Historical Review*, 41 (1954-55), 623-640. Murray was a political disciple of John Adams, who was ambassador in London when Murray was writing his essays, and addressed the essays to Adams. Adams himself was then writing his *Defence of the Constitutions . . . of the United States of America* (3 vols., 1787-88), which similarly disparages Montesquieu's ideas. In a long passage in volume III (1788), Adams followed Murray's ideas closely and, independently of Webster and Stevens, developed views similar to theirs as well. Adams, *Works*, VI, 206-216, quotations at 208, 211.

With all of this, Noah Webster agreed, but for him Murray's critique did not go far enough. In 1785, in his *Sketches of American Policy,* he too had questioned the precept "that *virtue* is the foundation of republics." What was meant by virtue? "The great Montesquieu," Webster assumed, had meant "*patriotism,* or disinterested public spirit and love of one's country." But had that ever, truly, existed in human society? If *that* is what virtue means, and if one is talking about actual, operational human motivation, then virtue has never been, and is not now, the peculiar attribute or "principle" of *any* form of government, republican, monarchical, or aristocratic. There is only one "real principle that is predominat in every individual and directs all his actions," Webster wrote, and that is "self-interest," and self-interest operates differently in different forms of government.

Two years later Webster elaborated. In his pamphlet *An Examination into the Leading Principles of the Federal Constitution . . . by a Citizen of America,* which he wrote at the request of the federalist leadership shortly after the ratification debate had begun, he said that Murray had been right in his criticism of Montesquieu, but he had failed to show the correct principles that had eluded the great man. After an introductory passage of much learning followed by a refutation of various criticisms of the Constitution, Webster developed his view of liberty and then turned to the concept of power. "In what," he asked, "does *real* power consist?" Not simply military force, and not cultural forces like religion. "The answer is short and plain — in *property.*" The "inseparable connexion between property and dominion" can be seen throughout Roman history and throughout British history. "Wherever we cast our eyes we see this truth, that *property* is the basis of *power.*" Therefore *"a general and tolerably equal distribution of landed property is the whole basis of national freedom,"* and it is this that Montesquieu, wise as he was, had never understood.

373

The system of the great Montesquieu will ever be erroneous till the words *property or lands in fee simple* are substituted for *virtue,* throughout his *Spirit of Laws. Virtue,* patriotism, or love of country never was and never will be, till mens' natures are changed, a fixed, permanent principle and support of government . . . An equality of property, with a necessity of alienation constantly operating to destroy combinations of powerful families, is the very *soul of a republic.* While this continues, the people will inevitably possess both *power* and *freedom;* when this is lost, power departs, liberty expires, and a commonwealth will inevitably assume some other form.

All the rest — "liberty of the press, trial by jury, the Habeas Corpus writ, even Magna Charta itself" — though no doubt "palladia of freedom," were all "inferior considerations when compared with a general distribution of real property among every class of people . . . Let the people have property and they *will* have power . . . The liberties of America, therefore, and her forms of government, stand on the broadest basis." Abstract virtue — absolutely disinterested love of country — is unreal and has nothing to do with the matter.[51]

But it was the fervent federalist John Stevens, writing a month after Webster's pamphlet appeared, who poured the bitterest scorn on applying the classical dicta on republicanism to the American situation. Everything Stevens wrote in the early numbers of the "Americanus" series was explicitly or implicitly a criticism of Montesquieu, but in the fifth paper (December 12, 1787) he confronted the central issues directly. Aside from its being "evidently defective" as a work of "philosophic precision," *The Spirit of the Laws* had been written to soften the rigors of monarchy, hence it was largely irrelevant in America.

---

[51] Webster, *Sketches* (facsimile ed., New York, 1937), p. 24n; *Examination,* in Ford, *Pamphlets,* pp. 57, 59, 60 — echoed in Webster's "To the Dissenting Members of the Late Convention of Pennsylvania" (December 31, 1787), *Doc. Hist.,* XV, CC 399 (195). For the federalists' request to Webster, see Thomas FitzSimmons to Noah Webster, Philadelphia, September 15, 1787, in Noah Webster Collection, New York Public Library; reproduced in microfiche addenda to *Doc. Hist.,* II, at mf. pp. 707–708.

Montesquieu's threefold classification of the types of government — republican, monarchical, and despotic — jumbles up distinctive categories, and his definition of the principles, or "springs of action which set these different species of government in motion," is "certainly a very fanciful piece of business . . . an ingenious conceit." By the virtue that he believed animated republics Montesquieu had meant ascetic self-denial and "an enthusiastic attachment to the political system of the country we inhabit." But one had only to look at the results in his favorite example, the "monstrous political prodigy" of Sparta, to see "the absurdities mankind are capable of." If Americans tried to imitate the Spartans, "we should soon become mere nests of hornets . . . Away with this Spartan virtue and black broth; we'll have none of them."

There were, Stevens wrote, only two truly animating principles, and they were everywhere the same "though compounded in various degrees" for the different types of government: *fear,* or the dread of punishment; and *attachment* — that is, "customs, manners, habits, prejudices." Further, Montesquieu's notion that ambition is pernicious in a republic is precisely wrong: no form of government needs the "laudable desire of excelling in whatever we undertake" as much as a republic. "Montesquieu may talk of virtue as the spring of action in a republican government, but I trust its force would be found too feeble to produce great exertions without the aid of ambition . . . It is ambition that constitutes the very life and soul of republican government. As fear and attachment insure obedience to government, so does ambition set its wheels in motion."[52]

[52] "Americanus" [Stevens], VI, *New York Daily Advertiser,* December 12, 1787; remarks on Sparta are in paper I, November 2, 1787. Cf. Hamilton's comment in *The Continentalist* (1782) that it is folly to urge pure disinterestedness in republican politics: "We might as soon reconcile ourselves to the Spartan community of goods and wives, to their iron coin, their long beards, or their black broth . . . it is as ridiculous to seek for models in the simple ages of Greece and Rome, as it would be to go in quest of them among the Hottentots and Laplanders." Quoted in Stourzh, *Hamilton,* p. 70.

4

So the federalists questioned the classical formulation that bound republicanism in some unique way to the principle of virtue. For most, it was sufficient to say that some degree of virtue was necessary for *any* free and secure government whatever its constitutional form, and that there was virtue enough in republican states to make the complex system of the Constitution work. But a very few others went further, probed the meaning of "virtue," questioned its applicability if defined either as asceticism, disinterested patriotism, or the denial of personal ambition, and suggested more realistic principles of political motivation and of the means of securing the permanence of free republican governments.

All of this was part of the effort to come to terms with their inheritance. They felt the necessity to build a power center in the national government, but their inherited understanding of the dangers to liberty — fragile in its nature and easily destroyed — warned them against such an effort. At the Philadelphia convention, with exquisite care and with delicate nuances, they devised a complex constitution that would generate the requisite power but would so distribute its flow and uses that no one body of men and no one institutional center would ever gain a monopoly of force or influence that could dominate the nation.[53] But that blueprint for a self-correcting power system, which they labored to explain in the minutest detail throughout the vast ratifying debate, was not enough. Something more was required. Their ideological inheritance, which so clearly warned them of the dangers of what they were doing and which fueled the antifederalists' objections to the Constitution, had to be confronted and assessed. The past would have to be laid to rest;

[53] All of the federalists' discussions of the Constitution are, in one way or another, commentaries on power, its uses and abuses; but for a particularly clear and cogent discussion of power, in the abstract and in practice, see "A Landholder" [Ellsworth], III, *Doc. Hist.,* XIV, CC 272.

not rejected in favor of some other, different set of beliefs, but refined, renewed, brought up to date — worked out, fulfilled.

Embarked as they were on a project they believed was without precedent in human history[54] — to construct a potentially powerful state, but one that would preserve the liberties of the people — they clung to the basic ideology of the early Revolution but, where necessary, turned its monitory, negative formulations to affirmative purposes. Anachronisms were weeded out; irrelevancies in the American situation were discarded; distended abstractions were lanced and drained of distortions; and the hard realities of the real, functioning world were everywhere revealed. Change was inevitably involved, but the movement of change was return as well as departure: revision, refinement, and reapplication of an earlier tradition, not repudiation.

So they dissipated the fear of "standing armies," not by abandoning the fear of military rule but by showing the irrelevance of that peculiar and distinctive concept in the American situation. They recognized the need for a regular, professional army, but they insisted that it remain under strict civilian control: the military must always, Tench Coxe wrote in the course of his defense of a national army, "be regarded *with a watchful eye, for it is a profession that is liable to dangerous perversion.*"[55] So they showed the irrelevance of the ancient "solecism" *imperium in imperio;* but despite Hamilton's assurances and despite the federalist structure of the Constitution, they continued to believe that a concurrence of powers *could* mean a repugnancy; that in certain situations you *could* have — to repeat Madison's words — "a sovereignty over sovereigns, a government over governments," and when you did you would find *"violence* in place of *law,* or the destructive *coertion* of the *sword* in place of

---

[54] Typically, Wilson's speech in the Pennsylvania convention, *Doc., Hist.,* III, 352–353, and that convention's general sentiment, p. 367; *Federalist* XIV [Madison], *ibid.,* XIV, CC 310.

[55] "An American Citizen" [Coxe], IV, *ibid.,* XIII, CC 183A (435).

the mild and salutary *coertion* of the *magistracy*." For, Madison prophetically insisted, "if a compleat supremacy some where is not necessary in every society, a controuling power at least is so, by which the general authority may be defended against encroachments of the subordinate authorities and by which the latter may be restrained from encroachments on each other." The supremacy of Britain's *Parliament* had not been necessary "for the harmony of that empire," but the Crown's negative "or some equivalent controul" *had* been necessary if "the unity of the system" were to have been preserved. The federalists did not dismiss the problem of dual sovereignties; they saw its deeper meanings, used it, and restated it.[56]

Federalism was a possible, not a certain, solution; its essence was not automatic harmony but an uncertain tension which statecraft alone could maintain. For the federalists there was no other solution, since they, as much as the eloquent antifederalist "Brutus," feared any comprehensive government whose power could be exercised without limitation. In their mind's eye they too could imagine and they too shuddered at the thought of a national government that could creep into every corner of the country, "wait upon the ladies at their toilett . . . accompany them to the ball, the play, and the assembly . . . enter the house of every gentleman, watch over his cellar, wait upon his cook in the kitchen, follow the servants into the parlour, preside over the table, and note down all he eats or drinks . . . attend him to his bed-chamber, and watch him while he sleeps." This they too, no less than their opponents, continued to believe was the ultimate tyranny.[57]

So, similarly, the federalists tested for its practical reality the venerable abstraction that the peculiar distinction and animating principle of republics is somehow "virtue" — showed the ambi-

[56] *Federalist* XX [Madison], *ibid.*, CC 340; Madison to Jefferson, October 24, 1787 (cited above, n. 46), pp. 209–210.
[57] See above, quotation on pp. 336–337.

guities of such a schematic notion. But they never abandoned the belief that only an informed, alert, intelligent, and uncorrupted electorate would preserve the freedoms of a republican state, and that sufficient virtue existed to sustain the American republic. So too they scotched the fear of an effective national executive, showed its necessity and benignity in the American situation. But they continued to believe, as deeply as any of the militants of '76, that power corrupts; that, in the words of the conservative Edward Rutledge of South Carolina, "the very idea of power included a possibility of doing harm";[58] that any release of the constraints on the executive — any executive — was an invitation to disaster; and that an unfettered collaboration between the executive and the military or the "secret services" was a certain catastrophe.

It was thus that the federalists corrected the cave — enlarged its dimensions, reshaped it, modernized it. We live in that more spacious world. Thanks to them, and to their antifederalist opponents who helped keep them close to their ideological origins, we know what obstacles are there, and so may weave and flitter, dip and soar in perfect courses through the blackest air. In that spirit we too — in the very happiest intellection — may continue to correct the cave.

[58] Edward Rutledge, speech in the South Carolina convention, Elliot, *Debates,* IV, 276.

INDEX

Aberdeen University, 35

Adams, Abigail, 133

Adams, Amos: *Concise Historical View,* 83; *Religious Liberty,* 262

Adams, John, 8, 20, 26, 99, 109, 118, 176; on nature of the Revolution, 1, 160; literary style of, 16; *Thoughts on Government,* 16, 45, 172, 272–273, 289, 290, 291; on Paine, 18, 288–290; on classical authors, 24–25, 26; "Novanglus," 35, 57, 76, 100, 110, 133, 137, 172, 233, 277, 280; *Works,* 35, 67, 68, 69, 74, 98, 292; and radical Whigs, 42, 45; *Dissertation on the Canon and Feudal Law,* 55, 57, 81, 83, 97–98, 102, 140; on power, 55–56; *Diary,* 56, 59, 61, 100, 107, 248, 268, 290; on weakness of liberty, 59; constitutional views of, 67–69, 74, 82, 175; on Saxon constitution, 82; on presumed conspiracy to subvert colonial liberty, 98, 121–122; on Stamp Act, 101–102; on plural officeholding, 109–110; on Boston Massacre, 117; on corruption in England, 135–136, 137; on destiny of American colonies, 140; on enslavement of colonies, 233; on religious establishment, 166–167, 248, 268–270; on Mayhew-Apthorp controversy, 256–257; on colonial nobility, 279; on democracy and republicanism, 282–283; and Murray (W. V.), 372; *Defence of the Constitutions . . . ,* 372

Adams, Samuel: on power, 60; "A Puritan," 98; on fixed constitution, 181, 337

Adams, Zabdiel, *Grounds of Confidence,* 61

Addison, Joseph, 8, 77; *Cato,* 44

Administration of Justice Act, 118–119

Admiralty, Court of (Vice-), 108–109

Africa, 79, 138, 243

Agents, colonial, 166

"Agrippa" (pseud. of James Winthrop), 322, 343, 349, 366

Allen, John: literary style of, 18; sketch of, 18; *American Alarm,* 18, 38, 107, 122, 123, 125, 233, 255, 267, 268, 274–275, 306; *Oration upon the Beauties of Liberty,* 18, 107, 116, 123, 124–125, 310; *Watchman's Alarm,* 77, 240–241; on slavery, 240–241; on religious establishment, 267–268

Almon, John, 88, 148

Ambition and desire for power: antifederalists and, 344–347, 368; federalists and, 368–369, 375, 379. *See also* Power

"Americanus" (pseud. of J. Stevens, Jr.), 329, 330, 363–365, 374, 375

Ames, Fisher, 370

Andrewes, Lancelot, 315

Anglicans, *see* Church of England

Antifederalists, 331–351; writings of, 326–328; fear concentrated power, 330–331, 331–332, 333, 338, 345–347; and Tories, compared, 332; oppose uniformity, 343; view of human nature, 345–347; on size of republic, 347–349

Aplin, John, *Verses,* 11–12, 96–97

Apthorp, East: and Mayhew controversy, 5, 96–97, 254–257; *Considerations,* 255

Arbuthnot, John: *Art of Political Lying,* 13; *History of John Bull,* 13

Argument Shewing That a Standing Army, see Trenchard

Aristocracy, 65, 70, 300; federalists and, 334. *See also* Nobility

Aristotle, 23, 70

Army, standing: fear of, 36, 48, 61–63, 65, 84, 112–119; antifederalists and,

INDEX

INDEX

Brady, Robert, 31, 82

Braxton, Carter: *Address*, 66, 124, 143, 291, 292; constitutional ideas of, 291–292

Brown, Dr. John, *Estimate of the Manners*, 87

"Brutus" (pseud.), 330, 335–337, 339–340, 347–348, 358

Brutus, Marcus Junius, 26

Bryan, Samuel, 333

Burgh, James, 132; *Political Disquisitions*, 40, 41, 344; *Britain's Remembrancer*, 40, 86, 87

Burk, John Daly, 157

Burke, Edmund, 147, 163, 169, 315; *Thoughts on the Present Discontents*, 134, 146; on conspiracy, 146, 158–159; on representation, 163

Burlamaqui, Jean Jacques, 27, 28, 29; on internal and external obligations, 210

Burnet, Bishop Gilbert, 45

Bute, Earl of, *see* Stuart, John

Butler, Bishop Joseph, 315

Caesar, Julius, 24

Caldwell, David, 340

Caligula, 131

Calvin's Case, see Coke, Sir Edward; Bacon, Sir Francis

Cambridge, Mass., 96, 254, 255

Camden, Earl of, *see* Pratt, Charles

Camm, John: dispute with Richard Bland, 5, 252–253; *Critical Remarks*, 11, 236; on slavery, 235–236; on religious establishment, 154–155, 252–253; *Single and Distinct View*, 254. *See also* Two-Penny Acts

Canada, 84, 126, 155, 280

Care, Henry, *English Liberties,* 44

Carlisle Commission, 227

Carmichael, John, *Self-Defensive War Lawful,* 6–7

Carroll, Charles (Sr.), 56, 82, 91–92, 213

Carroll, Charles, of Carrollton, 91–92, 131, 132, 137

Carter, Landon, 252

Carthage, 282

Cartwright, John, 41

Cassius Longinus, C., 26

"Cato" (pseud. of New York writer), 346–347, 348. *See also* Addison

Cato, M. Porcius, 24

Cato's Letters, see Trenchard

"Centinel" (pseud. of S. Bryan), 333, 333–334

Chalmers, James: and enlightenment authors, 29; *Plain Truth*, 29, 66, 248, 287, 288; *Additions to Plain Truth*, 85, 282

Champion, Judah, *Brief View*, 83

Chandler, Thomas Bradbury, 318; *American Querist*, 11, 12, 15, 313; *What Think Ye*, 184, 226, 281; on rights, 188; on sovereignty, 226; on colonial nobility, 281; on obedience to authority, 313–314; *Friendly Address*, 313, 314

Chaplin, Ebenezer, *The Civil State Compared to Rivers*, 9, 15

Charles I, 28, 29, 53, 118, 145, 200; *His Majesties Answer*, 71

Charles II, 121

Charters, as written constitutions, 191–193

Checks and balances, 323, 324; Henry (P.) on, 345–346; "Americanus" (Stevens) on, 363–364; federalists' reliance on, 368–369, 369, 371

Church, Benjamin, Massacre Oration, 169

Church of England: Hoadly and, 38–39; desire of, to become established in colonies, 95–98; establishment of, 248–249; in Virginia, 251–253; and Mayhew-Apthorp controversy, 254–257. *See also* Society for the Propagation of the Gospel

Cicero, Marcus Tullius, 23, 24, 25, 26

"Cincinnatus" (pseud.), 342

Civil disobedience, *see* Authority, civil

Classics, use of by pamphleteers, 23–26

Coercive Acts, 4, 126, 148

Coke, Sir Edward, 43, 54, 171, 177, 179, 180, 201; citation of, by colonists,

INDEX

appointments by, 102 ff., 276–279; and presumed conspiracy to subvert colonial liberty, 122–130; supremacy of, over colonies, 202 ff. *See also* Constitution, British; Power

Curtius Rufus, Q., 24

Customs: Commissioners of, 102–105; regulations and officers, 343

Dana, Edmund, 102

Dana, James, 83

Danbury, Conn., 129

Dartmouth, Lord, *see* Legge, William

Davies, Samuel, 251

Debt, national, 335

Declaration . . . for Taking up Arms, 126

Declaration of Independence, 14, 152–153, 155, 156, 237, 246

Declaratory Act, 202, 227

Defoe, Daniel, 8, 13; *Shortest Way with the Dissenters,* 13

Delaware, 150, 194, 245

Delolme, John Louis, 27

Democracy, 70, 278, 282–284, 300, 301; in America, and virtue, 372–373. *See also* Commons; Constitution, British

"Democratic Federalist" (pseud.), 339

Demosthenes, 171

Denmark, 65, 79, 113. *See also* Molesworth, Robert

Devotion, Ebenezer, *Examiner Examined,* 168

Dialogue Between the Ghost of General Montgomery . . . and An American Delegate, 12

Dialogue Between a Southern Delegate and His Spouse, 12

Dickinson, John, 8, 11, 58, 82, 123, 129, 130, 370; *Essay on the Constitutional Power,* 23, 58, 170, 223, 226, 227; scholarship of, 23, 26; *Farmer's Letters,* 37, 42, 63, 64, 75, 102, 104, 145, 215, 232–233, 238, 283, 337, 344; *Speech Delivered . . . 1764,* 39, 187, 192; on rights, 77, 187; *Address to . . . Barbados . . . ,* 78, 187; views of En-

gland, 89–91, 137; on ministerial conspiracy, 100–101, 119–120, 145; *Late Regulations,* 121; "Address to the Inhabitants of the Colonies," 153–155, 173; on charters, 187, 192; constitutional views of, 215–216, 223, 226, 283; on colonies and state of slavery, 232–233

Dilly, Edmund, 135

Dio Cassius Cocceianus, 24

Divine right, *see* Crown, British

Documentary History of the Ratification of the Constitution, 326

Doddridge, Philip, 40

Douglass, William: *Summary, Historical and Political,* 75, 165; on qualifications for legislators, 165

Dougliad, The, 279

Downer, Silas, *Discourse,* 104, 187, 217, 238

Drayton, William, 17; *Letter from Freeman,* 64, 107, 110, 279, 280, 284; *Charge,* 137; on colonial nobility, 279–280; on democracy, 283

Duché, Jacob, 315

Dulany, Daniel (Sr.), *Right of the Inhabitants,* 43–44

Dulany, Daniel (Jr.), 28, 42, 144; *Considerations,* 60–61, 66, 67, 79, 168, 171, 212, 215; on power, 60; on representation, 167; on distinction between external and internal authority, 211–212, 215

Dunk, George Montagu, 3rd Earl of Halifax, 151

East India Company, 132

Eclipse, The, 233

Economic basis of politics, 324–325

Economic growth, American, 351–352

Economic Interpretation of the Constitution (Beard), 326

Edes, Peter, [*Massacre*] *Orations Delivered at the Request of Inhabitants,* 6

Edwards, Jonathan, 243

Egypt, 63

Elections, Congressional, 332, 338

Eliot, Andrew, 283; *Sermon,* 6, 59, 93,

INDEX

Fowle, Daniel, *Appendix to the . . . Eclipse of Liberty,* 165

France, 66, 129, 238, 305; despotism in, 63, 66, 79, 118

Franklin, Benjamin, 43, 87, 102, 127, 149, 214, 215, 333; as writer, 13; and European Enlightenment, 27; on corruption in England, 88–89, 130, 136; on placemen, 102; and distinction between external and internal taxes, 213–215, 337

Franklin, James, 43, 44

Freedom, *see* Liberty

French Revolution, 19, 38, 314

Gaius, 24

Galba, Servius Sulpicius, 131, 132

Galloway, Joseph, 136, 156, 187, 280, 335; and Enlightenment authors, 29; *Candid Examination,* 30, 143; on corruption in England, 137; *Historical and Political Reflections,* 157; *A Reply,* 157, 223; on sovereignty, 223, 226; Plan of Union, 226

Garth, Charles, 166

Gay, John, 49

Genoa, 66

Genuine Principles of the Ancient Saxon . . . Constitution, 61, 183–184, 297

George I, 133

George II, 38, 106

George III, 82, 124, 134, 145–146, 147, 156, 224, 226, 303, 304; on presumed conspiracy in the colonies, 152–153

Georgia, 248

Georgia (Russia), 66

Germany, 79, 138

Gerry, Elbridge, 322

Gilbert, Sir Geoffrey, 31

Glorious Revolution, 35, 46, 52, 81, 105, 123, 132, 147, 173, 201

Goldsboro (Goldesborough), John, *Reports,* 31

Gordon, Thomas, 39, 40, 45, 133; translation of Tacitus, 22, 42, 43, 45; *Cato's Letters,* 22, 36, 37, 39, 40, 43, 44, 45, 48–49, 52, 53, 57, 58, 59, 60, 61, 64, 68, 77, 80, 86, 132, 137, 283–284; influence on colonists, 35–36, 44, 53; *Independent Whig,* 36, 43, 45, 53; translation of Sallust, 42, 137

Gordon, William, *Discourse,* 104

Government: by consent of governed, 172–174; and balance of powers, 72, 273–281, 284–301; and control of factions, 273, 300; qualifications for leaders of, 309–311; distinction between internal and external spheres of, 209–219; and equality, 316–318; American forms of, 330–379 *passim.* *See also* Authority, civil

Graves, Henry, 213

Graves, William, 132

Great Awakening, 249

Great Britain, 131, 278, 313, 314. *See also* Church of England; Constitution, British; Crown, British; Customs, Commissioners of; England; Glorious Revolution; Normans; Parliament; Privy Council; Representation; *and kings by name*

Greece, 133, 287

Grenville, George, 150, 151, 168

Grotius, Hugo, 27, 43, 150, 177, 205, 206

Guthrie, William, 41

Hadley, Mass., 265

Hale, Sir Matthew, 30, 201

Halifax, Earl of, *see* Dunk, George Montagu

Hall, David, 87–88, 115, 133, 135, 149

Hall, John, 29

Haman (Biblical), 127

Hamilton, Alexander, 312, 330, 337, 356–358; and Enlightenment authors, 27; *Farmer Refuted,* 28, 64, 188, 197, 198; *Full Vindication,* 121; on English society, 137; on natural rights, 188; and Constitution, 352–353; on standing army, 356–357; on size of republic, 365–366, 368; on virtue, 370

Hampden, John, 132, 344

INDEX

Hancock, John, 17; *Oration,* 63, 116, 121
Hanover County, Va., 259, 260
Hanson, Alexander Contee, 328, 337, 353, 355–356; *Remarks on the Proposed Plan,* 328
Harrington, James, 34, 35, 45, 75, 210, 365
Hart, Levi, 247; *Liberty Described,* 77, 243; on slavery, 242–243
Hartford, Conn., 133
Harvard College, 254
Haven, Jason, *Sermon,* 310
Haverhill, Mass., 265
Henry III, 82
Henry VIII, 29
Henry, Patrick, 236, 253, 291; on corruption in England, 136–137; and Constitution, 322, 335, 336, 338, 343, 345–346
Herodotus, 24
Hervey, John, 38; *Ancient and Modern Liberty,* 42
Hicks, William, 181; *Considerations,* 57, 81, 176, 277; *Nature and Extent,* 58, 76, 82, 182, 217
Hill, Wills, 1st Earl of Hillsborough, 119, 331, 332, 344
Hillsborough, Lord, *see* Hill, Wills
Hitchcock, Gad, *Sermon,* 38, 310
Hoadly, Benjamin, Bishop of Winchester, 45, 52, 310; influence on colonists, 37–38; *Original and Institution of Civil Government,* 37; *Measures of Submission,* 37, 53; *Works,* 57
Hobbes, Thomas, 28, 173, 201, 229; on sovereignty, 199, 200
Holland, 66, 138, 238, 282, 287
Hollis, Thomas, 40, 87, 283; correspondence with Mayhew, 35, 37, 40, 42, 99; correspondence with Eliot, 35, 40, 99, 104, 114, 115, 116, 120, 123, 126, 131, 132, 141, 189, 263, 264, 266
Holmes, Abraham, 340
Holt, Sir John, 30
Homer, 24
Hooker, Richard, 201
Hooper, William, 85, 137, 141

Hopkins, Samuel, 148–149, 151, 243–245, 247
Hopkins, Stephen, 11, 42, 99; *Fall of Samuel the Squomicutite,* 10; *Letter to the Author,* 11, 17; *Rights of Colonies Examined,* 35, 100, 185, 212, 235, 344; on sovereignty, 211; on slavery, 234–235
Horace, 24
Hotman, Francis, *Franco-Gallia,* 72–73
Howard, Martin, Jr., 11, 17, 100; *Halifax Letter,* 100, 144, 181, 185, 207; and conspiracy, 144; on rights and the common law, 185
Howard, Simeon, *Sermon,* 28, 35, 38, 62
Howe, Sir William, 156–157
Hulme, Obadiah, *Historical Essay,* 61, 183–184
Human nature: antifederalists' view of, 345–347; Henry on, 345–346; federalists' view of, 368–373; Madison on, 369; Washington on, 369–370; Hamilton on, 370
Hume, David, 85, 339; *History,* 28, 42; "Of the Parties of Great Britain," 97–98
Hunt, Isaac, *Political Family,* 30, 311
Hunter, Robert: on colonial Assemblies, 75, 118
Hutcheson, Francis, 40
Hutchinson, Thomas, 72, 76, 131, 138, 157, 213, 332, 335–336; and Coke, 31; distrust of, 99, 121–122, 331, 344; *Copy of Letters Sent to Great-Britain,* 100, 280; and plural office-holding, 109–110; and presumed conspiracy, 121–123, 151, 152, 155–156; *Strictures,* 155, 156, 246; and distinction between external and internal taxes, 212; *Speeches . . . to the General Assembly,* 219–222, 225; on sovereignty, 220–222; on slavery, 246

Impeachment trials, 342, 342–343
Imperium in imperio, 223–229, 336, 358–360, 377; *See also* Federalism

388

INDEX

INDEX

INDEX

Ministerial Catechise, 10, 15, 104

Molasses, *see* Sugar Act

Molesworth, Robert, 1st Viscount, 39; *Account of Denmark,* 39, 65, 66, 98–99; definition of a "real Whig," 71–72, 73

Molière, 23

Monarchy, 70, 355
See also Crown, British

Montague, Mass., 265

Montesquieu, 27, 29, 30, 77, 150; and British Constitution, 71–72; *Spirit of the Laws,* 72, 87, 347, 348, 374–5; antifederalists and, 345; Hamilton and, 361; Stevens and, 363, 365; Murray and, 372; Adams (J.) and, 372; Webster and, 373

Moore, Maurice, *Justice and Policy,* 32, 82, 168, 172

Mordecai (Biblical), 127

More, Sir Thomas, 365

Morris, Gouverneur, 322

Morris, Lewis, 88

Morris, Robert, 322

Moyle, Walter, 62. *See also* Trenchard, *Argument Shewing*

Murray, William, 1st Earl of Mansfield, 123

Murray, William Vans, 371–372, 372, 373

Nasson, Samuel, 343

Neal, Daniel, 33

Nedham, Marchamont, 45; *Excellencie of a Free State,* 58

Negroes, *see* Slavery; Slave Trade

Nepos, Cornelius, 24

Neville, Henry, 34, 45

New Bern, N.C., 10

Newcastle, Duke of, *see* Pelham-Holles, Thomas

New England Courant, 43

New Jersey, 96, 240; tenure of judges in, 106; charters of, 191; "Laws, Concessions, and Agreements," 195

Newport Mercury, 30–39, 57

Newport, R.I., 244

New York, 44, 88, 96, 108, 115, 133, 194; Assembly of, 75, 118; Council of, 75, 118, 278–279; tenure of judges in, 106; charters of, 191, 195; *Act Declaring What Are the Rights,* 197; and religious establishment, 247, 248, 250; Committee of Safety in, 312

New York Evening Post, 57, 64, 77, 233, 235

New York Gazette, 80

New York Journal, 115

New York Mercury, 57, 61, 80

New York Weekly Journal, 43, 44, 85

Nicholas, Robert Carter, *Considerations,* 70, 142

Nicholas, Wilson, 356

Niles, Hezekiah, 160

Nobility, 274; lack of, in colonies, 275–277; proposals for creation of, in colonies, 278–280. *See also,* Aristocracy; Constitution, British

Noble, Oliver, *Some Strictures,* 61, 62, 121, 127

Normans, 80–81

Norris, Isaac, I, 43

North, Frederick (Lord North), 123, 128, 147, 227

North Carolina: tenure of judges in, 106; and religious establishment, 248; ratifying convention, 340, 346

Norwich, Conn., 10

No Standing Army, 62

O Liberty Thou Goddess Heavenly Bright, 85

Obedience, *see* Authority

Observations on Several Acts of Parliament, 104

O'Hara, Charles, 146

"Old Whig" (pseud.), 336

Oldisworth, William, *Dialogue,* 57

Olive Branch Petition, 126

Oliver, Andrew, 279

Oliver, Peter, *Origin and Progress,* 152, 157

Onslow, Arthur, 163, 164

Orders in Council, 103

Orwell, George, 2

Otis, James, Jr., 8, 69, 80, 99, 247; as

391

INDEX

writer, 18; and Enlightenment authors, 27; *Rights of the British Colonies,* 28, 31, 35, 67, 69, 81, 173, 178, 179, 205, 206, 207, 238; *Vindication,* 28, 79, 85, 186, 189, 207; and Coke, 31, 177; on power, 55; *Brief Remarks,* 56, 100, 206, 207; on rights, 78–79, 185–187; on representation, 168; *Considerations,* 169, 170; and writs of assistance case, 176–177; on constitutions, 176–181, 189–190; on sovereignty, 205–209; on slavery, 237–238

Ovid, 24

Paine, Thomas, 29, 180, 183; *Common Sense,* 5, 143, 175, 285, 286; as writer, 16; on balance in government, 285–286; attacks on, 287–291
Palfrey, William, 112, 132
Pamphlets: definition of, 1–2; use made of, in Revolution, 1–8; George Orwell on, 2; literary qualities of American Revolutionary, 9–19; and public opinion, 323
Paoli, Pasquale, 66
Pardon(s), presidential, 342
Parker, Henry, 200
Parliament: manipulation of, by Walpole, 47–51; supremacy of, 69, 222–223; role in British Constitution, 73–74, 176–177, 180–181; natural rights expressed by, 77–78; Saxon origins of, 81–82; elections to, 89–90; representation in, 162–164, 166–167; colonial representation in, 166–167, 176; jurisdiction in colonies, 186–187, 202–229; right to tax colonies, 202, 214–215; self-correction of, 205–209; efforts to restrict power of, 209–219; selection of members, 338. *See also* Authority; Constitution, British; Representation; Sovereignty; Wilkes
Parliament, Acts of, *see* Magna Carta
Parsons, Jonathan, *Freedom,* 247, 270, 271
Parsons, Samuel Holden, 360
Parsons, Theophilus, 298

Parsons' Cause, *see* Two-Penny Acts
Pelham-Holles, Thomas, 1st Duke of Newcastle, 146
Pemberton, Isaac, 167, 269
Pendleton, Edmund, 81
Penn, William, 84; as constitution maker, 191–192; "Laws, Concessions, and Agreements," 195
Pennsylvania, 115, 165, 182, 194, 240; Assembly of, 105, 187; tenure of judges in, 105–106; charter of, 187, 191, 192; and slave trade, 245; and religious establishment, 247; proposals for constitution of, 294–298; *Essay of a Frame of Government for,* 296; Proprietary party in, 308
Pennsylvania Chronicle, 115
Pennsylvania Gazette, 134
Pennsylvania Journal, 80
People the Best Governors, The, 294
Persia, 127
Petronius, 24
Petyt, William, 31, 82, 168
Philadelphia, 10, 43, 87, 126, 128, 133, 239, 268
"Philadelphiensis" (pseud. of B. Workman), 334
Pickering, Timothy, 352, 355
Pinckney, Charles, 368
Piso, 131
Pitt, William, 280; on corruption in England, 134–135; on conspiracy, 147
Pitt, William, the Younger, 156, 280
Plato, 24, 365
Pliny, 24
Philoleutherus Lipsiensis, *see* Bentley, Richard
Plutarch, 24, 25
Poland, 63, 64, 79, 138
Polybius, 24
Poor, and military service, 356
Pope, Alexander, 49
Power: colonial view of, 55–62; as opponent of liberty, 57–58; and standing army, 61; constraints and limitation of, 323, 349–351, 368–369, 376, 378–379; fear of (before Revolution), 323, 330–331; problem of establish-

INDEX

Robinson-Morris, Matthew, Lord Rokeby, *Considerations,* 133, 141

Rockingham, Marquis of, *see* Watson-Wentworth, Charles

Roman Catholic Church: as threat to liberty, 98, 207; in Virginia, 248

Rome, 26, 66, 79, 85, 88, 90, 102, 132, 133, 232, 282, 287, 295, 306; colonists' knowledge of history of, 25, 373; compared to England, 131, 133, 137

Rousseau, Jean-Jacques, 23, 27, 29

Rush, Benjamin, 230, 239, 328–329

Russell, Lord William, 132

Russia, 63

Russian Revolution, 19

Rutledge, Edward, 379

Rycaut, Sir Paul, *History of the Ottoman Empire,* 63, 64

St. George's Field Massacre, 115

St. John, Henry, Viscount Bolingbroke, 8, 28, 42, 49, 72, 75, 77, 85, 118, 151, 168; *Craftsman,* 39, 40, 42, 50, 53, 57, 72, 73, 86, 206; *Dissertation on Parties,* 40, 68; on the constitution, 68

Salem, Mass., 7

Salkeld, William, *Reports,* 31

Sallust, 24, 25, 26, 42, 137

Salter, Richard, *Sermon,* 127

Savannah, Ga., 169

Sawbridge, John, 149

Saxons, 67; and origins of British Constitution, 80–82

Seabury, Samuel, 27, 74, 119; writing of, 11; *Free Thoughts,* 11, 312; *Alarm to the Legislature,* 62; *View of the Controversy,* 121, 137, 143, 175, 184, 223, 226; on English society, 137; on representation, 174; on sovereignty, 226; on civil disobedience, 312; *Congress Canvassed,* 312

Selden, John, 315

Self-interest: antifederalists on, 345–346, 347; federalists on, 366, 367

Seneca, 24

Serious Address to . . . New York, 233

Seven Years' War, 84, 103, 113, 204

Shakespeare, William, 23

Sharp, Granville, *Declaration of the People's Natural Right,* 241

Shebbeare, John, *Letter to the People of England,* 13

Sheffield, England, 169

Sherlock, Thomas, Bishop of London, 252

Sherman, Roger, 322

Sherwood, Samuel, 104

Shirley, William, 121

Shuckford, Samuel, *Sacred and Profane History . . . Connected,* 33

Sibthorpe, Robert, 28, 29, 53, 199, 344

Sidney, Algernon, 22, 29, 38, 40, 45, 60, 132, 168, 299, 344; *Discourses,* 34; popularity of writings of, in colonies, 34–35

Silence Dogood, 43

Silliman, Ebenezer, 213

Singletary, Amos, 343–344

Size, of republics: antifederalists on, 347–349; federalists on, 360–368

Slave trade, 236; abolition of, 245–246

Slavery: colonies and state of, 119–120, 122, 232–233, 312; concept of, as political condition, 233–235; identification between causes of Negroes and of colonies, 235–246

Smith, Melancton, 322

Smith, William, Jr., 46, 280

Society for the Propagation of the Gospel in Foreign Parts (S.P.G.), 249; and Episcopal establishment, 96–98; Mayhew-Apthorp controversy, 254–257

Some Fugitive Thoughts, 17, 237

Some Observations of Consequence, 168

Sons of Liberty, 111, 244

Sophocles, 24

Soulé, François, *Histoire des troubles,* 124

South Carolina, 111, 166, 236; plural officeholding in, 110; and religious establishment, 248; ratifying convention, 339, 341

South Carolina Gazette, 59–60

South Sea Bubble, 36, 132

Sovereignty: of Parliament, 47, 200–

INDEX

INDEX

Virginia, 111, 119, 235, 236; and religious establishment, 247, 249, 257–261; Church of England in, 251; Declaration of Rights of, 260; constitution of, contrasted with England's, 276; proposals for state constitution of, 291–293; ratifying convention in, 335, 345–346, 353, 356, 360–361, 369. *See also* Tobacco; Two-Penny Acts

Virginia Gazette, 38, 66, 80, 102, 137, 152, 169, 259

Virtue, in government: antifederalists and, 344–345; federalists and, 351–352, 368–376, 378–379; Madison on, 369; Webster on, 373

Voltaire, 27, 29, 30, 84

Votes and Proceedings . . . of . . . Boston, 7, 61, 66, 78, 104, 107, 108, 109, 117, 206, 219

Wales, Princess Dowager of, 148

Walpole, Horace, 147, 303

Walpole, Sir Robert, 36, 39, 46, 47–50, 51, 52, 53, 72, 87, 121, 137, 206

Wanton, Gideon, 10

Ward, Samuel, 10

Warren, Joseph: *Oration,* 76, 116, 233, 275; on Stamp Act, 101–102

Warren, Mercy Otis: *The Blockheads,* 7; *The Group,* 7, 29; and Enlightenment authors, 29; *History,* 64, 102, 157; on Hutchinson, 331; *Observations on the Constitution,* 332

Washington, George, 17, 42, 120, 121, 333; on *Federalist* papers, 327; on virtue and American government, 369–370

Watson-Wentworth, Charles, 2d Marquis of Rockingham, 134, 135, 147–148

Watts, Isaac, 40

Wealth: and military service, 356; and virtue, 371–372; distribution of, 374

Webster, Noah, 327–328, 354; *Sketches of American Policy,* 373; *Examination . . . ,* 373

Webster, Samuel, *Misery and Duty,* 193

Wedderburn, Alexander, 29

Weems, Mason, 157

Wells, Richard: *Few Political Reflections, A,* 140, 235, 241; on slavery, 239–240

West Indies, 236

West, Samuel, 370

Whately, Thomas, 213; *Regulations Lately Made,* 166

Whigs, English: influence of radical, on colonists, 33–54; interpretation of history of, 41–42; radical, and corruption in England, 132–133; and sovereignty, 199, 201

Whitelock, Bulstrode, 41

Whitney, Peter, *Transgressions,* 59, 61, 67, 183, 310

Wilbur, Richard, "Mind," 322

Wilkes, John, 110, 111, 112, 115, 131, 344, *Number 45 North Briton,* 11; identification of colonists with, 110–112, 121

William III, 36, 46

Williams, Samuel, *Discourse,* 7, 66, 140, 271, 272

Williams, William Peere, *Reports,* 31

Wilson, James, 8, 174, 322, 329, 332, 368; *Considerations,* 42, 81, 104, 171, 225; on placemen, 103; "Address to the Inhabitants of the Colonies," 153–155, 173; on representation, 171; speech (Oct. 6, 1787), 328, 339

Winthrop, James, as "Agrippa," 322, 343, 349, 366

Worcester, Mass., 152

Workman, Benjamin, "Philadelphiensis" papers, 334

Wright, John, 57

Wyndham, Sir William, 171

Xenophon, 24

Xerxes, 66

Zenger, John Peter, 43, 52, 85

Zubly, John Joachim: *Calm and Respectful Thoughts,* 42; *Humble Enquiry,* 58, 169, 182, 217; *Law of Liberty,* 66, on representation, 169; on nature of constitutions, 181; on divisibility of sovereignty, 217

396